Unanimous raves for hardcover edition of

ETIQUETTE

"...revised to include up-to-date information, the most complete of the etiquette books...."
—*The Kansas City Star*

"...an ideal gift for the bride-to-be...."
—*House Beautiful*

"...the last word in good taste, an invaluable guide in reference to every social situation."
—*The Houston Post*

"...full of good sense and calculated to make life more pleasant...."
—*The Plain Dealer*

"...a genuinely helpful book, an excellent buy...."
—*Chicago Tribune*

"...the new edition maintains the high standard set by the original Mrs. Post...."
—*Cincinnati Enquirer*

Emily Post's Pocket Book of Etiquette is an abridgment, containing the essence of the Twelfth Revised Edition of *Emily Post's Etiquette,* published by Funk & Wagnalls, a division of Reader's Digest, Inc.

EMILY POST'S
POCKET BOOK OF
ETIQUETTE

New revised and enlarged edition by

ELIZABETH L. POST

PUBLISHED BY **POCKET** **BOOKS** NEW YORK

EMILY POST'S POCKET BOOK OF ETIQUETTE

Funk & Wagnalls edition published April, 1965

POCKET BOOK edition published November, 1967
2nd printing.......February, 1968

Revised and Enlarged POCKET BOOK edition published March, 1970

This POCKET BOOK edition is a revised, enlarged, and updated version of *Emily Post's Pocket Book of Etiquette*. It is printed from brand-new plates made from clear, easy-to-read type. POCKET BOOK editions are published by POCKET BOOKS, a division of Simon & Schuster, Inc., 630 Fifth Avenue, New York, N.Y. 10020. Trademarks registered in the United States and other countries.

L

PREFACE

to the Twelfth Edition

When my husband and I became engaged, one of the first things he wanted to do was to take to me to Edgartown, Massachusetts, and introduce me to his grandmother, Emily Post. In spite of his reassurances, and obvious devotion to her, I had all the natural reservations about meeting the famous First Lady of Etiquette, and I was a very nervous young lady when we arrived at her lovely island home that day in June, 1944. And I remained nervous for at least five minutes! In that space of time, I found that the supposedly unapproachable authority on all our manners and behavior was the sweetest, most natural, warmhearted, unaffected person I had ever met. From that day on, we were as close as two people separated by a span of some years can be, and I was never once made uncomfortable or self-conscious in her presence. That, to me, is the proof of the value of etiquette. To practice perfect manners without appearing to be "stiff" and at the same time to let those about you feel that *they* are equally well-mannered is a goal that can be achieved only by making consideration and unselfishness an integral part of your behavior.

My husband and I, and our children, spent a great deal of time with "Grandmama," as we always called her, and the children loved her as much as we did. Even they felt the gracious atmosphere that radiated from her and were almost invariably at their best in her presence, not because they had to be, but because they wanted to be.

We often discussed etiquette in those years, both the subject itself and the book she wrote about it. Emily Post was thoroughly aware of the changing pattern of modern living and made a point of keeping in constant touch with the changes both through her correspondence with readers and through the activities of the members of her own family. Furthermore, she fully realized that the time would come when etiquette would necessarily be affected by these changes. She herself eliminated and changed parts of her original work in frequent revisions over the years, and she foresaw that one day still other parts would no longer be applicable. And, conversely, she recognized that new aspects of modern life, nonexistent then and therefore unmentioned in earlier editions, would need to be considered.

As a result, Emily Post founded—in 1946—the Emily Post Institute. The purpose of the Institute was, and is, to perpetuate the traditions of gracious living by making available the most recent information on etiquette today. The staff of the Institute worked closely with Mrs. Post herself, and she actively supervised all phases of the work until her recent death. She insisted from the beginning that I take an active part, and it is for this reason that I have undertaken this revision of *Etiquette*.

All of us connected with this project have constantly kept in mind the need to maintain the high standards set by Emily Post, although in the less formal life that most of us lead today, some of the rules may seem more stringent than ever. If we have succeeded in making this revision of her book a useful, readable, and practical guide on all questions of etiquette for young and old alike, then we will know that we have carried on the work started by Emily Post as she would have wished.

ELIZABETH L. POST

CONTENTS

Part SEVEN
SPECIAL OCCASIONS

Part EIGHT
ENGAGEMENTS AND WEDDINGS

ents and responses—The wedding present—What to
wear to a wedding—At the church—From church to
reception—At the reception

Part NINE
ON THE SUBJECT OF INVITATION, INFORMALS, CARDS

PART ONE

THE ART OF CONVERSATION

1

Introductions, greetings, farewells

The words we say as we meet or take leave of someone can create an impression with far-reaching consequences. Therefore, the forms we use on such occasions may be of considerable importance. Automatic familiarity with them leaves our minds free for the more complicated arts of conversation and gracious listening.

UNBREAKABLE RULES OF INTRODUCTION

Though rules for introductions have become much less rigid in recent years, certain forms must be followed. A younger person is presented to an older person. A gentleman is always presented to a lady, even though she is no older than eighteen. No woman is ever presented to a man, with the following exceptions: (1) the President of the United States; (2) the recognized head of another country; (3) a member of a royal family; (4) a cardinal or other high church dignitary.

THE USUAL FORMS OF INTRODUCTION

The simplest introduction, suitable whenever two individuals are introduced, is the mere pronouncing of the two names: "Mrs. Woodman—Mrs. Norman." A man is also introduced:

"Mrs. Woodman—Mr. Norman." A mother introducing a man to her married daughter says, "Mr. Brown, I would like to introduce you to my daughter, Mary Smartlington."

To refer to one's husband as "Mr. Smith" or to one's daughter as "Miss Smith" is discourteous. But if the daughter has a different name, it may be said with a pause between that makes a parenthesis: "My daughter [pause] Mrs. Smartlington." The same pause may be used when introducing a stepparent and an acquaintance. To avoid confusion, if your names are likely to be thought the same, you say, "Mrs. Brown— my stepfather," then, after a pause, "Mr. Jones." This sounds much more pleasant than "Mrs. Brown—my mother's husband."

The name of the older or more notable person is said first. A woman's name is said before a man's, unless the preposition "to" is used before the lady's name. If, for instance, you find yourself saying Mr. Norman's name first, you can turn this slip into a polite gesture by saying, "Mr. Norman, may I introduce you to Mrs. Maddox?"

Formally, a man introduces another man to his wife: "Mr. Brown, I should like to introduce you to my wife." To a good friend, a husband would say, "Jim, I want you to meet my wife" (never "the wife"). Then, as though in parentheses, he says to his wife, "Mary, Jim Buyer" or "Mr. Buyer." Or if they are all young, he probably says, "Mary, this is Bob Ace."

A lady introduces her husband to friends as "John" and to acquaintances as "my husband." The two names of safety are "my husband" and "my wife" because they are proper no matter to whom you are talking. With other than friends, acquaintances and business associates, "Mr. Brown" and "Mrs. Brown" are quite correct.

An introduction prefaced by the phrase "This is," said with an enthusiastic inflection, expresses warmth and charm. London *Punch* once had a drawing of a small boy approaching his mother, holding an abashed small girl by the hand and radiantly explaining, "Mummy! THIS IS HER!" In the same way, a child would introduce a beloved teacher enthusiastically, "Mother, *this* is Miss Brown," or "Miss Brown, *this* is my mother!"—in the sense of "Behold! this is she—my mother."

Relatives-in-law:

A lady formally introduces her son's wife to acquaintances as "my daughter-in-law," but with friends she uses the less formal "Mary, Dick's wife." The warmth of voice is important. By tone alone, the same words may convey every shade of feeling from cool indifference to adoration. To introduce a parent-in-law as simply "Father" or "Mother" may be confusing. "This is my mother-in-law" is preferable, or "my husband's sister" and "my brother John's wife" (or "Jim's sister" and "John's wife" to one who knows who Jim and John are). Such identifications are clearer than "my sister-in-law."

Introducing stepparents:

When a child has always lived with his stepparents and has been given their name, he almost invariably calls them "Mother" and "Father" (or derivatives of those names) and introduces them in that way. When he has come to live with one stepparent, or two, later in life, the situation is different, because he may well retain his own name. Since this can be extremely confusing when introductions are necessary, the relationship should be made clear at once. There is nothing objectionable or derogatory in the terms "stepmother" or "stepfather," and the simplest form of introduction, said in the warmest tone to indicate an affectionate relationship, is, "Mrs. Jones, I'd like you to meet my stepfather, Mr. Casey," or "Mr. Fulbright, may I introduce you to my stepmother?" In the latter case it is not necessary, although perfectly proper, to say her name.

The same rule holds true when the parents are the introducers. A man would correctly introduce his wife's son by a former marriage, "Jack, I'd like you to meet my stepson, Jimmy Winters."

Teen-agers and young adults:

Informality is the rule among young adults and teen-agers. Muriel Manners, for example, taking a friend to a country club, greets a group of friends with "Hello, everybody. This is Sally Stranger." Everyone then calls Sally by her first name and further introductions are made in the same way: "Sally Stranger, Lucy and Bob Gilding." Or, "Lucy, this is Sally Stranger"; then to Sally, "That is Bob Gilding, and that is Tom

Brown," for a man is always introduced to a girl. The newcomer waits to be called by her first name before calling others by theirs. A younger person never calls an older person by his or her first name unless he is asked to; the choice lies with the older person.

Other permissible forms:

Other forms of introduction might be called conversational introductions. For example: "Mrs. Parker, you know Mrs. Robinson, don't you?" or "Mrs. Robinson, have you met Mrs. Parker?" Sometimes a few words of explanation make the introduction of a stranger pleasantly smooth. "Mrs. Worldly—Miss Jenkins. She writes as Grace Gotham." Or, "Mr. Neighbor, I should like you to meet Mr. Tennis. He has just won the tournament at Forest Hills." These explanations can be overdone, however, and may create the effect of trying to impress one's acquaintance with another's importance.

Forms to avoid:

Never say, "Mr. Jones, shake hands with Mr. Smith," or "Mrs. Jones, I want to make you acquainted with Mrs. Smith." In introducing one person to another, do not call one of them "my friend." You may say "my aunt" or "my sister" or "my cousin," but to pick out one person as "my friend" implies that the other person is not. "Mrs. Smith, I want you to meet Mrs. Jones" is correct, but never "Mrs. Smith, meet Mrs. Jones." The last phrase lacks friendliness and courtesy. Do not repeat "Mrs. Jones—Mrs. Smith. Mrs. Smith—Mrs. Jones," unless the name is foreign or difficult to pronounce. Then repeating the name a second time slowly is helpful.

To say "What is your name?" is abrupt and unflattering. If giving your own name doesn't elicit the information, find a third person later and ask, "Who was the lady with the gray feather in her hat?" The next time you see her, you will be able to say, "How do you do, Mrs. Green?"

FORMAL AND CEREMONIAL FORMS OF INTRODUCTION

The most ceremonious introduction possible is: "Mrs. Distinguished, may I present Mr. Traveler?" or "Mrs. Young, may I present Professor Gray?" "Present" is more formal than "introduce," but "may I introduce" is equally proper.

To the President of the United States:

The correct introduction of either a man or woman is: "Mr. President, I have the honor to present Mrs. [or Mr.] Williams" —or "Mrs. Williams of Chicago," if further identification is necessary. Mrs. (or Mr.) Williams simply bows. If, as is customary, the President offers his hand, Mrs. Williams takes it, but she does not offer hers first.

To a reigning sovereign:

Because one's name has been put on a presentation list beforehand, at the actual presentation the "accepted" name is repeated from one functionary to another and nothing is said to the king or queen except "Mrs. [or Mr.] Williams." Mrs. Williams curtsies. If the king offers to shake hands, she curtsies again as she gives him her hand. (If she objects to curtsying, she must not ask to be presented to the sovereign.) Mr. Williams follows the same procedure, bowing instead of curtsying.

On less formal occasions, a woman is presented to any member of a reigning family, "Your Royal Highness [or whatever the title], may I present Mrs. Williams?"

To a church dignitary:

To a cardinal, one says, "Your Eminence [or in England, "Your Grace"], may I present Mrs. Williams?" One who is not a Catholic behaves as he would to a king, but a Roman Catholic drops on the right knee, places the right hand, palm down, under the cardinal's extended hand and kisses his ring. A woman is always presented to archbishops, bishops, monsignors and priests. Mrs. Williams replies by saying to the archbishop or bishop, "How do you do, Your Excellency?" and to the monsignor, "How do you do, Monsignor Ryan?" To a priest she says either "Father Kelly" or simply "Father."

To other distinguished persons:

With the exception of state and high church dignitaries, distinguished persons are all presented *to* a woman by their proper titles. A foreign ambassador is presented, "Your Excellency, may I present you to Mrs. Williams?" —or a senator, "Mrs. Williams, may I present Senator Davis?" A senator is always "Senator Davis," even when he is no longer in office. But the

President of the United States, once out of office, becomes "Mister."

Former governors and ambassadors are "The Honorable." On ceremonial occasions, you would present "The Honorable John Jones, former governor of the State of Blank." Among friends he may be introduced simply as "Mr. Jones."

Doctors and judges are introduced and addressed by their titles. Protestant clergymen are "Mister" unless they hold the title of doctor, dean or canon, in which case the surname is added to the proper title. A Catholic priest, however, is "Father Kelly," whatever his other titles may be.

If the one making the introduction has neglected to use a title, the safest thing to say is "How do you do?" After that you may address any gentleman as "Sir." In fact, to avoid repetition of long titles like "Your Royal Highness" or "Mr. President," it is preferable to say "Ma'am" or "Sir" occasionally.

(For a chart of titles used in addressing and introducing important persons, see Chapter 5.)

WHEN TO INTRODUCE

Receiving lines:

When a large, formal party is given in honor of someone unknown to most of the people invited, the hostess receives with the special guest. People are presented to her as they arrive: "Mrs. Eminent, this is Mrs. Neighbor." Mrs. Eminent offers her hand. At a smaller, friendly party given for someone known to the majority of the guests, the guest of honor does not receive with the hostess, but sits or stands in a convenient place so that others can go up and talk with her. (If you should happen to arrive after the receiving line has dispersed, you must look for the guest of honor and present yourself; otherwise you will appear very rude.)

Formal dinners:

At a formal dinner all the people seated at the same table talk to each other, with or without a formal introduction. Strangers sitting next to each other usually introduce themselves. A gentleman says, "I'm Arthur Robinson." An older lady replies, "I'm Mrs. Hunter Jones," but a younger one says, "I'm Mary Brown," and perhaps adds, "Bob Brown's wife." When a young woman finds herself next to an unknown man at a dinner party, she may talk to him without telling him her name. But if he introduces himself to her as "John Blank," she says, "I'm Mary Smith"—not "Miss Smith."

One person to a group:

On formal occasions, one person is not introduced to each and every person already present. An arrival may be introduced to one or two people, or he may be left to talk with those nearby without exchanging names. But at a small lunch, for instance, let us suppose you are the hostess. Your position is not necessarily by the door, but near it. Mrs. King and Mrs. Lawrence are sitting close to you and Miss Robinson and Miss Brown farther away. Mrs. Jones enters. You go to her, shake hands, then you stand aside, as it were, to see whether Mrs. Jones goes to speak to anyone. If she apparently knows no one, you say, "Mrs. King—Mrs. Jones." Mrs. King, if she is younger, rises, shakes hands with Mrs. Jones, then sits down; or if she is about the same age as Mrs. Jones she merely extends her hand and remains seated. Without repeating Mrs. Jones's name you turn to the other lady sitting nearby saying, "Mrs. Lawrence." You look across the room and continue, "Miss Robinson, Miss Brown—Mrs. Jones." The two nod and smile but do not rise. Then the hostess seats Mrs. Jones next to one or more of the earlier arrivals and they all enter into conversation. When you are making such introductions, it is a good idea to say the name of the person already present first in order to get her attention, since she may be busily engaged in conversation.

Sometimes a hostess at a large party leads a guest on a tour around the room to make sure that he—or more especially she —is introduced to everyone. This results in the poor stranger being hopelessly confused by too many names. The better procedure is, as described above, to introduce her to a nearby group and let her sit down with them. They will make her feel comfortable and introduce her to others.

INTRODUCING ONESELF

At all informal gatherings, the roof of a friend serves as an introduction and everyone there *always* talks to those near them. But at a large party (a dance or a wedding reception), you are not required to speak with those whom you do not know unless you and another guest find yourselves apart from the others. Then you may comment on the beauty of the bride or on the weather. If you wish, you may introduce yourself with an identifying remark: "I am Sally's cousin," or "I am a neighbor of the groom." To talk or not to talk depends on mutual willingness. When you have a good reason for knowing someone, then you introduce yourself. For instance: "Mrs. Worldly, aren't you a friend of my mother? I am Jane, Mrs. John Smith's daughter." Mrs. Worldly says, "I am indeed. I'm so glad you spoke to me."

(For information on announcing oneself in business situations, see Chapter 2.)

WHEN INCORRECTLY INTRODUCED

We have all, at one time or another, been incorrectly introduced: one's title wrongly given or the name mispronounced. It is only kind that the person being introduced correct the error immediately. If, for example, a hostess introduces a man to a group as "a surgeon who has just moved to Greenwich" when he is really a general practitioner, he explains this to the new acquaintances—and the hostess, if she remains there—at once. He also makes a correction should she refer to him as "Mister" instead of "Doctor."

When someone is introducing a stranger to a number of people and consistently says the name wrong, the person being introduced corrects the host, not with annoyance but with as light a touch as possible. "My name is McDonald, not Donald."

WHEN NOT TO INTRODUCE

We all know introduction enthusiasts who cannot let one person pass another without insisting that they stop to be introduced. At a small "get-together," this is quite all right, but at a wedding reception or any general gathering, it is a mistake. A newly arrived visitor is not introduced to someone who is taking leave. Nor is an animated conversation between two persons interrupted—especially one between a young man and a young woman—to introduce a third.

INTRODUCING EMPLOYEES IN A HOME

There are occasions when a halfway introduction seems most appropriate. Suppose you wish to make a domestic employee known to a guest. "Olga, would you please take Mrs. Jones's bag to her room?" Or you might say to your guest, "Mary, this is Hilda, who will be glad to take your bag for you." Or in the case of a loved and respected servant, a young man might say to his new fiancée, "Mary, this is Lizzy Smith who has brought me up," and to Lizzy, "Lizzy, I know you will love Mary as much as I do."

Often one domestic helps in so many ways that she becomes almost a member of the family and rightfully expects to be treated as such. The thoughtful employer might say to a house guest, "Mary, this is Sally Jones, whom we couldn't manage without. Sally, this is my oldest friend, Mrs. Charles."

WHAT TO DO WHEN INTRODUCED
What to say:

If, in answering an introduction, you have not heard the new name clearly, it is perfectly correct to say simply, "How do you do?" But adding the name of the person you have met is the warmest, most polite response, and helps in committing it to memory. For example, when Mrs. Worldly had been introduced to Mr. Struthers, she replies, "How do you do, Mr. Struthers?" He simply nods, or he may say, "I'm very glad to meet you." If Mr. Struthers is someone whom she has long wanted to meet, Mrs. Worldly may go on to say, "John Brown speaks of you all the time"—or whatever may be the reason for her special interest.

When and how to shake hands:

Gentlemen always shake hands when they are introduced to each other even if they have to cross a room to do so. Ladies may do as they wish. When a gentleman is introduced to a lady, she generally smiles, nods, and says, "How do you do?" But if he should extend his hand, she gives him hers.

As to whether or not to shake hands on parting, there is no fixed rule. You are more likely to shake hands with someone whom you find sympathetic, but you can be courteously polite and at the same time reserved to someone who does not appeal to you.

Everyone dislikes to shake a "boneless" hand extended as though it were a wet rag or to have one's hand shaken violently. What woman does not wince at the viselike grasp that cuts her rings into her flesh and temporarily paralyzes her fingers? The proper handshake is made briefly, with a feeling of strength and warmth. At the same time one looks into the face of the person whose hand one takes. In giving her hand to a foreigner, a married woman relaxes her arm and fingers, as it is still customary in some Latin countries for him to lift her hand to his lips. Younger women usually offer their hand to the older; otherwise, women merely clasp hands, give them a dropping movement rather than a shake, and let go.

When to rise:

On formal occasions, the hostess always stands at the door and the host nearby. Both shake hands with each arrival. On informal occasions, they both rise and go forward to greet each guest. The children in the family rise for every grown person who enters the room and stand until the older person is seated. Grown as well as half-grown members of the family other than the host and hostess rise to greet guests, but do not necessarily shake hands.

A woman guest does not stand when being introduced to someone at a distance, nor when shaking hands with anyone, unless that person is much older. Should an elderly lady enter the room in which many other ladies are seated, only the members of the family rise, since seven or eight all getting up produces an effect of confusion.

Every gentleman stands as long as his hostess or any other lady near him does. Nor does he sit if any other gentleman with whom he is talking remains standing. Furthermore, a man always rises when a woman comes into a room. In public places, a man does not jump up for every woman who is a stranger to him if she happens to approach him, but if she addresses a remark to him, he stands as he answers her.

When a woman goes to a man's office on business, he stands up to receive her, offers her a chair and remains standing until she is seated. When she rises to leave, he gets up instantly, stands for as long as she remains, then goes with her to the door, which he holds open for her.

In a restaurant, when a lady greets him, a gentleman merely makes the gesture of rising slightly from his chair and nodding.

(For additional details, see Chapter 9.)

The young greet the old:

It is rude for young people not to go and shake hands with an older person of their acquaintance when they meet away from home, especially someone to whose house they have often gone. There is no need for them to enter into a long conversation. The older person should avoid detaining the young person with endless questions on his health and activities or those of his family.

NAME "BLACKOUTS"

When you are talking with someone whose name you are struggling to remember and are joined by a friend who looks inquiringly from you to the nameless person, all you can do is to introduce your friend to the stranger by saying to the latter, "Oh, don't you know Mrs. Neighbor?" The tactful stranger then announces her own name. If she says nothing, however, and Mrs. Neighbor makes matters worse by saying, "You didn't tell me your friend's name," the only solution is to be completely frank, admit you do not remember the name, throw yourself on their mercy and then ask them to complete the introduction themselves.

When meeting someone who may have forgotten you, never say, "You don't remember me, do you?" Unless the person you speak to greets you by name, say at once, "I'm Mrs. Brown, or Mary Brown," and then, if this does not bring a sign of recognition, "We met at the Roberts'."

INFORMAL GREETINGS

"Hello," the universal form of greeting in America, is acceptable in any situation except after a formal introduction. Even comparative strangers say "Hello" in passing, and among young people it is considered friendly after a first-name introduction. "Sally, I'd like you to meet Joan," and Sally says, "Hello, I'm glad to meet you, Joan."

In the business world, "Good morning" is the usual greeting before the lunch hour. After lunch, the somewhat stilted "Good afternoon" has been largely replaced by "Hello"; but it is still used as a phrase of dismissal, indicating an interview is ended, a class is dismissed, etc. Among friends or business acquaintances who know each other personally, "Good-bye" or "Good night" is said on parting.

GREETINGS IN PUBLIC

In Europe a gentleman bows to a lady first. In the United States a lady is supposed to greet a gentleman first, but today few people observe this formality. When one passes a casual acquaintance, a tipping or slight raising of the hat by the man and a smiling nod from the woman is all that is necessary.

In theaters, restaurants, shops or almost any public place, people speak to acquaintances as long as the greeting does not create a situation that may disturb others around them, as it would in the middle of a play. If they are too far apart to speak without shouting, they simply smile and wave.

Unless one has a good memory for people, it is always better to nod to someone whose face is familiar than to run the risk of ignoring an acquaintance. It is often difficult to recognize people whom one has met, when they are wearing a different type of dress or hat. One must be careful not to confuse such unintended rudeness as shortsightedness or absentmindedness with an intentional cut. A "cut," the direct stare of blank denial, insulting to its victim and embarrassing to every witness, is, happily, a rare occurrence.

THE ANSWER TO "HOW ARE YOU?"

Normally, the correct and conventional answer is "Fine, thank you" or "Very well, thank you." To one who is a chronic invalid or is in great sorrow or anxiety, a gay "Hello, Mrs. Jones! How *are* you? You look fine!" is tactless and unkind.

TAKING LEAVE

When a visitor is ready to leave, he or she merely stands. To one with whom he has been talking he says, "Good-bye, I hope I shall see you again soon," or, simply, "I'm glad to have met you." To the first, the other answers, "Thank you, I hope so too"; or to both, merely, "Thank you." In taking leave of a group of strangers—whether you have been introduced or merely included in their conversation—you nod and smile a "Good-bye" to anyone who happens to be looking at you, but you do not attempt to attract the attention of those who are unaware that you are leaving. When leaving a party early, you find your hostess and say good-bye without attracting any more attention than is necessary, in order to avoid being the cause of breaking up the party prematurely.

2

Names and titles

USE OF FIRST NAMES

In general, first names should indicate that people have met more than once. If, however, during the first meeting one person finds she is drawn to another by common interests or mutual friends, it is perfectly correct for her to say, "Please call me Sally." At an informal party in the home of friends, it is customary to use first names after having responded correctly to the introductions. If you don't, you will be thought stiff and unfriendly.

(For what to do when introduced, see Chapter 1.)

Many people of middle age and older think that being called "Sally" or "Jack" by Doris Sophomore and Bobby Freshman puts them on the same age level, suggesting a camaraderie which often does not exist. But if Mrs. Autumn and Mr. Sere prefer to be "Sally" and "Jack," no one else has a right to object.

CHILDREN AND OLDER PEOPLE
Parents:

Unfortunately, in America today respect for older people is not as prevalent as it was a few generations ago. Nevertheless one of the areas in which a parent should still insist on respect is in the way they permit their children to address them. *It is a flagrant violation of good manners for children to call their natural parents by their first names.*

Stepparents:

Because circumstances vary there can be no set rule about what children should call their stepparents. It depends only on what seems to be best in each case. Children should never be forced to call a stepparent "Mother" or "Father" or any nickname having that meaning, especially if their own parent is living. If they *choose* to do so, it is a compliment to the stepparent and should be encouraged.

If a child goes to live with a stepparent at a very young age, and if his own parent is dead or if the child is not and probably never will be acquainted with that parent, then he would consider his stepparent as his own and say "Mother" or "Father," particularly if he hears stepbrothers or stepsisters using those names. If the child is older when one parent remarries, the situation is quite different. If he has known the stepparent for some time, he may call him (or her) by a nickname or even by his first name. Actually, an appropriate nickname seems to be the best solution, provided it is not a derivative of "Mother" or "Father."

Names for parents-in-law:

A bride may call her parents-in-law by whatever names she chooses. Usually, and naturally, parents-in-law are called by names that mean mother and father but are not the names that the bride uses for her own parents. The ban against "Mother" and "Father" results from consideration for one's own parents who are not often happy to hear their own special names bestowed elsewhere. The less intimate relationships of aunts, uncles and even grandparents never come into question because the bride calls all such relatives of her husband's exactly what he does, and he does the same in speaking of hers.

Other adults:

A child or young person may call an older person by his first name *only* when that person has specifically asked that he do so. As long as the child understands that it is done at the request of the grown-up, it is quite acceptable. For example, some adults dislike being called "Aunt" or "Uncle" or "Cousin." Intimate friends, devoted to the children, may also feel that "Mr. (or Mrs.) Surname" does not express the close relationship they desire and suggest nicknames for themselves. Otherwise, a child addresses all friends of his parents as "Mr. (or Mrs.) Surname."

REFERRING TO HER HUSBAND OR HIS WIFE

Correctly a lady says "my husband" when speaking of him to an acquaintance. But to a friend or to the friend of a friend she speaks of him as "John." This does not give anyone else the privilege of calling him "John" unless asked to do so.

In the same way, Mr. Worldly speaks of "Edith" to intimate masculine friends and to every woman whom they both know socially, whether they themselves call her "Edith" or "Mrs. Worldly." But to a man not an intimate friend and to a woman who is a stranger, he speaks of her as "my wife." In most business situations, if he has occasion to speak of her, he would say, "Mrs. Worldly thinks thus or so . . ." Thus, when the Duke of Edinburgh, accompanying Queen Elizabeth II, was hailed by a former shipmate in the British Navy, he correctly introduced him to "my wife."

ANNOUNCING ONESELF

Arriving at the door:

When an adult member of the family comes to the door in answer to your ring, you never call yourself "Mr." or "Mrs." or "Miss" but announce yourself as "John Grant" or "Sally Smythe" and explain the purpose of your visit. If he obviously does not recognize you, you further identify yourself by a sentence or two: "I'm a friend of Jim's at the office" or "Susan and I met at the Barrys' cocktail party." If a child answers the door, you say, "I'm Mr. Grant [or Mrs. Smythe]. Would you please call your mother for me, if she is at home?"

If the door is answered by a maid who does not know you and if you are not expected, you announce yourself as "Mr. John Grant." If you are expected, you merely say, "Mr. Grant."

The businessman announces himself:

When you enter an unfamiliar office, say to the receptionist, "Good morning. My name is Rodger Salecurve. I have a ten o'clock appointment with Mr. Byre." At this point, you offer your business card (if you carry one)—it will help the receptionist to give your name correctly to the person you wish to see. If you do not have a specific appointment, you may add a little information about your business. "Good afternoon, I am Rodger Salecurve of the Schmid Corporation. I would like to see Mr. Byre about our line of lubricants."

The use of Doctor:

When the title "Doctor" indicates a degree required for the practice of a profession, as in medicine, dentistry or veterinary medicine, it is used instead of "Mister" at all times.

An earned title indicating that a man or woman has received a doctorate in divinity, philosophy, literature, etc., is always used professionally. In private life he may, if he prefers, continue to call himself "Mister." But in any situation where other people are introduced as "Mr.," "Mrs." or "Miss" rather than by first names, it is a mark of recognition and respect to use the title "Doctor." The distinction, then, is in the social setting rather than in the type of degree. He generally uses "Mister," or no title at all, on social visiting cards or in social directories, and the initials of his degree do not follow his name.

The use of Jr., 2nd and 3rd:

A man with the same name as his father uses "Jr." after his name as long as his father is alive. He may drop the "Jr." after his father's death, or, if he prefers, he may retain it in order not to be confused with his late father. This also helps to differentiate between his wife and his mother if the latter is still living and does not wish to be known as Mrs. Jones, Sr.

When a man is named after his father who is a "Jr.," he is called 3rd. A man named after his grandfather, uncle or cousin is called 2nd.

The following diagram may help to clarify these relationships:

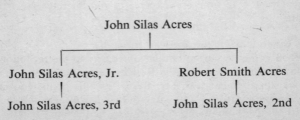

John Silas Acres

John Silas Acres, Jr. Robert Smith Acres

John Silas Acres, 3rd John Silas Acres, 2nd

The wife of each of these men uses the same suffix after her name as her husband does, i.e., Mrs. John Silas Acres, 3rd.

It is improper, unless he has a good reason, for a man to continue adding "Jr." to his name after the death of his father or grandfather. But he may wish to retain the "Jr." if he lives in the same locality as his mother and his wife might be confused with the older Mrs. Smith, or if the widow, who is perhaps the young stepmother of the son, does not wish to be known as "Sr." If a father has been so celebrated that the son cannot possibly take his place (and sometimes for other professional reasons), it may be practical for the son to keep his identity as junior.

The same considerations apply in continuing to call a boy "John Smith, 3rd" if John Smith, Jr. (or 2nd) has died. *Junior* always means the son—or possibly the grandson—of a man of the same name; *2nd* means the nephew or cousin of a man of the same name.

NAMES LEGALLY CHANGED

Whenever a name by which one has been known is changed, social and business associates should always be notified of the change quickly. The simplest way is to send out formal announcements in this form:

Mr. and Mrs. John Original Name
Announce that by Permission of the Court
They and Their Children
Have Taken the Family Name of
Miller

SPECIAL USAGE OF WOMEN'S NAMES

A divorcée's name:

Until recently, unless a divorcée took back her maiden name and used the title "Miss," her only possible form of address was her maiden name combined with her ex-husband's last name. Mary Jones who married John Smith after divorcing him became Mrs. Jones Smith. This is still absolutely correct but there is now an acceptable alternative.

Years ago when divorce was uncommon the divorcée was apt to remain in the same town or city where she was well known. Therefore her maiden name identified her and also declared her divorced state. But today many divorcées move:

they look for a new life in a new community where their maiden names mean nothing and may be a source of considerable confusion to new acquaintances. By using the formerly unacceptable title "Mrs. Mary Smith," however, she establishes both her identity and her divorced status.

A divorcée may also prefer to use her given name as opposed to her maiden name when the combination of the two last names is ludicrous or unmanageable. Mrs. Mary Lipwitz is certainly easier for both Mary and her friends than Mrs. Hobenzollen Lipwitz. Mrs. White Black could cause considerable amusement.

A married woman's legal name:

A woman's legal name consists of her given name, her maiden name and her husband's name. Except in a few instances—for example, on income tax forms—the middle name is shortened to an initial. The title "Mrs." is never used with the legal signature since it should be used only with a woman's husband's first name. The only possible exception is in the case of a professional woman who wishes it to be known that she is married, but does not wish her husband's name to appear. In that case she may put "Mrs." in parentheses before her signature.

She uses her legal name as her signature on all business correspondence, on bank accounts and all legal documents. On correspondence, to denote her marital status, she may write Mrs. Henry Smith below Barbara H. Smith.

Professional women in social situations:

A woman who has a degree in medicine, dentistry, etc., is always called "Doctor" professionally! She also may be introduced and referred to as "Doctor" socially. However, social correspondence to her and her husband is addressed "Mr. and Mrs. John Woods," since she forgoes her professional title in the interest of convenience and social convention.

3

The good conversationalist

A practical rule for a conversation is STOP, LOOK, LISTEN. "Stop" means not to rush recklessly forward; "Look" means pay attention to the expression of the person with whom you are talking; and "Listen" is the best advice possible, because the person whom most people love to sit next to is a sympathetic listener who really listens. A fixed expression of sympathy while your mind wanders elsewhere won't do. It never fools anyone.

PLEASANT TALK

Humor is the rarest of gifts. If you know anyone who is gay, beguiling and amusing, do all you can to make him prefer your house and table to any other, for where he is, there is the successful party. But beware of the forced wit; he is always a bore.

Fishing for topics:

If we want to be thought sympathetic, intelligent or agreeable, we must "go fishing." In talking to a person whom you have just met and about whom you are in complete ignorance, try one topic after another, just as a fisherman searches for the right fly. "Are you fond of the theater?" you ask. If the answer is "yes," you talk theater. When that subject runs down, you talk of something *you* have been doing—planting a garden, contemplating a vacation, or similar safe and natural topics. Do not snatch at a period of silence. Let it go for a little while. Conversation is not a race that must be continued at breakneck pace.

Introducing oneself is sometimes the most practical way to begin a conversation. You might say, "I'm Betty James. My husband and I live in the country, but we often come to town to go to the theater." The stranger may reply that he lives in the city, but his favorite occupations are golf and fishing. Talk of these leads to other things. It's really very simple.

Another helpful gamble, especially if you are a woman, is to ask advice. "We are planning to drive through the South. Do you know the roads?" Or "I'm thinking of buying a television set. Which make do you think is best?" It is safe to ask his opinion on almost anything: politics, sports, the stock market, the current fad. If you are a man talking to a young woman, ask her what she thinks about work, young people, amusements. If she is an older woman, she will probably talk to *you!*

Avoid criticism of a religious creed or disagreement with another's political convictions. Also be careful not to let amiable discussion turn into argument. A tactful person says, "It seems to me thus and so," but never "That's not so!" If another's opinion seems unreasonable, you quickly find a more pleasant subject. If you care so intensely about a subject that you can only lecture about your fixed point of view, don't mention that subject. But if you are able to listen with an open mind, you probably need put no barriers on any topic. Argument between cool-headed, skillful opponents can be a delightful, amusing game, but it is very dangerous for those who may become hot-headed and ill-tempered.

The tactless blunder:

Examples of tactlessness include the means-to-be agreeable elderly man who says to an old acquaintance, "Twenty years ago you were the prettiest girl in Philadelphia." Or to a mother whose only son has just married, "Why is it, do you suppose, that young wives so often dislike their mothers-in-law?"

Personal remarks:

It is always pleasant to hear something appreciative about something one has done. "Your speech was splendid!" "What a delicious dinner you gave us." "I've never seen such beautiful flowers." But it is bad taste to comment on physical attributes or ask about expense or other money matters. "What a lovely dress! How much did it cost?" is exceedingly rude.

The sympathetic listener:

The person who is seemingly eager for your news or enthralled with your conversation, who looks at you with a kindling of the face and gives you spontaneous and undivided attention, is the one to whom the "orchid" for the art of conversation would undoubtedly be awarded.

UNPLEASANT TYPES

The bore:

A bore might be described as one who insists on telling you at length something that you don't want to hear about at all. He insists that you hear him out to the bitter end in spite of your plainly shown disinterest. His constant repetition is deadly dull. But the most delightful people are those who refuse to be bored. One way out is to try being agreeable yourself; that helps and may break the stream of monotonous conversation. Boredom often comes with laziness, an unwillingness to shift one's point of view. So if you find yourself sitting in the hedgerow with nothing but weeds, don't shut your eyes and see nothing; instead find what beauty you may in the weeds.

The wailer:

Too many people use as the staples of their conversational subject matter misfortunes, sickness and other unpleasantness. Don't dwell on your own problems. Your audience has them, too, and won't be entertained by yours. Only your nearest and dearest care how many times you have been to the operating room.

The cutting wit:

Sharp wit tends to produce a feeling of mistrust even while it stimulates. Furthermore, the applause that follows a witty sally tends to make well-intentioned people more and more sharp-tongued; in the end it makes others uneasy and one's self unpopular.

The sentence-finisher:

Some people are quicker to find a word or phrase than others. They have an irresistible urge to supply that word or to finish a sentence for one who is slow in finding the exact expression he wants. If you are inclined to do this, use all your strength to resist the urge. It makes the other speaker feel inadequate, you may change his meaning by supplying a word he did not intend to use and, finally, you put yourself in the position of appearing to try to steal the limelight from him.

"I'd say it to her face!"

A good resolve to make and keep, if you would keep your friends, is never to speak of anyone without, in imagination, having him or her overhear what you say. One often hears the exclamation "I would say it to her face!" Be very sure that this is true and then—nine times out of ten—think better of it and refrain. Preaching is all very well in a textbook, schoolroom or pulpit, but it has no place in society. Society is supposed to be a pleasant place; telling people disagreeable things to their faces or talking behind their backs is not a pleasant occupation.

For those who talk too much:

Regrets are generally for what you said rather than for what you left unsaid. "Better to keep your mouth closed and be thought a fool than open it and remove all doubt." Don't pretend to know more than you do. To try to discourse learnedly about something you know very little about is to make others look on you as a half-wit. No person of real intelligence hesitates to say, "I don't know." Above all, stop and *think* what you are saying. This is really the most important rule. Know when to listen to others, but know also when it is your turn to carry the conversation. Then remember that nothing holds the interest of the listener when it is too long dwelt upon or told too often.

TOASTS

Men are frequently called on to make a toast, an often perplexing experience unless one knows he will be called on and can plan in advance. The best solution is simply to say exactly what you feel. Toasts never need be long. If you are called on unexpectedly, you can get away with something as brief as "To Joe, God bless him," or "To Jack—a wonderful friend and a great boss."

But if you wish to appear more poised and more eloquent, you must add a few remarks—a reminiscence, praise or a relevant story or joke. The toast is always in keeping with the occasion. Toasts at a wedding should be on the sentimental side, those in honor of a retiring employee nostalgic, and so on. A touch of humor is rarely out of place.

The following toasts are intended to give you some ideas for various occasions. They must be changed to fit the particular circumstances, of course—adding a word or two of your own feelings to give a personal touch.

A father's toast at his daughter's engagement party:

Now you know that the reason for this party is to announce Mary's engagement to John. I would like to propose a toast to them both.

A best man's toast at the rehearsal dinner:

John and I have been friends for a long time now, and I have always known what a lucky guy he is. Tonight all of you can see what I mean when you look at Mary and realize she is to become his bride tomorrow. Please join me in a toast to Mary and John. May this kind of luck continue throughout their lives together.

**A bridegroom's toast to his bride
at the wedding reception:**

I'd like you all to join me in a toast to the girl who's just made me the happiest man in the world.

A bridegroom's father's toast at the rehearsal dinner:

I don't need to tell you what a wonderful girl Mary is, but I do want to tell you how happy John's mother and I are to welcome her as our new daughter-in-law. To Mary and John.

Toast to a retiring employee or a member of the firm:

I know that every one of us here tonight thinks of Bob (Mr. Smith) not as an employee (employer) but as a friend. When he leaves, we will suffer a very real loss both in our organization and in our hearts. At the same time we rejoice that he will now be able to enjoy the things he wants to do, so let us rise and drink a toast to one of the finest friends we have known.

Anniversary toast:

Many of us who are here tonight can well remember that day twenty-five years ago when we drank a toast to the future happiness of Mary and Bob. It is more than obvious that our good wishes at that time have served them well, and therefore I would like to ask that all of you—old friends and new—rise and drink with me to another twenty-five years of the same love and happiness that Mary and Bob have already shared together.

Toast to a guest of honor at a testimonial dinner:

1) We are gathered here tonight to honor a man who has given unselfishly of his time and effort to make this campaign so successful. Without the enthusiasm and leadership that Bob Jones has shown all through these past months, we could never have reached our goal. Please join me in drinking a toast to the man who more than anyone else is responsible for making it possible to see our dream of a new hospital wing finally come true.

2) Ladies and gentlemen, you have already heard of the magnificent work our guest of honor has accomplished during his past two years in Washington. Right now we would like to tell him that no matter how proud we are of his success in his chosen career, we are even more pleased to have him home with us again. It's great to have you back, Jim!

PART TWO

CORRESPONDENCE AND GREETING CARDS

4

The appearance and style of your letters

The letter you write is a mirror that reflects your appearance, taste and character. You can, with practice, make yourself write neatly and legibly. Observe straight lines and regular margins on both the left and right sides of the sheet—the left-hand margin is usually a little wider than the right. It is perfectly correct to type letters to friends if you wish. All business letters—from home as well as office—should be typed if possible, but some forms of correspondence must always be written by hand.

Never type an invitation, an acceptance or a regret.

Never type letters of congratulations or thanks.

Never type letters or notes of condolence.

STATIONERY

A person whose handwriting is large should pick a larger size paper than someone whose writing is small. Low, spread-out writing looks better on a square sheet of paper, tall pointed writing on high and narrow paper. Rough or smooth paper is a matter of personal choice—but let the quality be good, the shape and color conservative. Do not use scented or oddly shaped paper and avoid excessive ornamentation.

The flap of the envelope should be plain and the point neither skimpy nor unduly long. When the paper is thin, use envelopes with colored linings so that the writing cannot be read through the envelope. Linings of unrestrained masses of red and gold, swirls of purple and green or other striking colors are not in good taste—though linings for Christmas card envelopes may be as gay as the ornaments that decorate a Christmas tree. Oblong envelopes are excellent for business, but those more nearly square are smartest for personal use.

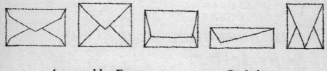

Acceptable Form   *Bad form*

Deckle-edged paper or clean-cut edges is a matter of personal choice. Both are correct.

Paper for a man:

A man's writing paper should always be conservative: plain white or cream, gray or granite, single sheet 7 or 7¼ by 10 or 10½ inches and engraved (or printed) at the top in black, dark gray or navy blue. His *business* stationery is engraved (or printed) in plain block letters with his name (without title), his address and, if he wishes, his telephone number. For his *social* correspondence, he uses paper of the same color and size, but he may use initials instead of his name, or a crest if he has one. The single sheet in each case is folded in threes to fit into a 7¼ or 7½ by 4-inch envelope. This stationery is correct for both typed and handwritten letters. Writing ink should be dark blue or black.

Paper for a woman:

White, cream, all blues, grays and, more recently, greens are in best taste. Paper should be of small or medium size, single or double sheets, plain or with colored border. It may be engraved (or printed) with either a monogram or initials. It may have only the address or it may have both monogram or initials and address. The color of the lettering must match the border.

Writing ink should be black or blue or green to match the color of the paper. A married woman's name is written "Mrs. William Frost," not "Mrs. Mary Frost" or "Mary Frost." An unmarried woman uses "Miss" only on the envelope.

Paper for everyone in the family:

A paper suitable for the use of all the members of a family has the address engraved or printed in plain letters at the top of the first page. Frequently the telephone number is put in small letters under the address. Or it may be put in the upper left-hand corner, with or without a small telephone device, and the address in the center.

350 Chestnut Street
Philadelphia 11, Pennsylvania
TELEPHONE ORMOND 4-7572

 GARFIELD 4-1986

18 Walnut Road
Peoria, Illinois

For the young correspondent:

A young teen-ager may use his or her name—Peter Frost or Elizabeth Jones—or a simple monogram. A young girl may

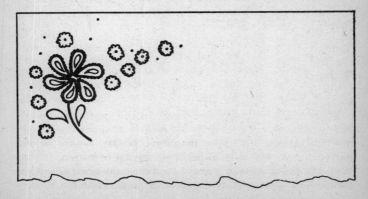

also use only her first name—Elizabeth (in full) or Betty if she prefers. Or her stationery may be decorated with a spray of flowers or other pretty design in the upper left-hand corner (this is never suitable for use by an older woman, however). A very young child—boy or girl—may use a drawing of a kitten or a puppy or some other animal.

Note paper:

For short notes or invitations, acceptances or regrets, a supply of fold-over note paper, half the size of a single sheet of a lady's writing paper, is invaluable. It may be of any color appropriate to the household, and engraved or printed with initials or with the owner's name and address and possibly with the telephone number.

Printing or engraving:

Paper upon which one's full name and address are printed has become indispensable to everyone who must write many letters. Therefore printed paper for informal social correspondence and for business letters is generally accepted as entirely correct. You may wish to have in addition a small supply of engraved paper, though no one will think any the worse of you if you do not.

Crests:

When an old family has used their family arms continuously since they brought the device—and their right to it as certified by the colleges of heraldry—from Europe to America, its use is proper, although, at the present time, somewhat conspicuous. The crest is the exclusive property of male members of a family, although it may be used jointly by husband and wife on some occasions. It never appears on the paper of a widow or spinster—a heraldic rule apparently unknown to most Americans. A widow may use the device on the shield of her husband's coat of arms, transferred to a diamond-shaped device called a lozenge. She may also, if she chooses, divide the lozenge perpendicularly into two parts and crowd the device from her husband's shield into the left half and the device from her father's shield into the right half. A spinster uses her paternal arms on a lozenge without crest or motto.

Your home address and the date:

If your stationery is not marked with your address, let your correspondent know where to reply by putting your address either on the upper right side of the first page of your letter, or, especially on a short note, at the far left, just below the level of your signature. Whether or not your stationery is already printed, the date goes either at the upper right-hand side of the first page of a letter or at the end and to the far left of the signature of a note.

Sincerely,
Mary Swenson
(Mrs. John Swenson)

45 Barton Street
Racine, Wisconsin (and the zip code number)
May 5, 1967

Recipient's address:

On business letters the address of the receiver is put at the left, below the level of the date and directly above the salutation, exactly as it appears on the envelope.

June 7, 1967

Mr. James Johnson
Smith, Johnson & Company
New York, New York (and the zip code number)

Dear Mr. Johnson:

Personal letters and notes, however, have the address of the receiver *only* on the envelope itself.

The salutation:

For business letters, the salutation "Dear Sir" or "Dear Sirs" is better than "Gentlemen" (never "Messieurs").

June 7, 1967

Smith, Johnson & Company
20 Broadway
New York, New York (and the zip code number)

Dear Sirs:

If a firm or organization is composed of women, the salutation is "Dear Madams" (never "Mesdames").

An impersonal business letter to a woman begins:

> Mrs. Richard Worldly
> 500 Fifth Avenue
> New York, New York (and the zip code number)
>
> Dear Madam:

A business letter from a man to a woman customer or client he knows personally begins with the same address form as above, but instead of "Dear Madam" the salutation is "My dear Mrs. Worldly" or "Dear Mrs. Worldly."

The most formal beginning of a social letter to a woman is "My dear Mrs. Smith." Increasingly intimate are: "Dear Mrs. Smith," "Dear Sally," "Sally, dear," and "Dearest Sally." A man is always addressed "Dear Bob" when something less formal than "Dear Mr. Smith" is desired.

(For forms used in addressing distinguished persons or those in special categories, see Chapter 5.)

The closing:

The best ending to a formal social note is "Sincerely," "Sincerely yours," "Very sincerely," or "Very sincerely yours." "I remain, dear madam," is no longer in use, but "Believe me" is still correct when a degree of formality is to be expressed in the close of a note.

> Believe me
> Very sincerely yours,

The close of a business letter is "Yours truly" or "Yours very truly." "Faithfully" or "Faithfully yours" is appropriate for a man when he is writing to a woman or for any non-commercial correspondence, such as a letter to the President of the United States, a member of the cabinet, an ambassador, a clergyman, etc. "Respectfully" is used only by a tradesman to a customer or by an employee to an employer.

"Sincerely" in formal notes and "Affectionately" or "Love" in intimate notes are the most used today, though "Cordially" is also widely used. "Yours in haste" or "Hastily yours" is allowable only if the communication indicates necessary haste. "Gratefully" is used only when a benefit has been received: to a lawyer who has skillfully handled a case or, possibly, to a friend who has gone to unusual trouble to do you a favor. In an ordinary letter of thanks, the signature is "Sincerely," "Affectionately," "Devotedly"—whatever your usual close may be.

(For forms used in letters to distinguished persons or those in special categories, see Chapter 5.)

The signature:

In America, John Hunter Titherington Smith, finding his name too much of a penful, chooses J. H. T. Smith for letters and documents, or perhaps at the end of personal letters, John H. T. Smith. Of course, if the letter is to a business associate whom he knows personally he may simply sign "Jack" over the typed "J. H. T. Smith." Mail is addressed to him in the typed form (or the printed form, if the letterhead carries his full name).

A married woman always signs a letter to a stranger, a bank, a business firm, etc., with her legal name. If her stationery is marked with her full married name and address, her signature —Mary Jones Mathews—needs no further explanation. Otherwise, she gives her married name (to which the reply will be sent) in one of several ways. When she writes by hand, she adds her married name in parentheses, beneath her signature, thus:

> *Very truly yours,*
> *Mary Jones Mathews*
> *(Mrs. John Mathews)*

When the letter is typed, her married name is typed beneath the space left for her signature, though not necessarily enclosed in parentheses.

> Very truly yours,
> *Mary Jones Mathews*
> Mrs. John Mathews

A woman uses "Mrs." in her signature only on a hotel register, on a business telegram or on an order letter to a tradesman thus: "Mrs. John Smith." To a servant in her employ it is "Mrs. Smith."

An unmarried woman uses much the same form in a typed letter:

> Sincerely,
> *Mary Jones*
> Miss Mary Jones

When she writes by hand, she may use this style:

> *Sincerely,*
> *(Miss) Mary Jones*

When an unmarried woman starts her career using her maiden name, she continues to do so throughout her professional life. She uses "Miss" in combination with that name even after she marries.

Many women start their careers after their marriage and wish to have it known that they are married. Professionally called Mary T. Forsyth or Helen Horton Hughes, they should use business stationery with their names printed that way. This can be confusing to a correspondent. In order to make it clear what title he should use in addressing a reply, Mary or Helen may precede her typewritten signature with (Mrs.). This should *never* be done except on business correspondence— in all other cases their husbands' names are used below the handwritten signature when it is necessary.

Folding a letter:

After signing a letter the paper is folded once for an envelope that is as deep as half the length of the paper, and twice for an envelope that is a third as deep. Paper that must be folded into thirds is used only as personal stationery for men or for business purposes. Note paper is the same size as the envelope and goes into it flat with only the original fold.

THE OUTSIDE ADDRESS

Write the name and address on the envelope legibly, including the zip code number, using a straight margin on the left:

Mrs. Harvey S. Simpson
4 Hillside Lane
Clinton
Ohio (and the zip code number)

Correct use of "Esq.":

"Esq." is seldom used today in the United States except by conservative members of the older generation, by lawyers and by justices of the peace. It may be used on handwritten invitations and personal letters. However, on any formally engraved invitation and its envelope Esq. should not be used.

A widow or divorcée:

Never address a note or social letter to a married woman—even if she is a widow—as Mrs. Mary Town. A widow always keeps her husband's name. If her son's wife should have the same name, she becomes Mrs. James Town, senior, or simply, Mrs. Town, if she is the only one in her community with that name. A divorced woman usually takes her own surname in place of her ex-husband's Christian name. If she was Mary Simpson before her marriage, she correctly calls herself Mrs. Simpson Johnson. However, to avoid confusion, some divorcées prefer to use "Miss (or Mrs.) Mary Johnson"; if they do, you must address them in that way.

Daughters, sons and children:

Formerly, the eldest daughter was correctly Miss Taylor, her younger sister, Miss Jane Taylor. Today Miss Alice Taylor and Miss Jane Taylor are invariably used. Envelopes to children are addressed to Miss Katherine Taylor and to Robert Taylor, the latter with no title. Little boys under ten years of age are addressed as "Master"; at college age they are called "Mr." In between, they are addressed with no title. "The Messrs. Brown" is correct only for unmarried brothers, never for a father and son.

"Personal" and "Please Forward":

If you are writing to someone at his home address, never write "Personal" on it. But on a social note to a friend's business address it is entirely correct. "Please forward" is correct if you know only a former address but not the current one, or if the person to whom it is addressed is traveling and you are not sure the letter will reach him before he leaves the last address you have.

Return address:

Customarily, a return address is put on the face of a business envelope at the top left-hand corner. On a personal letter, it used to be put on the flap—this was and still is particularly true on personal *printed* stationery. But today (in response to requests made by the United States Post Office) it is permissible and advisable on a handwritten envelope to put the return address on the face. The handwriting should be small and include the zip code number.

Unsealed letters:

Best form dictates that any letter given to a person (other than a commercial messenger) for delivery by hand be unsealed unless it has a valuable enclosure. If the envelope is sealed beforehand it is polite to explain why. Though not obligatory, customarily the person carrying it seals it immediately in the presence of the writer.

5

Addressing important persons

The following chart has been prepared to cover as many as possible of the situations likely to occur in the ordinary course of events—and some not so ordinary. Special attention has been given to the official and formal occasion; naturally Governor Marvin's friends will continue to call him Joe at purely friendly functions and their wives will continue to address their dinner and luncheon invitations to the Governor's wife. Only when a wedding or other formal invitation would be sent to both husband and wife is it necessary to use the special forms included below in the "Social Correspondence" column.

Federal custom in the United States bestows the title "Honorable," first officially and then by courtesy for life, on the following: the President, Vice President, United States Senators, United States Congressmen, members of the cabinet, all federal judges, ministers plenipotentiary, ambassadors and governors of all states. But this title is not used by the person himself on his visiting card or letterhead or in his signature. The people of the state address their state senators as "The Honorable Lawrence Hamilton, State Senator," as a courtesy title only. Best usage dictates that "The Honorable" (spelled out in full) appear on a separate line, as shown in the chart in this chapter, and that his wife, when she is included, have a line to herself below his name and slightly indented.

The correct forms for addressing representatives of other countries who are living in the United States are firmly fixed by governmental protocol. But whether their wives are addressed as Mrs., Madame, Señora or some other title depends upon the usage of the particular country (that is, the wife of the Mexican ambassador is Señora Ortega), but sometimes, especially when a difficult or little known language is involved, she uses Mrs. or Madame.

In this age of international travel, we may need information about the important personages of countries other than our own. Customs vary and no general rules can be made for the more than one hundred nations in the world. Should you find yourself about to leave for Ghana or Japan or Finland, try the consulate nearest you or the embassy in Washington or the mission to the United Nations in New York where information officers stand ready to facilitate your communication with their homelands. Of course, when you arrive in a foreign land, any American embassy or consulate is usually equipped to help traveling Americans in such matters.

Personage	ENVELOPE ADDRESS	SOCIAL CORRESPONDENCE	INFORMAL BEGINNING OF LETTER
THE PRESIDENT	The President The White House Washington, D.C.	The President and Mrs. Washington The White House Washington, D.C.	My dear Mr. President:
THE VICE PRESIDENT	The Vice President United States Senate Washington, D.C.	The Vice President and Mrs. Hope Home address	My dear Mr. Vice President:
CHIEF JUSTICE, SUPREME COURT	The Chief Justice The Supreme Court Washington, D.C.	The Chief Justice and Mrs. Page Home address	My dear Mr. Chief Justice:
ASSOCIATE JUSTICE, SUPREME COURT	Mr. Justice Katsaros The Supreme Court Washington, D.C.	Mr. Justice Katsaros and Mrs. Katsaros Home address	My dear Mr. Justice Katsaros:
CABINET MEMBER	The Honorable Gary George Gussin The Secretary of the Treasury or The Attorney General or The Postmaster General Washington, D.C.	The Honorable The Secretary of the Treasury and Mrs. Gussin Home address *or (for a woman cabinet member)* Mr. and Mrs. Henry Leo Woods	My dear Mr. Secretary: or My dear Mr. Attorney General: or My dear Mr. Postmaster General: or Madam Secretary:
FORMER PRESIDENT	The Honorable Alfred Edward Work Office address	The Honorable Alfred Edward Work and Mrs. Work Home address	My dear Mr. Work:
UNITED STATES SENATOR	The Honorable John Wandzilak United States Senate Washington, D.C.	The Honorable John Wandzilak and Mrs. Wandzilak Home address *or (for a woman senator)* Mr. and Mrs. John Row Doe	My dear Senator Wandzilak:
THE SPEAKER OF THE HOUSE OF REPRESENTATIVES	The Honorable Walter James Grevesmuhl The Speaker of the House of Representatives Washington, D.C.	The Speaker and Mrs. Grevesmuhl Home address	My dear Mr. Speaker:
MEMBER OF THE UNITED STATES HOUSE OF REPRESENTATIVES	The Honorable Henry Cobb Wellcome United States House of Representatives Washington, D.C.	The Honorable Henry Cobb Wellcome and Mrs. Wellcome Home address *or (for a woman member)* Mr. and Mrs. John Knox Jones	My dear Mr. Wellcome:
AMBASSADOR OF THE UNITED STATES	The Honorable John Wilson Smith The Ambassador of the United States American Embassy London, England	The Honorable John Wilson Smith and Mrs. Smith Home address *or (for a woman ambassador)* Mr. and Mrs. Leeds Walker Home address	My dear Mr. Ambassador: or My dear Madam Ambassador:

FORMAL BEGINNING OF LETTERS	INFORMAL CLOSE OF LETTERS	FORMAL CLOSE OF LETTERS	IN CONVERSATION	TITLE OF INTRODUCTION	PLACE CARDS FOR FORMAL OCCASIONS
Sir:	Very respectfully yours,	I have the honor to remain, Most respectfully yours,	Mr. President or Sir	*Only the name of the person being introduced is spoken*	The President (Mrs. Washington)
Sir:	Sincerely yours, or Faithfully yours,	Very truly yours,	Mr. Vice-President or Sir	The Vice-President	The Vice President (Mrs. Hope)
Sir:	*Same as above*	*Same as above*	Mr. Chief Justice or Sir	The Chief Justice	The Chief Justice
Sir:	Sincerely yours,	*Same as above*	Mr. Justice or Mr. Justice Katsaros or Sir	Mr. Justice Katsaros	Mr. Justice Katsaros
Sir: or Dear Sir: or Madam:	*Same as above*	*Same as above*	Mr. Secretary or Mr. Attorney General or Mr. Postmaster General or Sir or Madam Secretary	The Secretary of the Treasury or The Attorney General or The Postmaster General	The Secretary of The Treasury or The Attorney General or The Postmaster General
Sir:	*Same as above*	*Same as above*	Mr. Work or Sir	The Honorable Alfred Edward Work	Mr. Work
Sir: or Madam:	*Same as above*	*Same as above*	Senator or Senator Wandzilak or Sir or Madam	Senator Wandzilak of Alaska	Senator Wandzilak
Sir:	*Same as above*	*Same as above*	Mr. Speaker or Sir	The Speaker of the House of Representatives	The Speaker
Sir: or Madam:	*Same as above*	*Same as above*	Mr. Wellcome or Mrs. Jones or Sir or Madam	Representative Wellcome of Nebraska	Mr. Wellcome
Sir: or Madam:	*Same as above*	*Same as above*	Mr. Ambassador or Madam Ambassador or Sir or Madam	The American Ambassador or (*if necessary*) Our Ambassador to England	The Ambassador of The United States or (*if more than one present*) to (*name of country*)

Personage	ENVELOPE ADDRESS	SOCIAL CORRESPONDENCE	INFORMAL BEGINNING OF LETTER
MINISTER PLENIPOTENTIARY OF THE UNITED STATES	The Honorable James Lee Row The Minister of the United States American Legation Oslo, Norway	The Honorable James Lee Row and Mrs. Row Home address *or (for a woman minister)* Mr. and Mrs. Arthur Johnson Home address	My dear Mr. Minister: or My dear Madam Minister:
CONSUL OF THE UNITED STATES	Mr. John Smith American Consul Rue de Quelque Chose Paris, France	Mr. and Mrs. John Smith Home address	Dear Mr. Smith:
AMBASSADOR OF A FOREIGN COUNTRY	His Excellency Juan Luis Ortega The Ambassador of Mexico Washington, D.C.	His Excellency The Ambassador of Mexico and Señora Ortega Home address	My dear Mr. Ambassador:
MINISTER OF A FOREIGN COUNTRY	The Honorable Carluh Matti The Minister of Kezeah Washington, D.C.	The Honorable Carluh Matti and Mrs. Matti Home address	My dear Mr. Minister:
GOVERNOR OF A STATE	The Honorable Joseph L. Marvin Governor of Idaho Boise, Idaho	The Honorable Joseph L. Marvin and Mrs. Marvin Home address	Dear Governor Marvin:

State Senators and Representatives are addressed like U.S. Senators and Representatives, with appropriate addresses

MAYOR	His [or Her] Honor the Mayor City Hall Easton, Maryland	His Honor the Mayor and Mrs. Lake Home address *or (for a woman mayor)* Mr. and Mrs. L. T. Wayne Home address	Dear Mayor Lake:
JUDGE	The Honorable Carson Little Justice, Appellate Division Supreme Court of the State of New York Albany, New York	The Honorable Carson Little and Mrs. Little Home address	Dear Judge Little:
BISHOP, PROTESTANT	The Right Reverend John S. Bowman Bishop of Rhode Island Providence, Rhode Island	The Right Reverend John S. Bowman and Mrs. Bowman Home address	My dear Bishop Bowman:
CLERGYMAN, PROTESTANT	The Reverend David Dekker Address of his church *or (if he holds the degree)* The Reverend David Dekker, D.D. Address of his church	The Reverend David Dekker and Mrs. Dekker Home address	Dear Mr. [or Doctor] Dekker:
RABBI	Rabbi Paul Aaron Fine Address of his synagogue *or (if he holds the degree)* Paul Aaron Fine, D.D. Address of his synagogue	Rabbi [or Doctor] and Mrs. Paul Aaron Fine Home address	Dear Rabbi [or Doctor] Fine

FORMAL BEGINNING OF LETTER	INFORMAL CLOSE OF LETTER	FORMAL CLOSE OF LETTER	IN CONVERSATION	TITLE OF INTRODUCTION	PLACE CARDS FOR FORMAL OCCASIONS
Sir: or Madam:	*Same as above*	*Same as above*	Mr. Row or Mrs. Johnson	Mr. Row, the American Minister or *(if necessary)* Mrs. Johnson, the American Minister to Denmark	The Minister of The United States to (name of country)
Sir: or My dear Sir:	*Same as above*	Sincerely yours,	Mr. Smith	Mr. Smith	Mr. Smith
Excellency:	Sincerely yours, or Faithfully yours,	Very truly yours,	Mr. Ambassador or Excellency or Sir	The Ambassador of Mexico	The Ambassador of (name of country)
Sir:	Sincerely yours,	*Same as above*	Mr. Minister or Sir	The Minister of Kezeah	The Minister of (name of country)
Sir:	*Same as above*	*Same as above*	Governor Marvin or Sir	The Governor or *(if necessary)* The Governor of Idaho	The Governor of (name of state)
Sir: or Madam:	Sincerely yours,	Very truly yours,	Mr. Mayor or Madam Mayor	Mayor Lake	The Mayor of (name of city)
Sir:	*Same as above*	*Same as above*	Mr. Justice	The Honorable Carson Little, Judge of the Appellate Division of the Supreme Court	The Honorable Carson Little
Right Reverend Sir:	Faithfully yours, or Sincerely yours,	Respectfully yours,	Bishop Bowman	Bishop Bowman	Bishop Bowman
Sir: or My dear Sir:	Sincerely yours,	Sincerely yours, or Faithfully yours,	Mr. [or Dr.] Dekker	Mr. [or Dr.] Dekker	Mr. Dekker, or, *(if he holds a degree)*, Doctor Dekker
Dear Sir:	*Same as above*	Sincerely yours,	Rabbi [or Dr.] Fine	Rabbi [or Dr.] Fine	Rabbi Fine, or, *(if he holds a degree)*, Doctor Fine

Personage	ENVELOPE ADDRESS	SOCIAL CORRESPONDENCE	INFORMAL BEGINNING OF LETTER
THE POPE	His Holiness Pope Paul VI *or* His Holiness the Pope Vatican City		
CARDINAL	His Eminence Alberto Cardinal Vezzetti Archbishop of Baltimore Baltimore, Maryland		
ARCHBISHOP, ROMAN CATHOLIC	The Most Reverend Preston Lowen Archbishop of San Francisco San Francisco, California		Most Reverend and dear Sir:
BISHOP, ROMAN CATHOLIC	The Most Reverend Matthew S. Borden Address of his church		My dear Bishop Borden:
MONSIGNOR	The Right Reverend Monsignor Ryan Address of his church		Reverend and dear Monsignor Ryan:
PRIEST	The Reverend John Matthews [*and the initials of his order*] Address of his church		Dear Father Matthews:
MEMBER OF RELIGIOUS ORDER	Sister Angelica [*and initials of order*] *or* Brother James [*and initials*] Address		Dear Sister Angelica: *or* Dear Brother James:

UNIVERSITY PROFESSOR	Professor Robert Knowles
	Office address
	  or (if he holds the degree)
	Dr. Robert Knowles
	  or
	Mr. Robert Knowles
		Professor [*or* Doctor *or* Mr.] and Mrs. Robert Knowles
		Home address
			Dear Professor [*or* Doctor *or* Mr.] Knowles:

PHYSICIAN	William L. Barnes, M.D. Office address	Doctor and Mrs. William L. Barnes Home address	Dear Doctor Barnes:

FORMAL BEGINNING OF LETTER	INFORMAL CLOSE OF LETTER	FORMAL CLOSE OF LETTER	IN CONVERSATION	TITLE OF INTRODUCTION	PLACE CARDS FOR FORMAL OCCASIONS
Your Holiness:		Your Holiness' most humble servant,	*See Chapter Twenty-one*	*See Chapter Twenty-one*	His Holiness, The Pope
Your Eminence:		I have the honor to remain, Your Eminence's humble servant,	Your Eminence	*One is presented to* His Eminence, Cardinal Vezzetti	His Eminence, Cardinal Vazetti
Your Excellency: *or* Most Reverend Sir:	*Same as formal close*	I have the honor to remain, Your Excellency's humble servant,	Your Excellency	*One is presented to* The Most Reverend, The Archbishop of San Francisco	The Archbishop of San Francisco
Most Reverend Sir:	Faithfully yours,	I have the honor to remain, Your obedient servant,	Your Excellency	Bishop Borden	Bishop Borden
Right Reverend and dear Monsignor Ryan:	Respectfully yours,	Respectfully yours,	Monsignor Ryan	Monsignor Ryan	The Right Reverend Monsignor Ryan
Reverend Father:	Faithfully yours,	I remain, Reverend Father, Yours faithfully,	Father *or* Father Matthews *or* Your Reverence	The Reverend Father Matthews	Reverend Father Matthews *or* Father Matthews
My dear Sister: *or* My dear Brother:	Faithfully yours,	Respectfully yours,	Sister Angelica *or* Brother James	Sister Angelica, [or Brother James,] may I present Mrs. Jones	Sister Angelica *or* Brother James
Dear Sir:	Sincerely yours,	Very truly yours,	Professor [or Dr.] Knowles (*within the college*) Mr. Knowles (*elsewhere*)	Professor [or Dr.] Knowles	Doctor Knowles *or* Professor Knowles
Dear Sir:	*Same as above*	*Same as above*	Dr. Barnes	Dr. Barnes	Doctor Barnes

6

Personal letters

THE LETTER EVERYONE LIKES TO RECEIVE

The letter we all like to receive carries so much of the writer's personality that he or she seems to be talking to us. Here are suggestions to make your letters reflect your personality.

Don't stop too long to think of *how* to say it. Decide what you want to say, then write it as quickly as possible as if you were talking to your friend. Use the same colloquial, informal language you do when you speak. The clever use of punctuation adds interest and variety, much as the change in tone of a speaker's voice can. Underlining a word, if done in moderation, or using an exclamation point after a phrase or sentence gives emphasis where you want it. A dash instead of a grammatical phrase can be effective: "We went to a dance last night—what a party!" Contractions are also useful: "I don't know" instead of "I do not know." For a personal touch, occasionally use the name of the person to whom you are writing.

LETTERS THAT SHOULDN'T BE WRITTEN
Letters of gloomy apprehension:

Don't write needlessly of misfortune or unhappiness, yours or another's, even to members of your immediate family. Chronic calamity writers who luxuriate in pouring out all their troubles and their fears of trouble-to-come on paper to their friends are both a bore and a menace. "My little Betty has been feeling miserable. I am worried to death. The doctor keeps insisting there is nothing to worry about, but doctors don't seem to appreciate what anxiety means to a mother," etc., etc.

The dangerous letter:

Avoid writing a letter to anyone—no matter whom—that would embarrass you were you to see it in a newspaper above your signature. Every day letters that should never have been written are put in evidence in courtrooms where they sound quite different from what was innocently intended. If you are determined to write an emotional letter either in affection or anger, at least put it away overnight in order to reread it and make sure that you have said nothing that may sound different from what you intended to say. A gentleman never writes a letter that can be construed as damaging to any woman's good name.

Spoken remarks that would amuse can pique and even insult their subject when written. Without the interpretation of the voice, gaiety becomes levity, raillery, accusation, and words that should be of a passing moment are made to stand forever. Angry words in a letter always sound stronger and are more permanent than the spoken word. Admonitions from parents to their children are quite proper in a letter—they are meant to endure and be remembered—but momentary annoyance should be expressed briefly. The habit of writing in an irritable or faultfinding tone to children insures that these letters will not be read by their recipients.

THE DIFFICULTY IN BEGINNING

For most people the difficult parts of a letter are the beginning and the closing. Here are a few helpful suggestions.

Such beginnings are: "I know I ought to have written sooner, but I haven't had anything to write about," or "I suppose you have been thinking me very neglectful, but you know how I hate to write letters," are most ungracious. Instead of slamming the door in your friend's face, why not hold it open? "Do you think I have forgotten you entirely? You don't know, Ann, how many letters I have planned to write you." Or "Time and time again I have wanted to write you, but each moment that I saved for myself was always interrupted by—something."

It is much easier to begin a letter in answer to one that has just been received. The news contained in it is fresh and the impulse to reply needs no prodding. For example: "Your letter was the most welcome thing the postman has brought for ages," or "Your letter from Capri brought all the allure of Italy back to me." Then you take up the various subjects in Ann's letter, which will probably launch you without difficulty upon topics of your own. Always answer specific questions—it is maddening to have them completely overlooked.

ON ENDING A LETTER

Just as the beginning of a letter should give the reader an impression of greeting, so should its ending express friendly or affectionate leave-taking. Never seem to scratch helplessly around in the air for an idea that will effect your escape. "Well, I guess you've read enough of this" or "You're probably bored by now so I'd better close" are stupid. When you leave the house of a member of your family, you don't have to think up any special sentence in order to say good-bye. Leave-taking in a letter is the same. In personal letters to friends, instead of the standard forms of closing, try something like this:

> *Will write again in a day or two.*
>
> *Martin*

> *Lunch was announced half a page ago! So good-bye for today.*
>
> *Nancy*

> *Counting the hours 'til next weekend!*
>
> *Betsy*

THANK-YOU LETTERS

The most important qualification of a thank-you letter is that it sound sincere. Therefore, you use the expressions most natural to you, and write as enthusiastically as though you were talking. Even the letters of older people, although they are more restrained than those of youth, avoid anything suggesting smugness or affectation.

Letters of thanks for wedding presents:

All wedding presents are sent to the bride, but her letters of thanks are written as though the gifts had been sent to both the bride and the groom. For example:

Saturday

Dear Mrs. Beck,

To think of your sending us all those wonderful glasses! They are perfect, and Jim and I want to thank you a thousand times!

The presents will be shown on the day of the wedding, but do come over this Tuesday morning for a cup of coffee and an earlier view.

Thanking you again, and with love from us both,

Joan

Thanks for Christmas and other presents:

Thank-you notes for Christmas—and all other—presents should be written within two or three days of the time the gift is received. In the case of Christmas gifts, they should be sent before New Year's Day, and certainly before young people return to school.

Dearest Aunt Lucy,

We just love our armchair! Jack says I'll never get a chance to sit in it if he gets there first. We both thank you so much, and are looking forward to seeing you at Easter.

With much love,

Sally

Dear Kate,

I am fascinated with my jewel box—it is so unusual. You are really clever at finding what no one else can, and what everyone wants. I don't know how you do it!

Again, thanks so much.

With love,

Edie

Thanks for a baby present:

Dear Mrs. Cooper,

Thank you ever so much for the blanket you sent the baby. It is by far the prettiest one he has, and so soft and warm that I am really envious of him.

Do come in and see him, won't you? We love visitors, any day between 4 and 5:30

Affectionately,

Helen

BREAD-AND-BUTTER LETTERS

When you have been staying overnight, or for a longer time, at someone's house, a letter of thanks to your hostess *within a few days after the visit* is absolutely necessary.

Bread-and-butter letters are difficult for many people to write. You have been visiting a friend and must write to her mother, whom you scarcely know. You begin "Dear Mrs. Town" at the top of a page, then the forbidding memory of Mrs. Town stops you. It would be easy enough to write to Pauline, the daughter. Very well, write to Pauline then—on a piece of scrap paper—about what a good time you had, how nice it was to be with her. Then copy the note you composed to Pauline and on the page beginning "Dear Mrs. Town," add "Love to Pauline, and thank you again for asking me," end it "Affectionately"—and there you are! Even if you cannot write a letter easily, the most awkward note is better than none—for to write none is the height of rudeness.

After a house-party weekend:
Dear Franny,

You and Jim are such wonderful hosts! Once again I can only tell you that there is no other house to which I go with so much pleasure, and leave with so much regret.

Your party over this last weekend was the best yet, and thank you very, very much for having included me.

With much love to you all,
Betty

Dear Mrs. Farthingham,

Last weekend was the high spot of the summer. Everything you planned was wonderful, but the best of all was the trip to the country fair on Sunday.

I truly enjoyed every minute with your family, and thank you more than I can say for including me.

Very sincerely,
Elliot Sandstrom

From a bride to her new relatives-in-law:
The following letter, written by a bride after paying a first visit to her husband's aunt and uncle, won her at a stroke the love of the whole family:

Dear Aunt Anne,

Now that we are home again I have a confession to make! Do you know that when Dick drove me up to your front door and I saw you and Uncle Bob standing on the top step —I was simply paralyzed with fright!

"Suppose they don't like me," was all that I could think. Of course, I know you love Dick, but that only made it worse. How awful, if you didn't like—me! The reason I stumbled coming up the steps was that my knees were actually knocking together! And then you were both so perfectly adorable to me and made me feel as though I had always been your niece—and not just the wife of your nephew.

I loved every minute of our being with you, just as much as Dick did, and we hope you are going to let us come again soon.

With best love from us both,

> *Your affectionate niece,*
> *Nancy*

After visiting a close friend:

Dear Ellen,

It was hideously stuffy in town this morning after the coolness of Strandholm, and a back alleyway is not an alluring outlook after the beauty of your place.

It was so good being with you and I enjoyed every moment. Call me just as soon as you get back to town and we'll have lunch.

> *With love,*
> *Caroline*

Dearest Bett,

We both had a wonderful time! Bob's sunburn has turned to a beautiful tan, and the rest did him a world of good.

You were good to ask us so soon again, and we thank you very, very much. Call us as soon as you get home.

> *Yours,*
> *Mary*

To a stranger who has entertained you:

When someone has shown you special hospitality in a city where you are a stranger:

Dear Mrs. Duluth,

It was so good of you to give my husband and me so much of your time. We enjoyed and appreciated all your kindness to us more than we can say.

We hope that you and Mr. Duluth may be coming East before long and that we may have the pleasure of seeing you then at Cottswold.

In the meanwhile, thank you for your generous hospitality, and my husband joins me in sending kindest regards to you both.

Very sincerely yours,
Katherine Starkweather

LETTERS OF CONGRATULATION

On an engagement:

Dear Stella,

While we are not altogether surprised, we are both delighted to hear the good news. Ted's family and ours are very close, as you know, and we have always been especially devoted to him. He is one of the finest—and now luckiest—of young men, and we send you both every good wish for all possible happiness.

Affectionately,
Nancy Johnson

Dear Ted,

Just a line to tell you how glad we all are to hear of your wonderful news. Stella is lovely, and, of course, from our point of view, we don't think she's exactly unfortunate either! This brings our very best wishes to you from

Arthur and Nancy Jackson

Letter from a mother to her son's fiancée:

When it is impossible for a mother to go to meet her son's new fiancée, a letter should be written to her. The general outline is:

Dear Mary,

John has just told us of his great happiness, which, of course, makes us very happy, too. Our one distress is that we are so far away (or whatever else) *that we cannot immediately meet you in person.*

We do, however, send you our love and hope that we shall see you very soon.

Sincerely and affectionately,
Martha Jones

On the birth of a baby:

Dear Sue,

We were so delighted to hear the news of Jonathan Junior's birth. Congratulations to all three of you!

May I come to see you and the baby the first time that I am in town? I will call and let you know when that will be.

Much love,
Helen

Other letters of congratulation:

Dear Mrs. Steele,

We are so glad to hear the good news of David's success; it was a splendid accomplishment and we are all so proud of him and happy for you. When you see or write to him, please give him our love and congratulations.

Affectionately,
Mildred Bowen

Dear Michael,

We all rejoice with you in the confirmation of your appointment. The state needs men like you—if we had more of your sort, the ordinary citizen would have less to worry about. Our warmest congratulations!

Jim

LETTERS OF INTRODUCTION

A business letter of introduction is different from a social one, although it carries the same implicit approval of the subject. It also implies the writer's request that the receiver pay due attention to the one being introduced. Since these letters are often written to important men with little time to spare, it is imperative that they not be written casually nor for people who do not truly merit the introduction. A business letter of this type does not necessarily oblige the receiver to entertain the subject socially. If he wishes to, he certainly may, but generally his attention to the bearer's business is sufficient.

The social introduction is, in a way, more of a responsibility, because the writer must decide on the compatibility of the people he is introducing. Therefore, there is one firm rule:

Never *ask* for such letters of introduction, and be very sparing in your offers to write them.

Few people realize that a letter of social introduction carries an immediate obligation. The form might as well be "The bearer of this note has the right to demand your interest, your time, your hospitality—liberally and at once, no matter what you think of him." Therefore, it is far better to refuse to write a note of introduction in the beginning than to commit the greater error of inconveniencing a friend or acquaintance.

When you know someone who is going to a city where you have other friends and when you believe that it will be a mutual pleasure for them to meet, a letter of introduction is proper and very easy to write. But sent to a casual acquaintance—no matter how attractive or distinguished the person to be introduced—it is a gross presumption.

The more formal note of introduction:

Dear Mrs. Miller:

Julian Gibbs is going to Buffalo on January tenth to deliver a lecture on his Polar expedition, and I am giving him this note of introduction to you. He is a great friend of ours and I think that perhaps you and Mr. Miller will enjoy meeting him as much as I know he would enjoy knowing you.

With kindest regards, in which Arthur joins,

Very sincerely,
Ethel Norman

If Mr. Norman wishes to introduce one man to another, he gives his card to the visitor, inscribed as follows:

Introducing Julian Gibbs

Mr. Arthur Less Norman

Mr. Norman also sends a private letter by mail, telling h.
friend that Mr. Gibbs is coming.

Dear, Jack,

I am giving Julian Gibbs a card of introduction to you when he goes to Buffalo on the tenth to lecture. He is delightfully entertaining and a great friend of ours. I feel sure that Mrs. Miller would enjoy meeting him. If you can conveniently ask him to your house, I know he would appreciate it; if not, perhaps you could put him up for a day or two at a club or arrange for a reservation in a good hotel.

Faithfully,
Arthur Norman

Informal letter of introduction:

My dear Ruth,

I am giving this letter to George Perrin, a great friend of ours, who is going to be in Chicago the week of January seventh.

I want very much to have him meet you and hope that this will find you in town.

Affectionately,
Louise Hill

At the same time a second and private letter of information goes by mail.

My dear Ruth,

I have sent you a letter introducing George Perrin. He is young, about thirty-five or so, good-looking, very good company, and an altogether likable person.

Alas, he does not play cards, which is not important; but knowing how much you play, I thought it only fair to warn you so that you might invite him to something other than a card party.

I know you will like him; and I hope you will be able to get together.

Affectionately,
Louise Hill

Procedure on arrival:

A letter of introduction is always handed to you unsealed.
(It is correct for you to seal it at once in the presence of its

author.) You thank your friend for having written it and go on your trip.

If you are a man and your introduction is to a lady, you go to her house soon after you arrive in her city, leave the letter with your card, if you have one, at her door, without asking to see her. If she herself opens the door, you introduce yourself and give her your letter of introduction. She should—unless prevented by illness—at once invite you to cocktails, lunch or dinner, or at least name an hour when she would like you to come to see her.

If your letter is to a man, you mail it to his house, unless the letter is a business one. In the latter case, you go to his office and send in your business card and the letter. Meanwhile, you wait in the reception room until he has read the letter and calls you into his office.

If you are a woman, you mail your letter of social introduction and do nothing further until you receive an acknowledgment from the recipient. But the obligation of a written introduction demands that only illness or mourning can excuse her not asking you to her house—either formally or informally.

When a man receives a letter introducing another man, he calls the person introduced on the telephone and asks how he may be of service to him. If he does not invite the newcomer to his house, he may arrange a hotel reservation or ask him to lunch or dinner at a restaurant, as the circumstances seem to warrant. But it is absolutely necessary that he show this stranger what courtesy he can.

The indirect letter of introduction:

When the Newcomers go to live in Strangetown, an indirect letter of introduction is better than a direct one. By indirect is meant a letter written by Mrs. Neighbor at home to a friend of hers in Strangetown. Mrs. Neighbor merely writes to Mrs. Oldhouse, "My friends, the Newcomers, are going to live in your neighborhood"; this leaves the former free to make advances only insofar as she feels inclined.

Because, as has already been explained, a letter of introduction makes it obligatory for the recipient to do something for the Newcomers, no matter how inconvenient it may be, it can be a very real burden. If you are ill or in mourning—the only excuses possible—you must send a note explaining your lack of hospitality, and if possible, a deputy—your husband, your sister, or even your nearest friend—to explain and insofar as possible to take your place. But with the indirect letter, you and the Newcomers have the same opportunity to know each other well, if you like each other, and are bound only by inclination.

THE LETTER OF CONDOLENCE

Intimate letters of condolence to those close to you are too personal to follow a set form. One rule, and one only, should guide you in writing such letters. Sit down at your desk; let your thoughts be with the person you are writing, and say what you truly feel and nothing else.

Don't dwell on the details of illness or the manner of death; don't quote endlessly from the poets and Scripture. Write as simply as possible and let your heart speak truly but briefly. Forget that you are using written words. Think merely how you feel—then put your feelings on paper. Grace of expression is important, but sincerity counts most of all.

Suppose it is the death of a man who has left a place in the community that will be difficult to fill. You think of all he stood for that was fine and helpful to others and how much he will be missed. So you say just that: "Dear Steve—what a prince he was! I don't think anything will ever be the same again without him." Ask if there is anything you can do at any time to be of service to his people. Nothing more need be said. A line expressing a little of the genuine feeling that you had for Steve is worth pages of eloquence.

Sometimes a letter from one who has suffered an equal loss, who in sincerity writes words of encouragement and assurance that in time the pain will grow less instead of greater, is of genuine help. But such a letter must never be written by anyone whose own suffering has not been equally devastating. A glib list of qualities that did not exist is meaningless. A letter of condolence must, above everything, express a genuine sentiment. The following are merely guides for those at a loss to construct a short, appropriate message.

My dear Mrs. Neighbor,
We are so shocked to hear of the sorrow that has come to you. If there is anything that either my husband or I can do, I earnestly hope that you will ask someone to call upon us.
Alice Rivington Blake

My dear Mrs. Neighbor,
   I know how little words written on a page can possibly mean to you at such a time. But I must at least tell you that you are in our thoughts and in our hearts, and if there is anything at all that we can do for you, please send us a message.
                                   With deepest sympathy,
                                        Mary Newling

Where death comes after a long illness, and you want to express sympathy but cannot feel sad that one who has long suffered has found release, you might write: "Your sorrow during all these years—and now—is in my heart, and all my thoughts and sympathy are with you."

To whom are letters of condolence written?

Letters of condolence may be addressed in various ways. If you knew the deceased well but do not know his or her family, the note is addressed to the closest relative—usually the widow, the widower, or the oldest child. Some like to add "and family" on the envelope, and this is permissible when you feel that you are sending your sympathy to all rather than to one special person.

When you did not know the person who died but do know one of his relatives, you write to that person rather than to someone who might have been closer to him. In writing to a married person who has lost a parent, you may write to the one whose parent it was, or if the other partner was close to his or her in-law, the letter may be addressed to both.

Letters to children who have lost a parent may be addressed to Miss Lucy Field (the daughter), with Mr. John Field (the son) underneath. The salutation would read, "Dear Lucy and John."

(For letters of invitation and acceptance, see Chapter 46, Informal Invitations, and Chapter 48, Acceptances and Regrets.)

7

Greeting cards

Birthday, anniversary cards and other messages of friendship
are charming evidences of good wishes from family and
friends. But such cards are pleasant only if you take the trouble to add a little note in your own handwriting expressing
something of your own feelings about the occasion. *(See also
Chapter 34, Funerals, for the use of "Thank you for your
sympathy" cards.)*

Christmas cards:
   There is virtually no limit to the list of those to whom one
may send Christmas cards, beginning with dearest friends and
ending with the slightest acquaintances. However, the custom
in many communities of sending a card to everyone with whom
you have a nodding acquaintance is ridiculous and contrary to
the spirit of Christmas.
   Christmas cards should be sent to those whom you really
wish to greet, but who are not quite close enough to you to exchange gifts, to those good friends you may not have seen for
some time, and most of all to those who do not live near you
and with whom your Christmas card may be your only communication.

A Christmas card to someone in mourning:
   A card to someone who is in mourning can be kind if it
illustrates the promise of peace or if its message is a loving
friendly thought. But please do not send a picture of a grave or
gravestones, nor a gay card shouting "Merry Christmas and

Happy New Year." Whether or not those who are in mourning send cards depends entirely upon their own feelings. Naturally they would not send cards to mere acquaintances, but there is no impropriety in wishing their friends happiness.

Cards to business acquaintances:

When it is company policy to send a Christmas card to a client, it is preferable to send it, addressed to the man at his business address in the name of the company—"The Hollister Hardware Company wishes you a Merry Christmas and a Happy New Year"—rather than to his home in the name of the president or other officer. But if the client is known to the executive socially as well as through business, it may be addressed to husband and wife, even though she is not known to him personally. It should be signed, however, by the executive —not by him and his wife. This also applies to people working with you, or for you, in your own company.

Engraved cards:

Few people send engraved cards today unless they are prominent in public life or hold an official position. These cards are very simple—they may contain the message and a little decoration: a straight gold border or a simple design of holly leaves around the edge. The title is included in the signature and the message usually reads, "Mr. and Mrs. Christopher Holly send you their best wishes for a Merry Christmas and a Happy New Year," or "Governor and Mrs. Herbert Black wish you a Merry Christmas and a Joyous New Year." Engraving of names on Christmas cards (as opposed to printing) follows the rules for the engraving of names on visiting cards. For example, a woman's name should never be engraved without the title of Mrs. or Miss, although a man's card may be left without a title.

Is husband's or wife's name written first?

When the cards are sent by husband and wife, the one who writes the names courteously writes his or her own name last. To very close friends, the last name need not be written. When cards are printed, there is no rule about whether the husband's or the wife's name shall be first, but the last name is always used. However, when children's names are included, the father's name comes first—always. For example: "John and Mary and John, Jr." A baby's arrival at any time during the year is announced by adding his name on the Christmas cards—"John and Mary and their new son Timothy." Cards sent to intimate friends, by a family having several children, might be "From The John Smiths—All Five," or "From The Smiths—John, Mary, Johnny, Marie and Tim."

On printed cards sent by a widow and her grown son together, or a widower and his grown daughter, the name of the parent is on one line and that of the son or daughter on the line below. Or if written by hand, the parent's name comes first: "Henry Brown and Mary," or to those who call the parent by the first name, "Henry and Mary," each signing his or her name.

Engaged people often send cards together to their intimate friends with their first names either written by hand or printed to match the rest of the printing on an informal card.

When a card is intended for the whole family, the envelope is addressed to Mr. and Mrs. Brightmeadow; on the card itself and below the wording of the message write in ink "Love to the children, too" or "We all in our house send best Christmas wishes to all of you in your house," or whatever message is suitable.

PART THREE

AS OTHERS SEE YOU

8

The general rules

"Do not attract attention to yourself in public" is one of the cardinal principles of etiquette. Naturally, then, one should shun conspicuous manners and conspicuous clothes. Avoid staring at people or pointing at them. Noise is unattractive, so don't talk in strident tones, and avoid loudly pronouncing people's names or making personal remarks that may either attract attention or proclaim a person's identity. Do not expose your private affairs, feelings or innermost thoughts in public— you are knocking down the walls of your house when you do.

WALKING ON THE STREET

Older convention ruled that a gentleman, whether walking with two ladies or with one, took the curb side of the pavement to protect his fair companion from runaway horses. Today it seems senseless for him to keep circling behind the lady every time they cross a street. Modern rules of behavior approve of his walking either on the curb side of the pavement or on the lady's left, as he chooses.

A gentleman never sandwiches himself between two ladies when walking or sitting with them. From one side, he can look in the direction of both while talking with either one, whereas when he is between them, he must turn away from one when he talks to the other. In addition, the women may have a tendency to talk "across" him, forcing him to turn back and forth as if he were at a tennis match.

The problem of packages:

Today, the etiquette of toting is determined by practicality. A lady carries such feminine articles as her purse, gloves, umbrella and hatbox, and any lightweight packages. A gentleman carries the heavy items for her—suitcases, golf bags or groceries—for a reasonable distance and asks if he can assist her when she has many small packages.

Though a man willingly carries a woman's field glasses, camera, polo coat or anything that might seemingly be his own, he should not be asked to carry a slender, colored umbrella with a long, delicate handle or a conspicuously feminine coat. A woman makes sure that any packages she asks a man to carry for her are wrapped neatly and securely or she is likely to find herself wondering why John Newbeau never calls her any more.

THE PROFFERED ARM OR THE HELPING HAND

A gentleman offers his arm to an elderly lady, to an invalid or to any lady when he thinks she may need his support. In the daytime, she need not take it unless she wishes. At night, however, when walking for some distance or going down the steps of a house, she courteously accepts his offer. When he offers his arm, he says, "Will you take my arm?" or perhaps "Wouldn't it be easier if you took my arm here?"

The only other occasions on which a gentleman offers his arm to a lady are when he takes her in at a formal dinner or when he is an usher at a wedding. In crossing a ballroom, couples walk side by side rather than hand on arm.

A gentleman does not grab a lady by the arm or the elbow and shove her along. Only when he is helping her into a car, a taxi, or a bus does he put his hand under her elbow. When he helps her out of such a vehicle, he alights first and offers her his hand.

GENTLEMEN BEFORE LADIES

In all ordinary circumstances, indoors or out, the gentleman precedes only if the way is dangerous or uncertain. Over dangerous footing, he goes first and offers his hand, which the woman takes to steady herself. He gets out of a car or bus or train first and holds the door for her, as well as stepping ahead of her to open the door for her when she enters it. He also precedes her down a very steep or slippery stairway: "Let me go first; the steps are bad." He also steps into a boat first and offers her his hand.

ON GOING THROUGH DOORS

A gentleman always stands aside and allows a woman to pass through an open door ahead of him. When approaching a closed, heavy door, however, it is far more practical and simpler if he pushes the door open, goes through and holds the door while she follows. If the door opens toward them, he pulls it open and allows her to go through first.

A woman steps into a revolving door ahead of a man if it is already moving, or if there is a partition in such a position that he can push it to start the door turning. Otherwise he steps in first and gets the door moving slowly so that she may step into the section behind him.

A LADY NOT ON THE LEFT

In former days a lady was never seated on a gentleman's left, because according to the etiquette of the day a lady "on the left" was *not* a "lady." Today in America all that remains of this rule is that, when equally practical, it is always more polite that a gentleman seat a lady on his right. (The few surviving rules about sitting on the right include the seating of a guest of honor on the right of the host or hostess or chairman, and the military rule by which the senior officer walks as well as sits on his junior's right.)

In her own car a lady sits, if practical, on the right-hand side of the rear seat if she is being driven by a chauffeur. This can be awkward, however, because in getting into the car on the left side of a one-way street, the hostess would have to precede her guest to avoid climbing over her. Therefore, it is really more practical for the lady who enters first to sit in the farthest corner, whether right or left.

THE QUESTION OF PAYING

It is becoming less customary today for a gentleman to offer to pay a lady's way, especially if they meet by chance. For example, if a young woman and a man happen to find themselves taking the same train and she stops at the newsstand to buy magazines, the man instinctively starts to pay for them. If she knows him very well and the total is small, she perhaps lets him pay. But if he is someone she knows slightly or if the magazines she has bought are higher-priced ones, she answers, "Don't bother; I have it!" and puts the money on the counter, to which he makes no protest. She also buys her ticket and tips the porter for carrying her bag. On the other hand, if she has gone on his invitation to spend the day in the country, or to lunch or dinner, or to a theater, he of course pays for everything.

A group of people going on an excursion or dining together in a restaurant should agree beforehand on the handling of the finances. Going "Dutch" (each individual or couple paying his own way) is more often done than not. To avoid the confusion of several people trying to divide and pay the bill, it is better for one man (or woman, but only if it is a women's group) to pay the entire bill, and the others to pay him their share later.

LIFE IN CROWDED CITIES

In today's congested cities, behavior that was once strictly private can all too easily become public. In city apartments sound seems sometimes to be intensified by distance. In the same room with the children, their play does not seem overloud, nor does the radio or television set when we are engrossed in the program. But to the family living on the floor below, the patter of little feet sounds like a stable full of horses and the toys they drop seem made of iron! Certain noises can't be helped; babies must sometimes cry, children scream, dogs bark or someone gets a hacking cough. Considerate people try to soften such sounds by shutting a window temporarily and by trying to train both children and dogs.

In nearly all communal buildings there are always those few who show little feeling for others because their own sensitivity is, as it were, on another wave length. Sounds that greatly annoy some of us—the unceasing sound of a television set, for example, or a record player—do not disturb others at all, whereas some things which we don't mind can be unbearable to our neighbors. If we make every effort to remember this we will not be classed with the insensitive few.

Public cleanliness:

We are all aware of the increasing messiness—sometimes filthiness—of the lounges and dressing rooms of hotels, theaters and movie houses to say nothing of the waiting rooms at railroad terminals, and rest rooms of overcrowded department stores or sports stadiums. Food-eaters, gum-chewers and newspaper-discarders are conspicuous offenders, and wall-scribblers often do permanent damage. The present scarcity of employees responsible for keeping order makes the orderliness of these places the responsibility of the public—and more especially you and me.

I particularly appeal to people who throw ashes no matter where, set wet tumblers down on no matter what, drop wet raincoats on the nearest upholstered chair, burn table edges with forgotten cigarettes. Some women leave indelible lipstick on napkins and towels, shake face powder on whatever is near them and leave hairs in the sink when they arrange their hairdo. Their behavior suggests that in their own homes their beds are seldom made! They live in disorder and are unaware of the disorder they make others endure.

If everyone would act as a deputy warden, the situation would improve. Instead of courteously refraining from criticizing others, we must not only become conscious of our own behavior but do what we have been trained NOT to do—frankly correct others. If a woman tosses a used paper towel at a receptacle and leaves it lying on the floor when it misses its mark, why not pick it up and put it in the receptacle? We might even add, "Did you notice you missed the basket?"

Most troublesome to all who have the care of public places is the discarding of chewing gum. I was told by a railroad official that chewing gum ground into the marble floor of a crowded terminal meant patient hand-scraping at great cost to the building maintenance department. Washrooms in railroad stations and department stores and other public places are put completely out of order by people who carelessly throw all manner of waste into toilets. In washrooms without attendants, conditions sometimes become so bad that a locked door is the only answer. The owner of a big department store wrote me he had been forced to hang a large sign on the door leading from the customer's rest room into the washroom reading: "This washroom can remain open for your convenience only so long as you cooperate in helping to keep it in order."

Every city has the same problem in keeping its streets clean. All the campaigns, the "Keep our city clean" weeks, the signs, the trash receptacles and the fines imposed for littering fail to solve the problem. It is the duty of each one of us to take pride in keeping our cities and towns places of cleanliness and beauty and to impress others with the importance of the problem.

I was myself a witness to the following example of the length of carelessness to which a nice person can go: Just ahead of me on the street, a prominent citizen bought a Sunday paper, walked along the street ruffling through its pages hunting for a particular article. Finding it, he stopped, tore it out, then dropped the entire paper on the sidewalk at his feet, stepped over it and walked on.

CONSIDERATION FOR THOSE WHO SERVE YOU

To show lack of consideration for those who serve us in any capacity—whether in restaurants, hotels, stores or in public places—is always a mark of ill breeding as well as inexcusable selfishness. The person who is afraid to show courtesy and consideration save to one whom he thinks it would be to his advantage to please has an exceedingly insecure dignity and questionable values.

9

In restaurants

ON ARRIVING
Checking hats and coats:

On entering a restaurant, a man leaves his hat and coat in the checkroom near the entrance. A woman may either check her coat or wear it into the dining room. If she keeps it with her, she wears it until she is seated, then drops the shoulders of the wrap over the back of her chair with her escort's help. In the daytime, if she wears a hat, she keeps it on—though today's trend is toward hatlessness, a hat is always correct with a street dress. At night, she wears a hat with daytime clothes, perhaps an evening hat or small veil with a cocktail or dinner dress and no hat, ever, with a formal evening dress.

Being seated:

After the coats have been checked, the couple or the group wait just inside the entrance until the headwaiter comes forward to ask about the number in the group and preference as to the location of the table. If there is no host (or hostess), some one member of the group assumes for all the duties that are ordinarily assigned to the host. If many people are involved, an informal kind of appointment may be made beforehand: "John, won't you please handle things this noon?" This avoids the confusion of several people addressing the waiter at once. Naturally this temporary host assumes no financial burdens not properly his.

After the table is reached, the waiter pulls out the choice seat first (meaning the seat that faces the room or perhaps a lake view). If you are a woman with a man, you naturally take it, unless you prefer another. If so, you stand beside the other chair saying, "I think I'd like to sit here." A lady who has another lady as her guest offers her the best seat, but when the hostess is a much older person, the young guest naturally refuses, saying, "Oh no, Mrs. Friendly, won't you sit on the banquette?"

When no waiter is at hand to seat them, the man seats his guests. If he is with two women, he helps first one and then at least makes the gesture of helping the second. He always helps a guest before his wife, who by that time has probably seated herself.

The women generally follow the headwaiter and the gentlemen follow them. But if a man is giving a dinner for six or more, it causes less confusion if he goes in ahead of his guests so he may indicate where they are to sit. When a husband and wife are hosts, the wife seats the guests, usually going ahead with the most important lady.

If there are only four and none is married, the ladies seat themselves facing each other. When one married couple invites another to dinner, the host and his wife sit opposite each other exactly as they do at a table for six or ten. If, however, neither couple is giving the party, they may sit in any fashion they prefer. At a table of eight or other multiples of four, the most important gentleman sits opposite the host with the hostess on his left.

If there is dancing and an older or more important woman is a guest, the host invites her for the first dance; then he dances with the other ladies and finally with his wife. The other men invite the women on either side of them to dance before asking others from seats farther away. A woman should never be left alone at a table.

At a restaurant with continuous sofa-seats or banquettes along its walls, two people dining together are seated side by side against the wall and the table is pushed in front of them. If there are four, the ladies are seated on the banquette and chairs are placed for the gentlemen facing them across the table.

In a restaurant with booths, the women go in first and sit against the far wall, facing each other across the table. The men then sit next to them, also facing each other. If a woman and two men are lunching or dining, the woman takes her place first against the wall. If one of the men is related to her, he sits across from her and the one not related sits beside her. If this grouping is reversed, the two ladies sit next to the wall and the man who is the husband of one sits beside the other.

Meeting people at a restaurant:

When a group of women arrive separately to have lunch at a restaurant, the first arrival should wait for the second rather than go in and sit by herself. When two have arrived, unless they are early, they should ask to be seated, explaining to the headwaiter that others are joining them and asking him to see they are promptly directed to the table.

When a girl is meeting a man at a restaurant and arrives first, she may do one of several things. If she knows he has made a reservation she may say to the headwaiter, "I believe Mr. Rodgers made a reservation for us. Please show me to the table and tell him I'm here when he arrives." If no reservation has been made, however, it is better for her to wait in the entry for him rather than assume the responsibility of choosing the table. Finally, if it is a nice day, she may prefer to walk down the street, window shopping for a few moments, and return after she is sure he has arrived. This, however, is really a question of tactics rather than of etiquette. A man will always wait for a lady in the entry after first making sure she has not arrived.

COCKTAILS AND WINE

When the group is seated, the waiter may ask if anyone would like a cocktail. The host asks the others what, if anything, they would like and then gives the order to the waiter. No one should be urged to drink cocktails once he has refused. If there are some who say "no" to liquor, the host asks if they would like ginger ale or tomato juice perhaps, while the others are having their cocktails. To prolong the cocktails beyond one or two when others are left with nothing in front of them is impolite.

If wine is to be served, it is ordered after the food has been chosen from the wine steward if there is one, otherwise from the waiter. The host, or the best qualified man, chooses a wine that goes well with the greatest number of choices of food. For instance, if more people have ordered chicken or fish, choose a white wine; but if more are having a steak dinner, pick a red. A vin rosé, or pink wine, is often a happy compromise, as it goes well with almost any menu. However, if you have a definite preference for red or white wine, either is perfectly correct with any food.

You may choose expensive imported wines if you wish, but some of the domestic wines at lower prices are delicious, too, and one should not feel it necessary to spend a great deal to enjoy a fine wine with dinner. If you do not recognize the names on the wine list, ask your headwaiter's advice, explaining the type you prefer, dry or sweet, domestic or imported.

ORDERING THE MEAL

For many years the rule was that the woman told the man what she would like and he gave the order. Today when one couple is dining in a restaurant it is correct and practical to follow the old rule, but when there are more than two people and the waiter asks each one for his choice, the ladies should give him their orders directly.

When the man knows the restaurant and its specialties well, particularly if foreign food is served with which the woman is not acquainted, he suggests some choices to her. If they are both unfamiliar with the type of food served, he asks the waiter to recommend one of the specialties of the restaurant.

Unless a woman knows her host is well off, she should show some consideration for his pocketbook and avoid ordering the most expensive items on the menu. She may ask for a *table d'hôte* dinner if one is offered, or choose only a soup or appetizer, a main course and a dessert. The man may always add more, with her permission, but she should give him the opportunity of economizing.

Four people, or even six, may order in the same way, telling their choices to the host, who then gives them to the waiter. If the group is larger, however, it is easier for the waiter to go around the table, taking a complete order from each guest in turn.

Table d'hôte and à la carte:

Table d'hôte means a set price for a complete meal, irrespective of how many courses are ordered. "Club" breakfasts and lunches, "blue plate" dinners or any meals at fixed prices are *table d'hôte*. *A la carte* means that you order from a list of dishes and you pay for each dish ordered, often including the bread and butter.

Usually, the price follows each item on an *à la carte* menu, whereas no prices are listed on a *table d'hôte* bill of fare except at the top where the price for the complete dinner is generally printed. Often a separate card or a box inset on the *à la carte* menu reads, "Special dinner $3.00" or whatever the price may be; you order whatever you choose on this special list for three dollars, but any item taken from the regular bill of fare is charged for as an extra.

On another popular type of menu a price follows each entrée and it says below that this price includes the choice of an *hors d'oeuvre* or a soup, a salad and a dessert, choice of coffee, tea or milk. Any additional items are charged for.

RESTAURANT TABLE MANNERS

Although table manners are much the same whether you are eating at home or in a restaurant, a few special problems arise when dining out.

The appetizer knife:

Restaurants offering appetizers requiring the use of a knife often fail to supply an extra one for this purpose. Use the knife that has been provided originally, leave it on your appetizer plate and ask for a fresh one when the waiter brings the main course. Do not try to clean your first knife and then lay it on the table between courses.

Individual side dishes:

Many restaurants serve vegetables and potatoes in small individual side dishes which the waiter places strategically around your dinner plate. You may eat these vegetables directly from the small dishes, or you may put them on your dinner plate by using a serving spoon or sliding them directly out of the small dish. You then ask the waiter to remove the empty dishes.

Cutting bread and pouring coffee:

When an uncut loaf of bread is placed on the table, the host slices or breaks off two or three individual portions and offers them with the rest of the loaf in the bread basket or on the plate to the ladies next to him. This is then passed around the table, each man cutting or breaking off a portion for himself and the lady next to him.

If coffee or tea is placed on the table without first having been poured by the waiter, the person nearest the pot should offer to pour, filling his cup last.

Iced-tea and iced-coffee spoons:

If iced tea or coffee has been served in a glass with a saucer under it, the spoon used to stir the drink is placed in this saucer. If there is no saucer and paper napkins are available, put one on the table next to your glass and then put the spoon on the napkin. If no paper napkins are available place the spoon with the bowl upside down on the edge of your butter plate, or dinner plate if necessary. A used piece of silver should not be put on the table, especially when there is a tablecloth.

Sugar and straw wrappers:

Tuck these wrappers neatly under the edge of your dinner or butter plate; do not crumple them into an ashtray, lest they catch fire.

Special types of meals:

The *smorgasbord,* a delightful importation ·from Sweden, is a very special buffet, extremely popular in the United States. When a man invites a woman to dine in this fashion, he may leave her sitting at the table and go to the buffet alone and fill a plate for her, but this eliminates much of the fun of dining in such a restaurant. Few women would want to miss seeing the delectable displays of food and choosing a little of each appealing food that is offered.

At this type of meal, the individual tables are set as usual. The smorgasbord has one or more stacks of small plates to be served with reasonable amounts of food. Since you are expected to make as many trips as you wish from your seat to the smorgasbord and back, do not overload your plate, and if you choose foods which do not go well together, use a clean plate for each trip. Leave your used plate and silver at the table for the waiter to remove while you are helping yourself to your next selection. You are intended to take your time. Start with fish to whet your appetite, then select cold cuts, followed by cheeses and a bit of fresh fruit or jello. You then choose your hot food, and end with dessert. Plenty of coffee is served throughout the meal.

Japanese and Chinese restaurants often offer interesting variations in service and food. Some of the former have a section where the guests may, if they wish, remove their shoes and sit on cushions on the floor at low tables in Japanese style. In Chinese restaurants you may try eating with chopsticks. Some restaurants suggest that each person at the table order a different dish; these are placed in the center of the table so that the diners may serve themselves from any or all of them, a delightful way to experiment with various dishes and helpful in ordering the next time you go to a similar restaurant.

Summoning a waiter:

There is no fixed rule for the best way to summon a waiter. Ways considered proper in some countries are downright insulting in others. For example a waiter who is hissed, whistled or clapped at in the United States would probably run in the other direction, and yet those gestures are perfectly correct in certain other countries. The usual way here is to catch his eye, then raise your hand, finger pointing up, as if to say "attention." If this fails, you may call "Waiter" or "Waitress" quietly or, if he is too far away to hear you, ask any other waiter nearby, "Please call our waiter."

PAYING THE CHECK

When everyone has finished his meal, the host catches the eye of the waiter or headwaiter and says, "The check, please." The check is brought face down on a small plate and presented to the man who ordered the dinner. He checks it quickly for mistakes, and returns it to the plate with the necessary money. If he finds an error, he beckons the waiter and points it out quietly; the waiter makes the adjustment, either himself or with the help of the headwaiter or cashier. Never make a "scene." If the management is unpleasant about making a correction, simply pay the check, leave as quickly as possible and do not return to that restaurant.

When it says at the bottom of your check "Please pay cashier," leave the tip on the table, collect your coats or belongings, and leave, with the host following the group, who wait in the entry while he pays the bill. (If he needs change in order to have the right amount for a tip, he pays the check and quickly returns to the table so that the waiter knows he has not been forgotten.)

Credit cards:

Numerous credit-card companies exist, a great convenience for those who dine out or entertain frequently. A credit card, sent to you on request with your name, address and a number, may be used as identification at any restaurant or establishment that is a member of the credit organization. The customer signs the check and gives it and the card to the waiter for processing. The card is returned to its owner, and the restaurant sends the check in to the credit-card company, which in turn bills the customer at the end of the month. The tip may be added to the check, but remember that if you do this, the percentage charged by the credit-card company may be deducted from the amount your waiter receives. You should therefore adjust your tip accordingly.

TIPPING

It is impossible to give definite rules for tipping, because it depends upon where you go, what you order, and the service that is given you—or that you exact. If you patronize luxurious restaurants and wear expensive clothes or if you are critical and difficult to please, greater "compenstaion" is expected.

Waiter and headwaiter:

Fifteen percent for the waiter is standard in any restaurant, twenty percent in a night club or if you've been very exacting or the service has been excellent; ten percent is too little almost anywhere, except perhaps at a lunch counter and never less than ten cents there. Tipping waitresses less than waiters is not only unfair but incorrect—because the service rendered is the same.

If you are having a party of ten, twelve, or more, fifteen percent is quite adequate for the waiters who serve you and perhaps five dollars for the headwaiter if he has given you particularly good service. If he does nothing beyond seating you and handing you a menu, you give him nothing.

Wine steward and bartender:

If the wine steward serves you, he receives twelve to fifteen percent of the wine bill. The bartender receives ten percent if you have drinks at the bar.

Checkroom and dressing room:

The fee to the checkroom boy or girl who takes care of a man's hat and coat in most restaurants is twenty-five cents, in a very expensive one, fifty cents. Fees to the maid in the dressing room of any restaurant or hotel are the same.

In the ladies room there is usually a small plate with a few coins on it in a conspicuous place. If the attendant hands you a towel or performs some other service, you are expected to leave a coin of the same denomination as those on the plate— usually a quarter.

A HOST'S RESPONSIBILITIES

The host considers the choice of restaurant: do his guests like exotic food or good plain cooking? If they are from out of town, do they have the proper clothes with them for an elaborate restaurant? Do they wish to see a place with a world-wide reputation? Or if a man is taking a girl to dinner, would she like a small, intimate spot or would she prefer to dance to a good orchestra? If he picks a well-known restaurant, he reserves a table ahead of time, and on a weekend evening, it is always safer to make a reservation. If he has ordered the dinner in advance, he observes the dishes as they are served to make sure that everything is as he requested; if there are any omissions he quietly calls them to the attention of the waiter and tactfully makes sure that they are supplied. If dinner has not been ordered beforehand, the host takes his guests' orders and gives them to the waiter or, if the party is too large, makes sure that the waiter gets the order correctly from each person.

When paying the check, the host does not display the total, but puts the money (or the signed check if he pays by credit card) quietly on the plate and nods to the waiter to remove it. If he has not had the exact amount, including the tip, the waiter brings his change, but if the sum includes both bill and tip, the host thanks the waiter and indicates that he is ready to leave by rising or remarking, "Perhaps we should be moving along if we don't want to miss the overture."

If the headwaiter has been especially helpful, given him the best table or taken special care in serving the meal, the host unobtrusively slips a bill (from one dollar to five dollars, depending on the size of the group) into his hand and thanks him as he leaves the restaurant.

WOMEN DINING OUT
When a woman invites a man:

When a woman invites a man to dine with her for personal rather than business reasons and it is understood that she is paying the bill, embarrassment is avoided if she has a credit card or possibly a charge account at the restaurant. The act of signing a slip of paper simplifies the whole affair. Many women without charge privileges prefer to give their guest a sum of cash large enough to cover the bill before they enter the restaurant. This is also an excellent solution if the husband finds he has insufficient money with him (his wife saves him embarrassment by passing him the necessary sum without calling attention to his situation).

If a woman is entertaining a customer for her business company, the company usually has accounts in nearby restaurants, and she signs the check as their representative. If no such arrangements have been made, she pays cash. If her guest protests, she explains that he is her company's guest and the amount of this check is going on her expense account. Or, if she has a credit card, she may use it and present the bill to her employer.

When women dine together:

When several women are dining out together, the problem of the check is one that can cause confusion among the waiters, the nearby diners and the women themselves. One way to avoid such confusion is to get separate checks. Or one woman may pay the entire check and the settling up can be done later.

Women and makeup at table:

A well-bred woman always avoids making up in public; cosmetics and food do not go together. At the end of a meal, she may quickly powder her nose and put on a little lipstick, but that is all. One never-to-be-broken rule is: don't ever use a comb anywhere outside a dressing room. Don't even slightly rearrange or put your fingers on your hair in any place where food is served.

RESTAURANT COURTESY

When a group about to dine together enters and sees people whom some know and others do not, the members generally continue on directly to their table, nodding "hello" as they pass. However, there are occasions when introductions are suitably performed. The men at the table rise when a woman is being introduced, as they do whenever a woman stops to talk. But when a woman stopping at a table is introduced to other women seated there, the latter never rise—not even if they are young and the visitor quite old.

Men at the table do not rise when another man stops on his way by. When someone comes across the room to speak to one of the diners, that man only stands to shake hands. The visitor then asks him please to be seated while he finishes what he has come to say. But if he intends to say more than a few words of greeting, he asks a waiter for a chair or quickly makes a later appointment with the one he wishes to talk to.

Then there is the unobserving woman who, on entering a restaurant, passes a table where her friends the Evanses are dining; she stops for a greeting that lengthens into a prolonged dialogue, while the polite husband stands and watches the food on his plate grow cold. From time to time the visitor earnestly urges, "Oh, *do* sit down!"—which Mr. Evans may quite properly do Usually, however, the poor husband feels too conspicuous to sit down while the woman remains standing.

One husband solved the problem this way: Gustav Gourmet, just about to eat a perfect soufflé in a noted restaurant, was forced to stand for a friend of his wife's who stopped at their table. "Oh, *please* sit down! You must not let your soufflé fall!" said she and, having given this permission, went on talking. Thereupon he solved the problem by lifting the plate and eating—standing.

Lunch counters and cafeterias:

When a couple goes to a lunch counter that is so crowded that there are not two seats together, it is permissible to ask a person sitting between two empty stools if he would mind moving down one place. Conversely, a person in this position should offer to move before he is asked. At a crowded cafeteria tables are meant to be shared, but it is only friendly and courteous to ask "Is this seat saved?" or "May I sit here?" before grabbing an empty chair at a table that is already occupied.

10

The opera, the theater and other indoor entertainments

THE OPERA

Seating in a box at the opera:

When people dine with their hostess before the opera, they usually arrive together. The gentlemen help the ladies to take off their coats. If there is an anteroom, one of the gentlemen draws back the curtain between the anteroom and the box. The ladies enter, followed by the gentlemen, the last of whom closes the curtain again. If there are two ladies besides the hostess, the latter places her more distinguished or older guest in the corner of the front row nearest the stage. The seat farthest from the center is always her own. The older guest takes her seat first, then the hostess takes her place, whereupon the third lady goes forward in the center to the front of the box and stands while one of the gentlemen places a chair for her between the other two. If there are eight, one of the ladies sits in the second row with two gentlemen beside her and the other two in the back row.

A common practice today is for three or four couples to subscribe to a box at the opera together, sharing the cost. So that each member of the group may enjoy the better seats and no two men be always relegated to the back row, these friends may agree to switch their seating arrangements around, even though it violates the old rule of "no gentlemen in the front row."

Between the acts:

Both ladies and gentlemen may visit friends in other boxes between the acts, but the lady always has an escort. They may go out to enjoy the refreshments provided by the opera houses or simply to mingle with the other patrons at the opera. No lady is ever left alone in the box, however, and all who have been out of the box during the intermission return promptly when the signal is given for the raising of the curtain, a courtesy to the performers as well as to the audience. Their is never any conversation during the overture or the performance. An enthusiastic audience may applaud at the end of an aria and, of course, after each curtain.

Dressing for the occasion:

In the boxes, many of the men wear white tie and tails, and their companions wear long evening dresses and their most brilliant jewelry—this is particularly true on Monday evenings in New York and other large opera houses. Other men prefer a dinner jacket, and the ladies choose an evening, dinner or cocktail dress. In the orchestra or grand tiers, either a dinner jacket or a business suit is correct, and you will feel comfortable in whichever you choose. A lady may wear a long or short dinner dress or, if her escort is in a business suit, a silk dress or a cocktail suit.

In the balconies, daytime clothes are more commonly worn by both men and women.

THE THEATER

Dinner and a play:

When an unattached man invites friends to go to the theater, he may take them to dinner in a restaurant beforehand; but if a host and hostess have a house or apartment not too far distant from the theater, they are likely to have their dinner party at home. Young people especially like to dine out together, and the evening is usually Dutch treat. Or one member of the group may ask the others to meet at his (or her) home for cocktails and a chat, but the cost of dinner and the tickets is divided among them. However, many friends prefer to meet at the theater and, perhaps, have refreshments afterward at some convenient restaurant.

It is absolutely essential that a host arrange for theater

tickets well in advance. In New York, for instance, if you buy
your tickets at the box office, you must plan weeks ahead in
order to get the desired seats for popular plays. You may also
buy tickets from a ticket agency which charges a certain
amount more than the box-office price.

Arriving at the theater:

On arriving at the theater, the host (or hostess) holds the
tickets so that the ticket-taker may see them, but he allows his
guests to pass in ahead of him. At the head of the aisle, if the
usher is there, he gives her the stubs and steps back, and the
ladies precede him down the aisle. If, however, the usher is
already partway down the aisle, the host may lead the way
until he reaches her. For a large party, the hostess may tell
her guests in what order they are going to sit, so that they
may arrive at their row in more or less that order.

The only fixed rule about seating in the theater is that a man
sits on the aisle. In a group of four, it is more pleasant if one
man goes in first, followed by the two women, and finally the
other man. A woman would probably sit next to the man who
was not her husband. When the party is larger, a woman
usually leads the way into the row, and the others alternate,
men and women, leaving the host, or one of the men if there
is no host, on the aisle. In the case of a man and a woman
alone, she, of course, goes in first and he follows, sitting on or
nearest to the aisle. There are exceptions to this rule: Arthur
Norman, for example, is stone-deaf in his right ear and his
wife always sits on his left no matter where that position
happens to place her. Others for comparable reasons do the
same.

When the play is over:

The man on the aisle, or nearest the aisle, stands in the
aisle for a moment so that the lady who follows can walk with
him or precede him. Only when the crowd is really dense does
a man go first to make a wedge for her. In a theater party of
six, the first man lets the woman who sat next to him go ahead
of him, then joins her.

Dressing for the theater:

Today Mrs. Franklin who decides to combine her trip to the
theater with an afternoon's shopping may quite properly

appear at the theater in a wool dress or even a suit, although it should not be a sports suit. Many women carry an extra piece or two of jewelry in their purses with which to dress up their "basic" black dresses for the evening.

When a hostess plans a theater party, perhaps to celebrate an anniversary, she may wish to make the evening more gala by requesting that the men wear "black tie." The only other time more formal dress is required is the opening night when one sits "down front." Then ladies wear cocktail or dinner dresses, and gentlemen tuxedos.

Courtesy at the theater:

Don't be late! If your taxi breaks down or something else causes unavoidable delay, you should wait at the back of the theater until the first scene is over. Then the usher can show you quickly to your seat.

Hats off! Every woman should be agreeable about removing her hat if asked to do so. Even better, courteous women take them off without having to be asked. A high hairdo can also block the view of the one behind it. In such cases one can only wish the wearer had been more considerate.

"Excuse me, please" is the natural expression of courtesy when having to disturb anyone in order to get to or leave your seat. If someone is obliged to get up to let you pass, say, "Thank you," or "I'm sorry"; if you have to pass someone a second time, say, "I'm sorry to disturb you again," and "Thank you," as they let you go by.

In passing strangers, both men and women face the stage and press closely to the backs of the seats of the row in front of them and are careful not to drag a bag or a coat across the heads of those sitting in that row. When you are seated and others must pass you, you may either turn your knees sideways, if there is space enough, so passersby do not have to step over your knees; otherwise you must of course stand, but sit down again—quickly! Every second you stand, you are cutting off the view of all who are seated behind you.

Occasionally older men as well as women practically refuse to allow anyone to pass because of their reluctance to gather up opera glasses, program and bag and stand to let each person on a long aisle leave and come back. But if you haven't sufficient self-control to be amiable why not avoid all annoyances and stay at home?

Quiet, please! Finish that one important story or joke or find that misplaced glove at intermission time. If you want to discuss the plot or the performance, wait until the act is over.

Smoking between the acts:

A woman usually goes out to the lobby with a man who wishes to smoke between the acts. If she does not smoke, it is quite proper to leave her briefly during one intermission, but he should not leave her at each curtain-fall to sit alone until the house is darkened for the curtain's rise.

THE MOVIES

Except for a premiere or an elaborate benefit performance, casual clothes are proper—although "casual" must be determined by the location of the theater and the other activities of the evening. For example, slacks might be quite proper in the country, with a stop at your favorite ice-cream stand to follow, but quite out of place in the city, especially should your escort suggest, say, dancing afterward.

Talking, coughing, jingling bangles—not to speak of rattling cellophane when opening candy boxes—are annoying and disturbing to everyone in the audience. If those behind you insist on talking, it is bad manners and does no good to turn around and glare. The only thing you can do is to say amiably, "I'm sorry, but I can't hear anything while you talk." If they still persist, you can ask an usher to call the manager. Those who discuss private affairs might do well to remember that every word said above a whisper is easily heard by those sitting directly in front.

11

Conducting meetings

Almost all of us are involved in several kinds of meetings each year and most of us find ourselves from time to time in the position of having to take charge. Therefore, some generalized suggestions may be useful.

MEETINGS OF LARGE ORGANIZATIONS

The president or chairman of any large organization runs its meetings in strict accordance with the rules of parliamentary procedure found in the standard reference book, *Robert's Rules of Order*, available in any library or bookstore. In addition he controls the meeting politely but firmly, preventing unpleasant wrangling and keeping the discussion from wandering from the business of the day. His appearance is one of good grooming, appropriate for the time of day and the type of meeting.

Board meetings:

The chairman of the board of any organization holds meetings, probably once a month and possibly oftener. Meetings of a large organization (a hospital or a community fund drive, for example) are run with some degree of formality. Preparatory work includes providing adequate seating, pads, pencils and, if possible, copies of the minutes of the last meeting and the agenda for that day.

You open the meeting (no more than ten minutes need be allowed for latecomers) with "Will the meeting please come to order?" and a word of welcome. The secretary reads the minutes of the last meeting. Whereupon, you ask, "Are there any additions or corrections?" If there are none, you state, "The minutes stand approved as read." If there are corrections, the secretary makes them and you say, "The minutes stand approved as corrected." If the minutes have been distributed to each board member in advance, the reading of them may be dispensed with, provided you first ask for a motion and a second from the floor to that effect which may then be put to a vote. Next you call for the treasurer's report, then the reports of the committee chairmen. Those who have no report simply say, "I have no report to make this month." If there are no questions about the reports, you bring up the business to be discussed, following your prepared agenda.

As chairman you recognize those who wish to speak, one at a time, and see that no one speaks for too long, intervening if an argument gets too heated by saying, for instance, "I'm sorry, Mrs. Harris, but you have spoken for more than your allotted time, so I will have to ask you to sit down"; or you may rap for attention, saying, "The meeting will please come to order. Mr. Robertson, kindly confine your remarks to the subject and do not go into personalities." If he persists in going on, you can simply ask him to sit down, as he is out of order. By directing the discussion firmly along appropriate lines, limiting speeches, and staying in charge, a good chairman hastens immeasurably the successful conclusion of the business meeting.

MEETINGS HELD IN THE HOME

When a group is formed to raise funds for a charity, to back a political candidate or put on a play, meetings may be held in the home of the chairman or of any member of the group who volunteers. Coffee is usually served before or after a morning meeting, tea or coffee in the afternoon. The member at whose home the meeting is held may provide the refreshments or others may volunteer to contribute.

No matter how informal these gatherings, a chairman, appointed or elected to plan and direct the meeting, and a secretary to take notes or minutes, are essential for the orderly continuity of the work. If funds are involved, a treasurer is needed to handle them and keep an exact account of receipts and expenditures.

The group need not follow any particular rules but may run

its meetings as it wishes—semi-formally with minutes being read and the roll being called. Or it may be a social meeting with open discussion over a cup of coffee and a piece of cake—provided the chairman directs the discussion into the proper channels. Otherwise, friends tend to become involved in a discussion of babies or neighborhood politics and forget the purpose of the meeting. Each member should express views about the current topic and be willing to discuss and act on suggestions, so that the chairman is not left with all the responsibilities.

As to clothing, ordinary standards of neatness are observed; of course, this excludes mud-encrusted shoes or hair curlers. A skirt and sweater, or slacks if you live in the country, are perfectly acceptable. If the group is made up of young mothers, babies and children are usually brought along to play together in some safe spot other than the conference room!

any other elaborate accommodations they w

a painful budget

PART FOUR

ADVICE FOR TRAVELERS

12

Planning the trip

Planning a trip is "half the fun." But to the joys of poring over maps and collecting suggestions from friends, add certain practical preparation without which travel can be a nightmare instead of an adventure. Touring castles in Spain will be far more enjoyable if you fortify yourself with a good meal and a comfortable night's sleep.

RESERVATIONS
Advantages of a travel bureau:
The easiest way to plan your trip is to go to a travel bureau, preferably one recommended by a well-traveled friend. Tell the bureau where you want to go, when and how, and let them work out the best possible plan for you. They can do it not only better but much more economically than you can and at no extra cost to you, as they get their commission from the transportation company, the resort or the hotel.

An important point for the inexperienced traveler to realize is this: while a competent travel bureau will engage, if you wish, the best rooms in deluxe hotels, secure automobiles by the week or month, either with or without chauffeurs, and arrange any other elaborate accommodations, they will, with equal interest, provide the same quality service for those traveling on a limited budget.

Making your own reservations:

If you do not wish to use a travel agency, make your reservations well in advance. Arrangements for an extensive trip to a popular area may reasonably be made six months or more ahead of time. Reconfirm the reservations a week or two before your departure. Request a receipt or acknowledgment (and carry it with you) to be shown on your arrival to the innkeeper or hotel manager as proof of your reservations.

Make your travel reservations at the same time that you make hotel reservations, and secure your home-bound ticket then too. Many people have found themselves in Europe at the end of the tourist season with days of waiting for a plane seat still ahead of them.

A tip to parents: When your son or daughter sets off for a summer of traveling, possibly with knapsack on his back and no planned stopping places other than a list of youth hostels (inexpensive lodgings for bicyclists and motorcyclists found in every European country), be sure that he or she has a return reservation, either with him or held at the airline or steamship office for him. It is all too easy for a youngster to cable home, "Unable to get reservations until September 15" —three weeks longer than you had expected to finance him!

Using a guidebook:

If you are able to travel during the "off" season you may not need reservations. To be able to drive at random, following whatever highway or byway catches your fancy, stopping for the night wherever you happen to be, staying as long as you wish in some charming city, is the ideal way to travel. There is but one requirement—a good guidebook. Places recommended by all reputable guidebooks are visited regularly by their staffs and their information is as accurate and current as it is possible to make it. Thus you may avoid poor or dirty accommodations and dishonest proprietors.

(For additional suggestions about hotels and transportation, see also Chapters 13 and 14.)

Protection of your house:

When you leave an empty house or apartment, take these steps:

Cancel milk delivery and newspaper delivery. Ask the post office to either hold or forward your mail—mail and newspapers piling up at your door only advertise your absence to unwelcome intruders. Have all laundry and cleaning delivered before you leave.

In a house leave a light or two burning, or install an automatic light that goes on at dusk. Check all locks on windows and doors and be sure that you take a key with you! Leave a spare key with a friendly neighbor and ask him to check the house occasionally. Notify the police of your absence and ask them to keep watch over your house. Give them the names of anyone who might be coming into the house legitimately.

Never give your travel plans or dates to your local newspaper in advance. There are people who watch the papers every day in order to take advantage of just such information.

TRAVEL DOCUMENTS

Several weeks before your departure, apply for your passport, visas if they are required, and health certificates which must be attended to in person. After you have filled out the forms and paid the fee at the passport office, your passport may be sent to you by mail. You must also go in person to the consulate of the country from which you wish to get a visitor's permit or visa.

It is advisable to get some foreign money in small bills and change (check the amount you are permitted to take in or out of some countries). Be sure to take the bulk of your money in American Express or other traveler's checks which can be replaced if lost and are accepted everywhere as readily as cash. A letter of credit is a good idea if you want to have something to depend on for extra and unexpected expenses.

(See also Chapter 15.)

13

Motels and hotels

MOTELS

All over America, and recently in foreign countries, motels are becoming more and more luxurious. The larger ones, particularly those belonging to national chains, are equipped with every facility including swimming pools, shuffleboard courts, sunbathing areas, television sets and individual coffee-makers in each room. At one motel I know, a drive-in movie is directly behind the motel, so that you can sit comfortably in bed and see a movie before going to sleep with the sound piped into each unit through a private speaker!

Those motels connected with a chain generally have a restaurant on the premises, but if you are staying at a smaller motel, you may have to go a little distance to find a good eating place. Ask the clerk at the desk to recommend one or two. If you are looking for entertainment—dancing, movies and so on—you may be better off in a hotel in the heart of the city.

The advantages of motels:

Because the majority of motels are on the outskirts of towns you need not drive into heavy urban traffic to reach them. Your car is parked directly in front of your room or unit and you unload only what you need for the night. One may travel in shorts, slacks—whatever is most comfortable for driving. One simply goes to the office of the motel, registers, pays for the room (if you are staying for one night only), receives the key and drives to the allotted unit. No tips are necessary. In the morning you depart when you wish, without any further formality.

Because of the immense popularity of motels as stopping places, it is wise, especially for a woman alone, to make reservations in advance. If you stay in a chain motel, they will be delighted to call ahead to the member motel in or nearest to your next destination and reserve a room for the following night.

HOTELS

Accommodations:

If possible, write or telegraph in advance for accommodations. At the time of a convention or a big football game, or any other occasion of crowded hotels, you should write months in advance. Have your letter or telegram state clearly the hour of your arrival, number of persons, the accommodations you wish, the approximate length of your stay, and ask for a confirmation.

A typical telegram and letter follow:

KINDLY RESERVE DOUBLE ROOM WITH BATH FOR WIFE AND SELF AFTERNOON DECEMBER THIRD TO FIFTH. PLEASE CONFIRM.

JOHN G. HAWKINS

Manager of the Lake Hotel
Chicago, Illinois (and the zip code number)

Dear Sir:

Please reserve two single rooms with baths or with a bath between for my daughter and me. We are due to arrive in Chicago at five o'clock on the afternoon of December sixth and shall stay a week.

I prefer moderate-priced rooms not higher than the fourth floor.

Very truly yours,

Mrs. George K. Smith

Kindly confirm reservation to
Brightmeadows, Ill. (and the zip code number)

(This is one of the few occasions when "Mrs." belongs with a woman's signature.)

The arrival at a hotel:

At a first-class hotel, a doorman opens the door of your car or taxi and deposits your luggage on the sidewalk. A bellboy carries your bags into the lobby and deposits them near the registration desk, usually a long counter manned by one or more men.

You go to the desk, and, if you have wired ahead, you say to the room clerk, "I am Mrs. George K. Smith. I telegraphed you Tuesday and received your confirmation on Thursday." The clerk presents you with a form to fill in and sign.

A man registers: "John Smith, New York." If alone he does not use "Mr.," but if his wife is with him, he adds the title to their joint names: "Mr. and Mrs. John Smith, New York."

He fills in the blanks on the registration form, which includes one for his house address. If he is accompanied by his entire family, "John Smith and Family" is acceptable. Nurses, employees or those with a different name should be listed separately so that they may receive mail or messages.

If for any reason children are registered individually, "Miss" precedes the names of all little girls. Boys are registered with no title—just "John" or "Henry" or whoever—until they are eighteen or over.

One exceptional occasion when a lady signs her name "Miss" or "Mrs." is in a hotel register. "Miss Jean McLean" is correct, or "Mrs. George K. Smith"—never "Sarah Smith."

If Mrs. Smith arrives first, she fills in the blank for both herself and her husband. Then on his arrival, he says to the room clerk, "Mrs. Smith has already arrived and registered. What is the number of our room, please?"

After you have registered, the clerk hands the room key to the bellboy who gathers up your bags and starts for the stairs or the elevator. You follow. In your room, he turns on the lights and opens the window or tests the air-conditioning unit. His tip is usually twenty-five cents for each large bag, more if there are several small parcels, and an extra twenty-five cents for opening up the room.

Service in a hotel:

The telephone is your base of operations. You tell the operator the hour you wish to be called, ask for the desk, inquire about mail or messages, call the porter's desk about luggage or trains or reservations, or the newsstand for magazines, newspapers or theater tickets, room service when you want food or drinks sent up to you, and valet or maid service if you need a dress or a suit cleaned or pressed. If there is no regular valet service, you ask a chambermaid, "Where can I have my dress [or suit] pressed?" She answers, "I will do it for you," or tells you who will.

In the morning, for instance, if you want breakfast in your room (there is an additional charge for this), you say, "Room service, please," then give your order, chosen perhaps from breakfast menus in your room. Presently the waiter brings in a tray with your order, puts it on a table, or in a large hotel he wheels in a long narrow table completely set: cloth, china, glass, silverware, etc. You may pay him in cash, or sign the check and have it put on your hotel bill.

You may receive the waiter when you are sitting up in bed or clad in a robe. Waiters are used to carrying trays into the presence of wearers of all varieties of pajamas and negligées. He returns later for the table, or, if you do not wish to be disturbed, you may put it outside your door. His tip is the usual fifteen percent of the check.

Pilferage:

An inexplicable urge to pilfer small or large objects seems to come over many otherwise decent, honest citizens when they are guests in a hotel. Bath towels, mats, ashtrays, dining-room silver and even blankets and bed linen disappear in such quantities as to be a major expense in every large hotel. These pilferers, normally law-abiding persons, when accused of stealing, say, "Not at all—the management expects these things to disappear!" I suggest that any time you are tempted to take home such a souvenir, you say to yourself, "That ashtray [or bath towel] is the property of the hotel, and if I take it home with me, I am no better than a common thief."

Hotel manners:

If you have a private sitting room, you can have everyone you please take a meal in it with you, or visit with you, as long as you observe the ordinary conventions of behavior. But it is against the rules of any reputable hotel for a guest to receive a visitor of the opposite sex in a bedroom without first speaking to the desk clerk. Noisy parties and men or women visitors at unconventionally late hours are not permitted in any high-class hotel.

The woman staying alone in a hotel—and it is quite correct for even a very young girl to do so—and having no sitting room of her own receives her men visitors in any one of the public rooms of the hotel and entertains in the restaurant or dining room. It is not so much a question of suitable age as of suitable behavior. A woman or girl who is dignified and whose friends are the sort that pass that sharpest of character readers, the house detective, will never have an uncomfortable moment. But the woman who thinks a hotel is a brier-patch where she can hide away all the things she oughtn't to do will find that she might as well have chosen to hide in a show window.

A hotel guest—whether a woman or a man—going down to the dining room alone may wish to take a book or newspaper, because nothing is duller than to sit staring into space while waiting for one's order.

A woman may wear a hat in a hotel restaurant or dining room if she wishes. Of course, if she is dressed in evening clothes, she does not wear a hat.

When you call on freinds at a hotel, you either inquire for them at the desk and the clerk telephones their rooms or you go to the house telephone and ask the number of their room, call them, and then go up in the elevator. Or your friends may wish to join you in the lobby or the lounge.

When you leave the hotel:

When you are ready to leave, go to the cashier—or telephone from your room—asking that your bill be made out. Then you telephone for a bellboy to carry down the luggage. Downstairs you tip him, pay the bill at the desk, leave the key and a forwarding address for mail to be sent after you.

TIPS

The following schedule of tips applies to transient visitors staying in the hotel (or the motel with services) for not more than a week. Permanent or long-term residents tip on a monthly or even twice-yearly basis. The amount varies according to the quality of the service, and the quantity requested. Hotel residents must arrive at their own conclusions, possibly with the help of other permanent guests and even the hotel management.

To a dining-room waiter in a first-class restaurant: between fifteen and twenty percent of the bill, but never less than twenty-five cents in a restaurant with a tablecloth on the table. In an American-plan hotel, you give the waiter or waitress at the end of each week about ten percent of the week's board per person, but less if the family is large. When going to the dining room for the first time, you give from two to five dollars to the headwaiter if you would like a table in a particular location. When you leave, you tip him proportionately to the service rendered: one or two dollars a week, if he has done little, and five dollars for a family. For a one-night stay, no tip is necessary.

Other tips:

Chambermaid: one dollar a week a room, or fifty cents a week in a small inexpensive hotel. If you stay one night only, fifty cents for each person in a room in a large hotel, or twenty-five cents in a small one. If you cannot find her leave it in an envelope addressed "Chambermaid" on the bureau.

Doorman: nothing for putting a bag on the sidewalk; twenty-five cents if he helps take luggage into the hotel or calls a taxi

Bellboy: twenty-five cents for each large bag; twenty-five cents for paging

Porter: fifty cents for bringing a trunk to the room
fifty cents or one dollar if there is much baggage
twenty-five cents for ice, drink setups, newspapers, packages, telegrams, etc.

Checking a man's coat and hat: twenty-five cents

Attendant in the woman's dressing room of a hotel or restaurant: twenty-five cents

Attendant at the coat rack at the entrance to the dining room: twenty-five cents

Valet: tip only if he brings a large amount of clothing back to your room when you are there; his charge for cleaning or pressing is included in the hotel bill

Barbers, manicurists and beauty-parlor specialists: fifteen
    percent of the bill, but not less than twenty-five cents
Bootblacks: twenty-five cents

People who frequent expensive hotels and take first-class
accommodations on trains, ships or planes are expected to
give larger tips than people traveling economically.

One piece of advice: Whether or not you approve of the
system of tipping, you will not get good service unless you tip
generously but not lavishly. If you do not care to order
elaborate meals, do not go to an expensive hotel and expect
your waiter to be contented with a tip of ten cents for your
dollar snack!

EUROPEAN HOTELS

Large, first-class hotels in Europe are essentially the same
as our best hotels in the United States. When you leave the
beaten track, however, for those less well-traveled be prepared
for certain differences in facilities and service.

All services other than actual accommodations and meals
are provided by a concierge; he and his staff handle luggage
and mail, make reservations, rent cars, shop for you, deliver
packages, arrange tours, and are altogether indispensable.

Instead of a telephone in each room, many foreign hotels
have a pushbutton device with little pictures of waiters, maids
or valets beside each button to indicate which to push. This
system helps to overcome the language barrier.

Small hotels seldom have bathrooms with every room. Many
rooms do have washbasins; in small towns there may just be a
pitcher of water and a bowl. In these hotels, you use the
public bathrooms on each floor used by all guests; these are
usually marked "W.C."—a universally known abbreviation for
"water closet." Washcloths and toilet soap may or may not be
provided, so carry your own!

The hotels in small towns may not be luxurious, but the
friendliness more than makes up for the lack of comfort: the
chef who proudly invites you to see his spotless kitchen, the
chambermaid who smilingly brings you a cup of coffee when
she awakens you in the morning, and the concierge who is
eager to show you the beauty of *his* town, leave you feeling
that the physical comforts are not so important as you thought.

14

On plane, train or ship

PLANE TRAVEL

Large, scheduled airlines offer two main classes of air travel: first class and economy. Both classes fly on the same plane. The economy class, occupying two-thirds or more of the space toward the rear of the plane, is divided from first class by a partition. Seats are generally three on each side of the aisle. Meals and snacks are included in the fare, but you must pay for alcoholic drinks. On long flights, most airlines show movies in both economy and first class. The difference in cost between economy and first class on a long flight is quite astronomical. For this difference, in the first-class section the widely spaced seats are two on each side of the aisle with plenty of room to stretch one's legs; tables may be put between the seats so that passengers may play cards or spread out their business papers. Cocktails are free, meals more elaborate.

Luggage:

The ideal luggage is a lightweight, firm metal, such as aluminum, or a composition. (Soft bags can be damaged or pierced if handled roughly.)

Each piece of luggage is weighed when you check in for an overseas flight, including those you carry with you onto the plane. The exceptions are handbags, cameras, binoculars, briefcases, knitting bags, a book or two, etc. In general, overseas economy-class passengers are allowed approximately forty-four pounds, and first class, sixty-six. You may carry more, but you pay for the excess at a specified rate per pound. Any bag or package carried onto the plane must be capable of being stowed under you seat. No hard or heavy article is allowed on the shelf above the seats. On domestic flights each passenger is allowed two pieces of luggage free, regardless of weight. If you carry more than two, you will be charged at the usual rate for excess.

On arrival at the airport or terminal, a porter takes your luggage to be weighed in. If it is overweight on overseas flights, you pay the extra charge at this time. Tip the porter twenty-five cents for each suitcase. When your ticket is validated, the bags are tagged and the stubs given to you at the same time. You do not see the luggage again until it is brought into the "baggage claim" section at your destination.

Arriving at the airport:

On overseas flights, you are asked to arrive at the airport one hour ahead of departure time, half an hour for domestic flights. Seats are usually assigned as the passengers arrive, although some airlines allow you to choose from a chart displayed at the counter. Your boarding pass with the seat number on it is shown at the departure gate and again to the stewardess when you board the plane.

While in the air:

During the trip, the stewardesses, whom you signal by a light above your head, serve meals, bring magazines, hand out newspapers, bring extra blankets, even help care for babies by heating bottles, etc. Never tip a steward or stewardess or any other member of the crew.

Be sure to wear loose, comfortable, wrinkleproof clothing. On overnight flights some women like to change into slacks and bedroom slippers. Men may remove jackets, loosen ties, change into a sport shirt. A loose sweater and wool socks or slippers are a wise protection against low temperatures in the plane.

Obey "Fasten Seat Belts" and "No Smoking" signs promptly. (Only cigarette smoking is allowed.)

No animals are allowed in the cabin of a plane except a Seeing Eye dog. A pet must be in a carrier (his weight is counted as part of the amount of luggage you are permitted). He rides with the luggage or in a special pressurized compartment.

In the washrooms or lavatories on a plane, wipe out the basin thoroughly with your used towel before you throw it into the towel basket. Before combing your hair, lay a fresh towel over the washbasin or counter. When you have finished, throw the towel into the towel receptacle. All this is only good manners.

Friendliness among the passengers is characteristic of air travel. People talk freely to each other. But anyone can avoid conversation by simply saying, "I'd rather not talk if you don't mind, I'm very tired."

TRAIN TRAVEL

The official rate for a porter to take luggage from the entrance of a railroad station to a train is twenty-five cents for each piece unless otherwise posted; an additional tip is optional but expected. When traveling to an unknown destination, where there may be no porters, send larger bags and trunks ahead by railway express.

If you are spending the night in a single berth, upper or lower, carry a small overnight case with you, as the remainder of your luggage will be stowed at the end of the car. Even in a compartment or drawing room, avoid having to open large bulky suitcases.

On a day-long journey, speak or not, as you please, to your table companions in the diner. On a longer journey, if you happen to sit near the same person for a number of meals, it is good manners to enter into friendly conversation.

During the day in a Pullman section, the seat facing forward belongs to the occupant of the lower berth; the occupant of the upper berth rides backward. If your seat faces forward, courtesy demands that you ask the occupant of the other seat whether he or she minds riding backward—and if he does, to make a place at your side. The window seat naturally belongs to you—unless you prefer the other.

In a bedroom, compartment or drawing room, the porter should be called to make up the beds by ten o'clock or ten thirty at the latest. If you wish to have another drink or continue your talk, you may go to the club car or bar car. When you are in a berth in the open section of the car, divided only by curtains from the other passengers, all conversation ceases as soon as neighbors are in bed; if you are not sleepy, resort to a good book in your berth. Occupants of a section, even though strangers, consult each other on the time they like their berths made up for the night.

Going to bed in a Pullman:

The porter, on your ring, will make up your berth when you are ready to go to bed. If you have a roomette, drawing room, compartment or bedroom, you simply shut your door when he is finished, and go to bed. Since all bathroom facilities are included in your space, you do not go to the public dressing room at all. If, however, your berth is in the open car, you wash and prepare for the night in the dressing room while the porter makes up your bed. If you have an upper berth the porter brings a stepladder for you to get up and down to your berth. You may remove your clothes in the dressing room, put on a bathrobe and return to your berth. But most people, after washing, return to their berths, close the curtains and go through the gymnastics of undressing in an impossibly small space! In the morning you ring for the stepladder and dress, again as much as you can in your berth, because there is no privacy—and less space—in the dressing room.

Tips:

Tip dining-car waiters as you would in any restaurant: fifteen percent of the bill, never less than a quarter; waiters or stewards in the bar car or club car, fifteen percent of the bill, and a quarter if they bring "setups" (ice, glasses, water and soda) to you in the Pullman car; the Pullman porter receives fifty cents to one dollar for each person on an overnight trip—more if he has given additional service other than making up the berths.

TRAVEL ON A SHIP
Luggage:

On your arrival at a pier, a porter puts your luggage on the escalator or elevator to the upper level. His tip is twenty-five cents or more a bag. You go to the receiving end of the escalator where your porter puts the luggage on trucks for delivery on board the ship. (If another crew takes over upstairs, tips are also given to these porters.) You then show your passport and ticket at the proper desk and board the ship.

Be sure to arrive at the ship in plenty of time to be certain your luggage is on board. Your receipt stubs for trunks sent to the pier by express are turned in to the baggage master at his desk on the pier; the luggage will be stored in the hold or sent to your stateroom, as requested. If you are sharing a cabin with strangers, unpack all but one or two pieces and send the rest to the hold.

Reserving dining-room table and deck chair:
Immediately after being shown to your cabin, it is well to go to the dining room and reserve a table at the sitting you wish for the voyage. Next, go to the main deck and see the head deck steward about a steamer chair and tell him your preference for its location.

Social life on board:
When friends come to the ship to wish you "Bon Voyage!" you may want to give a party. If you have a large, comfortable stateroom, your steward will bring soda and soft drinks, hors d'oeuvres, ice and glasses to your cabin. If you are in a small room, possibly shared with strangers, you may have your party in one of the bars or lounges. In either case, board the vessel early and make the arrangements with your cabin steward or the headwaiter. During the rest of the trip you may entertain your new shipboard acquaintances in the same way. Tip the stewards who serve such a party fifteen percent of the bill at the time, rather than adding it to your regular tip at the end of the trip.

In first class, on a luxury liner, some people dress in evening clothes—tuxedos for the men and dinner dresses for the women—every night except the first on board. This is not necessary, however, except on the night of the Captain's party (usually the next-to-last night out), and cocktail dresses and business suits are acceptable on other evenings.

No formal introductions are necessary on board in any case—you introduce yourself to your neighbors and, with luck, you quickly find congenial people with whom you will become friends for the length of the voyage: in deck chairs, around the swimming pool, in the lounges or in the game rooms. Only remember that some people honestly wish to be left alone.

A cruise ship is like a large house party where the guests speak to each other as a matter of course. A "cruise director" (on small ships this is the purser) acts as host or hostess, arranges for deck or bridge games and introduces dancing partners. Any young girl or man on board who is without friends is expected to go to the director and ask to be introduced to congenial people.

On any ship, the Captain usually entertains at cocktails, once for first-class and once for tourist-class passengers. He may also give smaller parties for prominent persons, personal friends or those sitting at his table. These invitations should always be accepted, if possible, and a written refusal sent if you cannot attend. The Captain is always "Captain Sawyer" and the other officers "Mr." At mealtime, those seated at the Captain's table or that of any senior officer must treat him as they would a host in a private home. These passengers arrive at the same time as the officer. If he is delayed, they wait for him before starting, unless he sends word to go on without him. At other tables it is not necessary to arrive all together as long as each person or group sits down well within the limits of that sitting.

Tips:

There are definite minimum amounts that passengers are expected to give. In first class, your cabin steward receives ten dollars, the dining-room steward ten dollars and the head-waiter five dollars. One or two dollars to the busboy, if there is one, would make him very happy. Lounge and bar stewards receive fifteen percent at the time they render their services, the chief deck steward five dollars and his assistant, if he has one, three dollars. Fifteen percent of the amount of the wine bill goes to the dining-table wine steward.

All these suggestions for tipping are per person, on a transatlantic trip.

Tips in the cabin and tourist classes are lower, in proportion to the difference in the passage fare. A good general rule for shipboard travelers is to allow approximately ten percent of the fare for tips. Divide about half of this allowance between the cabin and dining-room stewards, and distribute the rest to others who have served you. Obviously, passengers occupying suites are expected to tip more generously than those in modest accommodations.

To anyone on the ship who has taken pains to please you, show by your manner in thanking him that you appreciate his efforts, as well as by giving him a somewhat more generous tip when you leave the ship.

On no account attempt to tip a ship's officer! Thank the purser as you would any other acquaintance for courtesy. If you go to see the doctor, or if he is brought to see you, he will probably send you a bill for his services. If he does not and you have had a real illness, it is proper to send him, in an envelope when you leave the ship, the amount that probably would have been charged by your own doctor. If you are ill enough to be hospitalized, an extra charge will be added to your fare.

15

Currency and language

MONEY MATTERS

The rates of exchanging dollars for each country's currency vary from time to time, but revised and inexpensive wallet-sized guides may be bought at stationery stores or gift shops and are distributed by many travel bureaus, ticket agencies, etc. It is wise to learn by heart the corresponding sum for such standard amounts as a quarter, a dollar and five dollars. The rough equivalent of a quarter is still a standard tip for small services all over the world and if you know the amount equal to one dollar, it is easy to arrive at that corresponding to ten dollars.

And a word about bargaining. In large city stores all over the world the prices are just as firm as they are at Macy's in New York City. In small towns or rural marketplaces, however, especially in Latin countries, bargaining is often part of the fun of making a sale. Not only is the tourist considered simple-minded if he pays the "asking price," but he has ruined the day for the vendor.

In most restaurants in Europe, there is a charge on the bill for service. When this is fifteen percent or more, you need not tip an additional fifteen percent, but you should leave something. If there is no service charge, or a very small one, you tip the usual fifteen percent.

THE LANGUAGE BARRIER

Although people will tell you time and again that it is not necessary to speak a foreign language because "everyone in Europe speaks English," it simply is not so. Outside the cities and areas frequented by tourists, there are literally millions of foreigners who never speak nor understand one word of English. I cannot stress enough the importance, first, of knowing a few words of the language of whatever countries you are planning to visit and, second, of carrying a small pocket dictionary with you.

You will find invaluable a few such words and phrases as: "yes" and "no," "please" and "thank you," "hello" and "good-bye," "how much?" "where is . . . ?" and "how do you get to . . . ?" and "ladies' room" and "men's room."

"Beautiful," "wonderful," "nice," "kind," etc.—these single words, said admiringly and sincerely about the place or people you are visiting, will warm the heart of any native. Nothing pleases a native of any country, including our own, more than realizing that a visitor has taken the time and made the effort to learn a little of his country's language. Anyone who has walked through a little alley in a tiny town on a Greek island and seen the beaming smiles and eager response of the old ladies who sit there in the sun and hear "Ka-lee-*meh*-ra" instead of "Hello" or "Good morning" will know that this is true.

16

Representing America abroad

As a result of travel by jet airplane, people at the farthest reaches of the earth have become our neighbors. Every traveler will increase his enjoyment of his trip if he attempts to make friends and exchange ideas with the people of the country he is visiting. When traveling we should know something of the customs that determine the different points of view. The best way to learn is to read books about the people and places you intend to visit.

OUR ATTITUDE

At first thought, it would seem that there could be no difficulties of understanding between us and those whose language is the same as ours—especially the British, the Australians and New Zealanders. But slight frictions develop even when there is no language problem. Sensitive perception of the feelings of others is something few possess instinctively. Therefore, we must train ourselves to see the point of view of the people of each country we visit, adapt ourselves to their ways and not expect them to adapt to ours.

Our travel attitude also determines the amount of enjoyment we get from our trip. Which one enjoys his travels more —the man who goes with an open mind, eager to see the best in each country and forget the inconveniences, or the man who finds it too hot in Spain, broods all day because he had no hot water for shaving, or can't find a hamburger stand to buy his favorite lunch? Do not voice your disappointments in public; rather attempt to find and dwell on the parts of your stay that you *do* enjoy. Don't hesitate to show your appreciation and enthusiasm for the country you are in.

Don't compare everything you see with the United States. Every country has something to offer that we do not. The people there do not necessarily envy us our material wealth— they may prefer their simpler, less complicated existence.

Adaptability is a happy, rewarding trait. Latins live in warmer parts of the world. The combination of temperament and the necessity of adapting themselves to hot weather has resulted in a relaxed, unhurried attitude in all things, and *"mañana"* is the order of the day. This is one of the most difficult adjustments for Americans to make. To arrive in a country where no one cares whether everything is ready, where one arrives for appointments hours late, and meals are served hours later than one is used to, is often quite a shock. Soon, however, if he is perceptive, the traveler finds that the Latin countries have something unique to offer, and it becomes as difficult to return to a clock-watching society as it was to leave it behind in the first place.

Our greatest fault, it is said, is that we think the best of everything should be eagerly handed to us because we can pay for it! Could anything be more ill-bred? We must learn how to pay for it graciously if we are going to be given more than just what dollars can buy! Dollars, pounds, francs, pesos, lire don't buy a single gesture of welcome, of admiration, of sympathy. But a little thought, a little preparation, a wish to learn and to understand, these will reap the beautiful reward —the foreigner's friendship.

OUR CONDUCT

Appearance:

Clothing should be appropriate: thin clothes for warm climates, dark clothes for large cities, a "dressy" suit or dress for dining out, and the proper clothes for any sports you intend to take part in. Do not wear shorts or slacks except at resorts, or for golf, tennis, boating, etc. Such attire only proclaims the ignorance of the tourist who so offends local custom. In fact, clothing is usually more formal in large cities abroad than in our cities. Men are seldom seen in anything but dark business suits, and well-dressed women wear dark suits or dresses. The tropics are different. There women wear sleeveless cottons; men wear a loose cotton or linen shirt-jacket, worn

utside the trousers and sometimes beautifully pleated or em-
roidered. Women should always carry some sort of head-
overing, if only a scarf, for some churches refuse them
dmittance without it.

Avoid talking in a loud voice or gesturing wildly even in
our effort to speak a strange language. When you see a
riend from home across the square or in a crowded restaurant,
on't shout and wave violently to attract his attention; approach
im quietly as you would ordinarily do at home. Europeans
re usually most polite about waiting their turns. We could
earn a lesson from them.

Don't stare or criticize customs different from those at
ome. When you see a Greek gentleman toy with his "worry
eads" or a peasant family, the mother burdened with a heavy
oad while the father rides the donkey, accept what you see
s an interesting facet of life abroad.

Taking pictures:

If you wish to include a native of the country in your
pictures, first ask his permission. He may quite naturally resent
t otherwise. In countries where the natives wear a national
costume, people are accustomed to being photographed by
ourists, but it is still polite to ask their permission unless you
re just taking a picture of a large crowd. Children's fears
may be overcome by the offer of a small tip or candy. Where
they are used to many tourists, they will often crowd around
you, offering their services as models.

Latin customs:

In Latin countries a man must not expect to meet a well-
brought-up girl one night and take her out the next. He must
be presented to her family, gain their approval, and then
arrange, at least on the first few dates, to include mutual
friends. A woman seldom goes out alone after dark; any
Latin man would consider himself un-masculine if he did not
attempt to approach her for a flirtation. Young girls should
stay in groups of three or four, and older women should be
accompanied by at least one friend.

The manners of Europeans and South Americans are more
"flowery" than those of Americans. Women always shake hands
when introduced, and hand-kissing is still practiced. European
gentlemen remove their hats to ladies and bow with a flourish.

Ladies are always seated on the gentleman's right, except in a theater when this would place her on the aisle.

Europeans, and especially Latins, have a great love of giving presents: foods and flowers—especially those baked in their own ovens or grown in their gardens—or any trifling or more expensive gift.

In accepting these, we show our pleasure warmly—and as soon as possible thereafter we respond to this gesture with a simple, appropriate gift. Flowers are always sent to the hostess when you are invited to dinner. They are also sent as a "thank you" and to greet visitors.

17

An audience with the Pope

Although there are often hundreds of people in a day who wish an audience with the Pope, no one is denied. The great majority of audiences are group or collective. Relatively few can be granted one of the three types of audience that are considered to be personal.

Requests by Americans for these group audiences as well as for the personal ones should be cleared by the North American College, and then sent to the Office of the Master of the Chamber known as *Ufficio del Maestro di Camera di Sua Santità* which is in the Vatican. They are presented in person, or sent on arrival in Rome, to the Monsignor in charge whose name and address can be obtained from the concierge of your hotel. One must fill out a form requesting the kind of audience desired and show his credentials, which for a Roman Catholic may be simply a letter of introduction from his parish priest or a prominent layman. The length of ne's stay in Rome, his address and telephone number, are also included on the form so that he can be notified of the day and hour of his audience. Non-Catholics as well as Catholics are granted audiences, and their requests for audiences must be arranged through prominent Catholic laymen or members of the Catholic clergy.

The reply, and the invitation if the answer is favorable, is sent within a few days. You may receive a general admission ticket, meaning no reserved seat, or, if you are considered sufficiently important, a reserved seat in a special section.

THE GENERAL AUDIENCE

General audiences are usually held at noon. It is not necessary to have tickets, and anyone may attend. Those without reserved places should arrive very early if they wish an advantageous location—people often start arriving as early as 10 A.M.

At noon, the audience rises as the Pope appears, seated on a portable throne called the Sedia Gestatoris, carried by eight Swiss Guards. At the end of the aisle, he usually leaves the portable throne for a fixed one. He delivers a short address; then the audience may kneel as he gives his benediction to all those present, as well as to all articles they have brought with them to be blessed. The group rises and if the Pope has time, he greets each person in the special area. He mounts his portable throne and is carried out, and the audience is over.

For general audiences women must have their hair covered, wear black or dark dresses with necklines that are not too low and skirts that are not too short; their forearms must be covered. Men wear jackets and long trousers.

OTHER AUDIENCES

The "private" audience is reserved for cardinals, heads of state, ambassadors or others of first importance. The second type of audience is the "special," which is almost as important as the "private," and is granted only to people of high rank or to those who have an important subject to present to the Pope. The third type of audience is the "baciomano," which is also considered personal, as each visitor comes into the personal presence of the Pope, kisses his ring, and exchanges a few words with him, addressing him as "Your Holiness."

In this third type of audience, visitors stand in a single file around the room and when the Pope enters they kneel and do not stand again until the Pope leaves the audience chamber or makes a sign for them to rise. He passes from one visitor to another, extending his hand to each so that all may kiss his ring. He also may ask a question and exchange a few words with each. It is customary, as it is in the general audience, for visitors to take with them one or more rosaries or other small religious objects, which, after the visitor has received the Papal blessing, are also considered to have been blessed.

The rules of dress for visitors to the Pope are not so strict as they once were. But even now for a private or special audience, men traditionally wear evening dress with tails or sack coat and women long-sleeved black dresses and veils over their hair. No one may wear any but the most functional jewelry.

NON-CATHOLICS

At a general audience, every person present must kneel, rise and sit at the prescribed time. Non-Catholics, if they do not ordinarily do so, need not make the sign of the cross.

In private audiences, those being received will be told when they arrive the proper manner of kneeling and kissing the Pope's ring. If they object to these requirements on the grounds of their religion, there may be some slight modification. But the procedures are strictly followed, and rather than make an issue, those who feel they do not wish to follow them would be wiser to forgo the private audience.

PART FIVE

FORMAL ENTERTAINING

18

Formal dinners

The requisites for a perfect formal dinners, whether a great one for two hundred people or a little one for eight, are as follows:

Guests who are congenial to one another (the most important requirement).

Good *food*, a suitable menu perfectly prepared and served, *table furnishings* in perfect condition, suitable to the occasion and the surroundings, freshly laundered linen, brilliantly polished silver, shining glassware, *service* competent and expertly suited to *your* requirements.

A *cordial, hospitable host* and a *charming hostess* whose tact, sympathy, poise and perfect manners are in evidence at all times.

For all dinners, these requisites are much the same, but the necessity for perfection increases in proportion to the formality and the importance of the occasion. A perfect dinner is not necessarily a *formal dinner*, which cannot be given without the help of servants. However, if the guests must help themselves from a buffet, or if the hostess has to rise to clear the table, the dinner immediately becomes informal.

EXPERT SERVICE WITH PERMANENT OR TEMPORARY HELP

The lack of butlers, footmen or kitchen maids need not keep you from entertaining formally. The hostess who wishes her dinner to be formal can either hire temporary help or resort to a catering service that provides not only servants but excellent meals, either prepared by a cook sent to your home or partially cooked in their kitchens and finished in yours.

A small (for no more than twelve) formal dinner may be beautifully handled by a cook, a butler and a footman or a maid (at a truly formal dinner, those who serve the meal should be men). More than twelve necessitates a second footman and a cook's assistant. Either the host's chauffeur or a man hired for the occasion assists the ladies from the cars or taxis, directs the parking and, later, brings the cars to the door when the party is over. (In the country his job is that of a chauffeur—in the city he acts as a doorman.) If there is a permanent cook in the house, she prepares the meal and only the butler and the footman are hired for the evening. They serve and also assist her with the cleaning up.

The hostess sets the table, arranges flowers and does all else that will relieve her help of responsibilities other than the preparation and serving of the meal.

The cook arrives early in the day, the butler and footman and doorman come a little later and take care of any last-minute polishing or arranging. If cocktails are served, the butler mixes them in advance and has them ready to serve as each guest arrives. Before the guests arrive, the footman takes his place in the hall to direct the guests or help with their wraps; the butler stands near the hostess to announce guests, pass cocktails or assist her in any way. It is up to him to see that all runs smoothly so that the hostess may devote her attention to her guests.

The butler, footman and waitress leave after all the guests have gone, the glassware is washed and the ashtrays emptied. The cook may leave after the cooking utensils and dinner service have been washed and the kitchen made immaculate. If the help has been hired from an employment agency, you may be billed later, but you tip those who have served you when they are ready to go. If hired by you personally, you

simply pay them before they leave at the rate you have agreed
upon. Be sure that you establish the method and amount of
payment at the time the servants are hired; this avoids any unpleasantness at the end of the evening.

SELECTING YOUR GUESTS

The proper selection of guests is the first essential in all
entertaining. It is a mistake to invite too many great talkers
to the same gathering. Brilliant men and women who love to
talk want listeners, not rivals. Very silent people should be
sandwiched between good conversationalists or at least volu-
ble talkers. Never seat the silly or dull near the learned and
clever, unless the dull one is a pretty woman with a talent
for listening and the clever one is a man with an admiration
for beauty and a love of talking.

Making a dinner list is a little like making a Christmas list.
You put down what *they* will like (you hope), not what
you like. Those who are placed between congenial neighbors
remember your dinner as delightful, but ask people out of
their own groups and seat them next to their pet aversions,
and wild horses will not drag them your way again.

THE IMPORTANCE OF DINNER INVITATIONS

Invitations to formal dinners may be engraved or written
by hand. Occasionally they are even issued by telephone.
(See Chapter 45.) They must be answered immediately by
return mail, or those which were telephoned, by telephone.
Only illness or an unavoidable accident excuses the breaking
of a dinner engagement. To break one engagement in order
to accept a more desirable one is inexcusable. The rule is:
Don't accept an invitation you don't care about.

If a guest is forced to drop out at the last moment, the
hostess tries to fill in by inviting an intimate friend by telephone. Good manners require the friend to accept if possible.

SEATING YOUR GUESTS
Who is the guest of honor?

The guest of honor is the oldest lady present, or a stranger
whom you wish for some reason to honor. The guest of
honor is *always* taken in to dinner by the host and placed
on his right. The lady of next greatest importance sits

on the host's left and is taken in to dinner by the gentleman on whose right she sits. The hostess is always the last to go into the dining room at a formal dinner unless the President of the United States or the governor (but only in his own state) is present. Then the hostess goes in to dinner with the guest of honor, who leads the way, and the wife of the President or governor follows immediately with the host.

In Washington, even though the dinner be given for a guest of medium rank, the ladies of highest rank have the honor-places on either side of the host. The lady for whom the dinner is actually given is merely "among those present," unless those of higher rank agree to waive precedence, which Mrs. Frances Perkins did when she was Secretary of Labor, saying always to seat her where no one else wanted to sit.

The order of table precedence:

The lady of highest rank is on the host's right. The lady of next highest rank is on his left. The third lady sits on the right of the man of highest rank, the fourth lady on the left of the man of second rank, and so on. The lowest in rank is nearest the center. If the dinner is not official and there is no particular distinction in rank or age, the hostess may seat her guests in whatever order she thinks will achieve the most congenial and pleasant conversation. The lady she places on her husband's right is automatically the guest of honor. The "lady of honor" is "taken in" by the host and seated at his right. At ordinary dinners, therefore, the hostess goes in to dinner with the man of the second highest rank. But if the man of honor is of such importance that she must go in with him as well as place him at her right, the lady who sits on the right of the gentleman of honor and the gentleman who sits on the hostess's left go in to dinner together and then separate. He sees her to her place, then goes around the table until he finds his card. The diagram (with arrow lines indicating ladies and gentlemen who go in together) makes this seemingly complicated situation clear:

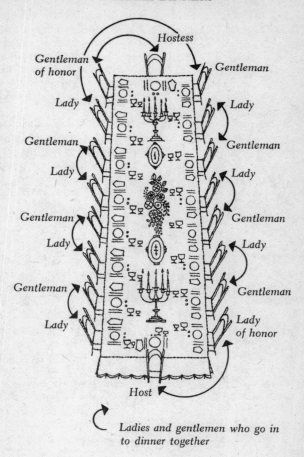

Ladies and gentlemen who go in
to dinner together

Seating a party of eight, twelve or sixteen:

At dinners of eight, twelve or sixteen, where either two
ladies or two men must sit at the head and foot of the table,
the hostess usually relinquishes her place and the host keeps
his. The hostess moves one place to her left rather than to her
right, and the male guest of honor is seated at one end of the
table on her right. An example of this, with the lines showing
service:

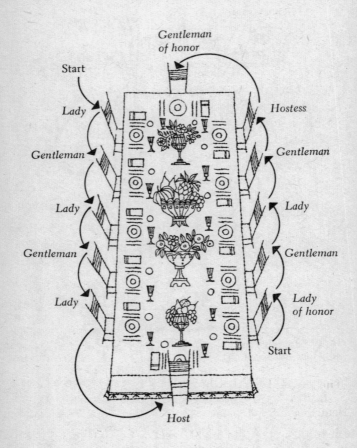

Gentleman of honor

Start

Lady

Gentleman

Lady

Gentleman

Lady

Hostess

Gentleman

Lady

Gentleman

Lady of honor

Start

Host

This diagram shows the correct seating arrangement for a group that has a hostess but no host:

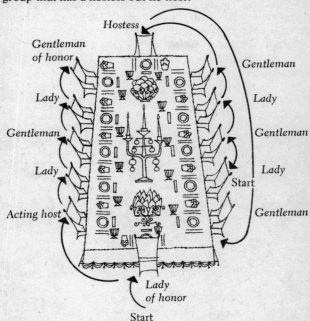

Hostess

Gentleman
of honor

Gentleman

Lady

Lady

Gentleman

Gentleman

Lady

Lady

Acting host

Gentleman

Start

Lady
of honor

Start

The order of table precedence for such special situations, for example when there is no host, can be worked out suitably by applying common sense to the standard forms.

The envelopes for the gentlemen:

In the entrance hall on his arrival, or just before he goes into the drawing room, each gentleman is offered a silver tray on which are small fold-over cards arranged in two or three neat rows. His name is on the front of one and his partner's name inside. Or, her name may be written on a small one- by two-inch card put into a matching envelope on which his name appears.

If there are many separate tables, the tables are numbered with standing placards (as at a public dinner) and the table number written on each lady's name card. (Do not call it an "escort card.")

The place cards:

The place cards are plain, about an inch and a half high by two inches long. The courtesy title and surname—"Dr. Gooding" or "Mr. Ashley"—are used except when there is more than one guest with the same surname; then it becomes Mr. Russell Albright and Mr. Lee Albright.

SETTING YOUR TABLE

One unbreakable rule is that everything must be geometrically spaced: the centerpiece in the actual center, the places at equal distances from each other, and all utensils balanced.

A tablecloth of white damask, best for a formal dinner, requires a pad under it. (Lacking a felt pad cut to the dimensions of your table, a folded, white blanket serves very well.) Naturally, the cloth must be smooth and perfectly laundered. Lace tablecloths are excellent on a refectory-style table. Handkerchief-linen tablecloths, embroidered or lace-inserted, are suited to all low-ceilinged, old-fashioned rooms. With either lace or linen, no felt or other padding is used.

The centerpieces may be an arrangement of flowers in either a bowl or a vase—low enough for guests to see over—or a distinctive ornament in silver, glass or china.

The individual places:

The distance between places at the table must allow guests elbow-room and room for the servants to pass the dishes properly. About two feet from plate center to plate center is ideal, though a small round table may require less room even if the seats touch at the front corners.

Plates are put around the table at equal distances. For the position of the silver, see diagrams A and B.

A

The silver is arranged so that one uses the utensils farthest from the plate first, taking the next in order for each succeeding course. Fork prongs are always up and the cutting edge of the knives toward the plate. Butter knives and plates are never used on a formal dinner table.

A dinner napkin folded square and flat is laid on each place plate. If the napkin is very large, the sides are folded in so as to make a flattened roll a third the width of its height. If the napkin has a corner monogram, it may also be folded diagonally in half and the two long ends folded under.

B

Napkins are put at the side only when food is put on the table before seating the guests. Bread should not be put in the napkin. The place cards are put on top of and in the center of the napkin or, if unsteady on a folded napkin, on the tablecloth above the napkin at the center of the place setting.

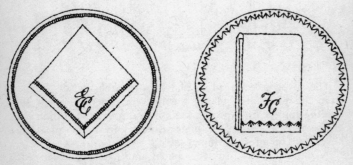

Finishing the table:

Two pairs of candlesticks are placed at the four corners about halfway between the center and the edge of the table, or two candelabra at either end halfway between the places of the host and hostess and the centerpiece. The candelabra are high enough and the candles as long as the proportion can stand, so that the light does not shine into the eyes of those at the table.

Dishes or compotes, holding candy, fruit, fancy cakes or other edible trimmings, go at the corners, between the candelsticks or candelabra and the centerpiece. Nuts may be put on the dinner table either in two big silver dishes or in small individual ones at each of the places, but they are removed with the saltcellars and pepper pots after the salad course. Pepper pots and saltcellars are put at every other place.

Olives and celery are passed during the soup course. When fish or meat or salad has its own accompanying condiment, sauce or relish, it is also passed. Pickles are incorrect on a dinner-party menu.

Cigarettes and ashtrays:

A small ashtray may be put at each place and cigarettes in a tiny holder in front of each diner or in larger holders spaced evenly about the table. The smoker does not light his cigarette until he has finished his main or salad course. Some hostesses even today prefer that their guests do not smoke until coffee is served, and no ashtrays or cigarettes are placed on the table. Others have them passed at the end of the salad course.

FOOD AND DRINK

Cocktails:

If cocktails are served, two or three varieties are prepared in the pantry or kitchen and passed (on a tray) to each

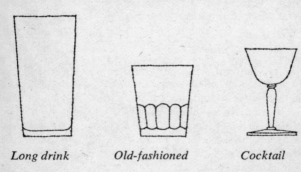

Long drink   *Old-fashioned*   *Cocktail*

guest as he arrives, the butler indicating what they are: "Would you care for an Old-fashioned or a martini?" Glasses of tomato juice or some other nonalcoholic beverage are always on the tray for those who do not care for liquor. Only one cocktail need be served. Formal dinners should start as nearly as possible at the hour stated on the invitation.

The menu:

The menu for a modern dinner, no matter how formal, consists of no more than six courses:

1) soup, fresh fruit cup, melon or shellfish (clams, oysters, shrimp)
2) fish course
3) the entrée, or main course (usually roast meat or fowl)
4) salad

5) dessert

6) coffee

Balance an especially rich dish by a simple one: for example, fish timbale with a thick creamed sauce followed by spring lamb or a filet mignon; broiled fish by an elaborate meat dish. Highly flavored Spanish or Indian dishes are not appropriate for a formal dinner. Avoid the monotony of too many creamed dishes: cream soup with creamed chicken; or too many sweet dishes: fish with apricot sauce and duck basted with currant jelly.

Vary the textures: for example, a poor menu is clear soup, smelts, broiled squab, miniature potato croquettes and string beans, lettuce salad with cheese straws, ice cream. There is no substance here. Substitute roast squab instead of broiled and a thick cream soup or a fish such as salmon. Too many women order trimmings rather than food and men go away hungry.

Wines:

Sherry, the first wine offered at dinner, is usually served only with a soup which contains sherry in the preparation. In other words, it should not be offered with cream of chicken soup or vichysoisse, but it would be an appropriate accompaniment to black bean or green turtle soup. Sherry is put into a decanter at room temperature and poured into small V-shaped glasses. It can stand being decanted almost indefinitely without spoiling. Sherry, also served at lunch or supper, or as a hospitable refreshment at any time, is often included as an alternate choice with cocktails.

A dry white wine is served with fish or with an entrée and is often the only wine at a woman's lunch or at the family dinner table. White wine, which should always be well chilled before being served, may be kept in the refrigerator for at least several hours or even days before being used. The most efficient way to chill a bottle of uncooled white wine is to place it in a bucket or cooler filled with a mixture of ice and cold water. The actual melting of the ice in the water will cool the wine faster than if it is immersed in cracked ice alone. Drawing the cork and turning the bottle from time to time will hasten the cooling. Unlike red wines, a white wine is good to the last drop, and the bottle may be upended when pouring the final glass.

Red wine is normally served with red meats, duck and game,

but at less formal dinners it may be drunk from the beginning of the meal to its close. This would more likely be true with a claret, a light red wine, than with a burgundy, which is much heavier. All red wines are served at room temperature, and the burgundy may be a degree or two warmer if the vintage is very good. It may be brought to this temperature by being left in a warm spot—never by warming over a burner or flame. The procedure for serving a fine vintage needs to be followed carefully if its excellence is to be appreciated: a day or two before it is to be used remove the wine from the wine cellar or closet, transferring the bottle into a straw basket as gently as possible, maintaining the bottle in a semihorizontal position. Once in the basket tilt it 15 or 20 degrees more toward the vertical than it was in the bin and leave it in this position for a day at least to permit any disturbed sediment to settle. If you do not have a wine cellar, purchase the wine several days before your dinner and follow the same procedure. An hour or so before serving, wipe the mouth of the bottle with a damp cloth to remove any accumulated dust and neatly cut away the foil to prevent the wine from coming in contact with it while being poured. Then carefully pull the cork and place it beside the neck of the bottle in its basket so that the host or interested guest may note that it is undamaged. During this hour the bottle is open, the wine is given an opportunity to "breathe" and rid itself of any musty or other unpleasant odor it might have absorbed in the cellar.

Serve the wine in the basket with the label showing to permit each guest to note what he is being offered. Pour the wine carefully in order to avoid any "backlash" or bubbling which would agitate the sediment resting in the bottom of the bottle. Do not pour the last inch or so from the bottle since this will be murky with sediment.

When a bottle of red wine is so heavy with sediment that the procedure given above will not result in a palatable drink, it may be decanted.

Champagne is, above all other beverages, that of the formal dinner party. When other wines are included, it is served with the meat course, but when it is the only wine, it is served as soon as the first course has begun. Its proper temperature depends upon its quality.

Champagne that is not of especially fine vintage is put in the refrigerator for a day and then chilled further by putting it into a cooler with a little salt as well as ice. Occasionally, holding the bottle by the neck, turn it back and forth a few times, taking care not to leave the bottle in the salt and ice too long or the champagne may become sherbet! When opening, wrap the bottle in a towel or napkin as a protection in case it explodes. An excellent vintage champagne is packed in ice without salt, which chills it just a little less. Champagne glasses ought to be as thin as soap bubbles.

Generally, champagne is served in a wide-brimmed glass (illustrated on the left), but the glass on the right is preferred by many connoisseurs as it tends to prolong the life of the effervescent bubbles.

Other types of wine glasses:

| Flute | German | Alsace | Bordeaux | Burgundy |

| Sherry | White wine | Red wine |

Wine glasses should be picked up by the stem rather than the bowl. In the case of white wine and champagne this helps to keep the wine cool, and in the case of all wines, including red ones, it enables you to appreciate the color.

THE GUESTS ARRIVE

The hostess receives:

The hostess stands near the door of her drawing room and as guests enter or are announced, she greets them with a welcoming smile, a handshake and says something pleasant to each: "I am very glad to see you," or "I am so glad you could come!" Elaborate phrases should be avoided. She takes your hand with a firm pressure and gives you—if only for the moment—her complete attention so that you go into her drawing room with a feeling that you are under the roof of a friend.

Although engrossed in the person she is talking to, she must be able to notice anything amiss elsewhere. No matter what goes wrong, she must notice it as best she can and at the same time cover the fact that she is noticing it. If a dish appears that is unpresentable, as quietly as possible she orders the next one to be brought in. If a guest knocks over a glass, her only concern seemingly is that her guest has been made uncomfortable. She says, "I am sorry! But the glass doesn't matter!" And she has a fresh glass brought (even though it doesn't match) and dismisses all thought of the matter.

If the conversation lags, both the host and hostess must keep it going. At the small dinner the skillful hostess displays what Thackeray calls the "showman" quality. She brings each guest forward in turn to the center of the stage. To a clever but shy man, she says, "Harold, what was that story you told me—" then repeats briefly an introduction to a topic in which Harold particularly shines. Or she begins a narrative and breaks off suddenly, turning to someone else—"*You* tell them!"

The duties of the host:

Mr. Oldname, who stands near his wife as the guests arrive, comes forward and, grasping your hand, adds his own greeting to his wife's gracious welcome. You join a friend standing near or he presents you, if you are a man, to a lady; or if you are a lady, he presents a man to you. At formal dinners introductions are never general and people do not as a rule speak to strangers except those next to them at the table or in the drawing room after dinner. The host therefore makes a few introductions if necessary.

A hostess who is either a widow or unmarried asks the

man she knows best to act as host. He gives his arm to the guest of honor and leads the way to the dining table, where he sits opposite the hostess. After dinner he leads the men to the smoking room and later to the drawing room to "join the ladies."

WHEN DINNER IS ANNOUNCED

It is the duty of the butler to "count heads" so that he may know when the company has arrived. As soon as he has announced the last person, he notifies the cook. Then he approaches the hostess, bows and says quietly, "Dinner is served."

Seating your guests:

The host offers his right arm to the lady of honor and leads the way to the dining room. All the other gentlemen offer their arms to the ladies appointed to them and follow the host, in an orderly procession, two and two; the only order of precedence is that the host and his partner lead, while the hostess and her partner come last. If by any chance a gentleman does not know the lady whose name is on the card in his envelope, he must find out who she is and be presented to her before he takes her in to dinner.

At a dinner of less than ten, the ladies are not escorted in to dinner but walk in with whomever they please, in groups of two or three to avoid crowding at the door.

The guests look for their place cards, assisted by the hostess, who may carry her seating plan with her. The gentlemen help the ladies on their right into their seats, with the exception of the male guest of honor, who seats the hostess, leaving the man on her left to walk around and seat the lady on the right of the guest of honor.

The late guests:

Fifteen minutes is the established length of time that a hostess may wait for a belated guest. When the late guest finally enters the dining room, she goes up to the hostess and apologizes for being late. The hostess remains seated, the guest shakes hands quickly so that all the men at table need not rise. The hostess simply says something conciliatory, such as, "I was sure you did not want us to wait dinner." The guest begins her dinner at the course presently being served.

CORRECT SERVICE

At a formal dinner in a house with a large staff, the butler always stands behind the hostess's chair except when giving one of the men under him a direction or when pouring wine. In a smaller house, where he has no assistant, he does everything himself or, if he has a second man or a waitress, he passes the principal dishes and the assistant follows with the accompanying dishes or vegetables.

No serving dishes are ever put on the table except ornamental dishes of fruit and sweetmeats. The meat is carved in the kitchen or pantry; vegetables, bread and condiments are passed and returned to the side table.

From the setting of the table until it is cleared for dessert, a plate remains at every place. If oysters or clams are served as a first course, the plate holding them is put on top of the place plate; so is a plate holding fruit or cold seafood in a stemmed glass. Only the used plate is removed and the soup plate is put in its place. But when the soup plate is removed, the underneath plate is removed with it; at the same time the plate for the next course is put down in their place. A first-course cold dish offered on a platter instead of being served on individual plates would have been eaten on the place plate, then a clean plate would have been exchanged for the used one, and the soup plate then put on top of that. *A plate with food on it must never be exchanged for one that has held food.* A clean one must come between. Dessert plates are put down on the table-cloth.

Dishes are presented at the left of the person being served, and plates are removed at the right unless, because of space, that is very inconvenient. Glasses are poured and additional knives placed at the right—forks are put on as needed at the left. Individual plates are not removed until the slowest eaters have finished.

Dishes are passed to the right or passed alternately right and left so that the same gentleman shall not always get the last piece on a dish.

The hostess is never served first:

To have oneself served first is the height of discourtesy to one's guests. In all first-class restaurants, each dish is presented to the host for his approval before it is passed or served to his guests but he does not help himself. Nor should a hostess in her own house. The person seated on the host's right is always served first.

Filling glasses:

As soon as the guests are seated and the first course is put in front of them, the butler goes from guest to guest, on the right-hand side of each, and fills the water goblet. He then serves the wine, asking each guest, "Sherry, sir?" (or "madam?"). All wines are poured at the right of each person and without lifting the glass from the table. Sherry is served with the soup (or Chablis with oysters) and then champagne is served straight through to the end from its own bottle with a napkin around it (put on like a shawl) and wrapped tight. *(For details about the traditional choices of wines, see "Food and Drink: Wines with Dinner.")*

Serving bread:

As soon as soup is served, dinner rolls, crackers and toast are passed in a flat dish or a basket. A guest helps himself with his fingers and lays the roll or bread on the tablecloth—there are no bread plates at a formal dinner because no butter is served. Whenever no bread is left at anyone's place at table, more should be passed.

Presenting dishes:

Dishes are presented held flat on the palm of the servant's left hand; every hot one has a napkin placed as a pad under it. A heavy meat platter is steadied by holding the edge of the platter with the right hand protected by a second folded napkin. Each dish is usually supplied with a serving spoon and a large fork. Peas, mashed potatoes, rice, etc., may be offered with a spoon only.

The serving table:

The serving table is in a corner near the door to the pantry or kitchen and hidden by a screen from the guests at table. It holds stacks of cold plates, extra forks and knives, the finger-bowls and dessert plates. At informal dinners all dishes of food are left on the serving table on a warming tray but at formal dinners, dishes are never passed twice and are therefore taken directly to the pantry after being passed. When clearing the table for dessert, the plates of whatever course precedes dessert are removed, leaving the table plateless. Saltcellars, pepper pots, unused flat silver and nut dishes are taken off on the serving tray and the crumbs brushed off each place at the table with a tightly folded napkin onto a tray held under the table edge.

Dessert service:

There are two methods of serving dessert. The first is to put the fork and spoon on a china dessert plate. After the dessert the fingerbowl is brought in on a separate plate. In the second method, the fingerbowl as well as the fork and spoon are brought in on the dessert plate. The diner puts the fingerbowl above his plate, and the fork and spoon each to its proper side. The fingerbowl is less than half filled with cold water; a few violets or a gardenia may be floated in it, but never a slice of lemon.

Fruit, when served, is passed immediately after the dessert or ice cream; then decorative sweets are passed: chocolates, caramels, peppermints, candied orange. Coffee is usually served elsewhere later.

AFTER THE MEAL

At the end of the dinner, the hostess looks across the table and, catching the eye of one of the ladies, slowly stands up. In a moment everyone is standing. The gentlemen offer their arms to their partners and conduct them back to the living room or the library or wherever they are to sit during the rest of the evening. Each gentleman then leaves his partner and, with the other men, follows the host to the room where after-dinner coffee, liqueurs and cigars and cigarettes are passed. At the end of twenty minutes or so, the host, at the first lull in the conversation, suggests that they "join the ladies" in the living room.

In a house where there is no extra room to smoke in, the gentlemen remain at the table for their coffee, etc., while the ladies go to the drawing room, where coffee, cigarettes and liqueurs are passed to them.

After-dinner coffee is served in one of three ways: (1) The footman proffers a tray of cups, saucers and sugar; the butler follows with the coffeepot alone and pours into the cup held in the guest's hand. (2) A tray with filled cups is proffered by the butler to the guests who help themselves. (3) The tray of cups and sugar is held on the servant's left hand. The guest puts sugar into one of the cups and the servant pours coffee with the right hand. Liqueurs are offered exactly as coffee in the second or third manner. The guests pour their own, or, saying "Cognac" or "Mint, please," their choice is poured for them. Cigarettes are arranged on a tray with matches or a lighter.

TAKING LEAVE

Today, although it is the obligation of the guest who sat on the host's right to make the move to go, it is not considered ill-mannered, if the hour is growing late, for another lady to rise first, go to her hostess and say, "Good night. Thank you so much." The hostess answers, "I am so glad you could come!"

In the dressing room or in the hall, the maid helps the ladies with their wraps. The butler at the door goes out on the front steps and says, "Mr. Sewell's car." The host's chauffeur (or a man hired for the evening) signals to Mr. Sewell's chauffeur; on the arrival of the car he reports to the butler who says to Mr. Sewell, "Your car is at the door, sir," Or, if Mr. Sewell is driving his own car, the chauffeur brings the car round and holds the door for him.

Bridge players leave as they finish their games, sometimes a table at a time or, most likely, two together. (Husbands and wives are never, if it can be avoided, put at the same table.) They stop to say good night to their hostess and thank her. She expresses her pleasure that they could come.

SOME ADVICE FOR THE GUESTS
Refusing wine or food:

If you do not wish wine, it is best to allow a little to be poured into your glass. A guest should, however, feel free to say "No, thank you," to anything offered him, if he wishes.

Gloves and napkins:

Ladies always wear gloves to formal dinners and take them off at the table—entirely off! It is hideous to leave them on the arm, merely turning back the hands. Both gloves and bag are supposed to be laid across the lap and the napkin, folded once in half across the lap, on top of the gloves and bag. However, both gloves and bag more often than not land on the floor. There is one way to keep these three articles from disintegrating—cover the gloves and bag with the napkin put cornerwise across your knees and tuck the two side corners under you like a lap robe with the gloves and bag tied in place, as it were. It is either that or have the gentleman next to you groping unhappily under the table at the end of the meal.

Conversation:

Guests, of course, are expected to converse with their neighbors on both sides of them. Not to do so is rude not only to one's neighbors but to the hostess as well.

19

Luncheons

The formal luncheon differs from the formal dinner only in minor details. I shall confine this chapter to the differences. *(For all other matters, see Chapter 18.)*

THE INVITATIONS

The word "lunch" is used much more often than "luncheon" —"luncheon" is rarely spoken but it is written in books like this one and sometimes in third-person invitations.

Although invitations may be telephoned, formal invitations to lunch are nearly always written in the first person and rarely sent out more than a week in advance. For instance:

Dear Mrs. Kindhart [or *Martha*]:

Will you lunch with me on Monday, the tenth, at half past one?

Hoping so much for the pleasure of seeing you,

Sincerely [or *Affectionately*],
Jane Toplofty

If Mrs. Toplofty's luncheon were given in honor of some-body, the phrase "to meet Mrs. Eminent" would be added im-mediately after the hour. At a very large luncheon for which the engraved card might be used, "To meet Mrs. Eminent" is written across the top. *(See also Chapter 45.)*

ARRIVAL OF THE GUESTS

The hostess sits in the living room in some place that has an unobstructed approach from the door. After leaving her wrap, each guest comes into the room preceded by the butler or the maid who quietly announces the new arrival's name. Or the guests may greet the hostess unannounced. The hostess takes a step forward, shakes hands and says, "I am delighted to see you." If the guest does not speak to anyone, she makes the necessary introductions.

When all the guests have arrived, or have had time to enjoy a cocktail if it is offered, the butler or maid notifies the kitchen, approaches the hostess and bows slightly. If necessary to attract the hostess's attention, he or she says quietly, "Luncheon is served."

If there is a guest of honor, the hostess leads the way to the dining room, walking beside her. The gentlemen stroll in with those they happen to be talking to or, if alone, fill in the rear, but never offer their arms to ladies in going in to a luncheon.

COCKTAILS

Cocktails may or may not be served before lunch. The preference leans toward sherry, Dubonnet or a cocktail made with fruit juice, such as a daiquiri. As always, tomato juice or plain fruit juice should be available for those who wish it.

THE TABLE

Although colored damask is acceptable, traditionally the lunch table is set with place mats of linen, needlework or lace. A runner, matching the mats but two or three times as long, may be used in the center of the table and on it are ar-ranged flowers or an ornament and two or four dishes of fruit or candy. No candles are used at a luncheon. On a large table, four slim vases with small sprigs of flowers or any other glass or silver ornaments may be added.

The places are set as for dinner with a place plate, a fork, a knife or a spoon for each course. The lunch napkin, matching the table linen, is smaller than the dinner napkin and is folded like a handkerchief in a square of four thicknesses and laid on the plate diagonally, with the monogrammed (or embroidered) corner pointing down toward the edge of the table. The upper corner is then turned sharply under in a flat crease a quarter of its diagonal length, the two sides rolled loosely under (*see diagram*). At a large luncheon, place cards are used as they are at dinner.

The bread-and-butter plate:

The bread-and-butter plate, part of the luncheon (and breakfast or supper) service goes at the left side of each place just above the forks with the butter knife on the plate placed diagonally from upper left to lower right, with knife edge toward the table edge.

Hot breads are an important feature of every luncheon—hot crescents, baking-powder biscuits, bread biscuits, dinner rolls or corn bread—and are passed as necessary. Butter in balls or curls rather than in squares is put on the plate beforehand and passed throughout the meal until the table is cleared for dessert. Bread-and-butter plates are removed at the same time as the large plate.

SERVING LUNCH

A formal luncheon may be served by one or two waitresses instead of by men alone. The service is identical with that of dinner. Carving is done in the kitchen and no food is set on the table. The places are never left plateless, except after the salad course when the table is cleared and crumbed for dessert. The dessert plates and fingerbowls are arranged as for dinner.

THE MENU

Five courses at most (not counting the ornamental sweets or coffee as a course)—and more usually four—are sufficient for the longest and the most elaborate luncheon possible. For example: (1) fruit or soup in cups; (2) eggs or shellfish; (3) fowl or meat (not a roast); (4) salad: (5) dessert. The menu in a private house is seldom more than four courses and eliminates either 1, 2 or 5.

A popular first course is melon, grapefruit or any sort of fruit cut into very small pieces and served in special bowl-shaped glasses set into long-stemmed larger ones, with a space for crushed ice between the two, or in champagne glasses, which are kept in the refrigerator until sent to the table.

Soup at a luncheon (or at a wedding breakfast or a ball supper) is never served in soup plates but in two-handled cups. It is eaten with a teaspoon or a bouillon spoon or is drunk from the cup which is lifted to the mouth with both hands. It is usually a clear soup: in winter, a bouillon, turtle soup or consommé; in summer, chilled jellied consommé, madrilene or vichyssoise.

Lunch-party egg dishes are innumerable (see any cookbook): substantial dishes such as eggs Benedict or eggs stuffed with pâté de foie gras and a mushroom sauce should be balanced by a simple meat course, such as broiled chicken served with a salad. With a light egg course, eggs in aspic for example, serve meat and vegetables. If you serve fruit *and* soup, omit the eggs.

For an informal luncheon, if you do not wish to leave out a course, choose the simplest dishes: a bouillon or broth, shirred eggs or an omelette, then chicken or a chop with vegetables, a salad of plain greens with crackers and cheese, and a pudding, ice cream, mousse or any other light dessert. There should always be at least one course of hot food. If you offer hot soup (or at supper, tea or chocolate), the rest of the meal may be cold.

The menus suggested above are for lunch parties. For women you know are dieting, the menu would be greatly modified. In other words, when lunching with intimate friends, you have the kind of food you know they like.

BEVERAGES

In the winter, one light wine such as a dry Rhine wine or a claret may be served with lunch. Sherry may also be served with soup. White wine might be served in the summer, but iced tea or iced coffee are the usual choices. Iced tea at lunch is prepared with lemon, sugar, and orange juice if you wish, and poured into ice-filled glasses (often decorated with sprigs of fresh mint) already at each place. But coffee is passed around in a glass pitcher on a tray that also holds a bowl of powdered sugar, a pitcher of cold milk and another of cream as thick as possible. The guests pour their coffee to suit themselves into tall gasses half full of broken ice and furnished with long-handled spoons.

After lunch, the men remain with the ladies and have coffee in the living room.

20

Teas and receptions

Afternoon parties range from the very dignified reception, through the more or less formal tea dance or tea, to the casual cocktail party. The reception today is primarily a public or semipublic gathering in honor of a prominent personage or an important event. Receptions usually take place on the diplomatic or civic levels and are handled by a competent staff. The major difference between a reception and a tea is one of atmosphere. A reception always takes itself seriously. A tea, no matter how formal, is friendly and inviting.

THE INVITATIONS

Afternoon teas are given in honor of visiting celebrities, new neighbors, or a new daughter-in-law, to "warm" a new house, for a house guest from another city, or just because the hostess feels hospitably inclined.

The invitation is a visiting card of the hostess with "Jan. 10, Tea at 4 o'clock" in the lower corner, opposite the address, and, if appropriate, "To meet Mrs. Harvey Montgomery" across the top of it. Or it may be telephoned. *(See also Chapter 45.)*

THE TEA TABLE

The tea and the coffee or hot chocolate may be passed on trays, but more often the hostess prefers to have them poured at a table. Many choose their dining-room table from which to serve; however, the tea table may be set up in any room with adequate space and easy access and exit so that the guests can circulate freely.

Except on a metal and glass table a cloth must be used. It may barely cover the table or hang half a yard over the edges. A tea cloth may be colored, but the conventional one is of white linen with needlework or lace, or both, or appliquéd designs.

A large tray is set at either end of the table, one for the tea and one for the chocolate or coffee. On one tray is the kettle, in which the water was boiling before being brought in. A flame under the kettle keeps the water hot. There are also an empty teapot, a caddy of tea, a tea strainer and slop bowl, cream pitcher and sugar bowl, and, on a glass dish, thin slices of lemon. On the coffee tray is a large coffee-filled urn or pot, also with a flame under it. A pitcher of cream and a bowl of sugar complete the tray. If chocolate is served instead of coffee, all that is needed is the pot of steaming chocolate.

If the trays are carried in by the maid, the flames under the pots are lighted as soon as the trays are set down but never before, to avoid any possibility of a spark catching fire to her apron.

The table:

The cups and saucers are placed within easy reach of the ladies who are pouring, usually at the left of the tray, because they are held in the left hand while the tea (or coffee) is poured with the right. On either side of the table are stacks of little tea plates, with small napkins matching the tea cloth folded on each one. Arranged behind these, or in any way that is pretty and uncluttered, are the plates of food and whatever silver is necessary. If the table is not large enough to hold all the plates and food, some may be placed on a sideboard or on a small table in a convenient location.

SERVANTS NOT NECESSARY

Because nothing needs to be passed to the guests, it is perfectly possible for a hostess to give a formal tea without the help of servants. The hostess would then set out the tray with everything except the boiling water before her guests arrive. After she greets the guests, she fills the tea-tray kettle from the kitchen kettle and carries it in to the tea table.

MAKING GOOD TEA

The most important part of the tea service is boiling water and plenty of it. Nothing is easier than tea-making; nothing is rarer than the hostess who knows how! To make good tea, first rinse the teapot with a little boiling water to heat it, and pour out. Then put in a rounded teaspoonful of tea leaves or one teabag for each person, or half this amount if the tea is superquality. Pour on enough *actually boiling* water to cover the tea leaves about half an inch. Then let it steep at least five minutes (for those who like it very strong, ten) before additional boiling water is poured on. Now pour half tea, half boiling water for those who like it "weak"; pour it straight for those who like it strong. The cup of *good* tea should be too strong without the addition of a little lively boiling water which gives it freshness.

When tea has to stand a long time and for many guests, the ideal way to make it is in a big kettle on the kitchen stove, very strong, and let the tea actually boil three to four minutes on the range; then pour it through a sieve or filter into your hot teapot. The tea will not become bitter. Moreover, you do not need a strainer at the table. It does not matter if it gets quite cold. The boiling water added to the strong infusion will make the tea hotter than most of us can drink immediately.

DRINKS SERVED AT TEA

At a tea or reception to which men have been invited, the hostess (or maid or butler) often asks a guest who has refused a cup of tea if he or she would like anything else, a whiskey and soda or a cocktail. If there is a servant, he will serve the drink after it has been made in the pantry. If the hostess has no help, she may ask the guest to mix his own drink from a bar that has been set up in an inconspicuous place separate from the tea table.

THE LADIES WHO POUR

The pouring is usually done by two intimate friends of the hostess especially invited beforehand. Sometimes after an hour, the first two are relieved by two other close friends of the hostess.

A guest says to the deputy hostesses pouring, "May I have a cup of tea?" (or coffee or chocolate). The one pouring smiles and answers, "Certainly! How do you like it? Strong or weak?"

If the visitor says, "Weak," *boiling* water is added and, according to the guest's wishes, sugar, cream or lemon. (Good tea calls for milk, though it seems always to be called cream.) If either hostess is surrounded with people, she smiles as she hands her the cup, and that is all. If the hostess is free, the guest makes a few pleasant remarks, such as an observation or two about the beauty of the table or how delicious the little cakes look. The guest then moves away with her tea or chocolate and joins a group of friends.

21

Balls, dances and debuts

FORMAL BALLS AND DANCES

There are two fundamental differences between balls and dances. First, only those of approximately one age are asked to a dance; ball invitations are sent to personal friends of the hostess, regardless of their ages. Second, because fewer people are asked to a dance, the decorations and refreshments may be but do not have to be simpler.

Great private balls have become almost unheard of in recent years. Two types of balls have replaced private ones all over the country—the charity ball and the debutante ball. Though you may never give a private ball, your daughter may be among the group of girls to be presented or you may be asked to serve on a charity committee.

How and where to start:

A public ball is run by a committee, whose chairman is comparable to the hostess, but without the full burden of responsibility. Special duties are allotted to each member of the committee: one takes charge of invitations, one of decorations; others are responsible for the orchestra, the food, the ticket money, etc. In the following paragraphs, however, wherever the word "hostess" is used, you may substitute "committee member" if the ball is other than a private one.

The hostess preparing to give a ball may enlist the aid of many people. The club or hotel where it is to be held provides the servants, the food and the drinks; or, if the ball is in her home, a caterer provides the same services. A good florist sees to the decorations, and there are social secretaries available to help the hostess with the lists and invitations. Nevertheless she must make the final decisions on all the details important to the success of the party.

The first thing the hostess does is to find out which evening the facilities of the club or hotel she prefers are free. She then telephones and engages the best orchestra she can for that evening. If possible, there are two orchestras, so that the moment one finishes playing, the other begins. Good music is of more importance than the choice of place. Also try to select an evening not already taken by another hostess or organization in order to avoid conflict either on lists or, in a small town, on the services of caterers, florists, etc. Next the hostess makes out her list and orders and sends out the invitations.

Asking for an invitation:

Invitations to balls, private or public, are always formal. There are, however, many variations in good taste. *(For these forms, and also for less formal invitations appropriate to the smaller dance, see Chapter 45.)*

It is always permissible to ask a hostess if you may bring a man who is a stranger to her; men who dance are always in demand, and the more the better. But it is rather difficult to ask for an invitation for an extra girl, no matter how pretty, unless she is to be looked after by the person asking for the invitation. In that case, the hostess is delighted to invite her. Invitations are never asked for persons whom the hostess already knows. This definitely established rule of etiquette assumes that she would have sent them an invitation had she cared to. However, an intimate friend may quite properly remind her of someone who, in receiving no invitation, has probably been overlooked.

The one who has arranged for the invitation for the stranger should, if possible, accompany him to the ball and introduce him to his hostess. "Mrs. Norman, I would like to introduce John Franklin, my roommate, whom you were kind enough to say I might bring." If the stranger arrives alone he introduces himself and identifies the guest who arranged for his invitation. "Mrs. Norman, I am John Franklin, Bob Whiting's roommate. He was kind enough to ask you if I might come, and he is joining me here later."

A ball in a private house:

A ball always has an awning and a red carpet down the front steps or walk of the house. A chauffeur at the curb opens the car doors. Appurtenances such as the awning, red carpet, coat racks and ballroom chairs, as well as crockery, glass, napkins, waiters and food, can be supplied by hotels or caterers.

The room selected for dancing should be emptied of furniture. If there are adjoining rooms such as a large hall or a library for those not dancing, the floor space of the dancing room is increased considerably by having no chairs at all in it— a far better arrangement than the stiff alignment of straight chairs around the dance floor. The floor itself must be smooth and waxed.

Decorations:

Decorations may be as simple or as elaborate as the pocketbook and the taste of the hostess or committee dictate. At Christmas there might be a beautifully decorated tree in one corner; at another time, Japanese lanterns and Oriental flower arrangements. Whether at home or in a public ballroom, some greens behind the orchestra, some flowers on the tables and wherever else they are most effective are all that are necessary for even the most elaborate ball.

The guests arrive:

The hostess is ready to receive on the stroke of the hour specified in her invitations. If the ballroom opens on a foyer or entrance hall, she usually receives there. Otherwise she receives in the ballroom near the entrance. Guests are announced as they arrive, and after shaking hands with the hostess, pass into the ballroom.

The perfect host and hostess:

The duty of seeing that guests are looked after, that shy youths are presented to partners, that shyer girls are not left at the wallflower outposts, that the dowagers are taken in to supper and that elderly gentlemen are provided with good cigars, falls to the perfect host. But both host and hostess try to see that their guests are having a pleasant time.

The perfect guest:

Guests have responsibilities too. Every young man must dance at least once with the hostess, the girl or girls the dance is given for, the hostess of the dinner he went to before the dance and both girls he sat beside at dinner. At a dance to which he has brought a girl, he dances the first dance with her. He also makes sure that she is not stuck too long with any one partner and he takes her home after the dance.

The helpful ushers:

The hostess chooses from among the young men she knows best a number who are tactful and self-possessed to act as ushers. The appointment cannot be refused. Ushers are identified as deputy hosts by white or other distinguishing boutonnieres. They see that the wallflowers remain chair-bound as little as possible and relieve any young man who has too long been planted beside the same "rosebud." An usher may introduce any man to any girl without knowing either one of them personally and without asking permission. He may also ask a girl (if he has a moment to himself) to dance with him, whether he has ever met her or not. The usher in turn must release every stag he calls upon by substituting another, and the second by a third, and so on. In order to make a ball "go," meaning to keep everyone dancing, the ushers have on occasion spent the entire evening in relief work.

The manners of the guests:

When a man is introduced to a girl, he says, "Would you care to dance?" She may reply, "Certainly" or "Yes, I'd like to very much," or she simply smiles, gets up and dances. At the end of the dance, whether it has lasted one minute or sixty, the man says, "Thank you" and perhaps he adds, "That was wonderful!" to which she replies, "Thank you, it was great fun."

If a girl is sitting in another room or on the stairs with a lone man, a second man should not interrupt or ask her to dance. But if she is sitting in a group, he can go up and ask, "Would you like to dance?" She smiles and either says, "Yes" or "Not just now—I'm very tired."

To refuse to dance with one man and then immediately dance with another is an open affront to the first one. A girl who is dancing may not refuse to change partners when another cuts in, even if she and her partner have taken only a dozen steps together.

When a stag sees a girl whom he wants to dance with, he

steps forward and places his hand on the shoulder of her partner, who relinquishes his place to the newcomer, who then dances with the girl until a third in turn does the same to him.

When cutting, the following rules must be observed: (1) The partner who was first dancing with a girl never cuts back on the man who took her from him. He can cut in on her next partner if he wants to, especially if he is giving her a rush. (2) He must not continue to cut in on the same man when the latter dances with other partners.

Supper is served:

A sit-down supper may be served by the caterer at an elaborate ball, but a buffet supper that begins at one o'clock and continues for an hour or more, to which people may go when they feel like it, is pleasanter and easier to manage. Small tables are set up at which guests may sit down to eat after they have served themselves at the buffet. They sit where they please, either a group making up a table or a man and his partner taking any two vacant chairs. A girl is always taken in to supper by the young man who is her escort. If there are unescorted girls at the party, the ushers (or the host, if there are no ushers) see that some of the stags take them to supper or that they are included in a group.

Hot dishes are still served at some balls, but many times the supper consists of a variety of sandwiches, platters of cold meats and accompanying dishes. There may be coffee, chocolate or bouillon or bowls of iced fruit punch. Champagne may be served if it is in accordance with the customs of your community and your own taste, and if guests are of legal drinking age.

SMALLER DANCES

Less formal dances may be given for any number of reasons, perhaps to introduce a new neighbor, or simply because your friends like to dance.

Evening dances:

Invitations are either telephoned or written on a visiting or an informal card. For a dance for young people, invitations are sent out on printed "party" invitations, which have attractive drawings on the outside and spaces for writing time, address and type of party on the inside. Include at the bottom an R.S.V.P. with a telephone number beside it and a hint about clothes. At young peoples' informal parties, even dances, clothing may be anything from suits for the boys and "party" dresses for the girls to Bermuda shorts for both. *(For additional details, see Chapter 46.)*

When the dance is held in your own home rather than a public room, the most important thing is a large enough clear space and a floor properly prepared for dancing. If possible, remove all the furniture from the room; if not, take out whatever you can and move the rest close to the wall, roll and put away the rugs and wax the floor. For decorations, a few flowers—on a mantle, for instance—are sufficient.

Tea dances:

An afternoon tea dance often takes the place of the old-fashioned debutante ball. It may also be given to introduce a new daughter-in-law or someone you feel responsible for who has moved to your community.

Invitations are written on the visiting card of the hostess with "To meet Mrs. Grantham Jones, Jr." across the top. It is equally correct to use the inside of a fold-over card or an informal, or they may be telephoned.

Nowadays houses large enough for dancing are comparatively few. As a result, the tea dance is usually given at a club or in a small ballroom of a hotel. Do not choose too large a room. An undecorated public room needs more people than a room in a private home to make it look filled and give the effect of success. A screen of greens back of the musicians, a few green vines here and there and flowers on the tables form the typical decorations.

Whether in a hotel, club ballroom or a private drawing room, the curtains are drawn and the lights lighted as though for a dance in the evening.

Usually only tea, chocolate (or sometimes coffee), breads, sandwiches and cakes are served. At the end of the table or on a separate table nearby are bowls or pitchers of orangeade or lemonade or punch for the dancers. Guests go to the table and ask whoever is serving for chocolate, coffee or tea and help themselves to the sandwiches or cakes, which they eat standing at the table.

Outdoor dances:

If you have a smooth terrace, a stone patio, perhaps beside a swimming pool, or even a built-in dance floor on the lawn, an outdoor dance on a summer evening is a romantic and gay way of entertaining. Small tables are set up near the dance floor, with enough chairs for all who are not dancing. The bar, if you serve liquor, and the table with refreshments are nearby.

Have plenty of light for the orchestra (if you have one) to see their music and also for the bartender and waiters. When your guests are ready to sit down, uneven ground or steps may be a hazard if not well lighted. For an outdoor dance, insure the guests' comfort in case of rain: either have a tent or marquee large enough to cover chairs, tables and dance floor, or be prepared to move the entire party into your house.

The importance of good music:

Good music is essential to the success of every dance. Therefore spend as much as your pocketbook can afford on it. Hire the best orchestra obtainable even though you have only three pieces. If you plan to use a phonograph, choose records specifically intended for dancing and ones that will appeal to your guests. If you borrow records from your friends—and many people do in such a situation—be sure the owner's name is clearly printed on the label in indelible ink or put on with marking tape.

Dance manners:

Good manners at a dance are the same for young and old alike. Whatever the local customs about cutting in, a man must dance with his hostess and he must dance the first and last dances with the lady he brought to the party, be it friend or wife. Where the guests are married couples and there are few extra men, the only time to change partners may be during the intermission or when the music starts again. At this type of party, there are almost always tables to which the couples return between dances, and the men must ask their wives, as well as the women next to them and their hostess, to dance. If the hostess is at another table, a man does not ask her to dance until all the women at his table have partners or there are several men and women remaining at the table, so no one woman is left alone. Under no circumstances should the men hold a "stag party" in the bar, leaving the women at the table without partners.

When the dance is over, every guest finds his host and hostess, thanks them and says "good night."

DEBUTS

"Presenting a debutante to society" may seem to echo social customs long past. Yet, when her daughter is eighteen, a mother may want to present the young lady to the adult world with a certain degree of formality. For this "coming-out," she has a choice of several forms:

(1) The most elaborate is a private ball; (2) less elaborate and more common is a small dance that presents the debutante to her own and her parents' friends; (3) a tea dance *(see Chapter 20)* and, (4) the most popular today, the big dance for all or several of the debutantes in the area. In a large city, a group of parents may get together and share the expense of a single coming-out party for their daughters. Or it may be given by an organization that invites a group of girls to participate. Many balls or cotillions of this kind are benefit affairs, handled by a committee of the sponsoring charity; the parents of the girls invited to participate are expected to give a substantial donation to the charity involved as a fee for their daughter's participation. *(For invitations and their answers see Chapters 45 and 48.)*

Debutante balls:

The debutante "receives" standing beside her mother, or whoever else may be hostess, and farthest from the entrance, whether that happens to be on the latter's right or left. As they enter, the guests approach the hostess first, who, as she shakes hands with each, turns to the debutante and, repeating the name that has been announced to her, says, "My daughter" or "You remember Cynthia, don't you?" or merely "Cynthia." Then each guest shakes hands with the debutante. If there is a queue of people coming at the same time, the guest need only say, "How do you do?" and pass on. If there are no others entering at the moment, each one makes a few pleasant remarks —for instance, "How beautiful your bouquets are!" A friend of her mother probably says, "Cynthia dear, how lovely you are tonight!" A young man exclaims, "My, you look wonderful tonight!" The girls assure her, "Your dress is simply divine!"

At a ball when the guests begin coming at eleven o'clock, the debutante receives until about twelve o'clock—or later if guests continue to arrive. Then she is free to join the dancing. She usually dances the first dance with her father and the next two with the young men she has asked to be her escorts for the evening.

It is still customary to send a debutante flowers at her coming-out party: bouquets or baskets or other decorative flowers. They are sent by relatives, friends of the family, and her father's business associates. Her escorts send corsages. The flowers are banked as a background for her when she stands to receive. The debutante always holds one of the bouquets while receiving, sometimes the same one, sometimes several in succession so as not to show partiality to any special giver.

The debutante goes to supper with her escorts. If she does not wish to center her attention on one man, an easy way out is to ask a brother or other relative. She makes up her own table which includes her most intimate friends. Her table is usually in the center of the dining room, is somewhat larger than the tables surrounding it and has a card on it saying "Reserved."

Debut dances:

Since many young people are at home only during school vacations, evenings available for parties are limited in number. In many communities, two girls whose guest lists overlap arrange for one of them to be presented at a dinner dance and the other at a late dance on the same evening, a convenient arrangement for both families. The one who serves the dinner provides drinks and refreshments for a limited time after dinner. The other girl only needs to worry about a light supper served around one o'clock, and the champagne, punch or whatever she chooses to serve for the rest of the night.

The two debutantes attend each others' parties. The one giving the second party leaves the first with her escorts immediately after dinner to help her mother with last-minute arrangements. The dinner dance usually starts at seven thirty or eight o'clock; the debutante and her hostess receive until dinner is served at eight thirty or nine. The late dance begins at approximately eleven o'clock.

Tea dances:

Tea dances are described earlier in this chapter. The only addition necessary to make it a "debutante tea dance" is the presence of the hostess and the debutante at the entrance as a receiving line.

Assemblies, cotillions and community dances:

Coming out as a member of a group, large or small, is becoming more and more common. These "mass debuts" are a great success because of the relatively small expense to each family involved. A girl's mother may give a small debut party or tea at home and still accept an invitation to participate in one of the assemblies or cotillions. Customs vary widely in different areas. Whatever local practices have become traditional and are accepted by the participants are, in that city or town, quite correct. Some committees invite both boys and girls (other than those "coming out") to the dance; others invite only the girls and request that they bring two escorts. When this is done, the girls send in the names of the escorts as soon as they have accepted and the committee then sends the boys a formal invitation. The girls pay for their escort's ticket if it is a charity-sponsored ball. At most multiple debuts, the committee itself does not invite guests, but each debutante's family is allowed a certain number of invitations and they pay for those they invite.

The party may be a dinner dance or, more often, a late ball. The members of the committee often have dinners beforehand for the debutantes and their escorts. This may also be done by the families of the girls themselves.

The father's part:

The role of the father at a private debut is that of the good host at any party. He does not stand in the receiving line but stays nearby, greets friends and acquaintances and sees that everything is running smoothly. He dances the first dance with his daughter, then he dances with his wife, with the grandmothers if they are present and wish to dance, and then with the other guests, young and old alike.

At many cotillions and community debuts, the fathers participate in a parade and a simple cotillion dance with their daughters. They cross the ballroom, one couple at a time, and each father presents his debutante daughter to the hostess or to the committee giving the dance. Although the young men

guests nowadays may wear tuxedos to debut parties, the escorts
of the debutantes who are coming out and the father must wear
white tie and tails.

The debutante's dress:

At a ball, the debutante wears the prettiest evening dress she
can buy, preferably white, suggesting something light, airy, gay,
and above all, young. A pastel color is acceptable, but not scar-
let or a bright blue, and never black. At a multiple debut, the
girls wear the same color, almost invariably white, but they
choose their own style. The mothers of the debutantes wear
evening dresses in any color except black.

At an afternoon tea the debutante wears a cocktail dress.
Her mother wears an afternoon dress. Both mother and daughter wear gloves, and neither wears a hat.

Some hints for the "belle of the ball":

Let us suppose that *you* are the debutante! Don't let your excitement overwhelm your sense of courtesy. Listen to a name
that is said—look at the one to whom the name belongs, put
out your hand cordially. As friends who have sent you flowers
approach, thank them; also later write an additional note of
thanks to older people. To your relatives or your own intimate
friends, your oral thanks are sufficient.

PART SIX

INFORMAL ENTERTAINING

22

Cocktail parties

Cocktail parties are a popular form of entertainment. They require little preparation, are limited as to time, and you can entertain many more people at once in a small house.

"PAY-BACK" PARTIES

An unattractive custom nowadays is that of giving large "pay-back" cocktail parties. A hostess who has been invited to many parties invites on one evening all those to whom she is indebted and creates one large horror! The guests are not chosen for compatibility, there are not enough places to sit down, the noise level reaches an intolerable pitch. If you incur social obligations with any frequency, do make the effort to give small parties from time to time and avoid the necessity of a yearly "pay-back."

COCKTAILS BEFORE A DANCE

A pleasant form of entertaining is having a group of friends for cocktails before a dinner dance or some other function. Invitations are sent out on visiting cards, note paper or a printed cocktail-party invitation card. They state "Cocktails before the dance at the Happy Course Golf Club, 6:00 to 8:00," the place and date. Add "R.S.V.P." because the hostess usually makes the reservations for those of her guests who wish to go on to the other event.

Invitations may be telephoned, a correct, practical method; the hostess knows immediately how many will be joining her at the club or dance and so can make the reservations sooner.

When you are the guest, you pay the cost of admission, dinner, drinks and anything else at the later party unless your hostess specifically says or writes that she expects you *as her guest*. If you are not a member of the club involved, find out in advance whether you may sign as a member of another club or pay in cash. If either is not permitted, ask your host if you may sign his name and add your initials so you may pay him for your share when he receives his bill.

COCKTAIL BUFFETS

Many hostesses choose the cocktail buffet for entertaining all except the smallest and most informal groups. Here the food offered is sufficiently substantial so that the guests need not have dinner afterward. Since they are expected to linger longer than at a regular cocktail party the invitation frequently states only the hour of arrival, perhaps six thirty or seven, and makes it clear that the gathering is a "cocktail buffet."

The menu may vary from simple to very elaborate. The least is a platter of sliced cold meat (ham, chicken or roast beef), slices of buttered breads, accompanying dishes such as carrot sticks, celery, olives, raw cauliflower, and possibly some sandwiches already made. This type of buffet may be eaten standing near the table without a plate. The meat is placed on a slice of bread and eaten like a sandwich and the raw vegetables picked up and dipped in a sauce. Often a smoked ham or turkey is placed whole on the table; when the platters of sliced meat are running low, the host, or any of the guests, carves additional slices as required.

The table is covered with a tablecloth and napkins are available. If there is room, a centerpiece of flowers or fruit is attractive, but it is better to leave it off and use a prettily decorated cake (or even one of the main dishes) in the center rather than crowd the table.

A more elaborate buffet includes one or more hot dishes, generally casseroles kept warm on an electric hot plate or served in a chafing dish over a flame. In this case, there are stacks of plates and rows of forks, or you may choose a hot dish such as bite-sized meat balls or frankfurters, tiny hot potatoes dipped in salt, and hot bread or rolls with a cheese fondue, all of which may be spread with a toothpick.

JUST COCKTAILS

If the number of guests is small, the invitation is almost always by telephone. For a larger party, they may be written on your own informal, on note paper or on a visiting card. *(See Chapter 46 for the correct forms.)* Or you may buy an attractively printed card made for the purpose.

The time is usually stated, "Cocktails *from* 5:00 to 7:00." Even though R.S.V.P. is omitted, thoughtful guests let the hostess know whether they are planning to attend the party. If there is an R.S.V.P., the telephone number is written beside it, as this type of invitation may always be answered by telephone. Every sort of hors d'oeuvre or appetizer is acceptable provided it can be eaten with the fingers: olives (chilled, or wrapped in bacon and broiled), tiny broiled sausages, thin bread rolled around cheese or bacon, skewered and toasted, crackers spread with sandwich paste, crabmeat or lobster in bite-size pieces, or shrimp on little wooden picks so that they can be dipped in mayonnaise or colorful sauces. Don't forget a pile of cocktail napkins—cloth or paper—on the tray.

WHAT DRINKS TO SERVE

As a general rule, a host should count on each guest having two or three drinks. In the winter, martinis, whiskey "on the rocks" and whiskey in a tall glass with water or soda are popular; in warm weather a cocktail mixed with fruit juice and gin or rum or tall drinks made from these same ingredients are excellent. Always have nonalcoholic drinks available: tomato juice, other fruit juices, Coca Cola, ginger ale. Never urge a guest to have a drink—or *another* drink—if he has once refused.

BARTENDERS AND WAITERS

For a cocktail party of more than twelve and if you have no maid in your home, it is wise to hire a bartender for the evening. The bartender attends to the drinks. He may stand behind a large table loaded with every sort of cocktail glass, ice, and bottles of each kind of liquor and soft drink to be served. The guests go to the bar themselves and request the kind of cocktail they wish. A gentleman usually asks the lady accompanying him her preference and she waits at a little distance from the bar while he gives the order to the bartender and brings her the cocktail. If a group of women are talking together, it is perfectly correct for one of them who wishes another drink to go to the bar herself.

You may prefer to have the bartender pass a tray of drinks, already mixed, to each guest as he arrives. After the first serving, he watches for empty glasses and, when he sees one, approaches the guest and says, "May I bring you another drink?" The guest replies, "Thank you, I am drinking bourbon and soda," and hands him the glass to be refilled.

One important note: Be sure that you instruct the bartender in advance exactly how you like your cocktails mixed and insist he use a measure. If you let him measure "by eye" your liquor supply may run out long before you had planned. Or you may have some unexpectedly boisterous guests on your hands!

HINTS FOR HOSTS AND GUESTS

At a small party, the hostess introduces a newcomer to all the guests, but at a large one, after introducing him to two or three people, she leaves him on his own, her roof serving as an introduction. There is no need to shake hands. A girl has trouble enough managing pocketbook, hors d'oeuvres, cigarette and cocktail.

Self-help:

When there is no extra help for the evening, the host is the bartender and the hostess the waitress. She passes the trays of hors d'oeuvres once or twice, often with a friend helping her, and then leaves the food in a conspicuous spot (on a hot plate or in a chafing dish if the hors d'oeuvres are hot) and the guests help themselves. She carefully removes trays or dishes even before they are completely empty. One cold limp shrimp in a dish, or a mayonnaise-smeared platter left on a table is most unappetizing.

If the choice is limited, the host-bartender may say, "Will you have a martini or bourbon?" Also, he may ask the men to refill their own glasses, as well as those of any ladies who wish another.

If there are only a few guests, the host hangs their coats in a hall closet. If there are more wraps than a closet can conveniently hold, the men and women put them in separate bedrooms, laid neatly on the beds. Or a rack may be placed near the door.

Overstaying your welcome:

Although the hosts must be ready on time, the guests may arrive as much as an hour or so after the start of the party. A late arrival, however, should not mean a late departure. After a half hour or so beyond the indicated departure time, the hostess may take steps to hurry the last survivors out. The most practical way is simply to remove the liquor and close the bar, after which the party will soon be over.

23

Informal dining

The degree of informality of a party depends entirely on the circumstances and taste of the host or hostess. The hostess who belongs to the great majority of women who entertain with no help at all, or with only a maid hired for the evening, should nevertheless consult the chapter on formal dinners. The rules for the informal dinner are derived from the rules for the formal dinner, and a knowledge of both will facilitate every step of the proceedings.

SIT-DOWN OR BUFFET?

The first consideration is the size of your party. Eight is the maximum number that can be served comfortably at a sit-down dinner without help. If your table can seat more than eight, you may have a semibuffet, with the guests serving themselves from a sideboard, but sitting together at the table. Otherwise, you must plan a buffet dinner. *(See Chapter 24.)*

PREPARATION AND PLANNING

Careful planning and preparing for a sit-down meal are of utmost importance. If you wish to enjoy the company of your guests, you choose dishes that can be prepared in advance and served with a minimum of last-minute fuss. Omit fancy hors d'oeuvres—salted nuts or "niblets" are preferable to elaborate spreads. Try to spread out your preparations over several days. Cigarette boxes may be filled, flowers arranged (choose those that will last several days), silver polished, and even your table set ahead of time. If you have a freezer, prepare in advance whatever dishes can be frozen.

THE INVITATIONS

Invitations may be written on visiting cards or note paper, but they are usually telephoned. They are extended between ten days and two weeks ahead of time and the person invited must answer promptly, either by mail or by telephone. *(See also Chapter 46.)*

SEATING YOUR GUESTS

Give considerable thought to the seating of your guests, for you can make or break a party by the congeniality of dinner partners. In a group of six or ten, the host sits at one end of the table opposite the hostess. If there are eight or twelve at the table, she must move one seat to the left, putting the male guest of honor on her right opposite her husband. The lady guest of honor sits on the host's right. If there is no particular guest of honor, the hostess might choose the oldest lady present or one who has not visited her house for some time. She alternates the men and women, spacing them as evenly as possible, keeping her place at the end of the table unless this puts too many women in a row. She still seats the honored guests at her right and her husband's.

SOME MENU SUGGESTIONS

There are certain practical aspects to consider. Try to avoid dishes that require many extra condiments or sauces; restrict your courses to two or three. If you decide on only two, a main course and a dessert, you may serve more substantial hors d'oeuvres beforehand. Some hostesses serve soup or a fish course, such as cold salmon or shrimp, in the living room. If this is done, the host helps his wife by removing the empty plates and ashtrays while she is seating the guests in the dining room in order to have the living room neat when they return there for coffee. If there is a maid, she does this tidying up while the guests are eating their main course.

A roast is always delicious, and there is something mouth-watering about watching the meat being carved. Creamed or curried chicken within a ring of noodles or rice is pretty. Or try a special dinner—shrimp steamed in beer, lobsters flown from Maine, a Spanish paella—in short any unusual treat.

A word of caution—don't experiment with a new dish at a party. Try it out at least once on the family. Because the appearance of a dish is almost as important as its flavor, choose a menu with variation in color and texture—never a white sauce on chicken served with rice and cauliflower.

CHOOSING AND SERVING WINE

Unless the meal is strictly formal, the host may choose any wine he thinks his guests would prefer. Whether that is the dry or the sweet variety is a matter of your own taste. The most important consideration is that the wine complement the food you are serving it with. *(For details about the traditional choice of wine, see Chapter 18.)*

The simplest way to offer wine at an informal dinner is to place the opened bottle on the table in front of the host, preferably on a coaster. If more than one bottle is needed, a second one is placed at the other end of the table and the host asks a man at that end to assist him in pouring. When the first course is served, the host (and his helper) informally fills the glasses of the guests at each end of the table. If a maid is present, she may pour the wine after she has served the first course. She removes the bottle from the table, serves the lady who is guest of honor, continues around the table counterclockwise serving the host last, and replaces the bottle in front of him. Anybody not wishing wine merely says, "No, thank you," but does not cover his glass with his hand or turn it upside-down. Incidentally, when drinking white wine finish the glass completely, but with red wine leave a sip in the bottom to avoid swallowing any possible sediment. Those pouring the wine offer to refill a guest's glass whenever it is empty or almost empty.

SETTING YOUR TABLE

Set the table as for a formal dinner, with a damask or lace cloth; or it may be set with individual place mats as for a luncheon. Gay, colorful cloths add much to a table set on a terrace or in an informal room.

If a tablecloth is used, you do not need butter plates, but with place mats, they are necessary to avoid soiling the polished surface with the buttered or crumbly rolls. All flat silver necessary for the meal is put at each place, the silver to be used last nearest the plate, the one to be used first on the outside. The service

plate is not used. In many houses, the salad dressing ingredients are arranged in a set of bowls and bottles that, with the salad bowl, are put in front of the hostess who mixes the dressing herself.

If a course is to be served before the entrée, it may be on the table when the guests come in to dinner. Fish or shrimp in long-stemmed glass bowls are brought in on a plate, and both removed to make way for the hot plates of the main course. If your first course is soup, practical soup dishes are little pots with lids; they keep the contents hot while the guests are seating themselves.

The butter should already be on the butter plates, the water glasses filled and any wine should either be chilling in a cooler beside the host or in a decanter on the table. Salad is often served with the main course on a salad plate or a bowl set at the left of each place.

If the host is to carve a roast, or serve the meat and vegetables, the stack of warm plates is placed in front of him along with the foods to be served and the necessary implements. If there is a course already on the table, however, the hostess or maid brings the entrée in from the kitchen after the plates have been removed.

GREETING THE GUESTS

The host and hostess stay near the door, or if the living room is out of sight of the door, they go together to greet their guests when the doorbell rings.

Dinner should be planned for forty-five minutes to an hour later than the time on the invitation if cocktails are served, or twenty minutes later if not, to allow late arrivals a moment of relaxation.

INFORMAL SERVICE
With one maid:

Before dinner, the maid may be on hand to take coats from the guests and serve hors d'oeuvres if cocktails are offered. Then she goes to make the last-minute preparations, and announces dinner, or signals the hostess, who tells the guests that dinner is ready.

If a first course is served, the maid removes the plates when everyone is finished and either replaces each one with a hot plate or places a stack of hot plates in front of the host, depending on how she is to serve the main course. She may do this in one of two ways.

First, if all the food is ready in the kitchen, she passes it to the guests, the meat first and then the vegetables. When the maid serves in this way she starts on the host's right with the lady who is guest of honor and continues around the table counterclockwise, serving the host last. Some hostesses insist that they be skipped and the maid return to serve them next to last, but this is awkward.

All dishes are served from the left and, if convenient, removed from the right. The condiments, breads, sauces and salad are usually passed around the table by the guests themselves; if the group is not large, the maid may pass one or more of them when she has finished with the main dishes. A competent maid may pass two vegetable dishes at the same time, holding one in each hand.

When the hostess sees that all her guests are finished, she rings and the maid clears the table. Everything is removed except the glasses and the silver for dessert. The maid then crumbs the table, using a clean folded napkin to sweep the crumbs onto a small plate held just below the edge of the table.

Dessert may be brought in from the kitchen already on the plates and placed before the guests in the same order as was the main course. Or the plates may be set before the guests and the dessert passed to each one in turn. If she prefers, the hostess may serve it herself at the table.

The less formal way, often used for family dinners when guests are not present, is to have all the dishes to be served arranged about the host; as he fills each plate, the maid lifts it and passes it to each person, from the left, starting as before, with the lady on the host's right. When everyone is served, she removes the serving dishes to be kept warm in the kitchen and passes them herself for a second helping when the hostess signals. Or if they have covers, they may be left where they are. When the host wishes to offer his guests another portion, he rings for the maid and says, "Mary, would you please bring me Mrs. Harris's plate"; she holds it for him to fill and returns it to Mrs. Harris. If dessert is served by the hostess, the maid passes the plates around in exactly the same manner as she passed the first course.

WITHOUT HELP

The ideal solution when one is giving a dinner party with no help is to have the guests serve themselves from a side table or buffet and then seat themselves at the dining-room table. This avoids the necessity of passing dishes around the table and makes dining easier and more pleasant for everyone. However, some hostesses do not have the facilities to do this, or prefer that the food be served at the table after the guests are seated. For this type of meal, start with the main course and provide the equivalent of a first course by serving plenty of substantial canapes with your cocktails or before you enter the dining room.

You receive your guests and stay with them until they

have all arrived and until the "cocktail hour," if you serve cocktails, is over. Then you leave them with your husband, bring the meat from the kitchen, set the vegetable dishes beside it and then invite everyone to "come in to dinner."

Your husband carves the roast or serves the casserole. Preferably he also serves the vegetables, but the vegetable dishes may be handed around. In either case, when the first plate is filled, the host hands it to the lady on his right, saying, "This is for you," since the guest of honor should be served first. The next plate is passed down the table on his right to his wife, or to whoever is seated at the opposite end. The rest of the guests on his right are served in order working back toward the guest of honor, and the process is then repeated on his left. He serves himself last. Since this procedure can consume considerable time and the food will be getting cold, the host or hostess asks the guests to start after three or four people have been served. If the host and hostess forget to do so, one of the guests is perfectly correct in beginning to eat.

When the coffee or tea is served with the meal, have the cups on the table when the guests sit down. After the meal is served, the hostess takes the coffee or teapot and goes around the table filling the cups, starting with the woman on her husband's right. She fills her own cup last. If she prefers to fill the cups while seated at her place, the guests pass them down the table from hand to hand. But this is inconvenient for the diners and may lead to an accident.

In most cases, when the guests see you start to rise to clear the table, they will stand up, saying "May I help you?" Firmly refuse, telling them, "No, really, it is easier to do it myself." The only exception is when you have a daughter, sister or very close friend at the table and have asked her in advance if she would mind helping.

You remove the dishes two at a time, not stacking them, and either put them on a side table or take them to the kitchen. Bread-and-butter plates, salts and peppers and condiment dishes are also taken off, but you need not crumb the table. Each time that you take something out to the kitchen, you may bring back dessert plates, salad and salad plates, or whatever is needed for the next course. If you wish, you may put a dessert plate at each place you have cleared as you return to take the next plate. Or as soon as you have removed your husband's plate, you may put a stack of dessert plates and the dessert in front of him so that he can serve it while you are finishing the table-clearing. Any system that speeds the changing of courses is acceptable, so that your guests do not feel that you are going to too much trouble.

You need not clear the dessert dishes; when everyone is finished, you say "Shall we have our coffee in the living room?" Don't accept a guest's offer to help do the dishes. The thoughtful guest does not insist.

AFTER-DINNER COFFEE

When the guests are seated in the living room, take the cream out of the refrigerator and pour the coffee into whatever pot you are going to serve it from—glass, silver, or, best of all, one that has a flame under it to keep the coffee hot. It may be made and served in an electric coffeemaker, which can be plugged in again in the living room. Arrange the coffee and cream on a big tray, set with sugar, spoons, cups and saucers. It is a nice gesture to offer either a large cup or a demitasse, so many hostesses put some of each size on the tray. When it is all ready, you or your husband carry it in and set it on a coffee table or on any table that has a chair nearby. You serve the coffee, asking each guest, "How many lumps of sugar?" and "Cream?" Either you or your husband may pass the cups around, or the guests may step up and you hand it to them directly. It is thoughtful to offer caffeine-free coffee as an alternate to regular after-dinner coffee.

HINTS FOR GUESTS

A guest should arrive within fifteen minutes of the time for which he is invited. When dinner is announced, you respond promptly, rise and encourage your companions to go with you —"Shall we go in to dinner? I think Nancy would like us to." Unless she says, "Please bring your drink with you," don't.

When you are told which is your place, wait for the hostess to seat herself before you sit down, unless she says, "Please sit down, I must bring in another dish." Men, as at any meal, help the women on their right to be seated. At a large party, you need not wait until all the guests are served to start. Your hostess should say, as the plates are passed, "Please start. I don't want your dinner to get cold," but if she neglects to do so, pick up your fork after four or five have been served. The others will follow suit.

When your hostess rises to clear the table, don't jump up to help unless she has asked you to beforehand. However, you may offer to pass the cups around when she serves coffee after dinner.

Most important—remember to talk to the guests on either side of you or to enter with enthusiasm into a general conversation if the table is small.

If games are suggested after dinner, no matter how you feel about them, look as though you think it's a fine idea. Often, especially if the guests do not have much in common, entertainment that you would ordinarily avoid can be the means of pulling a party together and making it a success.

FAMILY MEALS

If the family has a maid, the meals are served exactly as they would be if guests were present. She may serve from the kitchen, or if the family is large she may pass the plates as the man of the house fills them.

In most households where Mother is cook and waitress, she fills the plates and brings them to the table two at a time, giving her husband the first one. She may, and should, enlist the aid of any one of the children who is old enough to help her. If the family is small she may remove the dishes herself, but if there are a number of children, those old enough should take their own plates to the kitchen, after waiting until everyone has finished eating.

If the meal is served by the father at the table, the dishes are passed from person to person. The first one filled is sent down the table on the host's right and stops at the mother's place. The others are served in order working back up the table, first on the right side, then on the left. Aside from the fact that the first plate is not given to the person on the father's right, the order is the same as that described for an informal dinner party.

At large family meals the vegetable dishes, instead of being at the father's place, may be farther down the table. When this is done the person nearest the dish, as soon as he receives his own plate, helps himself and passes the vegetable in the direction of those who already have their meat.

When a person seated at one end of the table asks for something near the other end, the person nearest the food requested picks it up and passes it on. If he wishes he may help himself before passing it to avoid his neighbor having to send it back again.

24

Buffet dinners

Three great advantages of a buffet dinner are: you can accommodate many more guests than your dining-room table will seat, lack of service is no handicap, and it has enjoyable informality. If people are not sitting beside those they find particularly congenial, women as well as men are free to move elsewhere.

WITH OR WITHOUT HELP

Just before the hostess announces dinner, she attends to lighting the candles, putting out iced water, and arranging the platters, casseroles or serving dishes on the table. But the food can be all ready—in double boilers or chafing dishes or, if cold, in the refrigerator. After eating, the guests take their empty plates back to the dining room themselves, putting them on a side table—not on the buffet—and serving their own dessert. Their hostess and her husband may remove the dessert plates or the guests may do it themselves. If the dining room has a door, it can be closed, or a screen can be pulled across the entrance, once all the plates have been taken there. If, however, the dining area is a part of the living room, the hostess removes the soiled plates to the kitchen while the guests are drinking their coffee.

If she has a maid or a hired waitress, she advises the waitress when to put the food on the buffet table, watching to see that her guests are ready. The maid takes out empty plates as they set them down. She may, if the hostess wishes, pass the dishes around for second helpings. Because everyone will not finish simultaneously, she has adequate time to remove the food from the buffet table and replace it with dessert plates and dessert or salad and cheese or whatever is chosen to finish the meal.

After the waitress has removed the last of the plates, she brings in the coffee tray and the hostess pours; the maid is then free to clean up the kitchen and dining room.

THE INVITATIONS

The invitation is usually written on an informal, on your note paper or across the top of the face of your visiting card. *(See Chapter 46.)*

The invitation must be answered promptly either by telephone or sent on a visiting card, merely saying "Sat. Oct. 2 with pleasure." *(See also Chapter 48.)*

SEATING ARRANGEMENTS

There are two ways of seating guests at a buffet dinner. First, they may simply return to the living room, hold their plates on their laps and set their glasses on the nearest table. Your guests will be more comfortable if you set a small folding table by each chair.

The second way of seating guests is to set out small tables —sturdy card tables, perhaps—in your living room, dining room or library. If you have the space, most men and women prefer to be seated in this way. The tables are covered with bridge-table-size cloths. Places are set exactly as for an informal dinner with silver, napkins, glasses. The guests serve themselves, going for second helpings and removing their used plates. If the living room is used, the hostess takes the tables out after the meal to make room for after-dinner activities.

SEMIBUFFET

A pleasant way of serving a small group of friends or a family party is to arrange the food on the sideboard or a side table and set the dining-room table as for a sit-down dinner. Two variations are possible. First, after the guests are seated, the host serves each plate from the buffet, asking the guests, "Do you like your meat rare or well done?" or "Do you take cranberry sauce and stuffing?" The hostess passes the plate, seating herself with her own plate next to last, the host helping himself last. She may say as she hands the plates around, "Please start, so that your dinner won't get cold." In the other variation, the guests may serve themselves as at a regular buffet and carry their plates to the table. The hostess serves herself after the guests, and the host is the last.

THE INVALUABLE ELECTRIC HOT PLATE

I recommend an electric hot plate or tray, because, on them, plates can be heated and your meal kept warm for an almost indefinite period of time. Furthermore, with an electric appliance on the buffet table, there is no need to take the dishes to the kitchen to be kept warm for second helpings. And, finally, it is unnecessary to watch and replace fuel for flame-heated chafing dishes.

SETTING THE BUFFET TABLE

Unless there is ample space, ornamental objects are omitted. Flowers are lovely, but if it is a question of choosing between decorative flowers and edible fruit, a centerpiece of dessert fruit is preferable. If the table is crowded and candles are not needed to see by, they are better left off. Candelabra are more compact than candlesticks and give better light.

If the party is large, leave the table in the center of the room, so that two lines of guests may serve themselves at once. The most important dish is divided into two parts and one plate or casserole placed at each end of the table. The plates are in two stacks beside them, and the napkins and silver neatly arranged next to the plates. Dishes of vegetables, salads, bread and butter, and sauces and condiments are on each side of the table and the guests need to pass down only one side. If the table is set against the wall, arrange the utensils and food in a way that makes for the best flow of traffic, so that the guests need not double back.

If you use a white damask cloth, silver candelabra and an elaborate centerpiece, your buffet will appear quite formal. But you may just as properly use pottery dishes with a hot-plate pad under them and a bowl of fruit in the center of the table. It is not the elegance of the utensils and decorations you use that

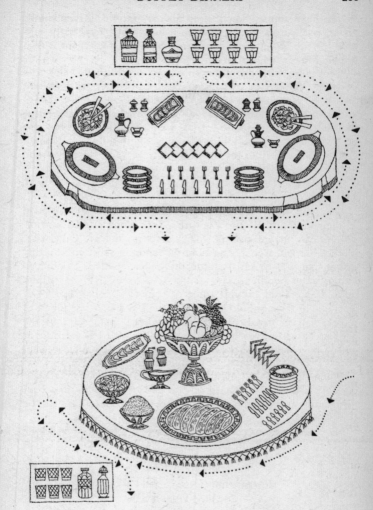

makes your table attractive, but the combination of dishes, linen, and silver and the way in which they are arranged on the table.

Color plays an enormous part in the beauty of a buffet table.

If you have copper bowls, keep all the autumn tints in mind: green, red, russet, and yellow on a bare table. Especially suitable for the buffet table are strong colors like eggplant, russet brown, lobster red, leaf green and dark blue.

Generally a punch or another cold drink, iced water and possibly beer left in its cans or bottles, together with glasses, are on the sideboard as well as a large urn of coffee.

Because the coffee is already there, the guests may serve themselves during the meal as well as afterward, but the hostess may take an additional tray, set with cups, a coffeepot, cream and sugar into the living room to serve those guests who did not want it with their dinner.

THE MENU

Whatever kinds of food you choose, be sure they are good of their kind and easy to eat with a fork alone (this is not important if you are seating your guests at tables). Otherwise, merely use a reasonable amount of common sense in selecting dishes that will be satisfying to the people invited. Don't feed hungry men bouillon, dabs of hors d'oeuvres, fruit salad and meringues; rather provide three or four substantial dishes—at least one of these should be hot. Substantial dishes include most meats, fish in a sauce such as Newburg, potatoes and the heavier desserts. Nearly everything made in a baking dish or casserole is ideal for a buffet meal as it is hearty and easily kept hot.

If you have many guests, you may serve two main dishes, possibly a lobster Newburg at one end of the table and beef Stroganoff at the other, but choose two dishes that will be complemented by the same vegetables and condiments.

Here are some menu suggestions, ranging from an elaborate buffet to a simple family-type meal. Use any combination that appeals to you, omitting or adding to each menu as you wish.

Veal Scaloppine or Roast Turkey
Mashed Potatoes
String Beans with Mushrooms
Cranberry Sauce, Stuffing, Gravy
Buttered Rolls
Fresh Fruit Compote
Cookies
Coffee

Italian Spaghetti and Meatballs or Lasagna
Mixed Green Salad
Choice of Roquefort, French, Italian Dressing
French or Italian Bread, Butter
Lemon Ice
Coffee

Hungarian Goulash or Beef and Kidney Pie
Noodles
Glazed Carrots
Green Salad with Mandarin Oranges
Buttered Rolls
Coffee

Curried Lamb or Chicken
Rice Ring
Chutney, Raisins, Ground Nuts
French Bread, Butter
Raw Spinach Salad
Ice Cream and Cake or Cookies
Coffee

For a summer evening:
Three or four varieties of cold sliced meats such as
Ham, Turkey, Roast Beef, Lamb, or Cold Cuts
Scalloped Potatoes
Vegetable Salad
Buttered Rolls
Vanilla Ice Cream with Green Mint Sauce
Cookies
Coffee

THE PARTY ITSELF

When the guests have arrived and the cocktails, if served, are finished, the door into the dining room is opened and people in more or less of a queue file around the dining table. The women as well as the men help themselves, although, quite correctly, a man may ask a woman what she would like, fill a plate and take it to her.

If people continue to sit and wait to be served, the hostess directs them, "Please go into the dining room and help yourself to what you like." If they stand blockading the table, carrying on a long conversation, she says, "Won't you please take your plate and go into the other room again and sit down?"

The only serving detail is the clearing away of used dishes. In a house with servants, every plate is removed as soon as it is put down, and filled ashtrays are constantly replaced; the glasses of those seated are refilled from time to time, and the main dishes passed for second helpings. But the servantless hostess asks one or two members of her family—or an intimate friend—to help her put used dishes in several spaces provided, from which she can stack them and take them away as unobtrusively as possible.

25

Informal luncheons

If you are one of those who have a very small dining room, or no dining room at all, but have a living room or a patio large enough to permit two or three small tables to be set up, a luncheon of eight or twelve, perhaps followed by bridge, is delightful. Each card table is set with a cloth, white or colored, a yard and a half square; any style will do, but they should, if possible, be exactly alike. Simple matched cloths are better than assorted, elaborate ones. A small flower arrangement makes a pretty centerpiece.

SERVING THE LUNCHEON
The hostess alone:

If you are serving without a maid, a buffet luncheon is the wisest. The food is set out as for a buffet dinner. For a ladies' luncheon, the fare is simpler than for a dinner. A delicious but light meal is more appreciated than one dressed with rich sauces and ending with "gooey" sweets.

After you announce that luncheon is served, your guests file past the table and help themselves, taking their plates to the card tables and seating themselves with whomever they wish. If you are having a course before the entrée, it is put on the tables before your guests arrive; they sit down and finish it before going to the table for the main course. If there is no maid, the guests take their empty plates and leave them on a side table, as they go to get their next course. While they are helping themselves, you remove the soiled dishes to the kitchen.

The same procedure is followed for the salad or dessert. You then ask them to leave the tables and sit on more comfortable chairs to have their coffee; you clear the tables and, if bridge is to follow, set out the cards, two decks, two score pads and pencils on each table. *(For further details about card parties, see Chapter 27.)*

With the help of a maid:

When you have a maid, she can serve eight or twelve guests quite easily if the first course is already on the table. She clears the plates by standing at the table corner, taking two at a time, one in each hand. A menu limited to a single dish and salad is best, as she must pass the food from each person's left. The salad may be all ready in small bowls or plates, which she brings in two at a time to place on the guests' left. Rolls, butter, iced water and any other beverage are put on the table beforehand.

When dessert is finished, the waitress carries the coffee tray to another room and readies the tables for bridge, while the hostess pours the coffee.

ON FOOD AND DRINK

If you wish to serve cocktails before lunch, the drinks should be of a milder type than those served before dinner. Sherry, Dubonnet, vermouth, either "on the rocks" or in a wine glass are ideal, but if you know your friends prefer them, serve martinis, daiquiris or Bloody Marys.

Two or three courses are sufficient at any informal luncheon. Four of the following menus have been planned with the idea that you can have all the preparation finished in advance. But the sole and the soufflé dishes must be cooked and served at the exact moment.

Fresh Fruit Cup
Filet of Sole Amandine
Spinach Salad with Chopped, Hard-Boiled Egg, Tart Dressing
Buttered Rolls
Orange Chiffon Cake
Coffee

Clam or Oyster Chowder with Oyster Crackers
Fruit Salad and Cottage Cheese
Melba Toast
Chocolate Mousse
Coffee

Cold Salmon with Green Mayonnaise Sauce
Sliced Cucumber and Tomato
Protein and White Toast
Lemon Chiffon Pie
Coffee

Curried Chicken with Rice Ring
Mixed Green Salad
Baking Powder Biscuits
Jell-O made with Fresh Fruit
Coffee

Little Neck Clams or Oysters
Cold Sliced Roast Beef, Horseradish Sauce
Potatoes au Gratin
Watercress and Tomato Salad
Fresh Strawberries and Sour Cream
Coffee

Cheese Soufflé
(if your guests can be trusted to arrive on time)
Asparagus Vinaigrette
Croissants
Fresh Fruit and Cookies
Coffee

Beverages:

In summer iced tea and coffee are delicious, or give your guests a choice by passing a tray with a pitcher of each, or have both available close to the buffet table. A bowl of fruit punch prepared with floating slices of orange and lemon and surrounded by glasses or cups adorned with fresh sprigs of mint looks refreshing. A pitcher of ice water, from which the guests may help themselves, should be in evidence.

26

Barbecues

If you have a built-in grill in your yard or patio, you are fortunate, but a portable grill serves just as well. A table near the fire holds the food and the plates, cooking utensils, etc. There must be seating facilities for every guest. A garden wall or steps leading to the patio may be used as seats, if cushions are provided. Small chairs can be rented for very little from a caterer.

You may give your flair for color and decoration a free rein: checked or striped tablecloths, ones with splashy designs of fruits or flowers are gay. They may be of cotton or linen, but plastic ones are more practical. If your cloth is patterned, solid-colored paper napkins and plates are best.

Disposable plastic or plastic-coated paper plates and cups are excellent if they are of a sturdy material—avoid the flimsy cardboard-paper type. For a hot drink, the cups must have handles (the package should be labeled "for hot drinks" or they will leak).

Some hostesses prefer the new hard plastic sets of "china" in lovely patterns; although unbreakable, they feel much like real china. Drink containers, too, come in a variety of unbreakable materials. The barbecue cook will like colorful enameled flameproof pots and pans.

For decorations, string lanterns above the table and make a centerpiece of gay paper parasols for a Chinese dinner. A fishnet tablecloth with colorful felt cutouts of fish sewed on is decorative for a lobster dinner. Fresh flowers arranged in a container that fits into the barbecue theme are always attractive —yellow daisies, for instance, arranged in a copper kettle.

At most barbecues, the host is the cook, but the hostess may also act as chef.

MENU SUGGESTIONS

I am going to give you some sample menus, intended only as a guide. In each, the main dish—meat, fish or fowl—is prepared on the grill, and unless specified, the others are prepared in advance and kept on the stove indoors or brought out to sit on a corner of the grill where the temperature must be neither too hot nor too cold.

The least expensive, but always popular, especially with young people:

Hamburgers and/or Hot Dogs
Buttered Rolls
Casserole of Baked Beans
Potato Chips
Celery and Carrot Sticks
Watermelon Slices

In the following menu, pieces of meat or shrimp, mushrooms, tomatoes, onions and bacon are marinated and threaded alternately beforehand on long skewers, ready to be laid on the grill:

Beef, Lamb or Shrimp "Kabobs"
Rice
Watercress and Tomato Salad
Hot Rolls
Chocolate Eclairs

Especially good for the seashore:

Grilled Swordfish
Casserole of Scalloped Potatoes
Spinach Salad
Croissants
Fresh Fruit Compote and Cookies or Cake

Messy to eat, but delicious:
Spareribs with Barbecue Sauce
Baked Potatoes
Coleslaw
Hard Rolls
Apple Pie with Vanilla Ice Cream

The classic barbecue menu:
Sirloin Steak
Potato Chips
French Fried Onions
Mixed Green Salad
French or Garlic Bread
Assorted Pastries

Beer, any soft drink and pitchers of milk go well with the informality of a barbecue, and, in very hot weather, iced tea and iced coffee. Pots of coffee kept hot on the grill are served either during or after the meal. If cocktails are served, instead of elaborate hors d'oeuvres, dishes of nuts or potato chips scattered about are sufficient.

A side table loaded with a variety of condiments is a nice touch. As each guest fills his plate (the host cuts and serves the meat), he passes by this table and helps himself to catsup, mustard, relish or sauce.

SOME GENERAL HINTS

Have plenty of light so the chef can tell whether the meat is done. Floodlights directed up into the trees give a beautiful effect. Japanese lanterns can be purchased strung on electric wires like Christmas-tree bulbs. Candles in hurricane lamps give a soft light. Some candles with insect repellent are excellent in summer.

A lunch-time barbecue may be followed by a swim if you have a pool or are near the beach, or you may organize a game

of softball or badminton. Many adults enjoy a game of catch
or touch football on a brisk day. Organized games and races for
the children are almost a necessity.

In the evening, a phonograph may be plugged in for dancing
if the patio or terrace has a suitable surface, or, with a stone
fireplace, the fire may be built up to a blaze and the guests
gather round it to sing or chat. If you notice your guests
putting on sweaters or coats, be prepared to move the party
into the house.

27

Other informal gatherings

Other ways of entertaining informally have special descriptive
names but do not otherwise differ much from the informal
gatherings discussed in earlier chapters. A housewarming, for
example, may be a cocktail buffet with a tour of the new
house added, or a surprise party might be an informal dance
given in someone else's home. Therefore, a hostess may want
to combine the suggestions made here with those from another
appropriate chapter.

HOURS FOR PARTY-GIVING

The hour chosen for a meal or a party or a game or a visit
should always be that of neighborhood custom. If weddings in
the evening are customary in your neighborhood, then have
your wedding in the evening too. If, on the other hand, a nine
o'clock dinner hour and a noon wedding are customary, then
even though you forage in the refrigerator an hour or more
before dinner, at nine you dine and at noon you marry.

If neighbors pay visits in the evening—or if morning is the hour preferred—you take your protesting husband with you in the evening—or go by yourself in the morning—no matter how inconvenient either hour may be to you. If you cannot manage to have a party at the time decreed by custom, find another way to entertain your friends.

HOUSEWARMINGS

You may invite your friends to a housewarming whenever you see them or by telephone. Invitations on visiting cards are quite suitable too. A housewarming is generally a cocktail party or a cocktail buffet. It may be as simple or as elaborate as you wish, but it is fun to keep the style of your house in mind when you plan your decorations. For instance, if it is an Early American type, a brown tablecloth set with copper or pewter may be more appealing than lace with crystal or silver. *(For additional suggestions, see Chapter 23.)*

The guest generally takes a small gift to a housewarming, something of permanent use, rather than flowers; a few pretty dish towels or place mats or a brush for the fireplace.

OPEN HOUSE

The door is open to all those invited at any time between the hours stated on the invitation. Most open houses nowadays are held to celebrate a holiday—New Year's Day, Christmas Eve or Fourth of July, and are decorated accordingly. They also may take the place of a housewarming.

Invitations are generally sent out on informals or commercial cards bought for the occasion. But an answer is never expected, refreshments are simple and expandable. Dips, bowls of nuts, or other "nibbles," and a punch rather than individual drinks are good choices. People drop in to greet their hosts and generally stay no more than a half hour to an hour.

Food and beverages are set out on the dining-room table or, if your refreshments are restricted to one or two plates of food and a punch bowl, on a table in the hall or living room. You may surround a bowl of eggnog with holly twigs or a fruit punch with flowers, but otherwise, only the attractive arrangement of glasses, little napkins (cloth or paper) and food is necessary to assure the charm of your refreshment table.

BRUNCHES

Brunch is a combination of breakfast and lunch that relies heavily on breakfast for its menus but is taken closer to the usual hour for lunch. Brunches are often given on the day after a large party, but no such excuse is necessary if you find the late morning hours convenient for you and your friends.

Informality is the rule. In the country, slacks or simple dresses are worn by the women, or if the party is beside a swimming pool, people may come in shorts and bring their bathing suits. In the city, any daytime dress or a suit is correct for a woman; a man usually wears a sports jacket rather than a business suit.

Invitations may be telephoned ahead of time, but with this kind of gathering the host may simply say to his friends as they are leaving someone else's party, "Would you come over around eleven thirty tomorrow for a late breakfast?" or "Would you all come for a late breakfast after church tomorrow?"

The food is attractively and conveniently laid out on a buffet table. Breakfast and lunch dishes are combined: a platter of scrambled eggs surrounded with bacon or little sausages, accompanied by hot rolls or toast, and sautéed potatoes and broiled tomatoes; or platters of waffles to be covered with maple syrup or with creamed chicken. Pitchers of fruit juice and pots of coffee are on a table beside the buffet.

CARD PARTIES

On planning your tables:

The first thing to do is to make a list of those to be invited. Then divide those who accept into groups of four and try to seat at each table only those who like to play together. The tables may all be different—one with good players, another with beginners, one where the stakes are high, another where they play for nothing—but do your best to put those who play approximately the same kind of game at the same table. Don't put people who take their game seriously with others who unceasingly chatter and keep asking, "What's trump?" Above all, don't seat players by drawing names out of a hat.

On each table you leave a slip of paper on which you have written the names of the four players who are to play there together. They cut for their seats and partners. See that each table is comfortably lighted, taking care that no light reflects the shiny surface of the cards. If you have any doubt about light, sit in each place, hold the cards in your hands, lay a few on the table and see.

Refreshments:

The kind of refreshments you offer at a card party depends, of course, on the time of day and the guests. Small sandwiches and tiny cakes, accompanied by tea or coffee, are suitable at four o'clock for a group of women. For the men at an evening gathering, a selection of cold meats and cheeses and a variety of breads for do-it-yourself sandwiches are served with coffee and beer. The food may be arranged on the dining-room table, and, having served themselves, the guests may return to the cleared card tables, or take their plates to comfortable chairs in the living room.

A note of warning: If you have invited avid card players, don't interrupt their game to serve some lavish concoction of whipped cream, etc. Give another kind of party if you wish to indulge yourself in the kitchen!

Prizes:

If it is customary in your community to play for prizes, select first prizes for the highest scores made by a woman and a man; at a party to which no men are invited, a second prize is usually given. All prizes are attractively wrapped before being presented. Those who receive the prizes open the packages at once and show appreciation when thanking the hostess.

DESSERT CARD PARTY

A dessert card party is a happy compromise for the hostess who wishes to do more than simply invite her guests to play cards. Dessert for four or eight may be served in the following way: The dining table is set for the dessert course only, with individual place mats, a china dessert plate, a lunch napkin on the plate, a fork at the left and a spoon at the right, and a glass of water. The table is set with a coffee tray in front of the hostess. While her friends are having their dessert, the hostess pours the coffee, and it is handed around the table. After coffee, they begin playing on tables already set up in the living room.

If there are more than eight, the dining table is set up as a buffet, using a pretty tablecloth or place mats or round lace doilies (paper ones will do) under the stack of plates and the dishes on which the dessert is served. The guests serve themselves and take their plates to the living room to eat, but unless the hostess asks them to, they do not sit at the card tables which have already been set up and readied for bridge. They help themselves to coffee; if they wish to start playing immediately, they may take their cups with them to the bridge tables.

STAG DINNERS

A man's dinner is called a stag or bachelor dinner. It is given by a man for men only. It usually celebrates some special event or person, as a welcome or farewell, or, most frequently, as the groom's last party with his good friends before his wedding. A man's dinner is usually given at the host's club or in a private room in a hotel or restaurant. If he gives a stag dinner in his own house, his wife (or mother or sister) should *not* appear. For his wife to come downstairs and receive the guests with him is definitely out of place. He discusses his plans and the menu with his wife, who will prepare it ahead of time and set out the dishes on a buffet table. After the men have eaten, she removes the plates and cleans up if they have gone to a room separated from the dining room; if not, she leaves the cleaning up until the next day.

THE SURPRISE PARTY

Surprise parties usually take place at a friend's house or possibly in a club. The couple to be honored is invited for a "quiet" dinner or evening by another couple, and when they arrive their entire circle of friends is there waiting to surprise them. Such parties always consist of a group of intimate friends and usually take place on John's or Mary's birthday or their anniversary, particularly an earlier one.

A husband may wish to give his wife a surprise birthday party, or she to surprise him with a party in honor of a special occasion—a promotion, for example. With the help of friends, the one planning the party arranges it in his own house.

Some caution is needed in arranging surprise parties and thought given to whether the people honored would really enjoy the occasion. For example, a word of warning is neces-

sary for persons who want to surprise their friends with a
party for their golden wedding anniversary. If the bride and
groom are young for their ages, they might like this type of
party. But if they were not married in their earliest youth, the
excitement of too great a surprise might very well have the
opposite of happy results.

SEWING GROUPS

The hostess at whose house a sewing group meets provides a
supply of different-sized thimbles, extra needles, and several
pairs of scissors and spools of thread. The purpose of the group
may be to make garments for a nursery, hospital or other
organization; or the members sew for themselves, do needle-
point or knit. Sometimes a sewing circle is also a lunch club
that meets weekly or fortnightly at the houses of the various
members. They sew from eleven until about one and then have
a sit-down or buffet luncheon. More often coffee and light
refreshments, such as coffee cake, cookies or doughnuts, are
served approximately halfway through a session that may run
from ten to twelve or from two to half past four.

SATURDAY NIGHT AT THE COUNTRY CLUB

In many communities the Saturday night dance at the local
country club has largely replaced small informal private
dances. Usually a group of friends will attend a country club
dance together after a cocktail party or similar gathering such
as the one described in Chapter 22. On arriving at the club
you ask to be shown to the table that your hostess at the
earlier party has already reserved—you will probably arrive
before her since she cannot leave her home before all her
guests have departed. If she has not arranged to have place
cards on the table, you leave seats free at each end or at opposite sides for her and her husband.

Generally, in deciding where to sit, husbands and wives
split up, since much of the fun of a dance is to enjoy the
company of different people.

As soon as possible a man should dance with the women
seated on either side of him, then with as many of the other
women at the table as possible, being certain not to forget
either his hostess at the cocktail party or his wife! When

she gets up to dance a woman leaves her bag, if it is a small one, on the table, or a larger bag on her chair.

When you make up a group for this type of party, try to choose couples who like to dance. It is inexcusably rude for the men to go off to the bar or otherwise ignore the women at the table. From time to time a man may cut in on a woman he knows who is sitting at another table, but at the end of that particular dance he escorts her back to her own table and then rejoins his original group.

At a late party you need not stay until the music stops. It is far safer to take your own car to the club than to share a ride with another couple since it can be disconcerting to have to stay on at a party because your car companions have decided to make a night of it.

28

Showers

Showers are friendly gatherings held in honor of a bride-to-be or in welcome of a new clergyman or in expectation of the arrival of the stork—for almost anything, in fact, that imagination can invent. The setting can be almost anything—a luncheon, a dinner, an afternoon tea, an evening party, or even a morning coffee. The only distinguishing characteristic of the shower is the giving of presents to the guest of honor.

Bridal showers are never given by members of the bride's immediate family, because a gift is obligatory. It is correct to give a shower for someone who is being married for the second time, whether she be widow or divorcée. But the hostess keeps in mind the elaborateness of the wedding plans and makes hers accordingly. The bride-to-be who is having a quiet, simple wedding might easily be embarrassed by an extremely elaborate shower.

THE INVITATIONS

Invitations to showers are often telephoned: "I'm having a kitchen shower for Betsy Jones on Tuesday at three o'clock." Or they may be written on a visiting card—"Larder shower for Dr. Smythe" or "Stork shower for Helen"—with the day and the hour. Or a shower card from a stationer's shop is entirely appropriate. Make it perfectly clear to the guests the kind of shower it is to be, including all details you have that may be helpful. For example, if you know that Betsy Jones's kitchen is to have red trim, let the guests know, too, so they can choose appropriately colored items.

THE HOUR

A shower for a bride may be given at any hour of the day or evening. Evening is chosen when men as well as women are invited. Originally shower presents were most often things to wear, and therefore showers were for girls only.

The shower for a clergyman is usually given in the early evening. A stork shower is always given in the early afternoon and only intimate girl or women friends are invited. Sometimes a combination of stork shower and surprise party is given at the house of the mother when the baby is five or six weeks old. Although a surprise party, it would be excusable for someone to give her a hint half an hour in advance, so that she and the baby will be found ready for company. The guests usually bring light refreshments with them, certainly in the case of a surprise shower for an unmarried clergyman.

GRANDMOTHER SHOWERS

When a women's club or social organization learns that one of their members is about to become a grandmother, the others may wish to give her a "grandmother shower." It is usually held during or at the end of their regular meeting or get-together with some special refreshments served and a few extra minutes devoted to the opening of the gifts. However, it may be given in the usual way—by a close friend or group of friends of the grandmother-to-be as an afternoon tea or a morning coffee.

The main distinction between a grandmother shower and any other is that the gifts are not for the use of the recipient. Often they are gifts for the baby or the new mother which are given through the grandmother. They may also be articles to be used by the grandmother when she is caring for the new baby—diaper pins, a bathinette, a teething ring, bibs, etc.

Whatever the arrangements, the grandmother shower is a delightful way to honor a friend, and to make the prospective grandmother feel an important part of the coming event.

THE GIFTS

The type of shower allows wide leeway in the choice of presents. At a stork shower, they include anything for a new baby. A larder shower, often given for a new clergyman, includes everything eatable. The shower for a bride is sometimes specified as a linen or a kitchen shower or a general shower.

At a "round-the-clock" shower, each guest is given an hour of the day on her invitation and brings a present appropriate for the hour. For example, at a bridal shower, if her hour is 10 A.M., she might take a dustpan and brush; if it is 6 P.M., she might take a set of four or six glasses.

PRESENTING THE GIFTS

When everyone—or almost everyone—expected has arrived, Betsy Jones opens the packages one by one and thanks each giver. "Thank you, Susie—how lovely!" The cards of donors should be enclosed.

If the party is at tea time, the guests are then offered light refreshments of tea or coffee and cakes. If it is in the evening, coffee or punch and sandwiches are suitable, as are cider and doughnuts, or liqueurs or highballs, especially if men are included.

Unlike wedding presents which are sent from the shop where they are bought, gifts for a shower are brought by hand and given personally. Sometimes the packages are taken at the door and put unopened with the others on a table in another room. In some localities all the presents are sent to the hostess several days beforehand. She leaves the packages as they are, but puts each in a uniform outer gift wrapping. When all are wrapped, the presents are piled on a table or behind a screen or perhaps in full view against one wall of the living room.

29

House parties and overnight guests

THE INVITATIONS

Invitations for house parties and overnight guests are generally telephoned, or, if your guests live in another town, written on your note paper.

June 15th

Dear Ellie,

John and I are hoping that you and Bob and the children can spend the weekend of the fourth with us in Edgartown. There is a 4:00 P.M. ferry that would get you here in time for dinner, and there are ferries leaving at 5:00 and at 8:00 on Sunday. The fishing should be great, and our children are counting on Sally and Jimmy for the annual picnic. Please come—we have wanted to show you our island for so long.

Affectionately,

Ann

With the rising popularity of winter sports, more and more people are acquiring lodges in the mountains, and ski weekends are becoming almost an institution in all sections of the country with nearby slopes.

January 4

Dear Joan,

The forecast is for snow and more snow, and Dick and I are hoping that you and Bill will spend the weekend after next skiing with us at Stowe. Come as early as you can on

Friday the 8th, and stay until Sunday night, so as not to miss a minute of it. The Hortons are coming, too, and perhaps you could drive up together. To find us, you turn off Route 7 on Skyline Drive, exactly three-tenths of a mile beyond the traffic light in Hampton; we are the second house on the right.

No formal clothes, only your ski outfits and slacks or a skirt for the evening. Plenty of woolies and flannels—it's cold.

We're counting on you, so do say "yes."

Love to you both,

Barbara

In your letter or on the telephone, always give the details of transportation or, if your guests are coming by car, the route. If they will be arriving by public transportation, tell them to be sure to let you know at what hour they will arrive, so that you can meet them at the station or airport. It is also wise to indicate what the main activities will be. "We're planning a deep-sea fishing expedition on Saturday," "The Joneses have asked us to a beach picnic on Sunday," or "There is to be a dance at the club on Saturday night."

ROOM FOR YOUR GUESTS

Temporary arrangements:

Few families today have a room in their house intended solely for the use of guests. When friends spend a night or a weekend (or more), the children are moved around to vacate a room, or the library or den is put in readiness. Toys are hidden from sight, clothes are removed from the closet (which should have an adequate supply of hangers), sufficient drawer space is cleared so that the guest may unpack his suitcase, and the room is made sparkling clean. If he is to share a bath with other members of the household, his towels are hung on a rack in his bedroom, so that children do not inadvertently use them. A vase of flowers on the bureau or table will make the room inviting.

PLANNING THE MEALS FOR YOUR GUESTS

When you must entertain without help, the more planning and preparation that can be done ahead, the more effortless and pleasant the result. House parties generally last for no more than two days and nights or possibly three. With the help of a freezer, or even the freezing compartment of your refrigerator, meals can largely be prepared in advance. A casserole, warming in the oven, can be ready at whatever hour your guests arrive, early or late. A steak cooked on the beach in summer or over the coals of the fireplace in winter, served with potato chips and salad, takes little effort. You may wish to treat your guests to a dinner in a local restaurant that specializes, perhaps, in foods native to the region. At most summer resorts, yacht clubs or night clubs provide dinner and dancing on Saturday night.

For lunches, you may prepare the ingredients for a chef's salad, lobster rolls, chowder and sandwiches in advance, ready to be mixed or spread at the last moment.

The one meal that the hostess cannot organize in advance is breakfast. Because one of the joys of a weekend away from home is being able to sleep as late as they want, guests should not be awakened unless there is an activity planned in which they truly wish to participate. The hostess precedes all her guests to the kitchen, makes coffee, prepares fruit or juice, and cooks sausage or bacon enough for all, keeping them warm on a hot plate or in a low oven. She puts butter, eggs and frying pan—or pancake batter and griddle—by the stove, bread by the toaster, and an assortment of cereals and milk and cream on the table, which she sets with places for everyone. She may wait for her guests, or she may eat her own breakfast and be ready to help the latecomers as they arrive. If some of the group want to make an early start to the beach or to ski, for instance, make plans the day before. The host and hostess may accompany the ones who are leaving, as long as everything is left in readiness for those who wish to sleep or relax and arrangements have been made for their joining the group later on if they wish.

A friendly custom is gaining popularity in many localities—when two or three couples go to visit good friends, they offer to bring a roast or a casserole to provide one evening's meal. There is no reason why the hostess should not accept such an offer. On this type of intimate party friends feel more comfortable if they can contribute.

THE PERFECT HOSTESS

The perfect hostess chooses guests who have the same interests and will enjoy each other's company. There is little pleasure in having one couple who enjoys staying up all night to play bridge, while the others wish to go to bed early in order to be up at sunrise to go on a fishing expedition.

Arrangements for activities you know your visitors will enjoy are made ahead of time. If they like tennis, sign up or reserve a court at a convenient hour, or if they would love to go to the dance at your club, make a reservation for a table. Leave time for your guests to relax and visit with you and the other guests; they may want to see a special landmark or shop in stores carrying merchandise made in the area.

Certain rules are easy to observe once they are brought to one's attention. A host or hostess never speaks of annoyance of any kind—no matter what happens. Unless actually unable to stand up, they should not mention physical ills any more than mental ones. If anything goes wrong with the household they must work a miracle and keep it from their guests. Should a guest be taken ill, the hostess assures him he is not giving the slightest trouble, at the same time doing all that can be done for his comfort.

And above all, they must not be "overanxious." The overanxious host or hostess is one who fusses and plans continually, who thinks the guests are not having a good time unless they are being rushed, tourist fashion, from this engagement to that, and crowded with activity and diversion every moment of their stay.

DO'S AND DON'TS FOR HOUSE GUESTS

Having accepted an invitation, guests may, in an emergency, shorten their visit, but they must not stay beyond the time they were asked for unless very especially urged to do so. Even then they would be much wiser to go early and be missed rather than to run the risk of outstaying their welcome.

You as a guest must conform to the habits of the family with whom you are staying, take your meals at their hour, eat what is put before you and get up and go out and come in and go to bed according to the schedule arranged by your hostess. And no matter how much the hours or the food or the arrangements may upset you, you must appear blissfully content. When the visit is over, you need never accept an invitation to that particular house again; but while you are there, you must at least act as if you were enjoying it.

The ideal guest not only tries to wear becoming clothes but tries to get into an equally becoming frame of mind, never mentioning the misfortunes and ailments he has experienced or witnessed.

The perfect visitor never keeps people waiting. You are always ready for anything—or nothing. If a plan is made to picnic, you like picnics above everything and prove it by enthusiastically making the sandwiches or the salad dressing or whatever you think you make best. If, on the other hand, no one seems to want to do anything, the perfect guest always has a book to be absorbed in, or a piece of sewing or knitting, or else beyond everything would love to sit in an easy chair and do nothing.

It is not necessary, but it is courteous to take your hostess a gift—or better, if she has children, to take presents to them. Some people prefer to send a present after their visit; having made note of something that their hostess would find useful or that would go perfectly in one of the rooms. As to the children, if they are young, a collection of small amusing articles from the ten-cent store often gives them more pleasure than a single present of value.

Condense your luggage in both quantity and size, especially if you are being taken in someone else's car or going by train to a place where there are no porters.

Besides the necessary sports clothes, a dinner coat (inquire of your host if one is necessary) and one or at most two sports jackets with the necessary shorts, shoes, ties, etc., will suffice.

If you are to swim, ride or play games, take your own bathing suit (preferably two in case of damp weather), riding habit, tennis racket or golf clubs.

The guest no one invites a second time is the one who dog-ears books, burns cigarette trenches on table edges, uses towels for cleaning shoes, stands wet glasses on polished wood, tracks into the house in muddy shoes. Other unwelcome guests are those who are late for every meal, help themselves to a car and go off and fail to come back for meals on time.

Aside from the more or less general rules of behavior, there are some specific rules worthy of mention: A guest in someone's home never suggests taking his hosts to a meal in a restaurant. If, however, your host suggests dining at a restaurant, you might well say, "That sounds wonderful, and we would love to be *your* hosts for dinner—you are giving us such a wonderful time!" Otherwise, you show your gratitude by inviting them to a restaurant when they are in town or by sending a suitable present.

If you have friends in the neighborhood and they invite you and your hosts over for a swim or to play tennis, never accept the invitation and then relay it to your hostess. Instead, make a noncommittal reply such as, "May I call you back, as I'm not sure about Joan's plans?"

If you are not needed to make up a foursome at bridge and you are tired and want to go to bed before your hosts and the other guests do, it is perfectly all right to say to your hostess that you've had a "rugged" week at the office and would like to go to bed.

When you are visiting a house run with one maid or none, avoid making your visit a burden through the extra picking up your carelessness may entail. If the housemaid offers to press a dress that has become mussed in packing, you accept her offer and later give her a larger gratuity—but do not ask for this service unless it is an emergency. A maid is always tipped by overnight guests. The amount for a weekend may range from two to five dollars, depending on the type of work she does. If the hostess does her own housework, you make your bed, tidy up your room and offer to help in clearing the table and cleaning up in the kitchen.

When you are one who wakes with the dawn and the household you are visiting sleeps on a Sunday morning, the long wait for your coffee can be most unpleasant. The farsighted guest with the early habit can prevent discomfort by carrying in a small case his own little electric water-heating outfit and a package of instant coffee or tea, sugar, powdered milk or cream, and a few crackers. He can then start his day all by himself without disturbing anyone. In an informal household, he may slip quietly into the kitchen and make himself a cup of coffee and a piece of toast to sustain him until the others are ready for a full breakfast.

Perhaps the entire guest situation may be put in one sentence. If you are an inflexible person, very set in your ways, don't visit! If you have confidence in your adaptability, go and enjoy yourself!

THE OVERNIGHT GUEST IN A CITY APARTMENT

Today an increasing number of people live in apartments where a guest room is a rarity. Sometimes a couch in the living room is converted into a comfortable bed at night for an overnight guest, or if a child is away at camp or boarding school, his room may be available. No matter how hospitable your host or hostess may be, a guest should remember that an extra person in small quarters is, inevitably, something of an imposition—no matter how charming the guest may be. Household regulations should be meticulously observed, and the visitor stays no longer than necessary, takes up as little room with his possessions as possible, and keeps his belongings neat. Above all, he should be prepared to fit in with the household schedule and not inconvenience his host or hostess.

PART SEVEN

SPECIAL OCCASIONS

30

The new baby

ANNOUNCEMENTS

Sometime before the birth of a baby, or immediately there-after, the prospective parents select an announcement card at a stationer's to be sent to their own friends, and those friends of the grandparents who are close to the family. After the birth and as soon as the name is determined, the father notifies the stationer and in a few days the cards are ready.

The nicest type of birth announcement, one that happily is coming back into general use, consists simply of a very small card with the baby's name and birth date on it, tied with a white or pastel ribbon to the upper margin of the "Mr. and Mrs." card of the parents.

A large variety of commercially designed announcement cards, with space for the baby's name, date of birth and parents' names to be written in by hand, are much less expensive and very popular. The least desirable include data on the baby's weight and length and a picture of a baby saying coyly: "My mommy and daddy want me to tell you I landed."

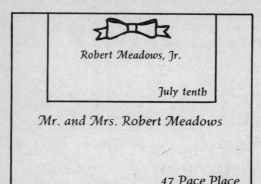

Announcement of adoption:

It is a nice gesture to send a card announcing this happy event to your friends and relatives. A card such as this will also bring assurance to the child later on of her place in the hearts of those who chose her to be their own.

> *Mr. and Mrs. Nuhome*
> *have the happiness to announce*
> *the adoption of*
> *Mary*
> *aged thirteen months*

Newspaper announcement of birth:

In the week following the birth, the father may send a release to the local newspapers: "Mr. and Mrs. Robert Meadows of 202 Park Avenue, New York, announce the birth of a son, Robert, Jr., on July 10, 1967, at Doctors Hospital. They have one daughter, Jane, 4. Mrs. Meadows is the former Miss Mary Gilding." Or, "A daughter, Mary Jane, was born to Mr. and Mrs. Robert Meadows," etc. The same announcement may be sent to the editor of the church newsletter or bulletin.

CHOOSING A NAME

Avoid giving the baby a name that is too long or difficult to pronounce clearly or that forms an unpleasant combination with the last name. Choose instead a simple or biblical name or one with some significance, perhaps because it is the name of some member of the family or a beloved friend. When a son is given the same name as his father, he may be given a middle name different from that of the parent; in adult life he may prefer to be known as "R. William Meadows," instead of "Robert Meadows, Jr." Roman Catholic baptismal certificates must record a saint's name as the baby's first or middle name. Most Jewish babies are traditionally named for a deceased relative.

PRESENTS FOR BABY AND MOTHER

Everyone who receives a birth-announcement card writes a note of congratulations to the new parents. Or a note may be enclosed if a gift is sent. It is not necessary to send a present, however, even if you receive an announcement.

Gifts for the baby are addressed to the parents at home or you may bring your present with you when you visit the hospital. It is thoughtful to bring something for the new mother too, handkerchiefs or a plant or flower arrangement.

CHRISTENINGS AND OTHER RELIGIOUS CEREMONIES
Time of christening:

In the Catholic church, the baptism takes place when the baby is very young—usually not over a month old—and always in the church or baptistry (unless its baptism is *in extremis*). In Latin countries, babies are often baptized in the hospital within a day or two of their birth. In Protestant churches, the average age for christening is from two to six months, although in some denominations or under special conditions, children may not be christened until they are several years old. In all churches, the mother is present if she is able.

The godparents:

If your faith requires godparents, before setting the day of the christening, the godparents are asked and their consent obtained. They may be asked to serve when the baby's arrival is announced to them and occasionally before; or perhaps when they visit the hospital. In Protestant practice, there are usually two godfathers and one godmother for a boy, two godmothers and one godfather for a girl. A Catholic baby has one godparent of each sex, who must be Catholics, too. (Catholics are not allowed to serve as godparents for children of other faiths.)

If the godparent lives at a distance, a note is sent to him or he may be asked by telegraph: "It's a boy. Will you be godfather?"

If a godparent is unable to be present, a proxy acts for him or her at the ceremony, the consent of the real godparent having first been given. It is considerate for the real godparent to send a note to the clergyman authorizing the proxy.

Only a most intimate friend should be asked to be a godmother or godfather, for it is a responsibility not lightly to be undertaken and also one difficult to refuse. Godparents are usually chosen from among friends rather than relatives, because one advantage of godparents is that they add to the child's stock of relatives. Should the child be left alone in the world, its godparents become its protectors.

The obligation of being a godparent is essentially a spiritual one; therefore, the godparent should be of the same faith as the parents. The godparent is supposed to see that the child is given religious training and is confirmed at the proper time. Beyond these obligations, he is expected to take a special interest in the child, much as a very near relative would do.

At the christening, he gives the baby as nice a present as he can afford. The typical gift is a silver mug or porringer, inscribed: *"Robert Meadows, Jr./December 5th, 1965/From his godfather/John Strong."* Other typical presents are a silver fork and spoon, a silver comb and brush set, a government bond, or a trust fund to which the donor may add each year until the child is grown.

Christening invitations:

Usually, christening invitations are given over the telephone or in a personal note to "Dear Linda and Jeff" or "Dear Mr. and Mrs. Kindhart," and signed "Mary" or "Mary Meadows."

> *Dear Jane,*
> *We are having Karen christened on Sunday at 3:00 in Christ's Church. Would you and Bob come to the ceremony at the church, and join us afterward at our house?*
> *Affectionately,*
> *Sally*

Or a message is written on the "Mr. and Mrs." card of the parents, saying: *"Baby's christening, St. Mary's Church, Jan. 10, 3 o'clock. Reception at our house afterward."* All invitations to a christening should be friendly and informal.

Clothes for the christening:

The baby's christening dress may be one worn by the baby's mother, father or even a grand- or great-grandparent. Custom requires that everything the baby wears on this occasion be white. The traditional christening dress is long, made of sheer, soft material with lace and hand-embroidery trim, and worn with delicate, long petticoats. If there is no family heirloom, any long, or even short, plain white dress will do. Some very pretty and quite inexpensive christening dresses are available in the new miracle fabrics.

In Protestant churches, when the children are no longer babies, little girls wear white dresses. Little boys, however, wear an Eton jacket, dark blue with matching shorts; older boys wear a dark blue or dark gray suit.

Guests at a christening wear what they would wear to church. The mother wears a light-colored dress, never black, and a hat or veil.

The church ceremony:

The ceremony may take place at the close of the regular Sunday service, the guests remaining after the rest of the congregation leaves. Roman Catholic parishes generally schedule baptisms for a specified time on Sunday afternoons, and the parents make an appointment at the rectory in advance. At all christenings, guests seat themselves in the pews nearest the front.

After the clergyman enters, the baby's coat and cap are taken off and the godmother, holding the baby in her arms, stands directly in front of the clergyman. The other godparents stand beside her and relatives and friends nearby.

The godmother holding the baby pronounces its given name or names distinctly; if the name is long or unusual, print it on a slip of paper and give it to the clergyman beforehand, because whatever name the clergyman pronounces is fixed for life. More than one baby has been given a name not intended for him. The godmother does not state the surname.

In the Presbyterian church and others that do not require godparents, the father holds the baby and gives its name. There is no separate service—it is done during or immediately after the regular Sunday service.

As soon as the ceremony is over, the baby and all the relatives and friends go to the house of the parents or grandparents for a reception.

Baptism is a sacrament of the church, for which no fee is required. A donation, however, is presented in an envelope to the clergyman after the ceremony, commensurate with the elaborateness of the christening.

A house christening:

If permitted by the church to which the baby's parents belong, the house christening is a pretty ceremony. The only necessary decoration is the font. This is always a bowl—usually of silver—put on a small, high table covered preferably by a dark rather than a white fabric: old brocade or velvet. Flowers may be arranged around the bowl in a flat circle, the blossoms outside, the stems covered by the base of the bowl.

At the hour set for the ceremony, the clergyman enters the room and takes his place at the font. The guests make way, forming an open aisle. The godmother, or the father if there are no godparents, carries the baby and follows the clergyman; the other participants walk behind and all stand near the font. At the proper moment, the clergyman takes the baby, baptizes it and hands it back to the godmother or father, who holds it until the ceremony is over.

After performing the ceremony, the clergyman, if he wears vestments, goes to another room, changes into his street clothes, then returns to the living room as one of the guests.

The christening party:

The only difference between an ordinary informal reception and a christening party is that the latter features christening cake and caudle. The christening cake is generally a white "lady" cake elaborately iced. A real caudle is a hot eggnog, drunk out of little punch cups. Today punch is often substituted for the caudle. Guests eat the cake as a sign that they partake of the baby's hospitality and are therefore his friends, and they drink the punch to his health and prosperity. But by this time the young host or hostess is peacefully asleep in his crib.

Jewish ceremonies for the newborn:

On the eighth day after birth, in the ceremony known as *Brith Milah,* a boy is initiated into the Jewish covenant between man and God. The circumcision is accompanied by a religious ceremony during which the boy is named. After the ceremony, there is a light collation, usually at home since today the mother rarely stays in the hospital more than a week. The guests drink to the baby's future and toast the parents, grandparents and godparents (there is always a godfather and usually a godmother). Relatives and close friends are invited to the *Brith* by telephone or informal note. They dress as they would for any service in a synagogue and both men and women customarily wear hats.

Girls are named in the synagogue on the first Sabbath after birth when the father is called up to the Torah. Sometimes the naming is postponed until the mother is able to be present. In some Reform congregations, boys are also named in the synagogue (in addition to being named at the *Brith*) when both parents are present and a special blessing is pronounced by the rabbi. The mother may be hostess at the collation following the service. Friends and relatives are invited to attend the religious service during which the baby is named.

The ceremony of redemption of the first-born (if it is a son), the *Pidyon Ha-Ben,* is performed when the baby is thirty-one days old. According to ancient custom described in the Bible, the first-born son was dedicated to the service of God. It became customary for a *Cohen* (a descendant of the priestly tribe) to redeem the child from his obligation, entrusting him to the care of his father for bringing up in the Jewish faith. The *Pidyon Ha-Ben,* consisting of a brief ceremony and a celebration, is held in the home, informal notes of invitation being sent about ten days previously to close friends and relatives.

31

Confirmations and bar mitzvahs

CONFIRMATION

Catholic children are generally confirmed when they are eleven or twelve, Protestants a year or two older. However, if one was not confirmed as a child, it may be done at any age, and there is a special confirmation for those who change their faith.

Candidates for confirmation in all faiths undergo a period of instruction. Those who complete these lessons satisfactorily are confirmed by a bishop or other high church dignitary in the manner of a graduating class. The service, which in the Protestant church is held at a regular Sunday service, and which in the Catholic church is separate from the regular Mass, is attended by members of the families and close friends of the young people.

Some churches hold an informal reception after the ceremony at which the parents and friends may have a chance to meet and chat with the visiting churchman who performed the confirmation. Afterward the family and a few friends may gather at the house for lunch and those who wish to do so give the newly confirmed youngster a gift. This is usually of a religious nature—a Bible with his name engraved on it, a prayer book, a gold cross, a medal or a charm of a religious nature.

Catholic girls wear white dresses and sometimes a short veil. Some Protestant clergymen request that the girls wear white but most simply ask that they wear simple, modest dresses in quiet colors. This is up to the discretion of the minister.

In both Protestant and Catholic churches, the boys wear dark blue or dark gray suits.

Confirmation is a religious occasion rather than a social one, the moment when the young person himself confirms the vows that were made for him by his godparents at the time of his baptism. It is a thoughtful and serious event and therefore is celebrated joyfully—but with restraint.

BAR MITZVAH

For a Jewish boy the ceremony which compares to the Christian confirmation is called bar mitzvah and celebrates his acceptance as an adult member of his congregation. In the Orthodox and Conservative branches, and in some Reform congregations, it takes place on the first Sabbath (Saturday) after the boy becomes thirteen, and has undergone a period of religious instruction. Other Reform congregations have replaced the bar mitzvah with a "confirmation" service at which both boys and girls are confirmed, sometimes at an older age than the traditional thirteen.

Bar mitzvah differs from the Christian confirmation in that, in addition to being a deeply religious occasion, it is always celebrated socially as well. Since it is one of the most important events in the boy's life, the family generally bends every effort to make it as wonderful an occasion as they can. The religious ceremony which takes place on Saturday morning may be followed immediately by a gathering in the social rooms of the synagogue. This is open to any member of the congregation who wishes to offer his congratulations.

The party—luncheon, dinner or reception—which follows later in the day usually includes all the close friends of the parents as well as friends and classmates of the boy. Only those who receive invitations may attend. Invitations may be formally engraved cards or handwritten notes, or they may be telephoned, but they must be quite explicit as to the hour, the place and the occasion. They must, like other invitations, be acknowledged promptly and in kind.

For the ceremony, guests wear the clothes that they ordinarily choose for a religious service. If the party is a luncheon, they go directly to it without changing. If the celebration is later in the day, they change into clothes appropriate for an evening party. If the affair is formal, this is specified on the invitation. Otherwise the women wear cocktail or dinner dresses and the men wear dark suits.

Everyone invited to a bar mitzvah is expected to send, or take, a gift. Something of a permanent nature to serve as a reminder of the occasion: a piece of jewelry, such as a tie clip or a set of studs for evening clothes, is typical, as well as a wallet, a leather desk set, a book on a favorite hobby—the list is limitless. Gifts of money are also acceptable. The boy writes thank-you letters promptly for each and every gift.

The reception itself is just like any other. Dinners and luncheons may be sit-down or buffet, and the party may be held at home or in a club, hotel or restaurant. An orchestra is optional, but if many young people are invited, they enjoy dancing after the meal is over.

23

Graduation

Graduation or commencement programs at the high school level are much the same as at the college, but on a modified scale. "Commencement week" festivities for the students start in advance of graduation day, but the events to which families and dates are invited take place only on the last day or two before commencement. The events usually consist of any or all of the following: a senior class ball, attended at some colleges by dates only, and at others by parents and brothers and sisters of the graduates as well; a senior class play, attended by everyone; fraternity parties, tea dances, to which all the graduates' dates are invited; a varsity baseball game. Winding up all commencement week festivities, and attended by every guest, are the baccalaureate service on a Sunday morning and the commencement exercises themselves that afternoon or the following morning.

INVITATIONS AND RESERVATIONS

Colleges and universities provide each graduating student with the number of invitations he is allowed to send. The list of announcements should be limited to those really interested, because the recipients usually feel that they must send a gift.

It is essential for the families of the graduates to make reservations well in advance of graduation day, even as early as some time during the fall term, especially if the college is in a small town that does not have too many accommodations. If the graduate is engaged or has a serious boy or girl friend, the family makes a reservation for him or her too.

REQUIREMENTS FOR THE SENIOR'S DATE

The senior's date, whether or not he or she is engaged to the graduate, stays with the family of the student and goes with them to parties or games to which all guests are invited. She takes care not to monopolize the attention of the graduate. If a young man's family cannot attend the commencement, he or his date finds another graduate's family willing to adopt her for the occasion. If this proves impossible, the young man may ask one of his favorite professors if it would be possible for her to stay in his house. Under no circumstances may she stay alone in a motel or an inn.

CLOTHING

Clothing is much the same as for similar social events elsewhere. The senior dance is always formal, requiring an evening dress or a tuxedo. Girls generally wear shorts or simple cotton dresses for daytime sporting events or picnics and the boys wear shorts or slacks and a sport shirt. For the baccalaureate and commencement services, mothers and girl friends wear cool, short-sleeved dresses, in a print or a pastel color (never black). Hats or veils are worn at a chapel service, but are not necessary if the commencement ceremony is held out-of-doors. Men and boys wear lightweight suits of any color for the formal services.

PRESENTS

Parents may give the graduate a fine watch, a set of evening jewelry, an automobile, or even a trip to Europe. If these gifts are beyond their means, anything lasting and of the best quality is always appreciated: a nicely bound book on a favorite subject or a set of cuff links or other simple jewelry. A fiancé or a "steady" boy friend might choose a charm or a locket and a girl friend might consider a handsome wallet or a gold or silver tie clip.

The gifts from other relatives and friends may depend on the future plans of the graduate. If he or she is taking a trip, a passport case or a suitcase would be a good choice; if marriage is contemplated, something for the new home—a silver tray with the graduation date on it. A check is always welcome.

A note of thanks, written by hand and on note paper, goes promptly to everyone who has sent a present whenever the giver has not been at the commencement to be thanked in person.

Dear Aunt Mary,

I can't thank you enough for the check you sent me which will be such a help toward my summer in Europe. I'm looking forward to seeing you in the fall to tell you all about the trip.

With much love,
Jane

Or:

Dear Uncle Jim,

Thank you so very much for the cuff links you sent me. How did you know I very much needed them? I was disappointed that you couldn't make the graduation, but I'll drive down to see you and thank you in person as soon as possible.

Thanks again,
Bill

33

Anniversary parties

Anniversary parties may be given in honor of any anniversary, but first, fifth, tenth, twenty-fifth and fiftieth are those most generally celebrated. The parties given for the first three are usually informal, not distinguishable from any other reception except for toasts to the bride and groom and gifts from close friends. The twenty-fifth and fiftieth anniversaries, however, are given more importance, and certain customs—almost rituals—are followed. Therefore this chapter will deal principally with the latter two.

When it is convenient, the party is given on the actual date of the anniversary, unless the couple prefer to have it on the Saturday night nearest to it. If one member of the couple is ill or absent at the time, the party may be held several weeks later, or if the illness or the absence is prolonged, it is preferable to celebrate the anniversary which falls on the following year. There is no rule which says one must recognize the twenty-fifth rather than the twenty-sixth.

WHO GIVES THE PARTY?

Early anniversary parties are always given by the couple themselves. By the time they reach the twenty-fifth, they may well have grown children who wish to make the arrangements, but it is perfectly correct for them to do so themselves if the young people do not, or cannot. Fiftieth-anniversary celebrations are almost invariably planned by the family of the couple.

PLANNING THE PARTY

The party may be held in the home of the couple or of the person planning the party, in a church parish house or in a room of a hotel, restaurant or club. If the party is a dinner or a small reception, the guests are primarily family, members of the wedding party and closest friends. A large reception or an open house may include business acquaintances, church and club members or—in very small communities—everyone in town.

INVITATIONS

The form of the invitations may range from an informal telephone call to an engraved "third person" invitation. The most common form is the handwritten note or the necessary information written on a visiting card or informal.

The invitation for the large open house may simply be an announcement in the local paper or the church or club bulletin. This has certain dangers: more people than the host and hostess expect may appear; some who are really wanted may fail to read the announcement or hear of the party. If the only invitation is the announcement in the paper, anyone who reads it is expected to attend, but if any invitations are extended personally, only those who receive them may go.

The following are sample invitations.

When the couple are giving the party themselves:

1943–1968
Mr. and Mrs. Harvey Langdon
request the pleasure of your company
at a reception
in honor of
their silver wedding anniversary
on Saturday, the eighth of December
at eight o'clock
Barrymore Country Club

R.s.v.p.
12 Corning Road

On an informal or visiting card (name engraved):

1943–1968
Mr. and Mrs. Harvey Langdon
March 1 at 6 P.M.
12 Corning Road
R.s.v.p.

When the children of the couple give the party:

Dear Anne (or Mrs. Franklin),
Will you and Joe (or Mr. Franklin) join us for dinner on Saturday, May 4, at 7:00 P.M. to help us celebrate Mom and Dad's twenty-fifth anniversary? Hoping to see you then,
Helen and Bill
(or Helen & Bill Porter)

Or, if they prepare an engraved card:

In honor of the
fiftieth wedding anniversary of
Mr. and Mrs. Harvey Langdon

Mr. and Mrs. William Porter
(or "their sons and daughters")
request the pleasure of your company
on Tuesday, the fourth of July
at seven-thirty o'clock
10 Glenwood Road
R.s.v.p.

The newspaper or church bulletin announcement reads:

Open House
to celebrate the fiftieth anniversary
of Mr. & Mrs. Harvey Langdon. Sunday,
March 4, 4 to 6 P.M., 12 Osborn Road

REFRESHMENTS

If it is a luncheon or a dinner, the hostess simply chooses whatever menu she thinks will please the couple and the guests most. Since the later anniversaries attempt to recreate the wedding day to some extent, the food might be the same as that served at the original wedding reception.

If it is a cocktail party, hors d'oeuvres are served and a wedding cake cut and passed with champagne or punch for toasting the couple before the guests leave. At an afternoon reception or an open house, the menu varies according to the formality of the party and the pocketbook of the host and hostess. Refreshments may consist of sandwiches, snacks and punch, or a complete buffet—cold ham, turkey, sliced fillet of beef and chafing dishes filled with hot snacks or hors d'oeuvres. Whatever the other food, a close replica of the couple's wedding cake is the main feature of the menu.

Drinks may range from tea and coffee at an afternoon reception to wine, champagne or highballs at an evening affair. Soft drinks should always be available for those who prefer them. Punch is often served at open houses and other daytime parties, made either with or without liquor. When the family does not object to alcoholic beverages, a glass of champagne is the traditional drink for toasts—at any hour of the afternoon or evening. Otherwise, the toasts may be made with punch or whatever drinks are available. *For suggested anniversary toast, see Chapter 3, The Good Conversationalist.*

DECORATIONS

Decorations need not be elaborate, but the twenty-fifth anniversary party should feature white and silver ornaments and flowers, and the fiftieth, gold (or yellow) and white. Flowers make the loveliest decoration of all, and the bride should always be presented with a corsage.

WITH OR WITHOUT MUSIC

There need not be any entertainment, but a strolling accordian player adds a touch of romance, and he can be asked to play the couple's favorite tunes, wedding music, etc. The host and hostess may prefer to hire an orchestra or provide records for dancing.

THE RECEIVING LINE

Except for a somewhat elderly couple celebrating their fiftieth, the couple and any members of their bridal party stand near the door as they did at their wedding reception. Their children may join them in the line; if the party is given by another member of the family, that person always heads the line as hostess. Older couples may prefer to be seated in a central spot—in front of a fireplace, for example. The guests, after greeting the hostess near the door, move on to find the honored pair and offer their congratulations.

GIFTS

Gifts are ordinarily taken to a couple celebrating an early anniversary, but it is perfectly correct to say "No gifts, please" on the invitations. However, it is *never* correct for a hostess to request a gift of money either for herself or for the person for whom she is giving the party. If she knows of something the couple longs for, she may enclose a note with the invitations explaining that the couple being honored wants terribly to go on a cruise, and if the guests would like to help make it possible, would they, instead of bringing a gift, send a small check to the "Anywhere Travel Agency." The hostess would then make up a packet of folders, tickets, boat plans and a card signed by all the guests, to be presented at the party. Thus, neither she nor the couple would know the amounts given.

Another solution is a card enclosed with the invitation, reading "In place of gifts, please, if you wish, send a contribution to Mother and Dad's favorite charity—the 'XYZ Research Foundation.'" The check may be sent with a note saying, "Please accept this contribution in honor of the fiftieth anniversary of Mr. and Mrs. John Doe."

Many people feel that it is more meaningful if gifts are the traditional material allotted to each anniversary. When an article of an original material cannot be purchased, something similar but not identical is acceptable—for example, a stainless steel or pewter platter instead of a silver one on a twenty-fifth anniversary. For all anniversaries a lovely flower arrangement or a plant is always appropriate.

Here are the traditional anniversary gifts:

*1. Paper or plastics
 2. Calico or cotton
 3. Leather or simulated leather
 4. Silk
*5. Wood
 6. Iron

---

* The eight anniversaries which are traditionally celebrated.

   7. Copper or wool
   8. Electric appliances
   9. Pottery
*10. Tin or aluminum
  11. Steel
  12. Linen
  13. Lace
  14. Ivory
*15. Crystal (includes china)
*20. China
*25. Silver (the best known anniversary)
  30. Pearls
  35. Coral and jade
  40. Ruby
  45. Sapphire
*50. Gold
*60. Diamond

THE MAIN TABLE

The table should be as much like the bridal table at the couple's wedding reception as possible. Bride and groom sit together at the center of a long table or at the head of a round one. Bridesmaids and ushers, if any are present, sit next to them; their husbands or wives are included at the table. Other places are filled by close relatives. If none of the bridal party is present, the couple's children are seated with them, the oldest son on the bride's right and the oldest daughter on the groom's left. Their husbands and wives, their older children, and brothers and sisters of the couple are arranged in whatever way they will enjoy most.

When the party is given by a married son or daughter of the anniversary couple, the host and hostess sit at either end of the table. But the couple sit together at the center rather than the bride sitting on the host's right and the groom on the hostess's right like ordinary guests of honor.

The table is decorated with white flowers or, for a fiftieth anniversary, gold or yellow flowers. The wedding cake may be in the center, but if it is large it is more convenient to place it on a side table.

---

* The eight anniversaries which are traditionally celebrated.

PICTURES

All anniversary couples enjoy having candid pictures made of their party. They are generally taken by one of the guests, although a professional photographer may be hired. An album of these pictures makes an ideal anniversary present for the couple.

REAFFIRMATION OF MARRIAGE VOWS

Some couples reaffirm their marriage vows on their twenty-fifth or fiftieth anniversaries, in as complete a reenactment of their original ceremony as is feasible, or with a simpler repetition of the vows. In either case, as many as possible of the wedding party gather for the service and the reception that follows.

34

Funerals

When a person makes a will, he may want to put into it his wishes as to how and where he would like to be buried. These wishes are not irrevocable, but the family will naturally give them every consideration. If he does not include them in his will, he should discuss the question with those closest to him so they may be able to carry out his wishes.

He should know whether there is space for him (and his wife, if she wishes) in the family plot at a cemetery, or think about purchasing a plot for himself and his own family. If he wishes to be cremated, the law requires that his nearest relatives give permission. Therefore, he makes his desires very clear to his wife (or husband, if we are speaking of a woman), his children, and his brothers or sisters.

The head of the family should have a space set aside for a copy of his will and the name of the attorney who drew it up, a deed to a burial plot if he has one, a list of the location of safe deposit boxes, mortgages, bank accounts, etc., and any personal instructions he may wish to leave in case of his death. The other members of the family should know the location of these papers and something about their contents. The small amount of effort necessary to put such a sensible precaution into effect is nothing compared with the help it can be to a stunned and confused family at the time of death.

IMMEDIATE STEPS

When you hear of the death of a close friend, you go at once to the house, and offer to help out in any way you can. For a less intimate friend, you write a letter to the family at once. Telephoning is not improper, but it may cause inconvenience by tying up the line needed for notifying members of the family.

You may help by preparing food for the family or for the children, sending telegrams and answering the door. *(See also Chapter 50.)*

A very good friend or a relative who is not of the immediate family can help immeasurably by taking charge of the funeral arrangements, thus relieving those closest to the deceased of making difficult decisions when they are prostrate emotionally.

Notifying family and close friends:

If members of the immediate family are not already present, the first act of someone at the bedside of the deceased is to notify them. In the case of a long illness, where the family has become attached to the trained nurse, she may be the best fitted to do this and to look after many details. Members of the family and very close friends should be called on the telephone. If expense is a factor, friends and more distant relatives may be notified by telegram.

The death certificate:

The death certificate is filled out and signed by the physician in attendance at the time of death. If the death was sudden or caused by an accident, or if there was no doctor in attendance, the county medical examiner or coroner must be called in immediately to sign the certificate since no other steps can be taken until the death certificate is properly signed.

Notifying an attorney:

The next step is to notify an attorney, preferably the one who has drawn up the will of the deceased. If he, or his firm, is unavailable, then any other reputable attorney, perhaps one who has been retained by another member of the family or one who is a personal friend, may be called.

The funeral director and the clergyman:

The next most immediate matter is that of selecting a funeral home. If the family belongs to a church or synagogue, they may call the church office which will give them all the information about the funeral directors in the area and probably recommend one who will suit their needs. The family doctor can also provide this information.

The funeral director comes to the home as soon as possible after he is called and removes the body to the funeral home. All arrangements are discussed with him at that time—how elaborate a funeral the relatives wish, if the service is to be held at the funeral home, in the home of the deceased, or in a church, and the day and hour. The clergyman must also be consulted as to the time. If the family is not affiliated with a church, the funeral director or a friend can recommend a clergyman of any faith the family chooses.

Newspaper notices:

Notices of the death go to morning and evening papers in a large city and to the local paper (daily or weekly) in towns or suburbs. These contain the date of death, names of immediate family, place and time of funeral, and, frequently, a request that a contribution be sent to a charity instead of flowers to the deceased. The notice may be telephoned by the person making the funeral arrangements, but often the funeral director handles it as part of his services. When the notice reads "Please omit flowers," this wish should be strictly followed.

CONSTANTINE—Mary Phillips, on March 19th, 1967. Beloved wife of Henry S. Constantine, devoted mother of Henry S. Constantine, Jr., and Barbara Constantine Franklin, sister of Dorothy P. Hill. Reposing at the Frederick

Carter Funeral Home, Farmingdale, Mass., Monday and Tuesday, 2:00 P.M.–9:00 P.M. Funeral Wednesday, 11:00 A.M., at Christ Church, Farmingdale. In lieu of flowers, please send donations to the New York Cancer Fund.

HASKELL—John Woods, suddenly, on February 12th, 1967. Beloved brother of Robert C. Haskell, George F. Haskell and Sally Haskell Simpson. Funeral service Friday, February 14th at 11:30 A.M. at the Riverside Funeral Home, 10 Lawton Street, Clinton, Mass.

When the notice reads "Funeral private" and neither time nor place is given, only very intimate friends are given this information, either by telephone or on the personal card of the relative or friend in charge: "Mr. Brown's funeral will be at Christ Church, Monday at eleven o'clock." Others are not expected to attend.

If the person who has died was prominent, probably the newspapers have a file on him and, in the case of an older person, an obituary already written. They should be notified immediately, and their information checked so that errors will not appear in the published articles. The paid notice of death is inserted as with less well-known people, when the details of resting place, funeral, flowers, etc., have been decided.

The clothing for burial:

The person in charge of arrangements, with the help of someone close to the deceased who would know of special preference, delivers the clothes to the funeral director. Members of some faiths, the Orthodox Jewish among them, still prefer to bury their dead in shrouds, but most religions have no restrictions on clothing for burial. Dresses in solid, subdued colors are of a style worn to church. Young girls are usually buried in white and children in their Sunday school clothes. Men are also dressed as for church. Wedding rings are left on, but other jewelry is removed.

Emblem of mourning on the door:

The funeral director may hang streamers on the front door if the family so desires: white ones for a child, black and white for a young person, or black for an older person. Flowers are usually ordered by the family directly from their own

florist, though the funeral director may order them. White
flowers are used for a young person, purple for one who was
older. Emblems are removed by a member of the funeral
establishment before the family returns from the services.

HONORARY PALLBEARERS

The member of the family who is in charge asks (either
when they come to the house or by telephone) six or eight men
who were close friends of the deceased to be the pallbearers.
For a man prominent in public life, there may be eight or ten
of his political or business associates as well as his six or eight
lifelong friends. Members of the immediate family are never
chosen as their place is with the women of the family.

One never refuses an invitation to be a pallbearer except
because of illness or necessary absence from the city. The
pallbearers meet in the vestibule of the church a few minutes
before the time set for the service.

Honorary pallbearers serve only at church funerals. They
do not carry the coffin. (This service is performed by the assistants of the funeral director, who are expertly trained.)
They sit in the first pews on the left and, after the service, leave
the church two by two, walking immediately in front of the
coffin, or, if there is no procession, ahead of the congregation.

USHERS

Ushers may be chosen in addition to, or in place of, pallbearers. Although funeral directors will supply men to perform
the task, it is infinitely better to select men from the family
(not immediate) or close friends, who will recognize those
who come and seat them according to their closeness to the
family, or according to their own wishes. When there are no
pallbearers, the ushers sit in the front pews on the left and
march out ahead of the coffin as pallbearers would. If there are
pallbearers, the ushers remain at the back of the church.

SENDING AND RECEIVING FLOWERS

If there is a notice in the papers requesting that no flowers
be sent, you send none. Otherwise, they are addressed "To the
funeral of [name of the deceased]," either at the funeral home
or the church. When you did not know the deceased, but only
his close relatives, flowers may be sent to them at their home,
with a card addressed to one of the family on which you might

write "With sympathy," "With deepest sympathy," or, if appropriate, "With love and sympathy." A few flowers sent to any bereaved person from time to time—possibly long afterward—are very comforting in their assurance of continued sympathy.

The one in charge of arrangements for the family appoints one person to take charge of flowers; he or she carefully collects all the accompanying cards and on the outside of each envelope writes a description of the flowers that came with the card. Sometimes this is done by the florist and the cards are delivered to the bereaved family after the funeral. For example:

> Large spray Easter lilies tied with white ribbon
> Laurel wreath with gardenias
> Long sheaf of white roses—broad silver ribbon

These descriptions are necessary when one comes to writing notes of thanks.

If friends have sent potted plants or cut flowers to the house, their cards are removed and noted for later acknowledgment.

If the family is Protestant, an hour before the time set for the service one or two women friends go to the church to help the staff arrange the bouquets or sprays, so that those sent by relatives are given a prominent position. But they leave the actual moving of heavy arrangements to the trained florist.

The sexton or one of his assistants will have collected the cards, noting the variety of flowers as above. He gives them to these friends who in turn deliver them to the one who is responsible for all the cards.

Friends of any faith may send a "spiritual bouquet" (a mass said for the deceased) to a Catholic family. Any priest will make arrangements for the mass and accept the donation. A card is sent to the family, stating the time and place of the mass and the name of the donor.

CALLING AT THE FUNERAL HOME

Usually the body of the deceased remains at the funeral home until the day of the funeral. Often the family receives close friends there, rather than at home. The hours when they will be there to accept expressions of sympathy are included in the death notice in the newspaper. People who wish to pay their respects but are not close to the bereaved may stop in and sign the register provided by the funeral parlor. Their signatures are formal, including their title—"Dr. and Mrs. Harvey Cross" or "Miss Deborah Page," not "Bill and Joan Cross" or "Debbie Page." This simplifies the task for those helping the family acknowledge these visits.

A visitor who sees and personally extends his sympathy at the funeral home need not write a note of condolence, unless he wishes to write an absent member of the family. Those who merely sign the register should, in addition, write a note. The family need not thank each and every caller by letter, but if someone has made a special effort or if no one of the family was there to speak to him, they may wish to do so.

The visit to the funeral home need not last more than five or ten minutes. As soon as the visitor has expressed his sympathy to each member of the family and spoken a moment or two with those he knows well, he may leave. If the casket is open, guests are expected to pass by and pay their respects to the deceased, but this is not obligatory.

WHO ATTENDS THE FUNERAL

All members of the family find out when the funeral is to take place and go to it without waiting to be notified. But if the notice reads, "Funeral private," a friend does not go unless he has received a message from the family that they wish him to come. The hour and location of the service in the paper is considered an invitation to attend. It is delinquent not to go to the public funeral of one with whom you have been closely associated in business or other interests, or to whose house you have been often invited, or when you are an intimate friend of the immediate members of the family.

Wearing black is not necessary unless you have been asked to be one of the honorary pallbearers, but dark, inconspicuous clothes are advisable.

Enter the church as quietly as possible and seat yourself where you think you belong. Only a very intimate friend takes a position far up on the center aisle. If you are merely an acquaintance, you sit toward the rear of the church.

FUNERAL SERVICES

At the church:

As the time appointed for the funeral draws near, the congregation gradually fills the church. The first few pews on one side of the center aisle are always left empty for the family and those on the other for the pallbearers.

The trend today is to have the casket closed. Protestants may follow their own wishes. At a Catholic or Jewish service it is obligatory that the casket be closed.

At most funerals, the processional is omitted. The coffin may have one or several floral pieces on it, or in some churches be covered with a pall of needlework—for a member of the armed forces or a veteran, it may be draped with the flag. It is placed on a stand at the foot of the chancel a half hour before the service. The family usually enters through the door nearest the front pews.

Should the family prefer a processional, it forms in the vestibule. If there is to be a choral service, the minister and choir enter the church from the rear and precede the funeral cortege. Directly after the choir and clergy come the honorary pallbearers, two by two; then the coffin covered with flowers, then the family—the chief mourner being first, walking with whoever is most sympathetic to him or her.

Usually each woman takes the arm of a man. But two women or two men may walk together. For example, if the deceased is one of four sons and there is no daughter, the mother and father walk together immediately after the coffin and they are followed by the two elder sons and then the younger, and then the nearest woman relative.

At the chancel, the choir takes its accustomed place, the clergyman stands at the foot of the chancel steps, the honorary pallbearers take their places in the front pews on the left and the casket is set upon a stand previously placed there for the purpose. The actual bearers of the casket, always professionals furnished by the funeral director, walk quietly to inconspicuous stations on the side aisles. The family occupies the front pews on the right side, the honorary pallbearers on the left; the rest of the procession fills vacant places on either side. The service is then read. Upon its conclusion, the procession moves out in the same order as it came in, except that the choir remains in its place.

If the family so wishes, one of the male relatives may stop at the back of the church to thank those who have attended the services. He need say nothing more than "Thank you" with perhaps a special word for close friends.

Outside the church, the casket is put into the hearse, the family enters automobiles waiting immediately behind the hearse; the flowers are put into a covered vehicle (open landaulets with floral offerings are in poor taste) to be taken in the procession to the cemetery. Or they are taken in the closed car by a different route and placed beside the grave before the hearse and those attending the burial service arrive.

At the house:

Many prefer a house funeral. It is simpler and more private and it obviates the necessity for those in sorrow to face people. The nearest relatives may stay in an adjoining room where they can hear the service, yet remain in seclusion. If the women of the family come into the living room, they wear hats, as in a church. All other women keep their wraps on. The men, if they are wearing overcoats, keep them on or carry them on their arms and hold their hats in their hands.

The coffin is usually placed in front of the mantel in the living room, or between two windows, but always at a distance from the door. It is set on stands brought by the funeral director, who also supplies enough folding chairs to fill the room without crowding. Phonographic recordings of organ and choir music are excellent and readily available.

It is unusual for any but a small group of relatives and intimate friends to go to the cemetery from the house.

At the funeral home or chapel:

The establishments of funeral directors generally have a nonsectarian chapel in the building. There are also reception rooms where the families may receive the condolences of their friends. Services are conducted in the chapel quite as they would be in a church. Sometimes there is a private alcove to one side, so that the family need not sit in the front pews.

The burial:

If the burial in the churchyard is within walking distance, the congregation naturally follows the family to the graveside. Otherwise, those attending the funeral, wherever the services

are held, do not expect or wish to go to the interment. Except
at a funeral of public importance, the burial is witnessed only
by the immediate family and the most intimate friends.

Cremation:

Many people prefer the idea of cremation to burial. The
service is exactly the same as that preceding a burial. The
family may or may not accompany the body to the cremato-
rium, as they wish. If they do, a very short service is held there
also. The ashes may later be delivered to the family, to be
disposed of in any way that the deceased would wish (as long
as it is not contrary to any law). Often, however, the urn is
deposited in a building or section set aside in the cemetery
or churchyard and sometimes it is buried in the family plot.

A memorial service:

In some circumstances a memorial service is held instead of
a funeral. Notice of this service is put into the obituary column
of the paper, or, in a small town, people are telephoned and
each given a short list of his own nearest neighbors whom he
is asked to notify.

These services are very brief. In general outline, two verses
of a hymn are sung, then follow short prayers and a very brief
address about the work and personality of the one for whom
the service is held. It is closed with a prayer and two verses
of another hymn.

Usually no flowers are sent except a few for the altar. On
those occasions when flowers are sent, they are arranged in
holders (not as sheaves) so that they may be put into the
wards of a hospital without having to be taken apart and rearranged.

Since this is more like a church service than a funeral, some
of the men in the family may, before joining the women, escort
guests to their seats as at a Sunday service.

After the funeral:

Today a quiet luncheon or reception at the home of one of
the relatives has taken the place of a real wake. If it is held at
the house of the immediate family, other relatives and close
friends provide the food. Members of the family who may not
have seen each other for some time have a chance to talk and

it provides a meeting place and a meal for those who came from out of town.

Because the mourners from out of town usually leave shortly after the funeral, the will is often read right after the luncheon, or at least that same afternoon. If this is not possible, it is done within the next day or two at the latest. It may be read either in the home of the deceased or, if more convenient, in the office of the lawyer in charge.

CHURCH FEES

No fee is ever asked by the clergyman, but the family is expected to make a contribution in appreciation of his services; the fee may be anything from ten dollars for a very small funeral service to one hundred dollars for a very elaborate one.

A bill rendered by the church office includes all necessary charges for the church.

ACKNOWLEDGMENT OF SYMPATHY

When messages of condolence mount into the hundreds (for example, when a public figure or a prominent business executive is involved) engraved or well-printed cards may be sent to strangers:

> *The Governor and Mrs. State*
> *wish gratefully to acknowledge*
> *your kind expression of sympathy*

> *The family of*
> *Harrison L. Winthrop*
> *wish to thank you for*
> *your kind expression of sympathy*

If such cards are used, a handwritten word or two and a signature *must* be added below the printed message when there is any personal acquaintance with the sender. Such cards are never sent to those who have sent flowers or to intimate friends who have written personal letters.

A most unfortunate custom has recently sprung up. The funeral director supplies printed cards and the recipient merely signs his or her name to it, a poor return for the thought behind a beautiful spray of flowers or even a bouquet of garden flowers.

A personal message on a fold-over card is preferable to any printed card; it can simply say, "Thank you for your beautiful flowers," or "Thank you for your kind sympathy," or "I cannot half tell you how much your loving kindness has meant to me."

If the list is very long, or if the person who has received the flowers and messages is unable to perform the task of writing, some member of the family or a near friend may write for her or him: "Mother [or whoever it is] asks me to thank you for your beautiful flowers and kind message of sympathy." The message should be written by hand.

(For suggestions on writing letters of condolence, see Chapter 6.)

MOURNING CLOTHES
For women:

An ever-greater number of persons today do not believe in going into mourning at all. However, a widow of mature years may still, if she chooses (and in some Latin countries they do), wear mourning for life. On the other hand, deep mourning for a year is now considered extreme and more than six months is very rare. The young widow, if she wishes to wear mourning, wears all-black for six months except in the country, where sports clothes of an inconspicuous nature are worn. She *never* remains in mourning for her first husband after she has decided to be married again.

A mother who has lost a grown son or daughter may wear all-black for six months or a year, depending on her inclination. A daughter or sister, if she wishes, wears mourning for one season. When going into mourning in the spring or summer, for example, wear deep mourning until winter clothes are appropriate, then go back to regular clothes.

Mourning that attracts attention is unsuitable in an office. Inconspicuous mourning, on the other hand, is entirely proper. The fact that a woman invariably wears a black dress or a gray mixture suit attracts no attention if she has a little white at the throat. But if a woman does not wish to go into mourning at all and arrives at her office a day or so after the death of a close relative in the clothes she ordinarily wears, no one looks in the least askance.

For men:

A man may go into mourning for a few months by the simple expedient of putting a black band on his hat and on the left sleeve of his clothes. Also, he wears black shoes, gloves, socks and ties, and white instead of colored linen. In the country a young man continues to wear his ordinary sport clothes and shoes and sweater without any sleeve band.

The sleeve band is from 3½ to 4½ inches in width, of dull cloth on overcoats or winter clothing and of serge on summer clothes. A sleeve band on business clothes implies a bid for sympathy, which most men want to avoid. Many men, therefore, go to the office with no evidence of mourning other than a black tie and black socks.

THE BEHAVIOR OF THE FAMILY AFTER THE FUNERAL

As soon as possible after the funeral, the life of the family should return to its normal routine. There are many things that must be attended to at once, and while these may seem like insurmountable chores to a grieving husband or wife, the necessity of having to perform them and, above all, in so doing, to think of others rather than oneself is in reality a great help in returning to an active life.

Letters of thanks must be written to the clergyman, the pallbearers and others who have performed some service for the family. The gifts of flowers must be acknowledged and each letter of condolence answered.

The return of the close relatives of the deceased to an active social life is, nowadays, up to the individual. If he or she is not wearing mourning, he may start, as soon as he feels up to it, to go to a friend's house, to a movie, play or sports event. A man or woman may start to have dates when he or she feels like it, but for a few months they should be restricted to evenings at the home of a friend, a movie, or some other inconspicuous activity.

Those who are wearing mourning do not go to dances or formal parties, nor do they take a leading part in purely social functions. But anyone who is in public life or business or who has a professional career must, of course, continue to fulfill his duties. In sum, each year the number increases of those who show the mourning in their hearts only by the quiet dignity of their lives.

Children:

A child should never be put into black at any time. They wear their best church clothes to a funeral, and afterward, whatever they ordinarily wear. Many people are uncertain about whether children who have lost a parent should participate in their usual school activities and after-school entertainments. The answer is "yes." The normal routine of a small child should not be upset—more than ever they need to romp and play. Older children take part in sports and school concerts or plays. However, they may not wish to go to a purely social party within two or three weeks, or even longer, after the death of a parent.

MEMORIALS

Many bereaved families wish to make a material gesture to honor their dead. For the very wealthy this may take many forms, from the building of a monument to the donation of a piece of equipment to the hospital that cared for the deceased. Because of its very nature this type of memorial requires careful consideration, and time is required for extensive planning before it can be done. Most people cannot provide such an expensive memorial. The gravestone they choose must be the only permanent memorial. Therefore, it, and the inscription on it, should be chosen with great care. It is a mistake to rush into ordering an ornate stone with sentimental carvings and a flowery inscription which later could prove a most unhappy choice. For example, an inscription bearing the words "the only love" or "the greatest love" of the spouse could cause considerable anguish to a future husband or wife.

The wisest course is to choose as handsome but simple a stone as one can afford and a warm sincere inscription. "Beloved husband of" expresses true devotion without excluding other members of a present, or future, family. Titles are not used for either men or women. A typical, correct inscription would read:

1900–1968
Helen Jones Schaeffer
beloved wife of
John Simon Schaeffer

PLANNING FOR THE GRAVE

In cemeteries where it is permitted, some people plant a veritable flower garden around a grave. Others simply plant grass and bring fresh flowers or potted plants regularly as an evidence of their continuing love. Both require constant care. A satisfactory solution is the use of evergreen shrubs and ground cover which look beautiful all year round with little attention.

35

Engagements

PRE-ENGAGEMENT

It is important during the pre-engagement time that young people do not avoid the company of others and that they get to know each other's friends. A marriage in which either partner is incompatible with those who have always been part of the other's life has one strike against it to begin with. This is true also of the couple's families. Each should be entertained in the home of the other so that they can see the surroundings and the family to which they will be expected to adjust. The family that is to entertain the young people should be advised of the situation beforehand by their son or daughter, in order to avoid embarrassing the guest.

Mother, may I bring Sally Foster up for the night next Saturday? We have been seeing a lot of each other, and I'm eager to have her see Waterbury and to introduce her to you.

Love,
Jim

or:

Dear Mom,
I recently met a most attractive man, Jerry Boy, from
Syracuse, and I'm eager for you to meet each other. I won-
dered if it would be convenient for us to spend next weekend
with you and Dad.
Please let me know as soon as you can.

Love to you both,
Sue

The parents receiving such a note or a telephone call realize that, unless they are told otherwise when the couple arrives, the engagement is still in the future.

THE FUTURE GROOM AND HIS FIANCÉE'S FATHER

After he proposes and she says "Yes" the prospective groom asks her father or whoever is head of her family for his consent. If her father refuses, the girl must either change her "Yes" to "No" or marry in opposition to her parents. The honorable young woman who has made up her mind to marry in spite of her parents' disapproval tells them that on such and such a day her wedding will take place and refuses to give her word that she will not marry. It is highly dishonorable for her to give her word when she intends to break it.

THE ENGAGEMENT RING

It is doubtful that the man who produced a ring from his pocket upon the instant that she said "Yes" often existed outside romantic novels. In real life, the fiancé first goes alone to the jeweler, explains how much he can afford and has a selection of rings set aside. He then brings his fiancée into the store and lets her choose from among them the ones she likes best, perhaps one of platinum and diamond design or a lovely ring in her own birthstone. Any good jeweler has a correct list of birthstones and can make suggestions as to the cut and color.

One popular trend today is that of using semiprecious stones, beside which the tiny diamond has lost its appeal: an aquamarine, amethyst, a topaz or transparent tourmaline is perfect for an engagement ring.

The engagement ring is worn for the first time in public on

the day of the announcement. But *the engagement ring is not essential to the validity of the bethrothal.* The wedding ring is a requirement of the marriage service. The engagement ring on the other hand is simply evidence that he has proposed marriage and that she has answered "Yes!" Countless wives have never had an engagement ring at all, many receive these rings long after marriage. Some brides prefer to forgo an engagement ring and put the money it would have cost toward furnishing their future home.

A WIDOW'S OR DIVORCÉE'S ENGAGEMENT RING

When a widow or a divorcée becomes engaged to marry again, she stops wearing her engagement ring from her first marriage, whether or not she is given another. She may continue to wear her wedding ring, if she has children, until the day of her second marriage. She and her new fiancé must decide together what they wish to do with her old engagement ring. If she has a son, she may wish to keep it for him to use some day as an engagement ring for his future bride. Or the stones may be reset and used in another form of jewelry—by herself or her daughters.

IF SHE GIVES HIM AN ENGAGEMENT PRESENT

The girl may give the man an engagement present or not as she chooses: a set of studs and a matching pair of cuff links, or a watch. But she does not give him an engagement ring.

THE PARENTS BECOME ACQUAINTED

The parents of the groom make the first move to become acquainted with the bride-to-be's family. If they live in the same town, the young man's mother calls the girl's mother and tells her how happy she and her husband are about the engagement. She suggests that they come over as soon as possible for coffee, cocktails, dinner or whatever she chooses. If they live in different cities, the groom's parents write—or telephone—first. A visit is arranged between the families as soon as possible; whichever one can travel most conveniently makes the trip. This time should be a happy one for the young couple and both sets of parents should act with spontaneity and in a spirit of friendship.

ANNOUNCING THE ENGAGEMENT

Personal announcement:

A few days—perhaps a week—before the formal announcement the girl and man each write to or call aunts, uncles and cousins and their most intimate friends telling of their engagement. This is done so those closest to them will not read of it first in the newspapers. These relatives telephone or write the bride-to-be as soon as they receive the news, and call, when it is convenient. She answers the letters as soon as possible.

His people may ask her with her fiancé to lunch or to dinner and, after the engagement is publicly announced, give a more general party in her honor. If, on the other hand, they seldom entertain, they merely call or write to show their welcome.

In case of a recent death in either immediate family, the engagement is announced quietly by telling families and intimate friends.

The formal announcement:

The formal or public announcement is made by the parents of the bride-to-be either by notes or at the engagement party and after that publicly through the newspapers. Engraved announcements are not correct.

A week or more before you wish it to appear, the announcement goes with all the necessary information (including perhaps a picture of the bride) to the society editor of all the papers in which it is to be printed. If you live in the suburbs of a large city or in a small town, a copy is sent to the local paper (which may be a weekly). The date should be stated clearly, so that the announcement comes out simultaneously in all the papers.

The usual form is as follows:

Mr. and Mrs. Herbert Coles Johnson of Lake Forest, Illinois, announce the engagement of their daughter, Miss Susan Bailey Johnson, to Dr. William Arthur Currier, son of Mr. and Mrs. Arthur Jamison Currier of Atlanta, Georgia. A June wedding is planned.

Miss Johnson was graduated from Bentley Junior College. She made her debut in 1965 at the Mistletoe Ball in Chicago, and in May will complete her nurse's training at Atlanta

General Hospital. Dr. Currier was graduated from the Hill School, Yale University, and the Yale Medical School. He completed his residency at the Atlanta General Hospital and is now in practice in that city.

When one parent is deceased: The announcement is worded the same way whether made by the mother or father of the bride.

Mrs. Herbert Coles Johnson announces the engagement of her daughter, Miss Susan Bailey Johnson, to Dr. William Arthur Currier . . . etc. Miss Johnson is also the daughter of the late Herbert Coles Johnson. . . .

If her parent has remarried:

Mr. and Mrs. John Franklin announce the engagement of Mr. Franklin's daughter, Miss Helen Susan Franklin, to . . . etc. Miss Franklin is also the daughter of the late Mrs. Sarah Ellis Franklin. . . .

If a parent of the groom is deceased:

Mr. and Mrs. Harry Brown announce the engagement of their daughter, Miss Mary Frances Brown, to Mr. Robert Lewis, son of Mrs. Allen Carter Lewis, and the late Mr. Lewis. . . .

When the bride is an orphan: The engagement is announced by the girl's nearest relative, a godparent or a very dear friend. If she has no one close to her, she sends the announcement herself:

The engagement of Miss Jessica Towne, daughter of the late Mr. and Mrs. Samuel Towne, is announced, to Mr. Richard Frost. . . .

This form may also be used if the parents live far away or if she has, for some reason, separated herself completely from her family.

If the parents are divorced: The mother of the bride usually makes the announcement, but, as in the case of a deceased parent, the name of the other parent must be included.

Mrs. Jones Farnham announces the engagement of her daughter, Miss Cynthia Farnham . . . Miss Farnham is also the daughter of Mr. Henry Farnham of Worcester, Massachusetts. . . .

If divorced parents are friendly: When divorced parents remain good friends and their daughter's time is divided equally between them, they may both wish to announce the engagement.

Mr. Gordon Smythe of Philadelphia, and Mrs. Howard Zabriskie of 12 East 72nd Street, New York, New York, announce the engagement of their daughter, Miss Carla Farr Smythe. . . .

If the bride is adopted: If the bride has been with the family since babyhood and has the same name as her foster parents, there is no reason to mention the fact that she is adopted. If she joined the family later in life, however, and has retained her own name, it is proper to say:

Mr. and Mrs. Warren La Tour announce the engagement of their adopted daughter, Miss Claudia Romney, daughter of the late Mr. and Mrs. Carlton Romney. . . .

Older women, widows and divorcées: A woman of forty or more, even though her parents are living, generally does not announce her engagement in the newspaper, but instead calls or writes her relatives and friends shortly before the wedding. A widow or divorcée announces her second engagement in the same way.

Parents of groom announce engagement:
Occasionally a situation arises in which the parents of the groom would like to announce the engagement. For instance, when a boy in the service becomes engaged to a girl from another country, her parents may not have the knowledge or means to put an announcement in the paper in his hometown.

Rather than announce it in their own name, the groom's parents word the notice:

> The engagement of Miss Gretchen Strauss, daughter of Mr. and Mrs. Heinrich Strauss of Frankfurt, Germany, is announced, to Lt. John Evans, son of Mr. and Mrs. Walter Evans of . . . etc.

THE ENGAGEMENT PARTY

Invitations to engagement parties are written on informals or visiting cards and do not necessarily mention the reason for the party. They are generally sent in the name of the bride's parents or of the relative who is announcing the engagement. Occasionally the parents wish to include their daughter's name with theirs, and add "To meet Mr. John Watkins." Or, they may prefer, "In honor of Sally Jones and Robert Coolidge," clearly indicating the nature of the occasion. The invitations also may be issued by telephone.

Presents are never taken to an engagement party because only intimate friends or relatives give gifts and it might embarrass other guests.

The engagement party may be of any type that the mother of the bride prefers. Generally it is a cocktail party or a dinner. The guests are relatives and close friends of the bride and groom and probably a few close friends of the parents. The news may be told by the girl herself, or by her mother, as the

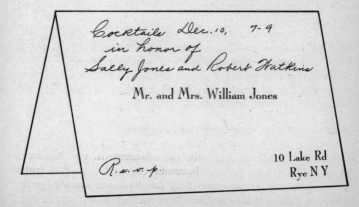

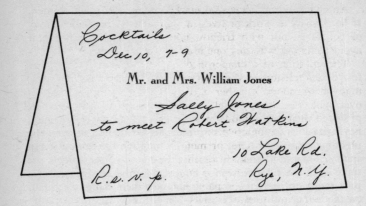

Cocktails
Dec 10, 7-9

Mr. and Mrs. William Jones

Sally Jones
to meet Robert Watkins

10 Lake Rd.
Rye, N.Y.

R.s.v.p.

guests arrive and find the fiancé standing with their hostess. Or, if the party is a dinner, it is announced by the father who proposes a toast to the couple.

As to a novel way of announcing an engagement, there is really no logical objection to whatever may be pleasing to you: you may float balloons with your names printed on them, distribute bouquets tagged with both names, or put it in telegrams used as place cards.

The toast:

When all glasses at the table are filled, the host rises, lifts his own glass, and says: "A standing toast: To my Mary and to her —Jim!"

Or: "I want you to drink to the happiness of a young pair who are close to the hearts of all of us: Mary [holding up his glass and looking at her] and Jim [looking at him]!"

Everyone except Mary and Jim rises and drinks a little of whatever the beverage may be. They then congratulate the young couple and Jim is called upon for a speech.

BEHAVIOR OF THE ENGAGED COUPLE

It is not necessary to demonstrate one's feelings with caresses and kisses in front of others. How much more attractive it is if the engaged couple indicate their affection by frank approval of whatever the other may do or say and by their radiant look. That is love as it should be.

An engaged man shows no marked interest in other women. If he is away at work or lives in another city, his fiancée may of course go out with friends, but both of the engaged pair avoid going out with any one man or woman alone.

The question of a chaperon differs with locality. There are few places left today where an engaged pair may not spend as many hours alone together as they wish, as long as it is not overnight. They may travel overnight by a public conveyance, provided their accommodations are not adjoining. They should never take an automobile trip that requires them to pass the night en route in a hotel or motel. Unmarried friends are not suitable chaperons, but married couples, even though of the same age, are. Otherwise, for any overnight stay, the engaged pair must be in the company of an older man, woman, or couple, either relatives or friends.

Presents that may and may not be accepted by the bride-to-be:

The fiancée of a young man who is saving in order to marry shows good taste by not allowing him to send her extravagant presents. If the bridegroom-elect has ample means, she may accept anything he chooses to select except wearing apparel or anything that can be classified as maintenance. He may give her all the jewels he can afford. He may give her a fur scarf, but not a fur coat; the scarf is an ornament, the coat wearing apparel. Her wedding dress and the clothes she wears away on her wedding day must not be supplied by the groom or, in most circumstances, by his family. Of course, if his mother has long known the girl, she may give her anything she chooses.

The engaged pair may properly open a joint bank account shortly before the wedding in order to deposit the checks they receive as gifts and draw on this account to help in furnishing their future home. She may select furniture for their home which he may rent, buy or have built. But she must not live in the house or use its furniture until she is given his name.

THE LENGTH OF THE ENGAGEMENT

The ideal duration is from three to five months. This allows time for the wedding arrangements to be made and for the couple to come to know each other well. If one or both are finishing school, but want to be engaged during the last year, or if a man is serving his military term and his fiancée wishes everyone to know that she will not be going out with other men, then it is proper to announce the engagement long before the wedding.

THE BROKEN ENGAGEMENT

If the engagement is broken, the ring and all other gifts of value must be returned to the former fiancé. Gifts received from relatives or friends are returned with a short note of explanation:

> Dear Sue,
> I am sorry to have to tell you that Jack and I have broken our engagement. Therefore I am returning the towels that you were so sweet to send to me.
>
> Love,
> Sara

A notice reading "The engagement of Miss Sara Black and Mr. John Doe has been broken by mutual consent" is sent to the newspapers that announced the engagement.

If the man dies before the wedding, his fiancée may keep her engagement ring. If it is an old family heirloom and she knows that his parents would like to have it remain in the family, she considerately offers to return it. She may keep any gifts that were given her by friends.

BUYING THE WEDDING RING OR RINGS

Shortly before the wedding, it is important that the bride go with the groom when he buys the wedding ring. Since she may not intend to take it off—ever—she should be allowed to choose the style she prefers. No ring is in better taste than the plain band of yellow or white gold or platinum. A diamond band is more suitable as a guard than as a wedding ring, since it will have to be taken off to be properly cleaned.

The wedding ring may be engraved with whatever sentiment the bridegroom chooses; today, this is usually only the initials and date.

If the bridegroom wishes to have a ring, the bride usually buys a plain gold band to match hers but a little wider. It may also be marked with initials or a sentiment. It is worn, like the bride's, on the fourth finger of his left hand.

ENGAGEMENT PRESENTS

A bride-to-be often receives a few engagement presents sent either by her relatives, her very intimate friends and her godparents or by members of her fiancé's family as special messages of welcome to her. Engagement gifts are usually table linen, towels, bed linen, such as a set of embroidered sheets, or possibly an inexpensive novelty gift. It is helpful if, shortly after the engagement is announced, the bride goes to the local stores and indicates her preferences in colors and styles so that engagement presents will fit in with her choice of trousseau.

Marking linen:

A monogram or initials on linen is most decorative. One initial with additional embellishment is more effective than two initials—and usually the cost is less.

The monogram should be in proportion to the size of the piece, neither too small nor too large. When articles are monogrammed, it is practical to mark everything with the bride's married initials.

Long tablecloths are marked on either side of the center, midway between the table center and the edge of the table. Small yard-and-a-half square tablecloths are marked at one corner midway between the table center and the edge. Square monograms look well set in line with the table edge; triangular or diamond-shaped ones look best at the corner.

Large damask napkins are marked in the center of one side, smaller ones in the corner—cross-cornered usually, but sometimes straight. To decide about the place for marking the napkins, fold the napkin exactly as it is to be folded for use, then make a light pencil outline in the center of the folded napkin.

Towels are marked so that when they are folded and hung on the rack the marking is centered.

Marking silver:

If the flat silver is monogrammed, use either a single letter—the initial of the groom's last name—or a triangle of letters. When Jane Ross marries Henry Cranmore, the silver may be engraved with the bride's married initials:

JR
C

Or with the last-name initial above and their two first-name
initials below:

C
JH

Initialing should be simple in style. Elongated Roman goes
well on modern silver, and Old English is best on the more
ornamental styles. A wedding gift of silver is safer to leave
unmarked so that it can be exchanged if desired.

Sheets are marked with base of the letters toward the hem—
when on the bed, the monogram is right-side up and can be
read by a person standing at the foot of the bed—and it is put
at half the depth at which the sheet is turned back. Pillowcases
are marked halfway between the edge of the case and the beginning of the pillow. On square French pillowcases the monogram is put cross-cornered with the top of initials at the corner.

PART EIGHT

ENGAGEMENTS AND WEDDINGS

36

Planning the wedding

A wedding, be it large and elaborate or small and simple, is always an important occasion—beautiful, impressive and the bride's day of days. But the groom is equally important and his wishes should be consulted from first to last. Because of the many details involved in even the simplest wedding, careful preparation is necessary if everyone is to enjoy the day itself. Without adequate preparation, father may be irritated, mother jittery, the bride in tears, the groom cross. This chapter and those that follow are dedicated to avoiding such miseries.

THE RESPONSIBILITIES, FINANCIAL AND OTHERWISE

All the expenses of the wedding itself belong to the bride's parents. A big fashionable wedding can total several thousand dollars; even a simple one may entail considerable outlay. Whatever size or style of wedding you choose, it is the careful, thoughtful planning—not the cost—that makes it beautiful. The simplest wedding is often the most tasteful. Whether a wedding is to be large or tiny, the reception is either at the house of the bride's parents or other relatives or close friends, or in rooms rented by her family. If, however, the bride were without family, she might perfectly well be married in the church or the rectory and go afterward to the house of the bridegroom's parents for the reception.

The bride's family's expenses:

1) The engraved invitations to ceremony and reception, and the announcements (true engraving is required for an extremely formal wedding, but today's simulated engraving is entirely suitable when cost must be counted).

2) The service, if needed, of a professional secretary who compiles a single guest list from the various ones provided her; addresses the envelopes, both inner and outer; encloses the proper number of cards; seals, stamps and mails all the invitations or announcements. She may also handle such details as making arrangements with florists, orchestra, etc.

3) The trousseau of the bride, consisting not only of her clothing but of her household linen as well.

4) Floral decorations for church and reception, bouquets for the bride and bridesmaids, corsages for the bride's mother and grandmother, and a boutonniere for the father of the bride. In some communities, the groom provides the bouquets carried by the bride and her bridesmaids, and the bride sends boutonnieres to the ushers.

5) Choir, soloists and organist at the church, and the fee to the sexton.

6) Orchestra at the reception. This may mean twenty pieces or one violinist or a phonograph.

7) Automobiles to take the bridal party from the house to the church and to the reception.

8) The refreshments, including the wedding cake and the beverages, for the reception.

9) The bride's presents to her bridesmaids.

10) Hotel accommodations for bride's attendants if they cannot stay with friends and neighbors.

11) A wedding present to the bride in addition to her trousseau.

12) Photographs taken of the bride in her wedding dress and candid pictures taken on the day of the wedding.

13) Rental of awnings, tent for outdoor reception and carpet for church aisle if desired.

14) A wedding present or a wedding ring, or both, to the groom, if the bride wishes to give them.

ATTENDANTS

___ t sister is always maid or matron of honor. ___ of suitable age, she chooses her most inti- ___ y also have bridesmaids, flower girls, pages ___ he last is a small brother or nephew who,

The bridegroom's expenses:

1) The engagement and wedding rings.

2) A wedding present to the bride, jewels or something for her of permanent value.

3) A personal gift to his best man and ushers, and their hotel expenses.

4) Wedding ties, gloves, boutonnieres for the ushers plus his own and his father's boutonnieres.

5) The bride's bouquet, where local custom requires it, and a corsage for her to wear when they go away.

6) His bachelor dinner (if he gives one).

7) The marriage license.

8) The clergyman's fee or a suitable donation to him.

9) Transportation for himself and his best man to the ceremony.

10) Expenses of the wedding trip.

WHEN, WHERE AND HOW BIG?

Before deciding the date of the wedding, the bride: (1) establishes the day her church or synagogue and the clergyman who will perform the ceremony are available and coordinates their time with that of the caterer, hotel or club; (2) decides the time of day for the ceremony, taking into account religion, climate, local custom, transportation schedules and the bride's and groom's own plans for their wedding trip; due consideration is next given to what is convenient for the relatives and friends who will be coming; (3) determines the number of guests based on the size of her house or the club and the amount she can spend. (Remember, a reception at a customary meal hour adds the expense of a substantial wedding breakfast or collation.)

THE INVITATIONS
When to order:

Two months before the wedding, the bride-elect and her mother go to the stationer's to select the size and texture of paper and the style of engraving for the estimated number of invitations or announcements that will be needed. Once the plates are engraved, the order may easily be increased if necessary. (*For details of forms, see Chapters 42 and 44.*)

Invitations are sent out three weeks before a formal wedding and two weeks or ten days before a small, informal wedding.

THE WEDDING LIST

Four separate lists of wedding invitations are made out: (1) the bride's, (2) the groom's, (3) the bride's family's (made out by her mother or other near relative), (4) the groom's family's (made out by his mother or a relative). If the families have long been friends and live in the same community, the invitations are divided more or less equally between them. If one hundred are to be included at the reception, some seventy names would probably be the same; each then could add fifteen of their own to the seventy already on their shared list. Otherwise each would limit her list to fifty. But if the groom's people live in another place so that not more than twenty will be coming, the bride's mother may invite up to eighty who will probably accept. Always allow for the few who accept but are unable to come.

Faraway friends are sent announcements or invitations to the church alone; these carry no obligation for a gift.

Invitations to a big church wedding are sent to all friends and relatives of both families, regardless of whether they can be present or not. Only a small church would limit the number of guests invited to the ceremony. For a house wedding or reception where the guest list is limited, the bride's family may tell the groom's family how many guests they may invite.

Lodging for out-of-town guests:

If the groom comes from another town, friends and neighbors of the bride, when possible, offer accommodations for his ushers and his immediate family. Otherwise they and his other relatives and friends stay at nearby hotels or motels for which the bride's mother reserves the necessary number of rooms, or she sends brochures and they make their own reservations. The rooms are paid for by those who stay in them.

CHOOSING THE ATTENDANTS

The bride's closest sister is always maid or matron of honor. If she has no sister of suitable age, she chooses her most intimate friend. She may also have bridesmaids, flower girls, pages and a ring bearer. The last is a small brother or nephew who, all dressed in white, walks ahead of her and carries the ring, lightly attached by a thread to a small firm white cushion. The bride may ask one or two young girls, usually between seven and twelve, to be junior bridesmaids.

The bridegroom asks his brother, brother-in-law, best friend or father to serve as his best man. He then asks as many ushers as he will need to seat the guests in the church—at least one usher for every fifty guests—and selects the head usher who becomes responsible for the promptness of the other ushers at rehearsals and the wedding ceremony. He also accompanies the mother of the bride when she takes her seat in the church—unless one of her close relatives is one of the ushers. A married man may act as usher or a married woman as matron of honor. The husband or wife not officiating is, of course, invited to the wedding, and is asked to sit at the bridal table.

The bride and groom usually ask their attendants to serve in their wedding at the time the engagement is announced or shortly thereafter. Bridesmaids pay for everything they wear except their floral bouquets which are presented to them by the bride. Ushers provide their own attire too.

Duties of the best man:

On the day of the wedding the best man is a combination of secretary, valet, and general manager of the entire wedding procedure, as well as the bridegroom's best friend.

His duties vary with the circumstances. The important thing is that he relieve the groom of as many details as possible. Any or all of the following suggestions will smooth the groom's way and add to the couple's enjoyment of their wedding day. The best man should take care of as many of these situations as pertain to the particular wedding.

Here are some ways in which he may aid the bridegroom: Help the groom pack for his honeymoon and see that the clothes the groom will change into after the wedding are packed in a separate bag and taken to where the reception will be held. Deliver the luggage of both the newlyweds to the airport, dock or station from which they will leave, check it and safely present the baggage-claim checks to the groom! If the couple are staying at a hotel or motel nearby, he checks their reservations, making sure the accommodations are adequate.

He may even register for them, delivering the key to the groom, so that they can go directly to their room.

When the couple are leaving the reception by car, the best man sees that the car is kept hidden until they are ready to go—to foil any practical jokes. He sees that their luggage is in the car, and he himself drives them to the hiding place or else arranges to have the car delivered at the moment of their departure.

As valet, he sees that the groom is dressed in plenty of time, stands ready with a remedy should the groom cut himself shaving, sees that the marriage license is safely stowed in the groom's wallet or pocket, asks for the wedding ring and the clergyman's fee and puts them in his own pocket. When the groom changes out of his wedding clothes, he again helps him dress, takes care of the discarded clothing and sees that he has everything necessary for the wedding trip: money, car keys, baggage-check stubs, required tickets.

After the ceremony, if the best man is not to walk out with the maid of honor, he leaves through a side door while the procession goes down the aisle and quickly goes around to the front of the church to give the groom his hat and coat. (The bridegroom or one of the bridal party helps the bride into her coat, which she has left at the entrance to the church when she came in.)

Sometimes the sexton takes charge of the groom's hat and coat and hands them to him at the church door. In any case, the best man sees the bride and groom into their car, which has been standing at the entrance to the church since she and her father alighted from it. Lacking a chauffeur, he delivers the newlyweds to the reception.

The best man gives the clergyman his fee on behalf of the groom before the ceremony while they are waiting to enter the church, or after the recessional. The amount may be from ten to twenty dollars for a simple ceremony, fifty for an average wedding with perhaps four attendants, one to two hundred (or more) for a very large wedding. If the fee is given in the form of a check, it is made out to the minister himself rather than to the church.

At the reception the best man sits on the bride's right and makes the first toast to the bride and groom. He is also the first man to dance with the bride after the groom, her father-in-law and her father have had their turns. When the couple are ready to leave, the best man escorts the groom's family to the dressing room for their farewells. He then leads the couple through the waiting guests to the door and when they have pulled away joins the rest of the wedding party in a final celebration.

ANOTHER WORD ABOUT ATTENDANTS

Unless attendants are limited to one or two, a brother of the bride, or if she has no brother, then her favorite cousin is usually asked by the groom to be an usher. The bride returns the compliment by asking the sister of the groom who is nearest her own age to be bridesmaid, or if he has no sister, she asks a cousin. If she is to have a number of bridesmaids and the groom has no sister, she asks him to name a close family friend. If the groom is choosing from six to ten ushers, he often includes one who is a special friend of the bride and asks him exactly as he asks the others.

When the homes of the bride and bridegroom are at such a great distance apart that none of the groom's immediate family can make the journey to the wedding, it is not unusual for him to choose (if he has no brother) his father or even stepfather as his best man. In such situations the ushers are chosen from among the friends of the bride.

It is entirely correct for a married man to act as usher, or for a married woman to be a matron of honor or a bridesmaid. Neither the wife of the first nor the husband of the second need be asked to take part. The one not officiating is of course invited to the wedding and sits at the bridal table. It is unusual for a husband and wife to be attendants at the same wedding, but if they are both close friends of the bride and groom there is no rule against it.

PLANNING THE CHURCH SERVICE

Some time before the wedding day, the bride and groom together visit the clergyman who will perform the ceremony, discuss the service they would like to have, whether they wish the choir or a vocalist to sing, possible pieces of music and any customs or rules peculiar to that church. If the marriage is to be performed by a minister or rabbi from another parish, the couple visit both him and the clergyman of the church or synagogue where the wedding is to take place.

THE FLOWERS

After the date and general plans for the wedding are decided upon, the bride and her mother get an estimate from the florist for church and reception decorations and for the bridesmaids' bouquets, and, if it is in accordance with the custom of the community, the bride's bouquet.

The bridegroom sends the bride a corsage to wear when she leaves the reception with him. He also buys the boutonnieres for his ushers, his best man and himself.

The church chancel is decorated as lavishly or simply as desired. There may be masses of flowers arranged as standards or a simple arrangement or two on the altar. Sprays of flowers may be tied to the pew ends. The colors, rather than being all white, may blend with those of the bridesmaids' costumes. At the reception the bridal couple often receive against a floral background, and a flower centerpiece may be used on the bridal table.

OTHER DECORATIONS AND ACCESSORIES

Other decorations may include a canopy at the church entrance and a carpet laid down the aisle of the church after the bride's mother is seated, to protect the bride's train. If the reception is held under a tent or a marquee, it is provided by the caterer for a home garden reception or by the club where the reception is to be held, and it is usually put up a day or two in advance.

MUSIC FOR CHURCH AND RECEPTION

At many weddings, the march from Wagner's *Lohengrin* is the choice for the wedding procession. The recessional is usually Mendelssohn's. But the bride and groom may select any music they are particularly fond of, providing, of course, that it is appropriate for a church ceremony. A singer, possibly a member of the bride's or bridegroom's family, may be asked to sing during the wedding ceremonies. All this is discussed with the organist.

The music at the reception may range from a full orchestra to a trio or even a phonograph to provide dance music. If there is to be no dancing, a wandering violinist or accordionist, playing the music chosen by the couple, acts as a happy background for toasts and conversation.

PLANNING THE "WEDDING BREAKFAST"

The "wedding breakfast" is the meal served at the reception, whether it be morning, noon or night. It may be an elaborate sit-down meal, a buffet, or simply sandwiches and hors d'oeuvres passed on trays. If the reception is held at a club or hotel, the bride and her mother discuss the menu and all other arrangements with the manager as soon as the wedding date is set.

The sit-down breakfast:

The sit-down breakfast is the most elaborate wedding reception possible. If not held at a club or hotel, it is supplied by a caterer, who brings all the food, tables, chairs, linen, china and glass as well as the necessary waiters. In the country a canopied platform is erected on the lawn. In the center a large table is reserved for the bridal party and another one for the parents of the bride and groom and specially invited friends. Place cards are provided for these two tables. Small tables are provided for the other guests who distribute themselves at them as they wish.

The menu may include: bouillon or vichyssoise, lobster Newburg or some other seafood; a main dish of beef Stroganoff with wild rice, or chicken in patty shells; any variety of aspic or salad; individual ices and little cakes. Small menu cards, perhaps with the initials of the surnames of bride and groom stamped on them, may be put on all the tables.

The stand-up breakfast or supper:

A single long table, set in the dining room of the home or club, is covered with a plain white damask cloth and adorned by a centerpiece of white flowers. On this table are piles of plates (white or white and gold), stacks of napkins and rows of spoons and forks at intervals. In evenly spaced places are cold dishes; chicken and celery salad or ham mousse with chopped hearts of lettuce and hot dishes such as creamed crabmeat, chicken à la king or chicken croquettes; besides these are finger rolls and sandwiches; for dessert, ice cream, fancy cakes and candies. On a side table are after-dinner coffee, champagne or punch.

The wedding cake, flanked by floral pieces, is placed either on the bridal table, if there is one, or in the center of the buffet table.

The simplest reception requirements:

An afternoon reception can be very simple: champagne or a fruit punch, in which to drink the bride's and groom's health, and the wedding cake are all that need be served. A slightly more elaborate reception would include either tea or coffee and thin sandwiches. The table decorations and wedding cake are white. The collation is set out on the dining table and the guests eat standing.

If there is to be no reception:

When the marriage takes place in a church and there is to be no reception, the bride and groom sometimes wait after the recessional in the vestibule of the church (with their parents and the bridal party) to receive the good wishes of their guests as they leave.

THE WEDDING CAKE

The wedding cake, usually ordered from a caterer, has several tiers and is topped by small figures of a bride and groom and flowers made of frosting or real flowers. Members of the wedding party, the families and as many guests as possible are offered a piece.

The groom's cake:

A nice if expensive custom still seen at some weddings is a separate fruitcake called a "groom's cake" cut and put into individual white boxes tied with white satin ribbon and ornamented with the combined initials of the bride and groom. These boxes are stacked on the table near the front door, and each departing guest is expected to take one. Though costly, it is a charming custom and is sometimes provided as a thoughtful wedding gift (after consulting with the bride) from a family friend skilled in the art of baking. When made as a gift, the individual pieces of cake need not be put into expensive boxes but wrapped in white paper and tied with white or silver ribbon and a little flower or greenery through the knot.

Another type of "groom's cake" is described above in "The Simplest Reception Requirements."

THE WEDDING PICTURES

Before the wedding, perhaps after the final fitting of the bridal gown, the photographer takes the formal wedding pictures of the bride. These are mailed to the newspapers two to three weeks before the wedding day.

Candid shots on the wedding day may be taken by a professional photographer or by a friend of the bride or groom who is an accomplished amateur. He may cover the entire day: the bride leaving the house before the wedding, the bridal party's arrival at the church, the bridal couple coming down the aisle after the ceremony, their departure from the church, the receiving line at the reception, shots of the bride and groom dancing, the guests, the toasts, the cutting of the cake and, finally, the departure of the happy pair on their honeymoon.

THE BRIDE'S TIMETABLE

In order to coordinate all the plans discussed in this chapter, the bride needs a definite schedule or timetable. The list below is based on the time necessary to plan and prepare a large wedding. But even those who are getting married simply and on short notice will find one list helpful.

Three months ahead of the wedding:

1) *Decide what type of wedding you will have,* formal, semiformal or informal, and if it will be held at a church, club, hotel or home. Always consult your bridegroom and your family whose expenses will be affected by the type of wedding you choose.

2) *Decide the hour of the ceremony and the type of reception to follow.* The degree of formality in your wedding ceremony must match your reception.

3) *Decide the date of the wedding.* Find out when your clergyman is free to perform the ceremony and when the church or chapel is available. Visit your clergyman with your fiancé to discuss both personal matters and wedding details; inquire about restrictions as to the time of year, day of week, musical selections, floral decorations or style of wedding clothes. Check with him on the rental fee for the church, organist's fee and if arrangements for a policeman or parking attendant may be made through the church secretary.

Before confirming the church date, be sure that the club, caterer or hotel can also accommodate you for the reception.

4) *Decide on the number of guests and attendants.* The bride

has at least one attendant—her maid or matron of honor; the
groom always has a best man.

5) *Compile your wedding lists for the church, reception and
announcements*. For a private ceremony, house wedding or
reception, where the guest list is limited, the bride's family
informs the groom's family how many guests they may invite.
Compile a special list of people to receive announcements only;
these are sent only to friends who are *not invited* to the
wedding or reception.

6) *Order your wedding invitations and announcements*.

7) *Order your bridal gown, select gowns for the bridesmaids*
and urge the mothers to get together to choose their clothes.

8) *Set a date with your photographer for your bridal portrait*
and/or candid pictures of your wedding.

9) *Begin to plan the decor of your new home or apartment*,
and to shop for both your household and personal trousseau.

Two months ahead of the wedding:

1) Make your medical, dental and beauty-shop appointments.

2) Select gifts for the groom and your bridesmaids.

3) Set the date for your bridesmaids' luncheon if one is
planned.

4) Register your wedding gift preferences in your local
stores.

5) Arrange for floral decorations for the church or ceremony, for the bride's and bridesmaids' bouquets and for reception decorations after getting an estimate from your florist.

6) Set up display shelves or a table if you plan to display
your wedding gifts.

7) Make transportation arrangements for cars to take the
wedding party and both sets of parents to the church. For a
large church wedding, hire a policeman or parking attendant
to direct traffic and parking.

The last month before the wedding:

1) Mail invitations so that they are received at least three
weeks before the wedding.

2) Record all wedding gifts and mail your thank-you notes
as soon as each gift is received.

3) Make hotel or housing arrangements for your attendants.

4) List items still needed for your new household; make moving arrangements if necessary.

5) Prepare a list of things needed for your honeymoon and begin to pack them in your luggage.

6) Set up display shelves or a table if you plan to display your wedding gifts.

7) Set aside everything you will use and wear on your wedding day and keep it together in one place; make sure bridesmaids' apparel and accessories are complete.

8) Check with your caterer, florist, photographer, church secretary or sexton on last-minute changes.

9) Send out wedding announcements and glossy prints of your picture to society editors.

10) Write out place cards for the bride's table, if there is to be one.

11) Change your name on all important papers: driver's license, personal bank account, social security records, insurance policies, etc.

Relax and get ready to enjoy the most glorious wedding day ever!

WEDDING PRESENTS AND OTHER GIFTS

If the presents, which begin to arrive as soon as the invitations are out, are likely to be many, each one should be entered at once in a gift book or "bride's book." There are many kinds published for the purpose, but any book with ruled pages about eight to ten inches square will answer the purpose. The usual model spreads across the double page as follows:

PRESENT RECEIVED	ARTICLE	SENT BY	SENDER'S ADDRESS	WHERE BOUGHT	THANKS WRITTEN
May 20	Silver Dish	Mr. and Mrs. White	1 Park Place	Criterion's	May 20
May 21	12 Plates	Mr. and Mrs. Hardy	2 South Street	Crystal's	May 21

All gifts as they arrive should be numbered with a paste-on sticker, and the corresponding number should be listed in the gift book. Since there might be many silver dishes and also dozens of plates, this sticker provides the only means of identification.

The bride's thanks:

In her own handwriting, she sends a separate letter for each present she receives, if humanly possible, on the day the present arrives. A note of thanks goes also to senders of congratulatory telegrams on the day of the wedding.

The inexcusable rudeness of the bride who sends a printed or an engraved card of thanks for wedding presents cannot be overemphasized.

In unusual cases, such as the hurried marriage of a bridegroom who is unexpectedly being sent overseas, or the marriage of a person of such prominence that the gifts arrive in overwhelming numbers, a printed acknowledgment, *always* followed later by a note of thanks, is permissible. There is no reason why a bride should not have every thank-you note written within two months. Even those who receive hundreds of presents can do so by determining to write a set number— say ten—each day.

When the presents are shown:

It is entirely correct to show the presents at the wedding reception. In a room other than that where the reception is being held, tables covered with plain white damask tablecloths or sheets are put like counters around the sides of the room and decorated perhaps with white ribbon and the sides with tulle net or pleated cheesecloth. The presents are arrayed in such a way as to make the prettiest display. The cards accompanying the gifts may be left or removed, as the bride wishes.

When checks are received, they must, of course, be displayed with the other gifts. This is done by overlapping them so that the signatures show but the amount is covered. A clear piece of glass is laid on top.

It is a time-honored custom to permit a bride to exchange duplicate gifts, except those chosen by her own or the groom's family. To keep sixteen saltcellars and have no coffee spoons would be putting sentiment above common sense.

Gifts for the bride's attendants:

The bride gives her presents to the bridesmaids at the rehearsal dinner, or when they arrive to help dress her for the wedding. (Or, if the bridesmaids give the bride a party before the wedding, she may give them her presents then.) Her present is usually something to wear: a bracelet, earrings, a pin, a clip or some other memento. The gift to her maid or matron of honor may match those given the bridesmaids or be quite different and more elaborate.

Gifts for the ushers:

The bridegroom's gifts to his ushers are usually put at their places at the bachelor dinner—if one is held. If not, they may be presented at the rehearsal dinner or just before leaving for the church. Cuff links, gold pencils and billfolds are popular gifts. The present to the best man is approximately the same as the gifts to the ushers.

The bride and groom exchange presents:

The bridegroom's gift to the bride may be a brooch, pendant, bracelet or perhaps a charm. The bride's gift to the groom is something permanent, ranging from cuff links to a watch or ring.

RETURNING WEDDING GIFTS

When wedding plans are cancelled, gifts which have already been received must be returned. If it is an indefinite postponement but the couple intend to be married as soon as possible, the gifts are carefully put away until the time the ceremony takes place. If there is doubt as to whether it will take place at all, the bride after six weeks to two months sends back the gifts so that the donors may return them.

"DOLLARS AND SENSE" PLANNING

An overall budget will avoid the nightmare of unsolved financial problems and unnecessary debts. The Wedding Expense Chart below gives a realistic picture of the actual expenses of four different weddings. However, these figures are offered only as examples.

A GUIDE TO WEDDING COSTS

	Total Wedding Budget			
	$500	$1,000	$2,000	$4,000
Type of Wedding	Informal or formal	Formal	Formal	Formal
Number of Attendants	1 or 2	2 - 4	2 - 4	6 - 8
Number at Reception	50	100	100 - 200	100 - 300
Place of Reception	Home or in church facilities	Home, club or restaurant	Club or hotel	Club or hotel
Type of Reception	Stand-up reception	Buffet or home or club, sit-down in restaurant	Buffet or sit-down	Buffet or sit-down depending on number
Refreshments	Sandwiches and snacks	Sandwiches and hors d'oeuvres	Sandwiches and hors d'oeuvres	Hot meal
Items to Budget:				
Wedding Clothes	$125	$200	$400	$ 680
Invitations, Announcements, etc.	25	40	80	200
Flowers, Attendants at Church and Reception	50	80	160	400
Music (Church and Reception)	35	40	160	400
Transportation for Bridal Party to Church and Reception	none	40	100	160
Photographs—Formal and Candids	50	100	200	240
Bridesmaids' Gifts	25	40	80	120
Reception (Food, Beverages, Wedding Cake, Catering Service)	185	430	760	1,600
Contingency Fund (Any additional expenses not planned in budget)	5	30	60	200

The inclusion of the chart above does not mean that a lovely wedding cannot be given for less than five hundred dollars. Actually, a beautiful and memorable wedding may cost only two hundred and fifty dollars or less. To illustrate, I will describe a wedding and reception I attended recently. The ceremony took place in the evening in a small chapel decorated with two vases of white flowers. The couple received on the church steps; then the wedding party (a maid of honor and best man) and the thirty-five guests went to the bride's home. Whiskey and soft drinks were offered but no hors d'oeuvres. At eight-thirty a buffet dinner was served, consisting of shrimp Newburg, sliced roast beef, salad, bread and rolls. A lovely wedding cake on display later served as dessert. At the time the bride and groom cut the cake, one round of champagne was passed to drink a toast to their happiness. The house was simply decorated with vases of greens and white flowers from the family's garden.

The bride could not afford to buy the wedding dress she wanted, but she was fortunate to be able to borrow a lovely one. Had this not been possible, she would have worn the prettiest dress she owned, as did her maid of honor.

The bride and groom issued the invitations by telephoning, eliminating that expense.

The total cost of this wedding was two hundred and sixty dollars. The expenses were as follows:

Food: 10 lbs. shrimp, $28; 9 lbs. roast beef (eye round), $11; cream, $2; salad, $6; rolls and bread, $5; miscellaneous, $5

Wedding cake: $20

Beverages: whiskey, 6 bottles, $36; mixes, soft drinks, $5; champagne (domestic), 8 bottles, $32

Catering help: cook and bartender, $60

Flowers: church, table centerpiece, bride's and maid-of-honor's bouquets, corsages and boutonnieres, $50

Though the wedding was planned and given in less than ten days' time, no element of a large wedding was missing. Every detail was simple but carefully planned, and it was a memorable occasion for all who attended.

37

Clothes for the wedding party

THE BRIDE'S WEDDING CLOTHES

A bride who has not been married before traditionally wears a white dress and a bridal veil. A bride over forty will probably feel more comfortable in a pretty cocktail dress in an off-white or pastel shade. Satin is suitable anytime, but is uncomfortably heavy for hot weather. Faille, velvet and moiré are excellent for autumn and midwinter. In the spring, lace and taffeta are lovely; in midsummer, chiffon, organdy, mousseline de soie, cottons, piqués and linens are cool and flattering. Lace adds dignity and is most becoming to a mature bride. The length of the train of the bride's dress depends somewhat upon the length of the church aisle and the bride's height. (A moderately short train extends one yard on the ground.)

For a civil ceremony before a justice of the peace, or a second marriage, the bride chooses the prettiest dress she has or can buy that will be appropriate to whatever the couple plan after the wedding ceremony—perhaps an afternoon or cocktail dress or suit. If they are leaving on a wedding trip immediately, she may be married in the suit or traveling dress she will wear away.

If the bride chooses to wear a veil over her face up the aisle and during the ceremony, the front veil is a short, separate piece about a yard square, gathered on an invisible band of some kind. It is taken off or thrown back by the maid of honor when she gives the bride's bouquet back to the bride at the conclusion of the ceremony.

The bride's slippers are of white satin or moiré and *com-*

fortable since she has to stand at the reception. If short gloves are the fashion, she merely pulls one glove off at the altar so that her ring can be put on. If elbow-length or longer evening gloves are worn, the underseam of the wedding finger of the glove is ripped for about two inches so that she may pull the tip off to have the ring put on. Or she may wear no gloves at all. A simple pearl necklace or possibly a pin of pearls or diamonds is the usual jewelry, but if the groom's present to the bride is jewelry, she always wears that on her wedding day.

THE BRIDEGROOM'S WEDDING CLOTHES

The groom plans his outfit according to the formality of the wedding. (The ushers' suits are the same style as the groom's.) The following are correct for every occasion:

1) *Formal wedding daytime:* Cutaway coat, or slightly less formal, black sack coat, waistcoat to match or gray (or white or fawn in summer); gray-striped trousers or black with white pinstripes; wing or fold-down collar for cutaway; stiff fold-down collar for sack coat; black and white tie or gray or white ascot; plain black shoes and socks (soles of the shoes should be blackened with waterproof shoe dye so that when he kneels at the altar, the soles look dark); white boutonniere; preferably white buckskin gloves or light gray; silk hat with cutaway; black homburg with sack coat—more often, no hat.

2) *Most formal wedding, evening:* Tailcoat, stiff white shirt, wing collar, white lawn tie, white waistcoat; white evening gloves; white boutonniere; patent leather pumps or oxford ties, black socks; silk hat or no hat.

3) *Informal wedding, daytime:* (when the bride wears a suit or daytime dress): Dark blue, black or very dark suit; white shirt; starched turn-down or soft-fold collar, bow or four-in-hand tie in conservative stripe or dark solid color; black socks and calfskin oxford shoes; white boutonniere; no gloves; gray or black fedora.

4) *Informal evening wedding:* (the bride wearing wedding gown or cocktail dress—if she is in a daytime dress, the groom wears outfit 3): Dinner coat (tuxedo) and black waistcoat or cummerbund; white shirt with piqué or pleated bosom; black silk bow tie; white boutonniere; no gloves; patent leather oxford shoes.

5) *Summer daytime wedding in the country:* Either dark

blue or gray flannel coat; white or gray flannel or white linen trousers; with blue coat, blue and white tie; with gray coat, black and white tie or plain gray; white buckskin shoes and white wool or lisle socks, or plain dark blue or gray socks (matching coat); no hat or gloves.

6) *Informal daytime wedding in torrid weather:* All-white Palm Beach suit; plain dark-blue tie, bow or four-in-hand; white socks; white buckskin shoes; white handkerchief.

7) *Evening wedding in a hot climate:* White dinner coat, double-breasted so as to avoid waistcoat; black tie, and other details same as (4).

(See Chapter 64 for correct accessories for evening and daytime formal wear.)

WHEN THE GROOM IS IN THE SERVICE

When our nation is not officially at war, a member of the armed forces may choose whether or not he wears his uniform when he is off the base or off duty. Therefore, officers and enlisted men—with their fiancées' help—may decide if they wish to be married in uniform. A professional serviceman will undoubtedly choose to wear his uniform and since his friends are probably regular service men too they will also be dressed in uniform. A reserve officer or enlisted man has the same choice. But if some of his ushers are civilians and some servicemen they have no choice—they must all dress in civilian clothes.

THE BRIDESMAIDS' COSTUMES

The costumes of the bridesmaids—slippers, dresses, bouquets, gloves and hats—are selected by the bride. The dresses may be long or short, straight or full, light or dark. Bridesmaids customarily wear and pay for what the bride chooses. They are always dressed exactly alike as to texture of materials and style, but their dresses may differ in color. The two who follow the ushers might wear green, the next two chartreuse, and the next two lemon yellow, and the maid of honor pale yellow. All carry the same kind of flowers.

The dress of the maid or matron of honor never precisely matches that of the bridesmaids; though it is usually similar in style, it is different or reversed in color. For an autumn wedding, the bridesmaids might wear deep yellow and carry rust and orange chrysanthemums and the maid of honor might wear rust and carry yellow chrysanthemums.

The bridesmaids almost always carry flowers. If sheaves, those walking on the right hold them on the right arm with the stems pointing downward to the left; those on the left hold their flowers on the left arm, with stems toward the right. Bouquets or baskets are held in front.

CHILDREN ATTENDING THE BRIDE

The clothes of junior bridesmaids are modified copies of those worn by the bridesmaids. Flower girls and pages may be dressed in quaint old-fashioned dresses and white suits of whatever period the bride fancies. Or they can be dressed in their ordinary white clothes, with wreaths and bouquets for the girls and white boutonnieres for the boys.

Tiny boys and girls wear kid slippers with a strap and white socks. Their slippers may match their clothes or contrast in color.

WHAT THE BEST MAN AND USHERS WEAR

At the formal daytime wedding, the best man wears precisely what the bridegroom wears. To make sure that his ushers will be alike, a bridegroom may send each one instructions after he finds out their sizes in gloves and collars. For example: "Please wear for the wedding black calfskin shoes; plain black socks; gray striped trousers—the darkest available; morning coat [cutaway] and single-breasted black waistcoat; white dress shirt; cuffs to show three-quarters of an inch below coat sleeves. Stand-up wing collar; bow tie and gloves are enclosed; boutonniere will be at the church." Or, having received their measurements, he may rent all the suits at a local agency.

The clothes of the bride's father need not match those of the ushers, nor should the clothes of the bridegroom, best man and ushers match too precisely. Their ties, boutonnieres and gloves are exactly alike, being gifts from the bridegroom and not bought individually. But there may be slight differences in the stripes of the trousers, the shape of the waistcoats and the materials and measures of the coats. Since few young men nowadays possess cutaways or tails, such suits are usually rented.

CLOTHES OF THE PARENTS

At a wedding held at any hour between 8 A.M. and 6 P.M., the mother of the bride wears a light-colored dress, varying in degree of elaborateness according to the other wedding preparations. At a formal wedding her dress should be formal—even, if she wishes, to a long skirt. She always wears a hat and gloves and usually flowers. A mantilla, veil or flowers may take the place of a hat. In the evening, dinner dresses are in best taste, though not cut too low. If the church is likely to be cool, she carries or wears a furpiece. Or a light wrap is put in the pew for her just before she herself comes up the aisle, so that nothing spoils the effect of her dress.

The bride's father wears whatever is becoming to him or whatever the bridegroom is going to wear.

Since the two mothers stand together to receive at the reception, the bridegroom's mother chooses a dress similar in type to that chosen by the bride's mother. At a formal wedding, the bridegroom's father may wear the same type of clothes as those worn by the bride's father: cutaway in the daytime, tailcoat in the evening.

(For clothes worn by wedding guests, see Chapter 41.)

38

Parties, dinners and the rehearsal

PARTIES BEFORE THE WEDDING
Bridesmaids' luncheon and the bachelor dinner:

In many American communities, the bridesmaids give the bride a farewell luncheon (or a tea) in addition to the regular showers. The only difference from other lunch parties is that the table is decorated with the bride's chosen colors for the wedding. *(For a full description of bridal showers, see Chapter 28.)*

Bachelor dinners are generally in the private dining room of a restaurant or in a club. Toward the end of the dinner, the bridegroom rises and proposes a toast. Every man rises, and drinks the toast standing.

THE REHEARSAL DINNER

A dinner is generally given the night before the wedding for the bridal party and the immediate families of the bride and groom. It may be followed by the rehearsal, but more often the rehearsal is in the late afternoon, followed at six or seven o'clock by the dinner. Customarily, though it is not obligatory, the parents of the groom give this party. If they come from another city, they may ask the mother of the bride to reserve a room in a club or restaurant for the dinner. If the groom's family does not, or cannot, give the rehearsal dinner, it is arranged by some member of the bride's family or by a close friend.

Invitations may be written on informals or in the form of handwritten notes. They may also be telephoned.

Rehearsal dinner for
Pat and Bob

Mr. & Mrs. John Goodfellow
Friday, June 6th, 7:00 P. M.
Short Hills Country Club
RSVP
1700 Low Street
Short Hills

or

Dear Joan (or Mrs. Franklin),
John and I are giving a rehearsal dinner for Pat and Bob on Friday, June 6, at 7:00 P.M. It will be held at the Short

*Hills Country Club, and we hope you and Bill (Mr. Franklin)
will be with us. We will look forward to hearing that you
can come.*

Affectionately (Sincerely),
Doris (Goodfellow)

1700 Low Street
Short Hills

All the adult members of the bridal party, the immediate
families of the bride and groom and out-of-town relatives who
have arrived for the wedding are invited.

A U-shaped table makes an ideal arrangement with the bride
and groom sitting at the base of the U with their attendants
beside them. The bridegroom's parents—or whoever are host
and hostess—sit at either end of the U. The bride's mother
sits on the right of the groom's father and the bride's father
sits on the groom's mother's right. Other members of the party
sit along the arms of the U. During the dinner the couple
present their gifts to the bridesmaids and ushers.

The host makes the first toast, followed by a return toast
by the bride's father and by numerous toasts proposed by the
ushers and anyone else who wishes to get to his feet.
(For suggestions on the content of these toasts, see Chapter 3.)

The entertainment may be a strolling violinist or a full
orchestra and after-dinner dancing. Or there may be none. The
bride and groom generally leave shortly after dinner to get a
good night's sleep, but the guests may stay on until the small
hours if the host suggests it. Decorations are simple—bowls of
flowers are all the adornment necessary.

THE REHEARSAL

Dress and behavior are appropriate for the church setting.
Girls wear simple dresses, never slacks or shorts, and the men
jackets and ties except in summer when a neat sports shirt is
acceptable.

A wedding rehearsal, essential for a smooth, dignified
ceremony, proceeds as follows: In order to determine the exact
speed at which the wedding march is to be played, the organist
is necessarily present at the rehearsal. The ushers try it out.
They line up at the door, walk forward two and two. The
bride and members of the families decide whether the pace

looks well. It must seem neither brisk nor slow enough to be funereal.

Once the organist has noted the tempo, the entire procession, including the bridesmaids and the bride on her father's arm, goes out into the vestibule and makes its entry. Each pair in the procession follows the two directly in front by four paces or beats of time, the pacemakers saying softly, "Left, left!" At the end the bride counts eight beats before she and the father put the left foot forward. The whole trick is starting; after that they walk naturally to the beat of the music, keeping the distance between them and the preceding couple as nearly the same as possible.

At the rehearsal, the bride takes her left hand from her father's arm, shifts her imaginary bouquet from her right hand to her left and gives her right hand to the bridegroom. The groom takes her right hand in his own right hand and draws it through his left arm, at the same time turning toward the chancel. If the service is at the altar, the bride approaches it holding the arm of the groom. If, however, the marriage ceremony is to be read at the foot of the chancel, he may merely take her hand in his left one and they stand as they are. No words of the service are ever rehearsed. The minister explains the order of the service and the responses.

The bride takes the bridegroom's left arm and goes slowly up the steps to the altar. The best man follows behind to the right of the groom and the maid of honor, or first bridesmaid, leaves her companions and moves forward at the left of the bride. The bride, in pantomime, gives her bouquet to the maid of honor; the best man, in the same way, hands the ring to the groom. This is rehearsed to see that they are at a convenient distance for the services they are to perform. The bride decides whether the bridal party is to leave the church in the reverse of the order in which they entered, or whether the ushers and bridesmaids are to pair off and go out together. They practice taking their places, then walk out briskly at their natural pace and the rehearsal is over.

ENTERTAINING AFTER THE RECEPTION

In some areas it is an accepted practice for the bride's family to invite out-of-town guests home for dinner or a late snack after the reception. But unless it is customary in your community, it is not necessary or expected.

39

The wedding day

BEFORE THE CEREMONY

The bridesmaids meet at the house of the bride, where they receive their bouquets. When everyone is ready, the bride's mother drives away in the first car, with perhaps others of her children or one of the bridesmaids with her. Maid of honor, bridesmaids and flower girls follow. Last of all come the bride and her father. This car remains in front of the church entrance.

Meanwhile, about an hour before the ceremony, the ushers arrive at the church. Their boutonnieres, sent by the groom, are waiting in the vestibule. The ushers most likely to recognize the friends and members of each family are detailed to the center aisle. Those who will escort the mothers of the bride and groom are designated.

A few front pews on either side of the center aisle are reserved for the immediate families of the couple. The left is the "bride's side" and the right the groom's. Guests may be sent pew cards *(see Chapter 42)* to show the ushers. If not, the ushers may be given a list of guests to be seated in the first few pews, generally marked by a bouquet or white bow on the end.

An usher offers his right arm to each lady as she arrives. If the vestibule is crowded and several ladies are together, he asks them to wait until he can come back or another usher is available. The usher, of course, does not offer his arm to a man.

If the guest has no pew card, the usher asks whether he prefers to sit on the bride's side or the groom's and seats him accordingly. Or, he may consult his guest list and if the guest's name is on it, seat him in a pew "in front of the ribbon."

SEATING DIVORCED PARENTS

If there is a friendly relationship between them, not only Mary's parents but both of her stepparents are present at the wedding. Her mother and stepfather sit in the front pew, her mother's immediate family behind them. Her father (after giving her away in a Protestant ceremony) sits with her stepmother and their family in the next pew.

According to the exactions of convention, the wedding of their daughter must be given by her mother. This creates a hardship if there is bitterness between divorced parents. The bride still drives with her father to the church, walks with him up the aisle and has him share in the marriage ceremony. After giving his daughter away, he sits in the pew behind the immediate family of her mother. His second wife may sit with him if the bride wishes, or she may not attend at all. The father does not go to the reception given by his ex-wife unless urged to do so.

If the wedding is given by the bride's father and stepmother while her own mother is also living, it means that the daughter has made her home with her father instead of her mother. The bride's own mother sits in the front pew with members of her family, but her second husband usually sits farther back. (Whether or not she attends the reception depends on the bride's wishes.) The father gives the bride away and then takes his place in the second pew with his present wife and their family.

The groom's mother and whomever she would like to have with her are given the first pew on the bridegroom's side of the church and his father and others of his family are seated in the third pew behind. At a large reception their presence need not be conspicuous nor make anyone uncomfortable.

THE LAST FEW MINUTES

Fifteen minutes before the wedding hour, the groom and his best man arrive at the church and enter the side door. They sit in the vestry or in the clergyman's study until the sexton or an usher comes to say that the bride has arrived. They then wait for and follow the clergyman to their places. *(See diagrams for procession.)*

The groom's mother and father wait in the vestibule. As the bride's mother drives up, an usher notifies the groom of her arrival. The bride and her father arrive last. When the entire wedding party is in the church, the doors between the vestibule and the church are closed. No one is seated after this except the parents of the young couple. Latecomers stand in the vestibule or go into the gallery.

The groom's mother goes up the aisle on the arm of the chosen usher to the first pew on the right; the groom's father follows alone and takes his place beside her. The same usher, or a brother or cousin of the bride, escorts the bride's mother to the first pew on the left. (When the bride has a stepfather he may follow her mother and the usher, in the same manner as the groom's father.)

If a carpet is to be laid, two ushers now pull it quickly down the aisle and drape white ribbon over the ends of the pews from the back of the church to the nearest reserved pew on each side of the center aisle. Then they take their places in the procession. The beginning of the wedding march should sound just as they return to the foot of the aisle.

THE WEDDING CEREMONY

The sound of the music is the cue for the clergyman to enter the chancel, followed by the groom and the best man. The groom stands on the right-hand side at the head of the aisle; but if the door opens onto the chancel, he sometimes stands at the top of the steps. The best man stands on his left, slightly behind him. The ushers and bridesmaids pass in front of him and take their places as illustrated.

The procession:

At a Protestant wedding with choral service, the choir may enter in advance of the hour set for the ceremony and so take no part of the wedding procession. However, at a formal Catholic wedding and also at Protestant weddings, if the bride and groom wish it and the minister and organist agree, the choristers lead the wedding procession, singing as they go. The ushers immediately follow them.

The procession is arranged according to height, the two

shortest ushers leading—unless others of nearly the same height are found to be more accurate pacemakers. Junior bridesmaids come next, if there are any. If not, the bridesmaids come directly after the ushers, two and two, also according to height, with the shortest in the lead. After the bridesmaids, the maid or matron of honor walks alone; flower girls follow, then the ring bearer, and last of all, the bride on the right arm of her father, with pages, if she has any, holding up her train. If there are both maid and matron of honor, the maid of honor immediately precedes the bride.

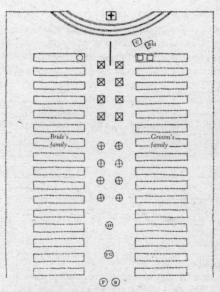

B, *bride*; F, *father*; FG, *flower girl*; MH, *maid of honor*; ⊕, *bridesmaid*; ⊠, *usher*; G, *groom*; BM, *best man*; ✠, *clergyman*

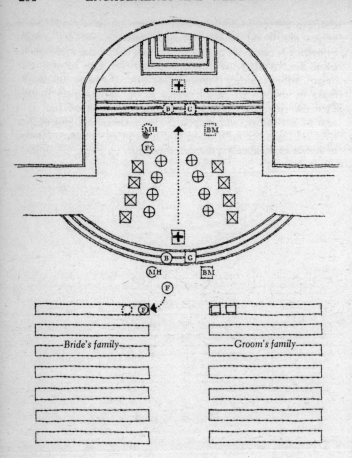

Bride's family

Groom's family

At the chancel:

At the foot of the chancel, the ushers divide. In a small church, the first two go up the chancel steps and stand at the top, one on the right, the other on the left. The second two go a step or two below the first. If there are more, they stand below. In a big church the ushers go up farther, some of them lining the steps or all of them in front of the choir stalls with the line sloping outward so that the congregation may see them better. The bridesmaids also divide, half on either side, and stand in front of the ushers. The maid of honor's place is on the left at the foot of the steps opposite the best man. Flower girls are put above or below the bridesmaids, whichever makes the prettiest arrangement.

In a Roman Catholic ceremony, the father of the bride joins her mother as the groom joins the bride. He does not give his daughter away.

In a church with two main aisles, the guests are seated according to aisles and not according to the church as a whole. All the seats on the right aisle belong to the bride's family and guests. The left aisle belongs to the bridegroom.

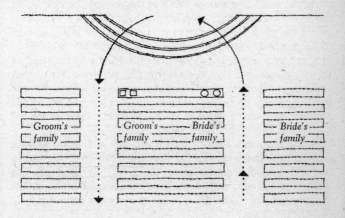

The bride's mother is seated in the front pew at the left (as always) of the bride's aisle—exactly as she would be in a center-aisle church. On the other side of the church the bridegroom's mother occupies the front pew on the right of the groom's aisle (also as always).

For the processional, the bride's (right) aisle is chosen. After the ceremony, the bride and groom come down the groom's (left) aisle. If the church is very large and the wedding small, the right aisle alone may be used. Then the bride's family sits on the left of this aisle and the groom's family on the right, while the marriage takes place at the head of this aisle.

The service:

As the bride approaches, the groom waits at the foot of the steps, unless he comes down the steps to meet her. If there are no steps, he waits at the head of the aisle. The bride relinquishes her father's arm, changes her bouquet from her right to her left arm and gives her right hand to the groom. The groom, taking her right hand in his right hand, puts it through his left arm—her fingertips resting near the bend of his elbow—and turns to face the chancel as he does so. It does not matter whether she keeps his arm, or whether they stand hand in hand or merely side by side at the foot of the chancel in front of the clergyman.

As the bride and groom stand at the foot of the chancel in front of the clergyman, he reads the betrothal. In a Protestant ceremony when the clergyman says, "Who giveth this woman to be married?" the father goes forward and the bride gives him her right hand. The father puts her hand into the hand of the clergyman and says "I do," (or if he prefers, "Her mother and I do"). He then takes his place next to his wife at the end of the first pew on the left. The clergyman, holding the bride's hand in his own right, takes the bridegroom's hand in his left and places the bride's hand in that of the bridegroom.

If the bride has neither father nor any near male relative or guardian, she may walk up the aisle alone. At the point in the ceremony where the clergyman says, "Who giveth this woman to be married?" her mother remains standing in her place at the end of the first pew on the left and bows her head to indicate "I do."

The organist then plays softly while the clergyman slowly moves to the altar before which the marriage is performed. The bride and groom follow slowly, the fingers of her right hand on his left arm. The maid or matron of honor moves out of line and follows until she stands behind the bride, slightly to her left. The best man takes the corresponding position behind the groom and to his right. At the termination of the anthem, the bride hands her bouquet to the maid of honor —or her prayer book to the clergyman. If the bride wishes her own prayer book to be used for her marriage, she carries it instead of a bouquet. And the bride and groom plight their troth.

When it is time for the ring, the best man produces it from his pocket, the minister blesses it, and the groom slips it on his bride's finger. (Since the wedding ring must not be put above the engagement ring, on her wedding day a bride either leaves her engagement ring at home or wears it on her right hand. Afterward she wears it above her wedding ring. At a double-ring ceremony, the maid of honor hands the groom's ring to the bride at the moment that the best man gives her ring to the groom, and the bride puts it on his finger immediately after she has received her ring from him. The ceremony then proceeds.)

AFTER THE CEREMONY

At the conclusion of the ceremony, the minister congratulates the new couple and the couple kiss. The organ begins the recessional. The bride takes her bouquet from her maid of honor, who then lifts the face veil, if one is worn. The bride turns toward her husband—her bouquet in her right hand—and puts her left hand through his right arm and they descend the steps. The maid of honor hands her own bouquet to a second bridesmaid while she arranges and straightens out the train and veil.

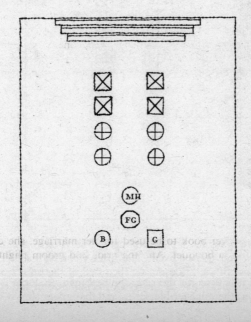

The recessional:

The recessional is played, and the procession goes out in one of two ways. In reversed order the bride and groom go first—she on his right arm—then the maid or matron of honor, bridesmaids and ushers, again all taking pains to fall into step with the leaders. In this form of recessional, the best man goes out through the vestry, picking up the groom's coat if he has one, and rejoins him at the front door.

In the other form of recessional, the maid or matron of honor and the best man walk out together behind the bride and groom. Then the bridesmaids and ushers pair off and follow two by two. One of the ushers or the best man will have put the groom's coat in the vestibule before the ceremony so that he need not go back to the vestry or waiting room for it.

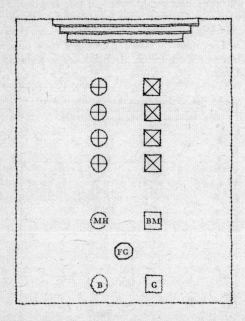

The automobiles are drawn up in the reverse order from that in which they arrived. The bride's car leaves first; next come those of the bridesmaids; then that of the bride's mother and father; next that of the groom's mother and father. The nearest members of both families follow.

As soon as the recessional is over, the ushers hurry back and escort to the door all the ladies who were in the first pews, according to the order of precedence; the bride's mother first, then the groom's mother, then the other occupants of the first pew on either side, then the second and third pews, until all members of the immediate families have left the church. Meanwhile other guests stay in their places. When the occupants of the first pews have left, the ribbons along the ends of the pews are removed and the other guests go out by themselves. If the best man has not already given the fee to the clergyman (see p. 240) he does so now and leaves for the reception.

ORTHODOX AND REFORM JEWISH WEDDINGS

The Orthodox wedding ceremony differs from the Reform Jewish ceremony. In the Orthodox ceremony, the bride is veiled and is escorted by her father and mother under a cloth canopy supported by four poles, usually held by hand. Or the posts may rest upon a stationary platform, and the bride's parents simply escort her up the aisle. Sometimes the canopy is of flowers instead of cloth. The groom is escorted by his parents. The principals stand under the canopy or "chupah" before the Ark of the Covenant. Hats are worn by all men attending the ceremony.

The service is read in Hebrew. The groom places a ring upon the finger of the bride, repeating the following formula: "Thou art consecrated unto me with this ring, according to the law of Moses and Israel." The officiating rabbi then makes the benediction over the wine, giving the groom and bride the goblet, from which they drink. A document is read in Aramaic, giving in detail the pledge of fidelity and protection on the part of the groom toward the bride and indicating the bride's contribution to the new household. At the conclusion of the ceremony, a glass is broken, symbolizing the fact that one must never overlook the possibility of misfortune.

In the Reform service, English (or the native language) is used in addition to Hebrew, and the canopy may be dispensed with. The young couple may decide to include many elements traditionally associated with the Christian wedding ceremony; they should consult with their rabbi about this a few weeks beforehand. The groom is usually ushered in by his best man, and the bride is escorted on the arm of her father although he does not give her away. The attendants function as in a Christian ceremony. The groom repeats either the Hebrew formula or its English equivalent. The bride and groom also drink wine out of the same cup, symbolizing the cup of joy. The clergyman delivers a brief address on the significance of marriage.

ROMAN CATHOLIC WEDDINGS

The wedding of the Roman Catholic Church is customarily centered around the Nuptial Mass celebrated between eight A.M. and noon. It is wise for the engaged couple to make arrangements at the rectory several months in advance. Marriage banns are usually proclaimed from the pulpit three times or are published in the church calendar prior to the wedding. Often, though it is not obligatory, the Catholic members of the bridal party receive Holy Communion at the Nuptial Mass.

Whether the bride and groom and best man and maid of honor, or the whole bridal party, are permitted within the altar rail is determined by individual church practice. The bride's father does not give her away, so after escorting her down the aisle, he steps into the front pew to join his wife.

Although afternoon weddings usually take place between four and five o'clock, they may be held at any time from one to six. A Catholic wedding may take place any time during the year, but during the closed seasons of Lent and Advent, the Nuptial Blessing is not given, unless, under extraordinary circumstances, permission is granted by the bishop.

THE RECEPTION

On arriving at the house where the reception is to be held, the bridal party may pose for pictures before the other guests arrive. This finished, they form the receiving line.

The receiving line:

The actual receiving line is made up of the mothers, the bride and groom and the bride's attendants. The ushers and best man have no place in it.

The bride's mother greets the guests at the beginning of the line nearest the entrance to the room. The bridegroom's mother stands next to her. The two fathers may join the line if they wish, standing on their wives' left, but it is not necessary, and they are generally more useful and happier circulating and greeting their friends.

At an elaborate reception there may be an announcer who asks each guest's name, then repeats it aloud. The guests shake hands with the hostess, make some polite remark about the "beautiful wedding" or "lovely bride," continue in line to the bridal pair. If there is no one announcing, guests unknown to the hostess announce their own names.

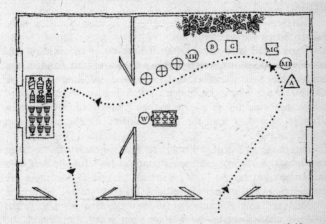

A, *announcer*; MB, *mother of bride*; MG, *mother of groom*; G, *groom*; B, *bride*; MH, *maid of honor*; W, *waiter*

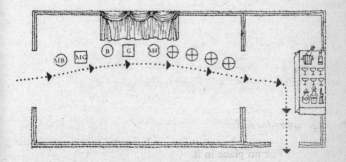

The bride stands on the bridegroom's right, the maid of honor next in line. The bridesmaids stand beyond the maid of honor, according to height.

Receiving their guests:

To a relative or friend of the bride, but a stranger to the groom, the bride always introduces her husband, saying, "Mrs. Neighbor, this is Jim," or, formally, "Mrs. Faraway, may I present my husband?" The groom says to an old friend of his, "Mary, this is Steve Michigan." And Mary says, "How do you do? Jim often speaks of you!" To all expressions of best wishes and congratulations, the bride and groom need only answer, "Thank you."

Refreshments are ready for guests as soon as they have passed down the receiving line.

When there is a bridal table, it may be at the side or end of a large room, decorated with white flowers. In front of the bride's place is its chief ornament, the wedding cake *(see Chapter 36)*. When the queue of arriving guests has melted away, the bride and groom go to their table or join their guests. Arm in arm they lead the way, followed by the ushers and bridesmaids.

The bride and groom always sit next to each other, she at his right, the maid or matron of honor at his left. The best man is at the right of the bride. Around the rest of the table are bridesmaids and ushers alternately. When there are no bridesmaids, the table is made up of intimate friends. The bridal table is always served by waiters even when the rest of the guests eat buffet style.

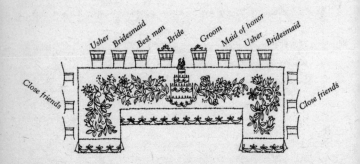

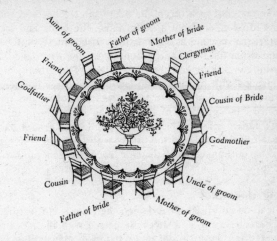

The table of the bride's parents:

When there is a table for the bride's parents, the groom's mother sits on the right of the bride's father, and opposite them the groom's father is on the right of the mother of the bride. The other places at the table are occupied by close relatives, very intimate friends of the parents or distinguished guests, who may include the clergyman who performed the ceremony.

The toast to the bride and groom:

At a sit-down bridal table, if champagne is served, it is poured as soon as the party is seated. The glass of the bride is filled first, then that of the bridegroom, and then on around the table, starting with the maid of honor at the groom's left and ending with the best man seated at the right of the bride. Then the best man proposes a toast to the bride and bridegroom. All (except the bride and groom) rise, raise their glasses and drink the toast. Then the groom rises and replies with thanks and a toast to his bride. At a small reception all the guests may join in drinking together to the couple's health and happiness.

Dancing at the reception:

If a regular two- or three-course meal, or wedding breakfast, is served, the first course is passed shortly after the bridal party sits down. The dancing starts after dessert has been eaten and the cake cut. But at a reception where sandwiches and snacks are passed or eaten from a buffet table, the bride and groom may start the dancing as soon as they wish. Guests watch and applaud while the bride and groom dance the first dance. Her father-in-law cuts in and then her father. The groom, meantime, dances with his mother-in-law and with his mother.

After this, the best man or a relative may cut in, the bride's father asks the groom's mother for the next dance and the groom's father asks the bride's mother. As the groom dances with each bridesmaid and the ushers with the bride, the guests may start cutting in, and dancing becomes general for the whole group.

Cutting the cake:

At a sit-down bridal table dinner, the cake is cut just before the dessert is served, and slices are passed with the ices or ice cream. If there is no bridal table, the cake may be cut later, often just shortly before the couple leave the reception.

The bride, with the help of the groom, cuts the first slice from the bottom tier (if it has more than one) with a silver cake knife. After this, a waiter cuts slices until the bottom tier has been cut away. The cake then is removed from the table, and the tiers are separated and cut into slices. The bride and groom may wish to save the figurines from the top.

THE DIVORCED FATHER SHARES IN THE WEDDING

When the divorced father of the bride wishes to have a share in his daughter's wedding, there is a practical solution. At the same time that the wedding invitations are sent out by her mother, the following invitations to a small second gathering are sent out by her father:

Mr. John Pater
requests the pleasure of your company
at the wedding supper of his daughter
Mary
and her bridegroom
James Martin
Saturday, the tenth of April
at seven o'clock
4 Monroe Place

If he has remarried, the invitation may read:

> Mr. and Mrs. John Pater
> request the pleasure of your company
> at the wedding supper of his daughter
> etc.

The mother chooses an earlier-than-usual hour for the reception. Then, instead of leaving the reception of the bride's mother in their traveling clothes, the bride and groom remain in their wedding clothes, and accompanied by her bridesmaids and his ushers, drive to the home of her father.

After the supper the bride and groom change into traveling clothes, which have been brought to her father's house earlier in the day, and depart.

THEY'RE OFF!

Unless the bride and groom have to catch a train, they usually stay until the crowd thins before going to dress for their journey. Then the bride signals to her bridesmaids and leaves the room. If the reception is in a house, they all gather at the foot of the stairs; about halfway up, she turns and throws her bouquet, and they try to catch it. If there are no stairs, she pauses at the entrance of the reception room to throw her bouquet. If the bride has no bridesmaids, she collects a group of other girls and throws her bouquet to them.

When the bridal pair appear in their going-away costumes, the guests all gather to bid them farewell, throwing confetti and rose petals after them as they run to the car.

40

Weddings in special situations

Not always do the bride-to-be and her fiancé choose to be married in church—and for a number of perfectly acceptable reasons. These occasions require our attention, for they should be as perfect of their kind as are the most elaborate of church ceremonies. Then, too, there are variations on the usual form, as when two sisters wish to be married at the same time or when the bride has been married before. Anniversaries, especially Golden Anniversaries, should be a re-echoing of the wedding day and so have been included here as special "situations."

THE HOUSE WEDDING

At a house wedding the procession advances through an aisle of white satin ribbons from the stairs or hallway to the improvised altar which may include a bench on which the bridal couple kneels. Chairs for the immediate families are placed within a marked-off enclosure, or if the room is small, all the guests stand.

The bride's mother stands at the door of the room in which the ceremony is to be and receives people as they arrive. The groom's mother takes her place near the altar with the rest of the immediate family. The ushers are purely ornamental, as no one is escorted to seats. The guests simply stand wherever they can find places behind the aisle ribbons. Just before the bride's entrance, her mother goes forward and stands in the reserved part of the room.

In a house, the procession starts from the top of the stairs.

In an apartment, it starts in the foyer or bedroom hall. The wedding march begins, and the ushers come in two and two, followed by the bridesmaids, exactly as in a church, the bride coming last on her father's arm. The clergyman and the groom and best man have, if possible, reached the altar by another door. If the room has only one door, they go up the aisle a few moments before the bridal procession starts.

For a very small wedding, the clergyman enters, followed by the bridegroom; the bride then enters with her father, or alone; and the wedding service is read.

There is no recessional at a house wedding. The couple turn around as the clergyman leaves, and greet their guests where they are.

For music there may be beautiful phonograph recordings of organ and choir made for such weddings. The collation may consist of ginger ale or fruit juice, wedding cake, and varieties of sandwiches, with the refreshments placed on a small table covered with a tea cloth, or it may be much more elaborate.

At a simple stand-up breakfast, the food consists of one hot dish and one salad. Bouillon, ice cream and wedding cake are served as at a large wedding.

When only the immediate families and a few friends are present, they often all sit together at one lunch or dinner table.

A home wedding may be performed in the garden, with the wedding procession under the trees, and tables out on the lawn.

The bride's dress:

At a home wedding, the bride may have a formal wedding gown, long or short (without long train, however), or a daytime dress or suit worn with a hat or small veil.

THE EVENING WEDDING

All through the South and generally throughout the West, many weddings are celebrated at eight or nine o'clock in the evening. The details are precisely the same as those for the morning or afternoon. In large Southern cities, the bride and bridesmaids may wear dresses that are perhaps more elaborate and more "evening" in type, and the bridegroom and ushers wear full evening clothes. Guests, both men and women, dress as though going to a ball. For the church ceremony, the women wear light scarfs of some sort around their shoulders and over their hair.

At simpler ceremonies, especially in smaller communities, the guests wear what they would wear to evening service in church—a good dress and hat for a woman, and a dark day-time suit for a man.

THE EARLY MORNING WEDDING

Among Roman Catholics, an eight o'clock morning wedding is not unusual. The wedding may be carried out as follows:

The bride wears any simple dress. She would probably wear a veil, of tulle rather than lace, either falling to the hem of her dress or of finger length. She carries a bouquet of moderate size, unless she carries a prayer book, and she wears no gloves. Her attendants wear the simplest sort of morning dresses and hats; the groom and his best man, business suits or flannels. And the breakfast menu—really breakfast—might be fruit, coffee and hot biscuits.

MARRIAGE AT THE RECTORY

Marriages are often performed in the clergyman's study or in another room at the recory or parish house.

When the bride and groom decide on a ceremony in the rectory, the clergyman is consulted ahead of time as to the date and hour. The bride and bridegroom go together and are met at the parsonage by the members of their families and the two or three friends invited. The bride and bridegroom stand before the clergyman, and the service is read. Afterward those present congratulate them, and that may be all. Or they may all go to the house of the bride or of a witness or to a res-taurant and have lunch, tea or dinner together. At such a mar-riage, the bride rarely wears a white wedding dress and veil, but she may if she chooses—especially if there is to be a wed-ding dinner at someone's home afterward.

MARRIAGE BY A JUSTICE OF THE PEACE

The general procedure is the same as that for a marriage at the rectory. There are always two guests, preferably relatives but often friends, who act as witnesses as well. The bride wears a pretty daytime dress or suit.

THE RUNAWAY MARRIAGE

An elopement means that a young couple have run off and been married without the consent of the young girl's parents.

When the parents had approved before the marriage or when they have accepted it afterward, they send out the announcements in their name. Should the parents not send out the announcements, the married pair may, if they wish, send them out themselves. *(See Chapter 44.)*

If the bride's mother and father wish to give a belated reception after the marriage, the invitations are telephoned or sent on informals, and, if written, include the bride's married name—"in honor of Mr. and Mrs. Harvey Kirk, Jr."

THE DOUBLE WEDDING

At a double wedding, the two bridegrooms follow the clergyman and stand side by side, each with his best man behind him, the groom of the older sister nearer the aisle. The ushers —half of them friends of the first, and the others friends of the second bridegroom—go up the aisle together. Then come the bridesmaids of the older sister followed by her maid of honor who walks alone. The older sister follows, holding her father's arm. Then come the bridesmaids of the younger sister, her maid of honor, and last, the younger bride on the arm of a brother, uncle or the nearest male relative.

The first couple ascend the chancel steps and take their place at the left side of the altar rail, leaving room at the right side for the younger bride and her bridegroom. The father stands just below his older daughter. The brother takes his place in the first pew.

The ceremony is a double one, read to both couples, with the particular responses made twice. The father gives both brides away—first his older daughter and then his younger. Then he takes the place saved for him beside his wife in the first pew.

At the end of the ceremony, the older sister and her husband turn and go down the aisle first. The younger couple follow. The bridesmaids of the older are followed by those of the younger and the ushers follow last, or bridesmaids and ushers pair off and go out together.

A bride at a double wedding may serve as maid of honor for her sister. Each in turn holds the other's bouquet during her sister's ceremony. The parents of the two grooms must share the first pew, or draw lots for first and second.

Since most double weddings involve two sisters, there is only one hostess—their mother. At the reception she stands first in the receiving line. Next to her is the mother of the older sister's husband, and then the older sister and her groom. The younger sister's mother-in-law comes next, and then the younger couple. Both maids of honor stand next to them.

At a sit-down wedding reception, if there are many attendants, it is best to have two bridal tables. Otherwise, all the party may be seated at the same table. One couple sit at either end, or opposite each other at the center of each long side. The bride always sits on the right of the groom, the maid of honor on the groom's left and the best man on the bride's right. All the sets of parents sit together at one table.

Each couple should have their own wedding cake. They each cut their own cake, one right after the other.

REMARRIAGE

The groom's second marriage:

The fact that a bridegroom has been married previously has no bearing on the wedding preparations made by his maiden bride. She may wear a white gown and veil, and the wedding and reception may be as elaborate as she chooses.

The marriage of a widow:

The marriage of a widow differs from that of a maid in that she cannot wear a bridal veil or orange blossoms, emblems of virginity. Although a dress and hat of color are preferable, she may wear white. She does not have bridesmaids, though she may have a maid or matron of honor.

A widow either removes her first wedding and engagement rings or else transfers them to the fourth finger of her right hand as soon as she becomes engaged. When her second engagement ring is given her, she puts aside the first, and if her second marriage is to take place soon removes her wedding ring as well. She may keep the engagement ring for a daughter, have it reset, or, later she may again wear it on her right hand. This depends upon the feelings of her second husband.

Usually a widow writes personal notes of invitation to a quiet wedding, but this is no reason why she cannot have a lovely ceremony. Sometimes—especially if her family and the groom's are very large—she finds it necessary to send out engraved invitations. *(For the correct form, see Chapter 42.)*

The most tasteful wedding for a widow is held in a small church or chapel or in her home. A few flowers or some branched greens are placed in the chancel or at the altar rail. (Or flowers and greens decorate the improvised altar in her home.) There are a few ushers, possibly only honorary ones. There are no ribboned-off seats, as only very intimate friends are invited. Usually the bride wears an afternoon dress and hat or possibly a cocktail dress and tiny veil. There may be a fairly large reception afterward or the simplest afternoon tea. In any case, the breakfast, tea or dinner is, if possible, at the bride's house, and the bridal pair may stay where they are and have their guests take leave of them and then drive away afterward.

A divorcée remarries:

Whether or not a divorcée may be married in her church depends upon the circumstances of her divorce and the approval of her clergyman. Usually the remarriage takes place in her own house, performed either by a clergyman or a justice of the peace. A small reception follows. She wears a simple street-length gown with a hat, in any style she prefers, so long as it is not white; she does not wear a veil or orange blossoms. Engraved invitations are not in good taste. Handwritten notes or possibly messages on visiting cards are best.

Children of divorced parents are not required to attend the marriage ceremony unless they are fond of their future stepparent. They may, if they wish, attend the reception.

MILITARY WEDDINGS

The only way in which a military wedding ceremony differs from a civilian one is the arch of swords through which the bride and groom pass at the end of the ceremony. This only occurs when the bridegroom is a commissioned officer. As soon as the service is over, the ushers line up on either side of the aisle at the foot of the chancel steps and at the head usher's command, "Draw swords!" hold their swords up (blades up) in such a way as to form an arch. The couple pass through, and at the command, "Return swords!" the ushers return them to their sheaths. They then turn and escort the bridesmaids down the aisle.

If the weather is fine, the arch may be formed outside the entrance. The bridesmaids walk out two by two, unescorted, but stop short of the arch. Only the couple themselves pass through. Should there be some civilian ushers in the party, they line up also and merely stand at attention while the arch is formed.

THE BLESSING OF A CIVIL MARRIAGE

When a couple have been married in a civil ceremony and have had the approval of their church, they may later wish to have a religious ceremony held in a church or chapel to bless that marriage. There is such a service in the *Book of Common Worship* similar to the marriage service, except that the minister says, "Do you *acknowledge* (rather than *take*) this woman . . . ," and makes other appropriate changes. No one, of course, gives the bride away, nor does the groom give the bride her ring again. It is a lovely and most satisfactory ceremony for those who wanted but could not have a religious wedding originally.

The service is only attended by family and closest friends and there are no attendants. The bride wears a street dress, and the groom a dark suit. She may carry a bouquet or wear a corsage. There may be music and the altar is decorated with flowers.

If a reception follows the ceremony, it may be as simple or as elaborate as the couple wish. Presuming the blessing takes place shortly after the civil marriage, the reception may have all the trimmings of any other wedding reception.

WEDDING ANNIVERSARIES

The eight universally recognized anniversaries are:

> 1 year, Paper
> 5 years, Wood
> 10 years, Tin
> 15 years, Crystal
> 20 years, China
> 25 years, Silver
> 50 years, Gold
> 60 years, Diamond

Because the first wedding anniversary is of great importance and the selection of paper gifts is comparatively limited, the trend is now toward making plastics also an accepted first-year gift.

Suitable parties to celebrate any of the earlier wedding anniversaries are a housewarming or a stork shower, a fancy-dress party, a barn dance, a treasure hunt. It can be a surprise party arranged for the bride and groom by their friends. The Silver Wedding is often celebrated by a big dinner or a dance to which everyone who was a guest at the wedding is invited, including the clergyman who performed the ceremony. The most important anniversary, the Golden Wedding, is usually celebrated by a somewhat formal afternoon or evening at home or by a family dinner either in the evening or at midday, after which other relatives, friends and neighbors come in to offer their congratulations. Some couples may wish to reaffirm their marriage vows on an anniversary such as the twenty-fifth or even the fiftieth.

Gifts not obligatory:

A gift is not obligatory, especially when the anniversary year is one that suggests an item of value. Sometimes the invitation carries a line reading "Please omit gifts." Intimate friends usually take or send something; flowers are always appropriate.

41

The wedding guest

The mere fact of receiving a wedding announcement or even an engraved invitation to the church obligates you to much or to nothing, according to your own personal situation or your impulse of the moment. In other words, an announcement informing you that a marriage has taken place between Mary

Anthony and John Ballard may require no more attention than it takes to change the name of the bride in your address book. On the other hand, the wedding of a dear friend or a godchild necessarily entails certain responsibilities.

"THE HONOUR OF YOUR PRESENCE . . ."

When an invitation to the ceremony, the reception, or both includes R.S.V.P., you must reply at once, so that the family can make definite preparation. Failure to reply causes extra trouble and expense. *(For the correct form of acceptances and regrets, see Chapter 48.)*

An invitation reading "and Family" includes every member of the family living under the same roof from the child of walking-and-talking age up to great-grandparents. Married daughters or sons who live in their own houses are sent separate invitations. However, guests should not take small children unless they have been specifically invited.

WHERE TO SEND PRESENTS AND RESPONSES

When the bride's address does not appear on the invitation, either under an R.S.V.P. or on the envelope flap, it may be difficult to discover where presents are to be sent. If you have no way of getting her address, or her family's, the only solution is to send gifts and responses in care of the club, hotel, hall or whatever is given as the site of the reception.

THE WEDDING PRESENT

Wedding presents should, if at all possible, arrive before the ceremony. If you are not an intimate friend of the bride or groom or of their families and are invited to the church ceremony only, you are not expected to send a present. When you accept an invitation to a wedding reception, however, you should send a present. An invitation by written note indicates that you are considered an especially dear friend, and you will therefore want to send a gift.

An occasional few special friends and perhaps close relatives send presents to someone being married for a second time, particularly if one of the couple has never been married before.

An announcement of an elopement does not require a

present, though affection for the bride or the groom or their families may prompt you to send one.

If, because of illness or absence, your present is not sent until after the wedding, a note accompanies it, giving the reason for the delay. Delayed presents are sent to Mr. and Mrs. Newlywed at their own new address or, if you do not know their address, in care of the bride's family.

What kind of gift:

Typical wedding presents include almost anything ornamental as well as useful for the furnishing of a house or the setting of a dining table, from a piece of silver, or an ashtray, to a lamp or an occasional table or chair. Objects of plain silver or untooled leather are enhanced by engraved or tooled initials; linen is more personal when it has an embroidered monogram or initials. But unless you know for certain that your gift will not be duplicated, it is safer to send presents unmarked.

Even if you have never met the bride, your present is sent to her. Often friends of the bridegroom pick out some things suitable for him, such as a masculine-looking desk set, which is sent to her, though obviously for his use.

Checks given as wedding presents are not necessarily drawn to the bride, but to the couple jointly. The check to be cashed after the wedding is drawn to John and Mary Smith.

A visiting card or a signed blank card is always enclosed with a wedding present with some such sentiment as "All best wishes for your happiness." If you know the bride well you sign it "John and Mary Friendly." If a friend of her parents or John's, you write "With best wishes from" and place it so that "Mr. and Mrs. Your Name" engraved on your card forms the signature. Unless you are certain that the bride knows it, be sure your address is included.

WHAT TO WEAR TO A WEDDING

Today few men wear anything more formal than plain business suits, whether dark blue or dark gray. During hot weather, especially at simple seashore and country weddings, light suits or white or light gray flannel trousers with plain flannel coats are suitable. The sport coat is out of place.

In the South and wherever evening weddings are customary,

tailcoats are still seen. More frequently, the tuxedo coat is the one worn in the evening. In simpler communities, men wear plain navy blue suits on all dress occasions in the evening as well as during the day.

At a formal evening wedding the women wear low-necked, sleeveless evening dresses, with flowers or clips or hair ornaments or perhaps a lace scarf over their hair and shoulders in church. At a very simple wedding in the evening or during the day, they wear afternoon dresses, with small hats.

When not going to the reception, clothes worn habitually to church are correct.

Children wear their best party clothes.

AT THE CHURCH

If you have arrived early enough to be given an aisle seat, it is entirely proper for you to keep it, no matter who or how many enter the pew later. *(For additional details on seating arrangements, see Chapter 39.)*

When the service is over and the recessional has passed by, those in the pews farther back wait in their places until the immediate families in the front pews have left.

FROM CHURCH TO RECEPTION

When invited to the reception, you provide your own transportation from the church to wherever the reception is to be held.

AT THE RECEPTION

At the house, club or hotel, someone at the entrance tells you, "Ladies' dressing room to the right, men's through the hall on the left." A woman leaves her wrap but retains her hat and gloves. Men remove coats and hats. At the door of the room in which the reception is held, there may be an announcer who asks your name. You give it with title: "Miss Pauline Panic" or "Mrs. John Jones" or "Dr. Henry Roberts." He then repeats in a clear voice, "Miss Pauline Panic," and you start down the line. The bride's mother offers you her hand and greets you. You comment on the bride's beauty, the day, or the wedding in general. If the groom's mother is standing next to her, you shake hands with her too. Make your remarks brief in order not to keep those behind waiting. You congratulate the groom and wish the bride happiness; a thoughtful guest mentions his or her name if it is not known to either of them. You greet any of the bridesmaids with whom you are acquainted. Otherwise you walk by with a smile for each.

The bride's father sometimes stands beside his wife, but he usually circulates among his guests just as he would at a ball or any other party where he is host. Therefore, you speak to him either on your arrival or whenever you encounter him elsewhere.

It is courteous, especially if he is a stranger, to introduce yourself to the groom's father and tell him how much you like his son or his new daughter-in-law.

After greeting the bride and groom, you mingle with the guests and make your way slowly to wherever refreshments are being served. You either ask one of the waiters to serve you or help yourself to what you want, lingering as long as you wish.

If you are a stranger at a sit-down breakfast, you sit down at an unoccupied table and let others join you.

When you wish to leave, you do so without formal leave-taking of any kind.

PART NINE

ON THE SUBJECT OF INVITATIONS, INFORMALS, CARDS

42

Wedding invitations

The engraved forms of invitations and announcements are governed by fixed rules. All formal invitations are recognized as such because they are worded in the third person; their acceptances and regrets are answered in this same form and by hand.

Invitations to the largest and most elaborate of weddings consist of an invitation to the church ceremony, a card of admission or "pew card," and, for relatives and close friends, an invitation to the reception. But many variations are possible and perfectly correct, as we shall see.

When a guest is expected to attend the church service only, no invitation to the reception is enclosed. When the wedding is in a small church or chapel and the reception in a very big house, many receive invitations to the reception and few to the ceremony. If both the church and the reception are limited to the few who are sent handwritten invitations or are given oral invitations, then engraved announcements in place of invitations of any kind may be sent to the friends who could not be included as well as to acquaintances.

Invitations to a large wedding are sent three weeks beforehand; those to a simpler wedding may be mailed as late as ten days before the wedding day.

(For wedding announcements and reception invitations, see Chapters 43 and 45.)

CORRECT STYLE

Correct invitations to any wedding, whatever its size, are engraved on the first page of a double sheet of heavy paper, ivory or white, either plain or with a raised margin called a plate-mark or panel. Its size is governed by the current fashion, but usually it is about 5½ inches wide by 7⅜ inches deep and folds once for insertion into its envelope. Or it may be about 4⅜ by 5¾ inches and go into the envelope without folding. The engraving is in whatever lettering style the bride chooses at her stationer's.

If the family of the bride's father has a coat of arms, it, or a crest only, may be embossed without color at the top center of the sheet. When the invitations are sent out by the bride's mother (or any woman alone), a coat of arms is not used. With a crest, plain script is the best taste for the engraving.

Two envelopes:

Two envelopes are used: the inner one has no mucilage on the flap and is addressed to Mr. and Mrs. Brown with neither first name nor address. Then it is put into an outer "mailing envelope" that has mucilage on its flap; this envelope is then addressed by hand.

The names of children under thirteen are written on the inner envelope, "Joan, Robert and Frederick," and inserted in an envelope addressed to "Miss and the Messrs. Greatlake" or "Miss Joan Greatlake" and below "Robert and Frederick Greatlake."

Addressing the envelopes:

In all formal correspondence never abbreviate the state name. Neither does one use initials for the first name—"Mr. and Mrs. Harold T. James" is correct rather than "Mr. and Mrs. H. T. James." When the middle name is known, that is written out also.

When every member of a family under one roof is included in the invitation, the envelope is addressed:

Mr. and Mrs. Joseph Truehart and Family

A daughter's name is written below her parents'—"Miss Helen Truehart," or "The Misses Truehart." Boys under twelve or thirteen, however, are more correctly sent separate invitations.

It is thoughtful to send invitations to members of the bridal party as mementos. These invitations are addressed exactly as they are to the other guests.

Folding and inserting:

When preparing to send out the invitations, all the envelopes are addressed first. An envelope-size invitation is inserted in the inner envelope, folded edge down, with the engraved side toward the flap. An invitation designed to fit an envelope half its size will require a second fold, which should be made with the engraving inside, and inserted, folded edge down, into the envelope. With the unsealed flap of this filled inner envelope away from you, insert it in the mailing envelope. If the invitation is folded, all insertions (such as the reception card or pew card) are placed inside the second fold with the type facing the flap of the envelope. If the invitation is not folded a second time, they are inserted in front of it (nearest you), with the reception card next to the invitation and any smaller cards in front of that.

Engravers generally use tissue sheets to protect the pages from the fresh ink and recommend that they be kept to prevent the ink from smearing.

CORRECT WORDING

The wording of the wedding invitation never varies. For example, the invitation to the ceremony itself always "requests the *honour*"—spelled with a "u." The invitation to the reception "requests the *pleasure* of your company." But it is perfectly proper for communicants of the Roman Catholic Church to use a form in which the phrase "at the marriage of" is replaced by *"at the marriage in Christ* of" and, where appropriate, add beneath the name of the groom the lines *"and your participation in the offering of the Nuptial Mass."*

In the examples of correct wording, spacing and styles of

engraving that follow, note the omission of punctuation, except after abbreviations and initials and when phrases requiring separation by punctuation occur in the same line.

Mr. and Mrs. Charles Robert Oldname

request the honour of your presence

at the marriage of their daughter

Pauline Marie

to

Mr. John Frederick Hamilton

Saturday, the twenty-ninth of April

at four o'clock

Church of the Heavenly Rest

New York

Doctor and Mrs. John Huntington Smith
request the honour of

Miss Pauline Town's

presence at the marriage of their daughter
Mary Katherine
to
Mr. James Smartlington
Tuesday, the first of November
at twelve o'clock
St. John's Church

General forms:

The wording of an invitation to a house wedding gives a house address in place of the name of a church, and R.S.V.P. is added at the bottom left.

Wedding and reception invitation in one:

Occasionally, the invitation to the reception or to the breakfast is included in the invitation to the ceremony.

Mrs. Alexander Oldname

requests the honour of your presence

at the marriage of her daughter

Barbara

to

Mr. James Town, junior

Tuesday, the twenty-first of October

at three o'clock

Church of the Resurrection

Ridgemont, New York

and afterwards at the reception

Bright Meadows

R.s.v.p.

Invitation to a wedding in the house of a friend:

Invitations are issued by the parents of the bride even though the wedding takes place at a house other than their own. The names of the parents at the head of the invitation means that *they* are giving the wedding, though not in their own house.

Mr. and Mrs. Richard Littlehouse

request the honour of your presence

at the marriage of their daughter

Betty

to

Doctor Frederic Robinson

Saturday, the fifth of November

at four o'clock

at the residence of Mr. and Mrs. James Sterlington

Tuxedo Park, New York

R.s.v.p.

When the reception follows a house wedding, it is not mentioned in the wedding invitation, as it is assumed that everyone invited will stay on.

When the bride has a stepfather:
When the bride's own father is not living and she has a stepparent, or her mother has divorced and remarried:

Mr. and Mrs. John Huntington Smith
request the honour of your presence
at the marriage of her daughter
Mary Alice Towne
etc.

When the bride's mother is widowed or divorced:
If the bride's mother is giving the wedding alone:

> *Mrs. Bertram Jones*
> *requests the honour of your presence*
> *at the marriage of her daughter*
> *Helen Jeffrey Jones*
> *etc.*

When the bride's parents are divorced:
When the bride's parents are divorced, the wedding invitations are issued in the name of the parent who pays for and acts as host at the reception. If relations are so friendly that they share the expenses and act as co-hosts, both names appear on the invitation.

> *Mr. and Mrs. Henry Smith*
> *(or Mrs. Jones Doe, if she has not remarried)*
> *and*
> *Mr. and Mrs. Robert Doe*
> *(or Mr. Robert Doe)*
> *request the honour of your presence*
> *at the marriage of*
> *Mary Doe*
> *to*
> *William Hughes*
> *etc.*

The bride's mother's name, whether she has remarried or not, appears first. If neither parent is remarried the wording would be:

> *Mrs. Jones Doe*
> *and*
> *Mr. Robert Doe*
> *request the honour of your presence*
> *at the marriage of their daughter*
> *Mary*
> *etc.*

When the bride is an orphan:
Though good taste does not permit "Miss" or "Mrs." as

titles before the bride's name, the three cases that follow are exceptions.

If the bride has no relatives and the wedding is given by friends:

Mr. and Mrs. John Neighbor
request the honour of your presence
at the marriage of
Miss Elizabeth Orphan
to
Mr. John Henry Bridegroom
etc.

If she has brothers, the oldest one customarily sends out her wedding invitations and announcements in his name. When another relative takes the place of a parent, his or her name is used. The bride whose several sisters or brothers are younger than she may prefer to send her invitations in her own name. The following form might be used:

The honour of your presence
is requested
at the marriage of
Miss Elizabeth Orphan
to
etc.

When the bride is a widow or divorcée:

Invitations to the marriage of a young widow or divorcée are sent in the name of her parents exactly as were the invitations for her first wedding, except that her name, instead of being simply "Priscilla," is now written "Priscilla Banks Loring," thus:

Doctor and Mrs. Maynard Banks
request the honour of your presence
at the marriage of their daughter
Priscilla Banks Loring
to
etc.

A more mature woman, or one whose parents are dead, may send out her own invitations:

The honour of your presence
is requested
at the marriage of
Mrs. John Kerr Simons
to
etc.

This same woman would drop the "John" and use "Mrs. Kerr Simons" if she were a divorcée.

The fact that the groom has been divorced does not change the invitation to, or announcement of, his new bride's marriage.

When the bride has a professional name:

When the bride has a career, uses a professional name and therefore has many professional friends to whom she would like to send invitations, but who are unlikely to recognize "Pauline Marie Oldname," the invitations may have her professional name engraved in very small letters and in parentheses under her Christian name:

Pauline Marie
(Pat Bond)

to

Mr. John Frederick Hamilton

This is most practically done by having the name (Pat Bond) added to the plate after the order for regular invitations has been completed. As many invitations as are to go to her professional friends are then struck off with this addition.

When principals are in the services:

On the wedding invitations, the name of a bridegroom whose rank is below Commander or Lt. Colonel is given:

John Strong
2nd Lieutenant, United States Army
or
Ensign, United States Navy

The title of higher ranking officers precedes their name, and the service may or may not be included on the line below.

Colonel John Spring
United States Air Force

The name of a noncommissioned or an enlisted man in the armed forces is engraved John Strong, and Signal Corps, U.S.N.R., or whatever designation is his, in smaller type directly beneath the name on the wedding invitations. Or if the bride chooses to include Pvt. 1st Class, U.S.A., or Apprentice Seaman, U.S.N.R., she may do so.

The name of the bride who is in the armed forces is engraved:

marriage of their daughter
Alice Mary
Lieutenant, Women's Army Corps

When the bride's father is in the armed forces and absent on duty, his name appears as follows:

Major (overseas) and Mrs. John Jones
request the honour of your presence, etc.

An officer in the Reserves does not use his title unless he is on active duty.

High-ranking officers continue to use their title and include their service on the line below with "retired" following the service.

General George Harmon
United States Army, retired

The double-wedding invitation:

Mr. and Mrs. Henry Smartlington

request the honour of your presence

at the marriage of their daughters

Marian Helen

to

Mr. Judson Jones

and

Amy Caroline

to

Mr. Herbert Scott Adams

Saturday, the tenth of November

at four o'clock

Trinity Church

The elder sister's name is given first.

When two brides who are friends wish to have a double wedding, the wording includes the surnames of both parents and brides:

Mr. and Mrs. Henry Smartlington

and

Mr. and Mrs. Arthur Lane

request the honour of your presence

at the marriage of their daughters

Marian Helen Smartlington

to

Mr. Judson Jones

and

Mary Alice Lane

to

Mr. John Gray

etc.

When the bridegroom's family gives the wedding:

When the young bride comes as a stranger from abroad, or from any distance, without her family, the groom's family may give the wedding and send the invitations in their name. This is the only other case where the title "Miss" is used.

Mr. and Mrs. John Henry Pater
request the honour of your presence
at the marriage of
Miss Marie Mersailles
to
their son
John Henry Pater, junior
etc.

Announcements, but not invitations, may be sent from abroad by her own family.

Including the bridegroom's family in the invitation:

On occasion the bridegroom's family, even though the bride's parents are alive and nearby, share in, or even pay for the major part of the reception, which is sometimes held in their home. Therefore their names as co-hosts are included on the invitation:

Mr. and Mrs. Charles Goodman
and
Mr. and Mrs. George Gonzalez
request the pleasure of your company
at the wedding reception of
Julia Goodman
and
Roberto Gonzalez
etc.

A separate invitation to the wedding ceremony is sent in the name of the bride's parents.

In some foreign countries the groom's family is included in the wedding invitation also and the invitation is a double one —with the name of the bride's family on the left inside page and the groom's parents on the right. This form is sometimes followed by these nationalities here in the United States and is a thoughtful and friendly custom.

On the left inside page:

> *Mr. and Mrs. Bruno Cairo*
> *request the honour of your presence*
> *at the marriage of their daughter*
> *Julia*
> *to*
> *Mr. Francisco Conti*
> etc.

Facing it, on the right inside page:

> *Mr. and Mrs. Roberto Conti*
> *request the honour of your presence*
> *at the marriage of their son*
> *Francisco*
> *to*
> *Miss Julia Cairo*
> etc.

Personal invitations:

The most flattering wedding invitation is a note of invitation personally written by the bride:

Dear Mrs. Kindhart,

Dick and I are to be married at Christ Church Chantry at noon on Thursday the tenth. We both want you and Mr. Kindhart to come to the church and afterward to the reception at the home of my aunt, Mrs. Salde, at Two South Beach Street.

With much love from us both,

> *Affectionately,*
> *Helen*

When the bridegroom is about to receive a degree:

When the bridegroom is a medical student at the time the invitations are sent, but will be a graduate by the date of the wedding, his name is written with his title—"Doctor John Jones." This holds true for any man in a profession in which the title is ordinarily used.

When the wedding date is changed:

When the wedding date must be changed after the invitations have already been engraved, instead of ordering a new set of invitations the bride encloses a small printed card saying, "The date of the wedding has been changed from . . . to . . ." or, if the number of guests is small, she writes the same information on the card by hand.

If a wedding may be postponed indefinitely after the invitations have been mailed, the news must go out as fast as possible. If cards can be printed in time, that is the best solution. If not, the bride and members of her family and bridal party send out handwritten notes at once. The wording, depending on the cause, would be:

Owing to the sudden death of
Mrs. Henry Miller
The marriage of her daughter
Sarah
to
Mr. Robert Sage
has been postponed

CARDS FOR RESERVED PEWS

To the family and those intimate friends who are to be seated in specially designated pews, a card (approximately 2 by 3 inches) may be enclosed, with "Pew No.   " engraved and the number filled in by hand. The style matches that of the invitation.

A more usual and less expensive custom is for the mother of the bride and the mother of the bridegroom each to write on her personal visiting card the number of the pew that each intimate friend or member of the family is to occupy.

Pew No. 7

Mrs. John Huntington Smith

600 East Fifty-Seventh Street

A similar card for a reserved front pew and inscribed "Within the ribbon" may be enclosed with the invitations, or "Within the ribbon" may be written on a visiting card and included with the invitation.

Pew cards are often sent, or given in person, after acceptances have been received, when the families of the bride and groom know how many reserved seats will be needed.

ADMISSION CARDS

Except in the case of a wedding held in a cathedral or other church which attracts sightseers, admission cards are no longer used. If it is necessary, a card of approximately 2 by 3 inches is engraved in the same style as the invitations:

```
┌─────────────────────────────────────────┐
│                                         │
│                                         │
│                                         │
│         Please present this card        │
│                                         │
│                    at                   │
│                                         │
│          The Washington Cathedral        │
│                                         │
│         Saturday, the first of August    │
│                                         │
│                                         │
│                                         │
└─────────────────────────────────────────┘
```

Only the holders of these cards will be admitted to the church at the time of the wedding.

AT HOME CARDS

If the bride and groom want their friends to know what their address is to be, an At Home card is included with the invitation. The size of the card is about 4 by 2¾ inches, slightly smaller than the reception card.

Many people receiving these cards put them away, intending to enter them in an address book or file. Later they come across the card, only to find they have entirely forgotten *who* would be at home at 1730 Taylor Street after October 16. Even though the couple are not married at the time the invitation is sent, in the interests of helpfulness and practicality, these cards should be engraved:

At home

after the fifteenth of November

3842 Olympia Drive

Houston 19, Texas

(For At Home cards to accompany wedding announcements, see Chapter 44.)

43

Invitations to wedding receptions

INVITATIONS TO A RECEPTION FOLLOWING THE CEREMONY

The invitation to the breakfast or reception following the church ceremony is usually engraved on a card to match the paper and engraving of the church invitation. If the latter is folded for the envelope, the card is a little smaller than half the full size of the invitation. For the smaller invitation that does not fold, it is approximately 2½ to 3 inches high by 3½ to 4 inches wide:

Reception

immediately following the ceremony

Essex County Country Club

West Orange

The favour of a reply is requested
Llewellyn Park, West Orange

Although better suited to the unfolded church invitation because of its larger size, this longer form is also perfectly correct:

Mr. and Mrs. John Huntington Smith

request the pleasure of

Miss Pauline Town's

company at the reception

following the ceremony

43 Park Avenue

R.s.v.p.

R.s.v.p. and R.S.V.P. are both correct. In France and in diplomatic circles the capital letters are the correct form.

Reception at the club of a friend:

When the wedding reception is given at a club through the courtesy of a friend of the hostess, the following announcement is always engraved in the lower right corner: "Through the courtesy of Mrs. John Smith Jones." This is put in the right corner because the left corner is reserved for the R.S.V.P.

INVITATION TO THE RECEPTION ONLY

On occasion, the church ceremony is private and a big reception follows. In these circumstances, the invitations to the ceremony are given orally and general invitations to the reception sent out for a somewhat later hour. The size and style of these invitations are exactly the same as those to the wedding itself:

Mr. and Mrs. John Huntington Smith
request the pleasure of
[name or names written in] *company*
at the wedding breakfast [or reception]
of [or for] *their daughter*
Millicent Jane
and
Mr. Sidney Strothers
Tuesday, the first of November
at half after twelve o'clock
555 Park Avenue
R.S.V.P.

A RECEPTION FOLLOWING A HOUSE WEDDING

When the reception follows a house wedding, no separate invitation is needed, as it is assumed that those attending the wedding will stay on.

INVITATIONS TO A BELATED WEDDING RECEPTION

A belated wedding reception is frequently held some time after the ceremony—perhaps after the honeymoon, or when the couple returns after an extended absence. In such a case the engraved invitation for the belated reception omits the word "wedding" thus:

Mr. and Mrs. Henry Peterson
request the pleasure of your company
at a reception
in honor of
Mr. and Mrs. Floyd Smith
on . . . .

A less formal invitation may be written on an informal; at the top write "In honor of" the young couple.

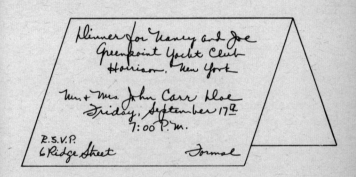

44

Wedding announcements

When the number of guests who can be accommodated at the marriage service or the reception is limited, announcements are sent to those friends of both families who would otherwise have been invited to be present. They require no gift or acknowledgment except what your own interest and impulse suggest. Announcements are never sent to anyone who has been invited to the wedding or the reception. And they should always be sent as soon after the wedding as possible.

CORRECT STYLE AND WORDING

The form (paper, engraving, envelopes) of the wedding announcement is the same as the wedding invitation in almost everything except wording. *(See Chapter 42.)*

Three forms of phrasing are equally correct: "have the honour to announce," "have the honour of announcing," or merely "announce." Although "Tuesday, April 24, 1967" is not incorrect, "Tuesday, the twenty-fourth of April" on one line and "One thousand nine hundred and sixty-seven" on the next is most formal.

Mr. and Mrs. John Fairplay

have the honour of

announcing the marriage of their daughter

Madeleine Anne

to

Mr. George Followes Highseas

Ensign United States Navy

Tuesday, the twenty-seventh of March

One thousand nine hundred and sixty-five

Washington, D. C.

The variations in wording necessitated by special circumstances (when the bride has a stepfather, or professional name, etc.) correspond to the variations in wedding invitations *(see Chapter 42)* with the following exceptions.

Whenever possible, announcements go out in the name of the bride's nearest kin, whether they have been present at the wedding or not. For example, invitations to a wedding given by the groom's parents carry their names, whereas announcements of the same marriage carry the names of the bride's parents.

Announcements for a young widow's marriage are the same as for a first wedding:

> *Mr. and Mrs. Maynard Banks*
> *announce the marriage of their daughter*
> *Priscilla Banks Loring*
> etc.

The announcement of the marriage of a widow of maturer years reads differently:

> *Mrs. William Phillip Hoyt*
> *and*
> *Mr. Worthington Adams*
> *announce their marriage*
> *on Monday, the second of November*
> *One thousand nine hundred and sixty-five*
> *at Saratoga Springs*
> *New York*

The parents of a young divorcée may announce her second marriage in the same form as if she were a widow:

> *Mr. and Mrs. Harvey Strong*
> *announce the marriage of their daughter*
> *Mary Strong Brooks*
> etc.

Or a divorcée may, with her husband, announce her own marriage:

> *Mrs. Strong Brooks*
> *and*
> *Mr. Robert Hanson*
> *announce their marriage*
> *on Saturday, the tenth of May*
> etc.

The bride who is an orphan and the bridegroom may announce their own marriage this way:

Miss Elizabeth Orphan
and
Mr. John Henry Bridegroom
announce their marriage
etc.

Or, if the wedding was given by a relative or friend, the announcement may be made in this way:

Mr. and Mrs. John Neighbor
announce the marriage of
Miss Elizabeth Orphan
etc.

AT HOME CARDS

When announcements are sent, the At Home notice may be engraved in the lower left-hand corner:

After the first of December
25 Elm Street, Greattown

Or cards in the same form as those used with wedding invitations may be enclosed *(see Chapter 43)*. Either form is perfectly correct. There is a third possibility, also. Because the marriage has already taken place, the card may read:

Mr. and Mrs. John Newlywed
will be at home
after November twelfth
25 Elm Street
Greattown

45

Other formal invitations

All formal invitations are engraved on white cards, either plain or plate-marked like those for wedding receptions, or written by hand on personal note paper.

Formal third-person invitations are sometimes written on paper headed by a very small monogram, but are never engraved on paper headed by an address. If the family has a coat of arms, it or the crest may be embossed without color on engraved invitations.

The size of the card of invitation varies with personal preference. The most graceful proportion is three units in height to four in width, or four high by three wide. The lettering is a matter of personal choice; the plainer the design, the safer. Punctuation is used only when words requiring separation occur on the same line, and in certain abbreviations, such as R.S.V.P. The time is never given as "nine-thirty" but as "half past nine o'clock" or, the more conservative form, "half after nine o'clock."

If the dance or dinner or whatever the entertainment is to be is given at one address and the hostess lives at another, both addresses are given.

BALLS AND DANCES
To a private dance:
   The form most often used by fashionable hostesses is this:

Mr. and Mrs. Harold Gilding

request the pleasure of

Miss Sally Waring's

company at a small dance

Monday, the first of January

at ten o'clock

400 Lake Shore Drive

R.s.v.p.

The expression "small dance" is often used no matter what the size of the ball, but it is not absolutely necessary.

Mr. and Mrs. Sidney Oldname

request the pleasure of your company

at a dance

Monday evening, January the third

at ten o'clock

The Fitz - Cherry

Kindly send response to
Brookmeadows,
Long Island

Even when the ball is given for a debutante daughter, her name does not necessarily appear, and the above forms may be used.

Other proper invitations in such cases are these:

Mr. and Mrs. Alexander de Puyster

request the pleasure of

Miss Rosalie Grey's

company at a dance in honour of their daughter

Miss Alice de Puyster

Monday, the tenth of January

at ten o'clock

One East Fiftieth Street

R.s.v.p.

Mr. and Mrs. James Town

Miss Pauline Town

request the pleasure of

Mr. and Mrs. Greatlake's

company on Monday, the third of January

at ten o'clock

400 Lake Shore Drive

Dancing

R. s. v. p.

The most formal invitation:

The most formal invitation to a private ball, no matter where it is given, announces merely that Mr. and Mrs. Somebody will be "At Home"—both words written with capital letters; the word "Dancing" is added in the lower left or right corner. It is engraved, usually in script, on a card of white bristol board about 5½ inches wide and 3¾ inches high. Like the wedding invitation, it is plain or it has an embossed crest without color. The precise form is this:

Mr. and Mrs. Davis Jefferson

At Home

Monday, the third of January

at ten o'clock

Town and Country Club

(It may be engraved in whatever style of lettering the family prefers.)

The invitation to a public ball:

The word "ball" is rarely used except in an invitation to a public one, or at least a semipublic one, such as may be given by a committee for a charity or by a club or association of some sort. For example:

The Entertainment Committee of the Greenwood Club
requests the pleasure of your company
at a Ball
to be held at the club house
on the evening of Thursday, the seventh of November
at ten o'clock
for the benefit of
The Neighborhood Hospital
Tickets five dollars

Invitations to a debutante assembly:

An invitation to present the debutante at an assembly reads thus:

The Committee of the Westchester Cotillion

invites

Mr. and Mrs. David S. Williams

to present

Miss Penelope Williams

at the Cotillion

on Friday, the ninth of September

at ten o'clock

Shenorock Shore Club

Rye, New York

An invitation to debutantes not being presented at the ball reads thus:

The Committee of the Mayfair Assembly

has the honor to extend to

Mrs. David S. Williams

an invitation for her daughter

Miss Penelope Williams

to attend

The Mayfair Assembly Dinner Dance

on

New Year's Eve

Saturday, December 31, 1964

Hotel Pierre Roof

nine o'clock

R.s.v.p.

An invitation to other guests invited to the ball:

The Governors of the Tuxedo Club
invite you to subscribe to
The Autumn Ball
to be held at
The Tuxedo Club
on Saturday, the twenty-second of October
Nineteen hundred and sixty-six
at eleven o'clock
Tuxedo Park, New York

R.S.V.P.

These invitations are accompanied by a card stating the amount of the subscription, where it should be sent, etc. A list of the debutantes being presented, the committee, and some-times the patrons, is printed inside the invitation.

INVITATION TO BE A PATRON

When patrons are asked to serve by written invitation, the correct wording is as follows:

> *The Committee of the Midwinter Ball*
> *has the honour to invite*
>
> *to be a Patron of the Ball*
> *for the benefit of*
> *The Children's Hospital*
> *at the Hotel Grand*
> *Friday evening, the thirtieth of October*
> *at nine o'clock*

Usually a card with return envelope is enclosed with the invitation for the convenience of the patron's answer.

INVITATIONS TO RECEPTIONS AND TEAS

Invitations to receptions and teas are somewhat smaller than those to a ball. The words "At Home" with capital letters may be changed to "will be at home" with small letters or "at Home" with a small "a." The time states a beginning and a terminating hour. A man's name appears only on a very unusual occasion. If the tea is given for a debutante, her name is put under that of her mother, and sometimes under that of her sister or the bride of her brother.

To a tea dance:

> *Mrs. Grantham Jones*
> *Miss Muriel Jones*
> *at Home*
> *on Tuesday, the third of December*
> *from four until seven o'clock*
> *The Hilton Hotel*
> *3751 Wildwood Boulevard   Dancing*

Or to a tea for a debutante:

Mrs. James Town
Mrs. James Town, junior
Miss Pauline Town
will be at home
Tuesday, the eighth of December
850 Fifth Avenue

When a man's name is included:

Mr. Town's name might appear with that of his wife if he were an artist and the reception were given in his studio to view his pictures; or if the reception were given to meet a distinguished guest, such as a bishop or governor, in which case "In honour of the Right Reverend William Ritual" or "To meet His Excellency the Governor of California" would be engraved at the top of the invitation.

Suitable wording for an evening reception:

To meet the Honorable George Stevens
Mr. and Mrs. James Town
at Home
Tuesday, the eighth of December
from nine until eleven o'clock

Note the use of the small *a* and a capital *H*.

THE CARD OF GENERAL INVITATION

Invitations to important entertainments are nearly always especially engraved so that nothing is written except the name of the person invited. But for the hospitable hostess, a card engraved in blank, so that it may serve for dinner, luncheon, dance, reception or whatever she may care to give, is a great help.

Mr. and Mrs. Harold Foster Stevens

request the pleasure of

company at

on

at   o'clock

Two Knob Hill

Already engraved cards similar to the example below may be purchased at any stationers.

Mr. and Mrs. Charles Watson James

request the pleasure of the company of

Mr. and Mrs. Maxwell

at Cocktails

on Tuesday, December 4th

at 6 o'clock

R. s. v. p.   185 Meadow Rd.

INVITATION BY MORE THAN ONE HOSTESS

The name of the hostess at whose house the party will be is usually put first. If one is a great deal older, her name may head the list. The invitation should make very clear where the event is to take place and where the acceptances and regrets are to be sent. For example, for the luncheon at Mrs. White's house:

> *Mrs. Walter David White*
> *Mrs. Henry Edward Black*
> *Mrs. Theodore Jamison Gray*
> *request the pleasure of your company*
> *at luncheon*
> *Tuesday, the tenth of November*
> *at half after one o'clock*
> *123 Sutton Place*

R.S.V.P.
Mrs. Walter David White

For the luncheon at a club or hotel:

> *Mrs. Walter David White*
> *Mrs. Henry Edward Black*
> *Mrs. Theodore Jamison Gray*
> *request the pleasure of your company*
> *at luncheon*
> *Tuesday, the tenth of November*
> *at half after one o'clock*
> *Hotel Pierre*

R.S.V.P.
Mrs. Walter David White
123 Sutton Place

INVITATION SENT BY AN ORGANIZATION

For example:

> *The Alpha Chapter*
> *of*
> *Beta Chi Delta*
> *requests the pleasure of your company*
> *on Monday, the twenty-third of February*
> *at four o'clock*
> *at a tea dance*
> *at the Beta Chi Delta House*
> *2 Campus Row*

INVITATION TO COMMENCEMENT

Each school, college and university follows its own established customs for Commencement Week. *(See Chapter 32.)*

Of the varying forms of invitation to commencement exercises sent, the following is the most usual:

The President and Faculty
of Hotchkiss College
request the pleasure of your company
at the Commencement Exercises
on Wednesday morning
the twentieth of June
at eleven o'clock
in the Sterling Gymnasium

HANDWRITTEN INVITATIONS

When the formal invitation to dinner or luncheon is written instead of engraved, note paper stamped with a house address or personal device is used. The wording and spacing follow the engraved models.

Mr. and Mrs. John Lindhost
request the pleasure of
Mr. and Mrs. Robert Gilding Jr.'s
company at dinner
on Tuesday, the sixth of December,
at eight o'clock.

If the device stamped on the paper does not contain the address, it is written below the hour. A telephone number never appears on a formal invitation. Note: "Jr." is used when appropriate.

An invitation should never be written like this:

Mr. & Mrs. J. Kindhost request the pleasure of Mr. & Mrs. James Town's company at dinner on Tuesday etc

This incorrect example has three faults: (1) Invitations in the third person must follow the prescribed form, and this does not. (2) The writing is crowded against the margins of the note paper. (3) The full name "John" should be used instead of the initial "J."

46

Informal invitations

With the exception of invitations to house parties, those sent to out-of-town guests, and those requiring a certain amount of formality, the invitation by note is almost a thing of the past. On informal occasions, the telephone is used almost exclusively. Be perfectly clear, however, about dates and hour and leave your guests in no doubt about what is intended. If you feel

that a written invitation is needed, you have a choice of
several possibilities.

VISITING-CARD INVITATIONS

For an informal dance, for a tea to meet a guest, or for
bridge, a lady may use her ordinary visiting card. *(See Chapter
49.)* Because the Post Office will not accept very small envelopes, a practical size should be ordered for mailing. Although larger, they match the card in color and texture.

The following examples are correct in every detail—including the abbreviations; they are written in black ink.

> *To meet*
> *Miss Millicent Gordon*
>
> **Mrs. John Kindhart**
>
> *Tues. Jan. 7*
> *Dancing at 9 o'ck.*
>
>   1350 Madison Avenue

> *Wed. Jan. 8.*
> *Bridge at 2 o'ck.*
>
> **Mrs. John Kindhart**
>
> *R. s. v. p.*   1350 Madison Avenue

INFORMALS

The use of informals *(small folding cards, described in Chapter 49)* for invitations is correct and practical. When the card is engraved with your name:

> *Cocktail Buffet*
>
> **Mr. and Mrs. Allen Burns**
>
> *Sunday, June 9th*
> *6:30 o'clock*
>
> *10 Haverstraw Rd.*

If the card is monogrammed or unmarked, the informal invitation includes your name. If the card is going to a close friend, the signature need only be the first name, but to others you must include the last name.

> *GBT*   *June 6*
>
> *Dear Sally,*
> *Could you and Jim*
> *join us for a barbecue*
> *dinner on Sat. June 12th?*
>   *Lucy Brooks*
>
> *9 Holly St.*

THE "SINGLE NOTE" CARD

A useful variation of the informal is an unfolded card, about 4½ by 3½ inches, with the address engraved in the upper right corner and the name slightly above the center, leaving room beneath for the message.

HANDWRITTEN NOTES AND ANSWERS

Informal invitations are written in the second person, and, though called informal because they have greater latitude than the prescribed pattern of the third-person invitation and reply, they too follow a fairly definite formula. The colon is not used after the salutation in a social note—either no punctuation or a comma, as you prefer.

The informal dinner and luncheon invitation is not spaced according to set words on each line but written in two paragraphs. From a younger to an older couple:

Jan. 2, 1964

Dear Mrs. Steele,
Will you and Mr. Steele dine with us on Thursday, the seventh of January, at eight o'clock?
Hoping so much to see you then, I am
Very sincerely,
Caroline Robinson Town

Or to a woman engaged to a man unknown to the writer of this invitation:

Jan. 2, 1964

Dear Phyllis,
Will you and your fiancé lunch with us this coming Saturday, at one o'clock?
Looking forward to meeting him,
Affectionately,
Caroline Town

Acceptance:

> *Dear Mrs. Town,*
> *We would be delighted to dine with you on Thursday the seventh at eight o'clock.*
> *Thanking you for your kind thought of us,*
> > *Sincerely yours,*
> > *Jane Steele*

Regret:

> *Dear Mrs. Town,*
> *We are so sorry that we cannot accept your kind invitation for Saturday because of another engagement.*
> *With many thanks for thinking of us, and I will bring John over to meet you soon.*
> > *Sincerely,*
> > *Phyllis Steele*

(For invitations to a house party, see Chapter 29; to an engagement party, see Chapter 35.)

A BACHELOR'S INVITATIONS

The bachelor's invitations are the same as those sent out by a hostess. In giving a party of any size he may write on his visiting card.

Saturday, April 7.
at 4. o'ck.

Mr. Anthony Dauber

To hear Tonini play.

Park Studio

47

Recalling and requesting invitations

WITHDRAWING AN INVITATION

If because of illness or for some other reason, invitations have to be recalled, the following forms are correct. They are always printed, because there is no time for engraving.

> *Owing to the sudden illness of their daughter*
> *Mr. and Mrs. John Huntington Smith*
> *are obliged to recall their invitations*
> *for Tuesday, the tenth of June*

When an engagement is broken off after the wedding invitations have been issued:

> *Mr. and Mrs. Benjamin Nottingham*
> *announce that the marriage of their daughter*
> *Mary Katherine*
> *to*
> *Mr. Jerrold Atherton*
> *will not take place*

REQUESTING AN INVITATION

Ordinarily one never asks for an invitation for oneself anywhere. But when regretting an invitation, it is quite proper to explain that you are expecting weekend guests. Ordinarily the hostess-to-be says, "I'm sorry!" But if she is having a big buffet lunch or a tea or cocktail party, she may say, "Do bring them. We will be delighted to have them!"

An invitation for any general entertainment may be requested for a stranger—especially for a house guest—still more especially for a man.

> Dear Mrs. Eminent,
>   My nephew, David Park, is staying with us. May he come to your dance on Friday?
>
> > Very sincerely yours,
> > Caroline Robinson Town

If the nephew had been a niece instead, Mrs. Town would have added, "If it will be inconvenient for you to include her, please do not hesitate to say so." This gives Mrs. Eminent a chance to answer that since her list of men was rather short she would be glad to have Mary come if Mrs. Town can find a man to escort her. A young girl may ask her hostess if she may bring a man to her dance.

48

Acceptances and regrets

The form of acceptance or regret depends upon the form of the invitation received, for the degree of formality or informality must be the same. The telephone presents no problems. For the handwritten answer, there are formulas that are invariably used.

THE FORMAL ACCEPTANCE OR REGRET

Whether the invitation is to a dance, a dinner, or whatever, the answer is identical save for the name of the occasion. (In the following form you may substitute "a dance," etc., for "dinner.")

> *Mr. and Mrs. Donald Lovejoy*
> *accept with pleasure*
> *the kind invitation of*
> *Mr. and Mrs. William Jones Johnson, Jr.*
> *for dinner*
> *on Monday, the tenth of December*
> *at eight o'clock*

The formula for regret:

> *Mr. and Mrs. Timothy Kerry*
> *regret that they are unable to accept*
> *the kind invitation of*
> *Mr. and Mrs. Harvey Brent Smith*
> *for Monday, the tenth of December*

In accepting an invitation, the day and hour are always repeated. But in declining an invitation this is not necessary.

To more than one hostess:

If the names of two or more hostesses appear on an invitation, the envelope is addressed to the one at whose house the party is to take place; or if it is to be at a club or hotel, to the name and address indicated below the R.S.V.P. (Without such indication, you must address it to all of them at the hotel or club.)

But when you write your answer, you repeat the same order of names that appeared on the invitation, no matter how the envelope is to be addressed:

> *Mrs. Donald Lovejoy*
> *accepts with pleasure*
> *the kind invitation of*
> *Mrs. White and*
> *Mrs. Black and*
> *Mrs. Grey*
> *for Tuesday, the tenth of November*
> *at half after one o'clock*

TO A WEDDING

An invitation to only the church requires no answer (unless the invitation is a personally written note). An invitation to the reception or breakfast is answered on the first page of a sheet of full-sized letter paper or on fold-over note paper; although it is written by hand, the spacing of the words must be followed as though they were engraved.

Acceptance:

Mr. and Mrs. Robert Gilding, Jr.
accept with pleasure
Mr. and Mrs. Smith's
kind invitation for
Tuesday, the first of June

Regret:

Mr. and Mrs. Richard Brown
regret that they are unable to accept
Mr. and Mrs. Smith's
kind invitation for
Tuesday, the first of June

The alternate form, "The kind invitation of," is equally correct.

Combination acceptance and regret:

It is entirely proper for a wife or husband to take it for granted that either one alone will be welcome at a general wedding reception and to send an acceptance worded as follows:

Mrs. John Brown
accepts with pleasure
Mr. and Mrs. Smith's
kind invitation for
Saturday, the tenth of June
but regrets that
Mr. Brown
will be absent at that time
or
will be unable to attend

If the wife could not attend, the wording would merely transpose Mr. and Mrs.

FORMULAS FOR OTHER OCCASIONS
To an organization:

> *Miss Mary Jones*
> *accepts with pleasure*
> *the kind invitation of*
> *The Alpha Chapter*
> *of*
> *Beta Chi Delta*
> *for Monday afternoon, February 23rd*

To a committee:
If the name of the committee or its organization is long or complicated, you may write your reply in the following form:

> *Mr. and Mrs. Geoffrey Johnson*
> *accept with pleasure*
> *your kind invitation*
> *for a Ball*
> *on Saturday, the first of January*

To a multiple debut:

> *Doctor and Mrs. Ronald Graham*
> *Miss Joan Graham*
> *accept with pleasure*
> *your kind invitation*
> *for a dinner dance*
> *Saturday, February 10th*
> *at nine o'clock*

INFORMAL REPLIES

When an invitation is sent on a visiting card or an informal, the reply may be telephoned or written briefly on your own card.

Visiting-card replies:

Accepts with pleasure!
Wednesday at 4.

Mrs. Robert Gilding, junior

14 Water Street

Sincere regrets
Wed. Jan. 8

Mr. and Mrs. Henry Osborn

Informals:

In replying on an informal, use the same degree of formality as was used in the invitation.

EPL   June 4

Dear Sue

We'd love to come
to dinner on June
10th at 8:00.

Thanks so much
Betsy

Brook Street   Holyoke   Mass.

So sorry we can't
make it on the sixth.
We'll be at the Cape.

Gloria

If your informal is engraved as a visting card:

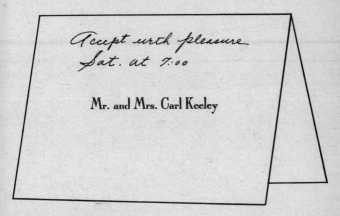

Accept with pleasure
Sat. at 7:00

Mr. and Mrs. Carl Keeley

On a plain informal:

Accept with pleasure

Saturday at 7:00

Fran and Carl Kelley

ANSWER CARDS

Regrettably the custom of sending "answer cards" with invitations to debut parties and subscription dances is too widespread to be ignored. It arose out of sheer necessity because teen-agers appeared at parties without having answered the invitation sent to them. Today, when parties are served and food prepared by catering services, a hostess must be able to tell them the exact number of guests expected. Therefore, while we deplore the lack of good manners which makes sending these cards necessary, we recognize that it seems the only way to obtain the answers.

The small answer card is engraved in the same style as the invitation:

Most invitations include a self-addressed return envelope.

Having returned the card, the receiver does not send a formal reply.

WHEN IT IS NECESSARY TO CHANGE YOUR ANSWER

If you find you cannot attend a function which you have already accepted, let the hostess know immediately. In most cases a telephone call is best, as it is quick and gives you a chance to explain your problem and express your regrets. If you prefer, and there is ample time, you may write a short note, giving the reason and your apologies.

Sometimes a person refuses an invitation for perfectly legitimate reasons and then finds that circumstances change and he can attend after all. If the affair is a party involving a limited number, such as for bridge, a theater party or a seated dinner, he must swallow his disappointment and hope to be asked again, as the hostess will have filled his place. If the party is a large reception, a cocktail buffet, a picnic where another guest or two would not cause complications, he may call the hostess, explain his situation and ask if he may change his regret to an acceptance.

49

Visiting cards, informals and business cards

VISITING CARDS

Nowadays, the visiting card (in its matching envelope) has taken the place of the written note of invitation to informal parties of every description. A card with "With deepest sympathy" written at the top is enclosed with flowers sent to a funeral, or it may be left at the home of the deceased. They are also enclosed with presents. (Most shops provide small white cards and envelopes if you do not have your own with you.)

A married woman's card is usually 3 to 3½ inches wide and 2¼ to 2½ inches high. (Very young girls use a small card.) A man's card is narrower: from 3 to 3¼ inches long and 1¼ to 1⅝ inches high. The cards are white or cream-white glazed or unglazed bristol board of medium thickness, and they are not plate-marked. (Those made of thin parchment paper are convenient if a greater quantity must be carried.)

Either shaded Roman or script is good form. Matching envelopes, large enough to obey postal regulations, may be ordered at the same time.

People in cities often have the address in the lower right corner. People with both town and country houses occasionally have separate cards for each.

Initials are used only when names are awkwardly long. A man may have his cards engraved "Mr. John H. T. Smith" or "Mr. J. H. Titherington Smith." His wife's card uses the same form.

A married woman's card (approximately 3¼ inches by 2¼ inches):

Mrs. John Foster Hughes

"Mr. and Mrs." cards:

Mr. and Mrs. John Foster Hughes

14 Willow Road

A married man's card: A man's card is engraved with his title, Doctor or Mr., even though he has "junior" after his name. (Doctor is preferred to Dr.) The size is 3¼ inches by 1½ inches.

Mr. John Foster Hughes, Jr.

A widow's name: A widow always continues to use her husband's Christian names: Mrs. John Hunter Titherington Smith (or Mrs. J. H. Titherington Smith), but never Mrs. Sarah Smith. If a widow's son has the name of his father, the widow may add "Sr." to her name when her son marries, especially if they live in the same village where no street address is used.

John Smith, Jr., John Smith, 2nd, and their wives: The fact that a man's name has "Jr." added at the end in no way takes the place of "Mr." His card is engraved "Mr. John Hunter Smith, Jr." and his wife's "Mrs. John Hunter Smith, Jr." "Junior" may be engraved in full; when it is, it is not spelled with a capital *j*. John, second, or John, third, may have 2nd or 3rd after their names, but II or III in Roman numerals is preferable.

A divorcée's card: Some women, if they have no children and if their divorce has been a bitter one, prefer to give up their married name entirely and return to being "Miss Susan Coleman." This is permissible. The proper name for a divorcée, however, is her maiden name combined with her husband's surname. Miss Susan Coleman, who is divorced from Franklin Butler, becomes Mrs. Coleman Butler, and her cards are engraved in this form.

A professional woman's card: A woman who has earned a professional title uses her title or professional name in public, while in private life she uses the name of her husband. A spinster who is a practicing physician uses the title of Doctor socially as well as professionally. (If she is a doctor of philosophy, she calls herself "Doctor" only in a classroom or when she is introduced as a speaker.)

The solution for a woman who is a medical doctor is to have two cards—one for business, engraved "Helen Corbin, M.D." or "Doctor Helen Corbin," and one for social use, engraved "Mrs. Richard Ford Corbin." On a "Mr. and Mrs." card, she remains "Mrs." If her husband is also a doctor, the card reads "Dr. and Mrs. Richard Ford Corbin."

A boy's card: A boy never puts "Mr." on his cards until he leaves school or becomes eighteen: many use cards without "Mr." until they have finished college.

Cards of a young girl: A young girl's cards, after she is fourteen, have "Miss" before her name: "Miss Sarah Smith," not "Miss Sally Smith."

Titles on cards: A doctor, a clergyman, or a military officer in active service, and holders of title-bestowing offices all have their cards engraved with their titles: Doctor Henry Gordon (an M.D.); The Reverend William Goode; Colonel Thomas Doyle; Judge Horace Rush; Senator James Widelands. A person holding high degrees does not add their letters to his name, and his cards are not engraved "Professor." The double card reads Doctor and Mrs. Henry Gordon, Judge and Mrs. Horace Rush, etc. It is always best to engrave titles in full.

Card of a governor:

The Governor of Nevada

on a card slightly larger or more nearly square than an ordinary man's card.

Card of a mayor:

The Mayor of Chicago

or, if he prefers,

Mr. John Lake
Mayor of Chicago

A diplomat uses his title and United States of America rather than America or American. Titles of courtesy have no place either in a signature or on a visiting card: The American title of courtesy, "The Honorable," is never correct on a card.

The professional card of a doctor or surgeon is James Smith, M.D. His social card is Doctor or Dr. James Smith, as he prefers. (Dr. is not incorrect; but Doctor is somewhat better form.)

(For the use of visiting cards as invitations, see Chapter 46; as messages of condolence, see Chapter 35.)

INFORMALS

The small fold-over cards known as informals are convenient when you want, for example, to write a very brief note but one that requires more space than is afforded by a visiting card. If you wish, you may have them engraved. Or you may simply have your monogram in the upper left corner.

Mr. Harold Hicks Harrison

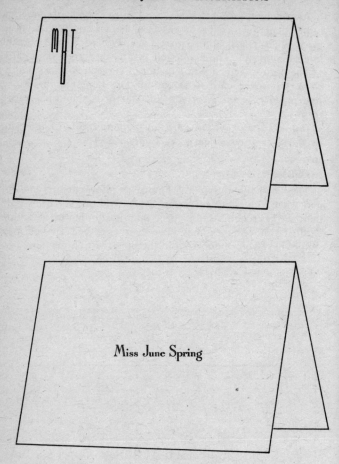

Informals are correct and practical for invitations *(see Chapter 46)*, but they cannot substitute for visiting cards when you make a formal call. They are enclosed with a gift only if you wish to write a personal message on the inner page.

BUSINESS AND PROFESSIONAL CARDS

Business cards are never used for social purposes and must not be confused with visiting cards. When an employee or an executive of a company makes a business call on another company or on a client or a prospective client, he sends in his card or leaves it as a record of his visit.

The card of an employee usually has the name and address of the company in the center of the card with the employee's name in the lower left corner and the telephone number in the lower right corner. An executive has his or her name in the center with his or her position in the company in smaller letters under the name. The name and address of the company are then put in the lower left corner. The telephone number is usually put in the lower right corner.

Business cards are approximately 3½ inches by 2 inches. They do not require the use of full names; that is, a man's business card may read "Mr. John Smith" (whereas his social card reads "Mr. John Hunter Titherington Smith") if he is known simply as "John Smith" in his business life and signs his letters in that form.

Professional cards differ from business cards in that no company name appears.

HAROLD HICKS HARRISON

500 WALL STREET
NEW YORK, N. Y.

MARKET 6-7272

50

Informal calls and informal visits

The custom of making formal calls is pretty much a thing of the past. But certain circumstances still require them. In Washington, members of diplomatic or military circles exchange calls. Members of the military or the diplomatic service arriving at a new post call on their superiors. Calls are exchanged between officers on military posts.

In addition, there are certain visits that all of us must make. A visit of condolence is paid at once to a friend when a death occurs in the immediate family. You ask if Mrs. Jackson feels like seeing you and, if you are admitted, you ask if there is anything you can do. If you barely know the family you may simply leave your card with "With deepest sympathy" written at the top. A lady does not call on a man, but writes him a note of sympathy. *(See also Chapter 34.)*

When going to see, or inquire about, a friend who has been very ill, it is thoughtful to take a gift of a book or fruit or flowers or perhaps, if you know of something she likes and is allowed to eat, you may take something from your kitchen.

Everyone invited to a wedding may call upon the bride on her return from the honeymoon. When a man marries a girl from a distant place, his friends and neighbors should go to see her as soon as she is at home.

A visit of congratulation is paid a new mother, and, of course, it is always very pleasing if you can take a present to the baby.

HOW TO MAKE A FIRST VISIT

In large cities, neighbors seldom call on each other. But when strangers move into a neighborhood in a small town or in the country, nearby residents usually call on them. The newcomers wait for the old residents to call on them, but by appearing friendly and outgoing they may hasten this "breaking the ice."

When a stranger moves in near you, you call, and if the lady herself opens the door—or you find her sitting on her porch—you say, "How do you do—I'm Nancy Jones, I live in the brick house across the street." The new neighbor says, "How kind of you to come to see me!" and invites you into her living room or asks you to join her on the porch. After ten to fifteen minutes, you usually leave, unless your hostess says, "Oh, do stay a little longer." When you are ready to go, say, "Do come and see me soon!" The new neighbor says, "I'll be glad to," and both of you make your farewells.

Returning a first visit:

First visits should be returned with considerable punctuality. When hospitality is shown you by two or more hostesses together, you are indebted to both or all equally, if you know them equally. If you know only one of the hostesses, you need not return the hospitality of the other (or others) unless the opportunity arises. When returning the hospitality of these several hostesses, it is never necessary that you invite them together.

INFORMAL VISITS

There are no rules for the casual visit between close friends except those which might be set up between them. Etiquette only requires that they be considerate to each other and offend no outsiders. However, many visits made between less intimate friends are not in the category of a formal call. Friends making or receiving these informal visits should know and follow certain rules.

THE UNEXPECTED VISITOR

No one, with the exception of closest friends and immediate family, should ever be an "unexpected visitor." Occasionally an unannounced "drop-in" works out well, but far more often it is most inconvenient to the one visited: she may have previous plans, her hair may be in curlers, her child may be sick, she may be in the middle of preparing dinner or she may simply be resting. Therefore, do not make a visit without making your intentions known, either by a telephone call, or, if you live some distance away, by a note, and allow enough time for a reply. Do not say, "We are coming on Saturday, etc." but rather, "If you and John are free Saturday, may we drop by . . . ?"

When you are the recipient of one of these unannounced visits, you have every right to carry on with any previous plans you might have. If Aunt Sally arrives unexpectedly from three hundred miles away and you had been planning to go to a church supper, suggest that she go along with you. If, however, you were expected at the Howards' for bridge, you simply ask her to make herself at home until your return, making sure there are enough ingredients in the refrigerator with which she can, if she chooses, make a light meal herself.

When the visitor is a friend from nearby, you merely say quite frankly, "I'm terribly sorry, but we were just leaving for dinner at the Hornsbys'. Could you come back another time?" And make the future date definite then and there. If you have just started your dinner when a caller drops in, try to make the meal stretch to include her. If she says, "Oh, no, thank you—I've just eaten," you pull up a chair for her and ask her forgiveness while you finish your meal.

CHILDREN AND PETS

Unless they are specifically invited, it is better to leave children—and pets—home when you visit friends.

A smart housewife who knows that she will have young visitors from time to time—either children of friends, nieces, nephews or grandchildren—makes preparations in advance: she removes breakable articles and those which might be dangerous from low tables, shuts the doors to rooms "off limits" and sees that doors to cellar steps and low windows are tightly closed. Then she checks her supply of recreational materials. A basket or sack of simple toys—coloring books, blocks, comic books, wind-up cars—makes the visit enjoyable for both mother and hostess. And, of course, this same clever lady has a supply of cookies and milk or soft drinks ready to fill in when the novelty of the toys wears off.

The mother herself can make her child a welcome guest in many ways: She does not take him visiting until he learns the meaning of "No"; she brings a basket of his favorite toys; above all, she sets a time limit for her visit.

Pets, no matter how well behaved at home, should not be taken along on visits unless they are invited. Fido may be irresistible to you, but to your hostess who has new rugs or upholstery, or may be allergic to dog hairs, he may be anything but a welcome visitor.

VISITING THE SICK

There are a few do's and don'ts that may be helpful for visitor and patient in a hospital or a home.

Don't bring as your gift foods such as chocolates or cakes that the patient may not be permitted to have.

Whenever possible, bring flowers with their own container. Most florists will arrange flowers in inexpensive (even disposable) containers at no additional charge. Of course, heavily scented flowers have no place in the sickroom. Potted plants give the patient many moments of pleasure.

Don't worry a patient about anything that you feel might upset or disturb him. If you wish to speed his recovery, bring him only cheerful, encouraging news. Don't talk to others about his illness in front of him, or ask him to discuss it unless he volunteers.

Make up your mind before you arrive that you will stay no more than fifteen or twenty minutes, and stick to it, no matter how much your friend may beg you to stay. If other visitors arrive while you are there, leave sooner, so that they may have their share of the patient's time without overtiring him.

The vast majority of hospital patients nowadays find themselves in semiprivate rooms or larger wards. Therefore voices of visitors are naturally kept lower. Any smoking that is done must have the permission of all the occupants of the room. When in doubt, don't smoke. If you are going to the snack bar or restaurant to bring a dish of ice cream or a candy bar to your friend, ask the other person in a semiprivate room if you can bring him anything at the same time.

If another patient in a room wishes to rest, draw the curtains between the beds to give him as much privacy and quiet as possible. On the other hand, if he and your friend have become friendly, include him in the conversation and your visit will be doubly appreciated.

It is perfectly proper for a woman to send flowers to any man she knows when he is seriously ill or convalescing—cut flowers, a plant, or terrarium which requires very little care.

PART TEN

PROTOCOL IN OFFICIAL CIRCLES

51

An invitation to the White House

FORMAL

An invitation to lunch or dine at The White House is a command and automatically cancels any other engagement not of the utmost importance. The reply is written by hand. It is mailed the day the invitation is received or delivered by hand to The White House. The reason for refusing such an invitation must be stated in the note of regret—unavoidable absence from Washington, the recent death of a close relative or actual illness.

The correct forms for replies are:

Mr. and Mrs. Richard Worldly
have the honor to accept
the kind invitation of
The President and Mrs. Washington
for dinner on Thursday, the eighth of May
at eight o'clock

Mr. and Mrs. Robert Franklin
regret extremely
that owing to Mr. Franklin's illness
they will be unable to accept
the kind invitation of
The President and Mrs. Jefferson
for dinner on Friday, the first of May

The note to a disappointed hostess:

Mr. and Mrs. Richard Worldly
regret extremely
that an invitation to The White House
prevents their keeping
their previous engagement for
Tuesday, the first of December

INFORMAL

Informal invitations to dinner or luncheon at The White House may be sent by letters, telegrams or telephone messages from the President's secretary or his wife's secretary. The replies are sent in the same form to whoever issued the invitations and are written on personal stationery.

A typical invitation:

Dear Mr. Heathcote,
   Mrs. Harrison has asked me to invite you to have lunch with her at The White House on Thursday, the sixteenth of May. Luncheon will be at one o'clock.
                                    Yours truly,
                                    Eleanor Smithers
                                    Secretary to Mrs. Harrison

The reply reads:

Dear Miss Smithers,
   Will you please tell Mrs. Harrison that I shall be delighted to lunch with her at The White House on Thursday, the sixteenth of May. Thank you very much.
                                    Sincerely,
                                    Frances Heathcote

To the luncheon Mrs. Heathcote wears a dress that she might wear to any similar gathering; a hat and gloves are obligatory.

DINNER AT THE WHITE HOUSE

An engraved invitation to The White House means black tie unless white tie is specified on the invitation. For black tie the men wear stiff shirts and collars and a dinner jacket. Women wear evening clothes, and if it is a white-tie dinner, long gloves.

All the names of guests expected at The White House are posted with the guards at the gate. You announce your name and wait a few seconds until you are recognized.

After the guests arrive, the President and his wife enter and speak to each guest and shake hands. Guests, of course, remain standing.

At a formal dinner, the President goes into the dining room first with the highest ranking woman guest. His wife follows with the highest ranking man guest.

DETAILS OF WHITE HOUSE ETIQUETTE

The following details represent the conventional pattern followed and adapted by each administration.

When you are invited to The White House, you must arrive several minutes before the hour specified so that you may be standing in the drawing room when the President makes his entry. The President, followed by his wife, enters, makes a tour of the room, shaking hands with each guest. When your turn comes, you bow. If he talks to you, you address him as "Mr. President." In a long conversation you vary "Mr. President" with "Sir" occasionally. You call the wife of the President "Mrs. Washington" and treat her as you would any formal hostess. You do not sit down as long as either the President or his wife remains standing. No one leaves until after the President has withdrawn from the room. Then the guests bid each other good night and leave promptly.

Requests to see the President on a business matter are made through one of the Presidential aides—the one closest to the subject you wish to discuss—or through your congressman. For a business appointment with the President, you always arrive a few minutes ahead of the appointed time. If a buzzer rings when you are in a corridor, an attendant will ask you to step behind a closed door. The buzzer means that the

President or members of the family are leaving or entering. This precaution is for their safety and privacy.

Don't smoke unless you are invited to.

Do not take a present unless you have cleared it with an aide, otherwise the Secret Service men may become alarmed.

Nor should you *send* anything to The White House without receiving permission from his secretary or one of his aides.

52

The flag of the United States

GENERAL RULES

The following rules and customs are followed to show our respect for our flag.

Every day in the year between sunrise and sunset is a proper time to fly the flag; although customarily it is not flown in inclement weather unless a particular occasion requires its display. It may also be displayed at night as part of a patriotic display.

On Memorial (or Decoration) Day, May 30th, the flag is displayed at half-staff until noon and at full staff thereafter till sunset. Flag Day is June 14th.

The flag is never used as decoration on a portion of a costume or athletic uniform, as embroidery on cushions, scarves or handkerchiefs, or on paper napkins or boxes. It is never so used that objects may be placed on it or over it. When the flag is used in the unveiling of a statue or monument, it is never used as a covering of the object to be unveiled. It is unlawful to use the flag in a registered trademark which comprises "the flag, coat of arms, or other insignia of

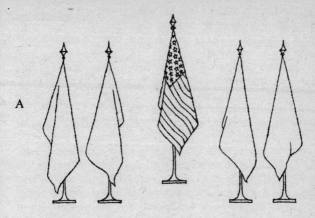

A

the United States or any simulation thereof." It is never displayed in connection with advertising of any kind. For festoons, rosettes or other draperies, bunting of blue (uppermost), white and red is used, but never the flag itself.

DISPLAYING THE FLAG

When displayed over the middle of a street, the flag is suspended vertically with the union (the blue field) to the north in an east-west street, or to the east in a north-south street.

When displayed with another flag from crossed staffs, the

flag of the United States is on the right (the flag's own right) and its staff in front of the staff of the other flag.

The flag is raised briskly and lowered slowly and solemnly.

When it is flown at half-mast, the flag is hoisted to the peak for a moment, then lowered to the half-mast position. Before lowering the flag for the day, it is again raised to the peak.

When flags of states or cities or pennants of societies are flown on the same halyard with the flag of the United States, the latter is always at the peak. When flown from adjacent staffs, the national flag is hoisted first and lowered last.

When the flag is suspended over a sidewalk from a rope, extending from house to pole at the edge of the sidewalk, it is hoisted out from the building, toward the pole, union first.

When the flag is displayed from a staff projecting horizontally or at an angle from a windowsill, balcony or the front of a building, the union of the flag should go clear to the peak of the staff (except when at half-mast).

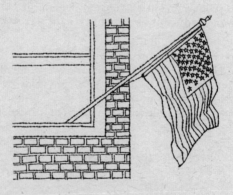

When the flag is used to cover a casket, it is so placed that the union is at the head and over the left shoulder. The flag is never lowered into the grave or allowed to touch the ground.

When the flag is displayed in a manner other than flown from a staff, it should be flat, not tucked or draped, whether indoors or out. When displayed vertically against a wall or in a window, the union is uppermost and to the observer's left.

When carried in a procession with another flag or flags, the American flag is either on the marching right or, when there is a line of other flags, in the center of that line.

When a number of flags of states or cities are grouped and displayed from staffs, our national flag is at the center or at the highest point of the group. If the flags of two or more nations are displayed, they are flown from separate staffs of the same height and the flags are of approximately equal size. International usage forbids the display of the flag of one nation above that of another nation in time of peace.

When the flag is used in a church, on the chancel or on a platform, it is placed on a staff on the clergyman's right, other flags on his left. When displayed in the body of the church, the flag is on the congregation's right as it faces the chancel.

When used as an identifying symbol on an automobile, it is flown on a small staff affixed on the end of the front bumper, on the right looking forward and within the line of the fender. When used this way, the staff should be tall enough so that the flag clears the car hood. Alternately, a small flag may be flown from the radiator cap. If the flag has become soiled or wind-torn, replace it promptly.

The flag is *never* hung upside down except as a signal of distress.

CARE OF THE FLAG

Every precaution should be taken to prevent the flag from becoming soiled or torn. Do not permit it to touch the ground or water or a floor, and in handling it do not let it brush against other objects. If it gets wet, hang it smoothly until dry; never roll or fold it while still damp.

Flags should be dry-cleaned, not washed.

PART ELEVEN

GOOD MANNERS FOR EVERY DAY

53

On the telephone

THE BUSINESS TELEPHONE

Answering the office phone:

When telephone calls go through a switchboard, the operator usually answers the ring by giving the name of the company, and sometimes adds some such greeting as "ABC Company, good morning." When the call is transferred or goes directly through, the person answering identifies himself and his department: "Mr. Hugo, accounting department." If answering for someone else, as a secretary does, she gives her employer's name as well as her own: "Mr. Carlson's office, Miss Norton speaking." If her employer is not in, or if she wishes to protect him from unnecessary calls, she offers to help the caller if she can or, if not, take a message: "He's not available at the moment. May I take a message?" or "He's attending a meeting this morning. Could I help you?" If he is in his office, she asks, "May I tell him who is calling?" With an evasive caller, she may have to ask for his name directly: "Who is calling, please?"

She should keep a pad and pencil next to the phone so that she can take a message.

Placing a call:

As soon as your call is answered, identify yourself, and unless the person you are calling knows you well, name your organization. "This is Robert Kramer, of the Hobbs Company. May I speak to Mr. Hughes?"

To a woman, a salesman announces himself correctly as, "This is Mr. Sales of the Blank Company." But to a gentleman, he may omit the "Mr."

A young woman in business says, "This is Miss Caesar of the Wheel Tyre Co."

A most discourteous telephone habit is that of the businessman who tells his secretary to call Mr. Jones and then is not waiting to take the call. The secretary, for example, dials the number; a voice announces, "A. B. Jones Company"; the secretary says, "Mr. Brown is calling Mr. Jones." Promptly Mr. Jones says, "Hello, Brown!" only to hear a secretary explain, "Mr. Brown is busy on another wire. He'll be with you in a moment." If you have placed a call, do not pick up another incoming call until you have finished your business with the person you called first.

THE TELEPHONE IN THE HOME

"Hello" correct at home:

The correct way to answer a house telephone is still "Hello." In all big cities, telephones are rung so persistently by every type of stranger who wants to sell something or to ask a favor that many prominent people keep their personal telephone numbers unlisted. The last thing that they want to do, therefore, is to announce, "Miss Star speaking." It is far more practical to say "Hello" and let the one calling ask for Miss Star. If she herself answers, a friend recognizing her voice says, "Hello, Mary. This is Kate."

Who is calling, please?

When the telephone in the home is answered by someone other than the head of the household, the response to "May I speak to Mrs. Brown, please?" is usually, "Just a moment, please." If, however, Mrs. Brown has told the maid (or a child) that she can only take certain calls, the one answering says, "Mrs. Brown can't come to the phone just now: may I have your name and she will call you as soon as she can?"

When a woman is alone in the house, she definitely *should* ask "Who is calling?" before giving out any information as to her husband's whereabouts or return. This is not only correct— it's a necessary safety precaution.

If the caller refuses to leave a message or give his name, he need not expect Mrs. Brown to speak to him.

Giving one's name:

When talking with strangers, titles are always used, but in other situations the following rules hold good: An older person announcing herself or himself to one who is much younger says, "This is Mrs. Elder" or "Miss Spinster" or "Mr. Elder."

A young lady, whether married or single, says, "This is Marie Manners," or to one whom she knows socially, but who is not on a first-name-calling basis, "Hello, Mrs. Knox? This is Marie Manners." Mrs. Knox answers, "Good morning, Mrs. Manners!"

A gentleman calling a lady always says, "This is George Smartling"—never "Mr. Smartling."

If a young man calls a friend and the answering voice is that of a friend or a member of the friend's family, he says, "This is Jim Brown" or "This is Jim." If the voice is that of a maid he says, "This is Mr. James Brown. May I speak to Mr. Gray?"

Invitations by telephone:

When Mrs. Jones issues an invitation by telephone, she says simply: "Is that you, Mrs. Smith [*or* Sarah]? This is Alice Jones [*or* Alice, if the other is an intimate friend]. Will you and your husband [*or* John] dine with us next Tuesday?"

Mrs. Smith: "I'm so sorry, we can't. We are busy that night." Or "We'd love to" and repeats, "Next Tuesday at eight," to be sure there is no misunderstanding of date or time.

Invitations for a weekend visit are often telephoned: "Hello, Ethel. This is Alice. Will you and Arthur come for the weekend on the sixteenth?" "The sixteenth? That's two weeks from tomorrow. We'd love to!" (*If Mrs. Jones is not telephoning herself and the message is given by or received by a butler or a maid, see the discussion of the formal invitation by telephone, Chapter 45.*)

It is a bad habit to preface an invitation with "Hello, John. Are you going to be busy Monday afternoon?" This puts John in an awkward position. If he answers, "No," he may feel he has to accept the invitation that follows whether he wants to or not. If he answers, "I have an engagement," he may lose out on an attractive invitation. A young woman who says she has an engagement and is then told, "Too bad you can't come because John Brilliant was looking forward to meeting you," cannot change her mind without being rude to all concerned.

Three important don'ts:

1) When the number you get is evidently wrong, don't ask, "What number is this?" Ask instead, "Is this Main 2-3456?"

2) Don't answer and then say, "Wait a minute," because the doorbell is ringing or the pot is boiling over; say instead, "I'll call you back in a few minutes!" And do so.

3) Don't let too young a child answer the telephone. The caller's message may be garbled beyond recognition.

Terminating telephone calls:

Under ordinary circumstances, the one who originates the call is the one who terminates it. The caller simply says, "I'm so glad I reached you—we'll be looking forward to seeing you on the seventh. Good-bye," or any appropriate remark. When you are trapped on the telephone by a long-winded caller and have made several tentative efforts to end the conversation, you may take more aggressive measures. At the first pause, or even interrupting if necessary, you may say, "I'm terribly sorry, but I simply must hang up—the baby's crying," or "I'm late for an appointment now."

A call should be terminated quickly if the one who receives it has a visitor—either in a business office or at home. To do otherwise is inconsiderate to your visitor. When you answer the phone and find it is not a call which can be terminated in a moment or two, postpone it for a more convenient time. At home you might say, "Joan just dropped in for a visit, so may I call you back in a little while?" The businessman could say, "I have a customer with me at the moment. If you will give me your number, I'll call you back when I am free." In either case, be sure to return the call as soon as you can.

LONG-DISTANCE CALLS

When making a long-distance call, do not shout—amplifiers on the circuits will step up your voice all the way. On overseas calls, wait for the other person to finish speaking before you start. It is a one-way-at-a-time circuit, and if both speak at once, both are shut off until one or the other stops talking.

If you call long distance often, especially in these days of direct dialing, a telephone timer, a small second-counting gadget that rings a bell before each three minutes, is a must for economy's sake. If you are making a personal call, you may ask the operator, when you put in your call, to interrupt when the three minutes are up.

ON A PARTY LINE

When it is realized that the usual number of families sharing a party line is four (and the maximum ten) and that as long as one person is talking, no outside call can reach any other person on that line, the consideration required of each sharer is obvious. For this reason the telephone company has taken pains to make—and expects the subscribers to keep— the following rules on a party line: When you find the line in use, hang up for three minutes before signaling again. In an emergency, call out clearly "EMERGENCY!" and then "Our barn is on fire," or "Johnny's had an accident," or whatever it is. But unless all on the line hang up, your telephone is cut off.

The operator is not permitted to cut in on a busy wire. But if a busy signal goes on and you must get through for some reason—such as missing a train or plane—ask for the supervisor of the station called and briefly explain. At her discretion, she may then cut in, and ask those talking to hang up.

PAYING FOR YOUR CALLS

Many guests mistakenly hesitate to proffer payment for their calls. The definite rule is this: Should one be obliged to make a single local call, one would not ordinarily offer payment for it, but one must pay for every long-distance call. Request in advance that the operator let you know the time and charges upon completion of your call. Then leave this amount with a slip, giving the date and the number called. Or if one has made many calls during a long stay, the complete list of telephone calls and telegrams sent, with the amounts of each and their total, may be handed to the hostess and paid for when one says good-bye. No matter how rich the host may be, it is correct to pay this debt.

If a guest does not offer to pay for his long-distance calls, it is quite correct—and fair to him and to you—to give him an itemized bill for them.

THE TELEPHONE COURTESY TEST

The number of times you can answer "Yes" to the following questions will show you how good your telephone manners are:

1) Do you make sure of the correct number so as not to risk disturbing strangers by "calling from memory"?

2) Do you make conversations with busy people as brief as possible?

3) When calling friends who do not recognize your voice, do you resist playing a game of "Guess who?" and announce yourself promptly?

4) Do you try to time your calls so as not to interfere with the occupations of those you call most often?

5) Do you make business calls well before the close of office hours, especially if calling a person you know is a commuter?

6) In a business office, do you explain to personal friends inclined to talk at length that you will call them after hours?

7) Do you treat wrong-number calls as a mutual inconvenience and answer, "Sorry, wrong number," in a tone of polite sympathy instead of showing ill-tempered annoyance?

8) On a dial telephone, do you always wait for the dial tone?

9) When the number you are calling is not answered quickly, do you wait long enough for someone to lay aside what she may be doing before you hang up?

10) Do you, when making a number of calls on a party line, space them so that others on the line may have a chance to use their telephones?

54

Motoring

Courtesy is essential to safe driving. The courteous driver constantly considers how his actions will affect those behind, in front of and beside him and is alert to what other cars are doing as well. Because of this attitude, he is invariably a safe driver. Many men and women whose behavior in all other circumstances is beyond reproach become transformed into bad-mannered autocrats behind the wheel of a car and become "accidents going somewhere to happen." Often the man who tries to force his way ahead of others in a line of cars would not think of trying to force himself ahead of others in a box-office line. However, let him get behind the wheel of a car, and his courteous instincts may fly right out the window.

"DO UNTO OTHERS . . ."

Every driver has innumerable chances to observe the golden rule each time he steps into his car. Are you that polite one who will pause to let a car in? Do you swear at the heavy pedestrian traffic slowing your turn in the city or do *you* wait patiently until there is a break in the flow? Don't just give lip service to the golden rule; act on it, and you will not only become a better driver, but a more relaxed and therefore a safer driver.

AT TRAFFIC LIGHTS

The courteous driver stops for a red light in a position that does not block the crosswalk. In heavy traffic he enters an intersection only if he is sure he can complete the crossing before the light changes. Nor does he start up with a rush when the light turns orange in the other direction or linger lazily after the light has changed so that the drivers behind him will be caught by the next red light.

Observe the right- or left-turn arrow at an intersection, and stay out of those lanes when you intend to go straight through so that you do not prevent others from turning with the arrow.

CASPAR MILQUETOAST

On many highways there is a minimum limit as well as a maximum, but where there is not, the offender against courtesy is not always just the fast driver, but also the slow! The snail who pokes along thirty miles an hour slower than the other cars is a menace to everyone. Impatient drivers pile up behind him, particularly on narrow and winding roads. These drivers take desperate chances, passing too close to a curve or the top of a hill and end up in a serious crash. If you wish to drive slowly, please stay off the super highways entirely, or if you must use them, have the courtesy to keep to the right where the slower traffic belongs.

OTHER OFFENDERS

Another discourteous menace is the "weaver." He scoots back and forth from lane to lane, cutting drivers off, causing them to jam on their brakes or swerve into the lane beside them. The well-mannered traveler on a highway always signals well in advance before he switches lanes or makes a turn. He keeps an eye on his mirror to be sure that drivers behind him have noticed his signals before he makes his move. A thoughtful motorist always gets into the proper lane well before he reaches his turn or exit. Few people are more dangerous on the road than the man who suddenly realizes that he has reached his turnoff and who cuts through the other lanes in order to reach his destination.

PASSING POINTERS

One of the worst offenders on the road is the driver who pulls out of a solid line of cars to steal his way forward, finds himself in sudden danger of a head-on collision and makes a frantic effort to push his way back into the line.

When you want to pass, wait until you have reached a safe stretch of road with adequate visibility, make your move smoothly, quickly and without changing your mind. And when you are the driver being passed, slow down a little to allow the other car plenty of space to pull back into line ahead of you.

NIGHT DRIVING

When driving at night, the careful driver lowers his speed in the darkness. He always dims his lights when meeting other cars. This automatically invites others to do the same. If you are driving with lights on low beam, turn them high momentarily to remind an approaching driver to turn his down, but keeping on your high-beam lights to "get even" with someone who has not dimmed his is both impolite and stupid. You can be the victim of the driver you "blind."

USING THE HORN

Blowing a horn in a traffic line when it can do no good is merely annoying to others. Sounding a horn at a pedestrian caught midstreet by a changing light is dangerous—it may cause him to jump into the path of another car. A polite young man does not announce his arrival to a lady by standing at the curb outside her door and yoohooing; neither should he sit at the wheel and blast away at the horn. He alights and rings the doorbell.

PARKING

The thoughtful driver never takes up more space than necessary and never parks so close to the car behind or in front of him that he will be unable to pull out.

Park as close to the curb as possible to leave more room for passing cars. When the car in front of you obviously wishes to back into a parking space, give him room to do it without rushing him by creeping forward or blowing your horn! Never sneak into an empty space when another car is about to back in.

Courteous drivers stay within the lines for parking spaces, take care not to block driveways and park off the pavement on rural roads or when forced to pull off a highway. Don't pull out without carefully looking in all directions. And look behind you before backing up to make sure there are no pedestrians about to step off the curb.

ENTERING A CAR

The custom of a man opening the door and assisting a woman into a car is still correct. However, when the car is parked on a busy street, he cannot be expected to help her in and then walk into the stream of cars to get in on the other side. In this case the man excuses himself for preceding her and slides in from her side. On a wide or lightly traveled street a gentleman naturally enters the car on his own side after first assisting any ladies into the car on the curb side.

DRINKING AND DRIVING

It should be unnecessary to emphasize the menace of the drunken driver. But not half enough blame is laid on the exhilarated driver who has had one or two cocktails and takes chances that he would not think of taking when he has had nothing to drink. Alcohol and gasoline do not mix. If you have had a drink or two, have the intelligence to refuse to take the wheel and ask some other man or woman to do the driving. A host, seeing a guest is showing signs of his liquor, should do his best to persuade him to stay away from the wheel.

IN AN EMERGENCY

If you have an emergency such as a flat tire or broken fan belt, it is not only essential to your safety but courteous to the other motorists to pull well off to the side of the road. Raise the hood and tie a white handkerchief or cloth to your door handle, the universal signal of distress. Any policeman or a kindhearted passerby will stop to offer assistance. On a super highway, stay in your car until help arrives. Walking for help on such a road is dangerous both for yourself and to the cars who swerve to avoid you.

MANNERS OF PEDESTRIANS

First rules for pedestrians include: Don't cross before the light turns green or the signal reads "Walk." Don't cross streets in the middle of a block. Don't dart forward after hiding behind a parked car. Don't, when the lights change while you are in the middle of the street, turn and run back to the side you started from. Keep on going exactly as you were. On a road that has no sidewalk, always walk facing the oncoming traffic.

SOME TIPS FOR MOTOR TRIPS

When starting out on a motor trip, make certain that your equipment is in the best possible condition. Check your tires, fuel, oil, brakes and automatic transmission before starting and during the trip. Replace windshield-wiper blades if rough or worn. Have headlights, turn indicators and brake lights checked.

Avoid fatigue. On long trips stop to stretch your legs, take some refreshment and allow your engine and tires to cool off. If you have a companion who is licensed to drive, stop and change drivers every two hours. Plan to arrive at your destination by four in the afternoon to allow time for a rest, a little sightseeing and a leisurely dinner.

Traveling with children:

Traveling with children who are old enough to read, write or play games need not be a problem. Take along a supply of papers, crayons or one of the excellent game books that are sold just for the purpose. Verbal games, such as "Twenty Questions," help to pass the hours. For little children, a mattress laid in the back of the station wagon or a little play-pen with a well-padded mat on the back seat is a boon. The baby can move about safely and the older child will enjoy the luxury of being able to stretch out and sleep for a while.

For comfort and safety:

Fatalities are far less frequent among drivers and passengers wearing properly installed belts or shoulder harnesses. They should be snugly fastened, so that you are not thrown hard *against* the belt by a sudden stop. The driver is quite correct in asking his passengers to use their belts. Keep a pair of sunglasses in the glove compartment of your car. Many people find that prolonged glare can cause severe headaches.

Your clothing should be loose and comfortable. Slacks or shorts are excellent for traveling and allow maximum mobility. A man, even though dressed in a business suit, will probably be more comfortable if he replaces his jacket with a loose sweater or, if it is warm, drives in his shirt with the collar loosened.

CAR POOLS

The "car pool" is a practical, economical arrangement for people who go to work at the same hour. There are several basic rules of courtesy.

Be on time! Don't carry quantities of articles or let those you must carry obstruct the driver's view to the side or in the rear-view mirror. Open or close windows only after asking permission of the other passengers. Observe the same rule of courtesy about smoking. Don't bring an extra passenger without asking the driver if there is room. Shake a wet umbrella (and raincoat) before getting into the car. Let the driver know in advance when he is not to pick you up.

55

For those who smoke

TIMES WHEN NO ONE MAY SMOKE

One may not smoke in a church or during any religious service or ceremonial proceedings. One may not smoke in a sickroom unless the patient himself is smoking or gives permission. Good taste still forbids smoking by a woman on a city street. No one should smoke or carry a lighted cigarette when dancing.

Smoking is forbidden on local buses, in theaters, in most museums, and in many big city stores.

SMOKING DON'TS

Never light a cigarette, pipe or cigar when a "No Smoking" sign is displayed.

Never lay a cigarette (or cigar) on the edge of a table or

other piece of furniture! Find an ashtray to put it in—or ask for one.

Striking a match directly toward someone is dangerous—the head may fly off and cause a painful burn. A lighted cigarette should not be thrown into a fireplace; it may start up an unwanted fire. Never toss a cigarette out the window—it may land on an awning or a pile of dried leaves. Don't throw filter-tipped cigarettes on a lawn or terrace where the fireproof, rainproof tip will remain until someone rakes or sweeps it away. Worst of all is the smoker who leaves his lighted cigarette in the ashtray to burn itself out, making others present ill from the smell.

A FEW HINTS ON SMOKING MANNERS

If each place at the dining-room table is set with cigarettes, a lighter and an ashtray, naturally people may smoke as soon as they choose. But in the houses of those who do not put them on the table or who have them passed only after dessert, it is bad manners to light one's own cigarette and smoke throughout the meal. And do be careful that the smoke from the cigarette you are holding is not blowing into the faces of your neighbors.

Smokers should carry their own cigarettes. When a man is about to smoke, it is polite to offer a cigarette to those next to him, or in his immediate group. And a warning—the feminine cigarette "sponge" is no more popular than the male.

A man should light a woman's cigarette if he is close to her, but not if he is on the other side of a table. A woman smoker carries her own matches or lighter and *uses* them.

Pipe smokers need to exercise caution when emptying a pipe, using only a large sturdy ashtray lest they break a fragile one, or spray their ashes over the table tops.

A word to cigar smokers: Don't leave cigar butts in ashtrays —dead cigars have a strong odor that is unpleasant. Ask permission to smoke a cigar in mixed company.

56

In clubs

Membership in many athletic associations may be had by walking in and paying dues and many country golf clubs are as free to the public as country inns. But to join an exclusive club, a man must have among the members friends who like him enough to be willing to propose and second him and write letters for him; furthermore he must be disliked by no one—at least not so much that a member might raise a serious objection to his company.

You may join a club by invitation or by having application made for you. To join by invitation means that you are invited to be one of the founders or charter members, or you may at the invitation of the governors become an honorary member; or in a small or informal club you may become an ordinary member at the suggestion of the governors. A charter member pays dues, but not always an initiation fee. An honorary member pays neither dues nor initiation fee; he is really a guest of the club—a mayor, for example, may be an honorary member just for the duration of his term in office. A life member pays his dues for twenty years or so in a lump sum and is thereafter exempted from dues even though they may be increased in later years or he lives to be a hundred.

Different clubs offer different types of memberships: at a country club, a "golfing member" uses only the golfing facilities, a "house member," only the restaurant and facilities of the clubhouse. Regular members of a club may be resident (that is, they live within fifty miles of the club) or nonresident (they live beyond that distance and pay smaller dues but have the same privileges).

BECOMING A MEMBER

"Putting up" a name:

Since no sensible man would want to join a club in which the members are not his friends, he says to a member of his family or an intimate friend, "Do you mind putting me up for the Nearby Club? I think that Dick would second me." The friend answers, "Delighted to do it!" and Dick says the same. A man has no right to ask anyone who is not really one of his best friends to propose or second him.

More likely the suggestion to join comes from a friend, who remarks one day, "Why don't you join the Nearby Club? Let me put you up, and I'll ask Dick to second you." And he arranges with Dick to do so.

Let us suppose that Jim Struthers is to be proposed by Donald Cameron and seconded by Henry Bancroft. Jim's name is written in the book kept for the purpose and signed by both proposer and seconder:

Struthers, James
    Proposer: Donald Cameron
    Seconder: Henry Bancroft

Then the name is posted with other names on the bulletin board in the clubhouse. Sometimes a list of proposed names is also sent to each member. Cameron and Bancroft each write a letter of endorsement to the governors of the club to be read by that body when they hold the meeting at which Struthers' name comes up for election.

Board of Governors,
The Nearby Club

Dear Sirs:
    It affords me much pleasure to propose for membership in the Nearby Club Mr. James Struthers. I have known Mr. Struthers for many years and consider him qualified in every way for membership.
    He is a graduate of Northsouthern University, class of 1941, and is a member of the Center Club. He is now with the firm of Jones, Fairbanks & Co.
                        Yours very truly,
                        Donald Cameron

Because in most clubs, the number of members is limited by the bylaws, there may be a waiting list. Therefore before making a decision as to which clubs you wish to join, find out about the length of waiting time and discuss the possibilities with your sponsor.

Meeting the governors:

Cameron selects with Struthers six or more of his friends who are members of the club (but not governors) and asks them to write letters endorsing Struthers. Since the candidate cannot come up for election unless he knows several of the governors personally so that they can vouch for him at the meeting, Cameron and Bancroft must personally present Struthers to several governors. At many clubs the governors appoint an hour on several weekend afternoons before elections when they are in the visitors' rooms at the clubhouse in order to meet the candidates whom their proposers must present.

Importance of good letters of endorsement:

Jim Struthers, having well-known sponsors and also being well liked himself, is elected with no difficulty. But young Breezy was put up by two not very well-known members who wrote halfhearted endorsements themselves and did nothing about getting letters from others. Two men who disliked his "manner" wrote that they considered him "unsuitable." As he had no friends strong enough to stand up for him, he was turned down. If a candidate is likely to be blackballed, the governors do not vote on him but inform the proposer that the name of his candidate had better be withdrawn. Later on, if the objection to him is disproved or overcome, his name may again be put up.

Qualifications for election:

When the candidate is elected, a notice is mailed to him next morning, telling him that he has been elected and the amount of the initiation fee and the dues, which he sends at once. Only now is he officially a member and free to use the club. A new member is given a copy of the club book, which contains a list of the members, the constitution and the bylaws or "house rules" which he must study and follow carefully.

COUNTRY CLUBS

Country clubs vary greatly in both characteristics and expense. It is as difficult to be elected to some of them as to any of the exclusive clubs in the cities, inasmuch as they are open to the family and friends of every member, whereas a city club is used only by the member himself.

Furthermore, many country clubs have one open door unknown to city clubs. People taking houses in the neighborhood or vacation visitors in a resort are often granted "season privileges." On being proposed by a member and upon paying a season's subscription, new householders are accepted as transient guests. In some clubs, this subscription may be indefinitely renewed; in others, a man must come up for regular election at the end of three or six months' or a year's time.

Hundreds of country clubs have very simple requirements for membership: one or two members who will vouch for a candidate's integrity and good behavior are sufficient.

In almost all country clubs the atmosphere is informal: members speak to each other without introductions, form tennis games and golf foursomes with comparative strangers.

WOMEN'S CLUBS

There is no difference between women's and men's clubs. In every state of the Union there are women's clubs of every kind and grade: social, political, sports, professional. Some are housed in enormous and elegant buildings designed especially for them and others in only a room or two, usually in a hotel. No clubs are more nearly perfect in appointment or more smoothly run than the best women's clubs.

IN THE CITY CLUB

There is no place where a person has greater need of restraint and consideration for the reserves of others than in a club. It is courteous of a governor or habitual member on noticing a new member or a visitor to go up and speak to him, but the latter should not be the one to speak first. In the dining rooms of many clubs, there is a large table, sometimes known as the social table, where members who are lunching alone may sit and where the conversation is general, and all are expected to talk whether they are friends or total strangers.

The fundamenal rule for behavior in a club is the same as

in the living room of a private house. In other words, heels have no place on furniture; ashes belong in ashtrays; books should not be abused; and all evidence of exercising should be confined to the courts or gymnasium, and the locker or dressing room.

VISITORS IN A CLUB

All men's clubs have private dining rooms where members can give dinners that include nonmembers, and many have a special dining room for women guests.

When a woman gives a lunch or any party in a club, either a women's club or in the "open" dining room of a men's club, she waits for her guests in the lobby, entrance hall, or, if there is one, the reception room. As her guests arrive, they join her and stand or sit near her. If the room is filled with others, she herds her own group, as it were, a little apart. When all have arrived, they go to the dining room and sit at the table prepared in advance for them. If they are more than four, the food is ordered in advance.

Almost always, a member is allowed to introduce a stranger —one who lives at least fifty miles away—for a varying length of time determined by the bylaws of the club. In many city clubs, the same guest cannot be introduced twice within the year. In country clubs, members usually may have an unlimited number of visitors. When these are golf or tennis players, the host is responsible for green's fees or court charges.

When a member introduces a stranger, he takes him to the club personally, writes his name in the visitors' book and introduces him to those who may be in the room at the time. If it is not possible for the stranger's host to take him to the club, he writes a formal letter to the secretary of the club for a card of introduction. This letter then goes in the club's files.

Secretary
The Town Club

Dear Sir [or *Dear Mr. Jones*]:
    Kindly send Mr. A. M. Strangleigh, of Wilkes Barre, Pa., a card extending the privileges of the Club for one week. Mr. Strangleigh is staying at the Carlton House.
                    Yours very truly,
                    Henry Bancroft

The secretary then sends a card to Mr. Strangleigh.

The Town Club
Extends its privileges to
Mr. Strangleigh
from Jan. 7 to Jan. 14
Through the courtesy of
Mr. Henry Bancroft

Mr. Strangleigh goes to the club by himself. A visitor who has been given a card to a club has, during the time of his visit, all the privileges of a member except that he is not allowed to introduce others to the club and he cannot give a dinner in a private dining room. The guest arranges at the club's office to have his charges rendered to himself, is scrupulous about asking for his bill upon leaving and pays it immediately. Otherwise his bill must be paid by the member who issued the invitation.

UNBREAKABLE RULES

Failure to pay one's debts or behavior unbefitting a gentleman is cause for expulsion from every club. If a man cannot afford to belong to a club, he must resign while he is still in good standing. If later on he is able to rejoin, his name is put at the head of the waiting list. If he was considered a desirable member, he is reelected at the next meeting of the governors. But a man who has been expelled—unless he can show that his expulsion was unjust—can never again belong to that club.

RESIGNING FROM A CLUB

To resign from a club, one writes a letter of resignation to the secretary well before the date on which the next yearly dues will be due. The letter would read something like this:

Mrs. James Town
Secretary, Colonial Club, New York

My dear Mrs. Town,
  It is with great regret that I find it necessary to resign from the club and to ask you therefore to present my resignation at the next meeting of the governors.
                              Very sincerely,
                                Mary Smartlington

57

At the table

THE "WHYS" OF GOOD TABLE MANNERS

Most rules for the table were made to avoid ugliness. To let anyone see what you have in your mouth is offensive. To make a noise is to suggest one of the lower animals. To make a mess is disgusting. Chairs scraped on the floor and knives and forks rattled against the plate are unpleasant to those nearby. But if you consider what impression your actions will make on the others at the table, few problems will arise that cannot be solved by common sense alone.

ARRIVING AT THE TABLE AND GRACE BEFORE MEALS

At the informal gatherings and family meals that all of us have each day, a man holds the chair for the woman on his right. But if the men or boys do not arrive simultaneously with the women, the women (and girls) seat themselves without delay.

Giving a family blessing or thanks before meals is a gracious custom. Some families sit with bowed heads and touch nothing until the grace has been said, others remain standing—both forms are correct. The mother or the father may offer the prayer, but it is sweet to allow the younger members of the family to take turns in asking grace. The following three are typical examples.

Bless us, O Lord, and these Thy gifts, which we are about to receive from Thy bounty, Through Christ our Lord. Amen.

Lift up your hands toward the Sanctuary and bless the Lord. Blessed art Thou, O Lord our God, King of the universe, who bringest forth bread from the earth. Amen.

Bless, O Lord, this food to our use, and us to Thy service, and make us ever mindful of the needs of others, in Jesus' name. Amen.

POSTURE

Sit at a distance from the table that is comfortable, but not so close that elbows are bent like a cricket's, nor so far back that food may be dropped in transit from plate to mouth.

Elbows are *never* put on the table while one is actually eating. To sit with the left elbow propped on the table while eating with the right hand or to prop the right elbow or forearm on the table while lifting fork or glass to the mouth is ugly and awkward.

Elbows are permitted when people are lunching or dining in a restaurant and it is difficult to hear above music or conversation, without leaning far forward. And in leaning forward, a woman's figure makes a more graceful outline supported on her elbows than doubled forward over her hands in her lap as though she were in pain! *At home* there is no reason for elbows. *At a dinner of ceremony,* elbows on the table are rarely seen, except perhaps at the ends of the table, where one has to lean forward in order to talk to a companion across the table corner. Even in these special situations, *never* when one is eating.

Slouching or slumping at the table is most unattractive and tipping one's chair is unforgivable. It not only looks dreadfully sloppy, but it is fatal to the back legs of the chair. Ideal posture at the table is to sit straight but not stiffly, leaning slightly against the back of the chair; when you are not actually eating, your hands should be in your lap; this will automatically prevent you from fussing with implements, playing with bread crumbs, drawing on the tablecloth, and so forth. Keep hands away from the face, from nervous scratching and from twisting or touching the hair.

It is correct to reach for anything on the table provided you do not stretch across your neighbor. When something is out of reach, simply ask the person nearest to it, "Would you please pass the jelly, Mrs. Betts?"

THE NAPKIN

As soon as you are seated, you put your napkin in your lap, unfolding it as much as necessary with both hands—avoid giving it a violent shake.

When using the napkin, blot or pat the lips.

When the meal is finished, or if you leave the table during the meal, put the napkin on the right side of your place, or if the plates have been removed, in the center. Do not refold it or crumple it; just lay it on the table in loose folds so that it does not spread itself out. At a dinner party, the hostess lays her napkin on the table as a signal that the meal is over; the guests then lay their napkins on the table—not before.

SERVING ONESELF AND BEING SERVED

Anything served on a piece of toast is lifted from the dish on it, unless you don't want the toast, in which case you help yourself to the asparagus and leave the toast. For sweetbreads, mushrooms on toast—foods that seem to be an arrangement— take the toast and all on the spoon and hold it in place with the fork.

When declining a dish offered by a waiter, you say, "No, thank you," in a low voice.

Gravy is put *on* the meat or potatoes, and the condiments, pickles, and jelly *at the side* of whatever they accompany. Olives, radishes or celery are put on the bread-and-butter plate if there is one; otherwise on the edge of the plate from which one is eating. Salted nuts are put on the tablecloth or place mat.

When passing your plate to the head of the table for a second helping, always leave the knife and fork close together across the center of the plate with the handles far enough on not to topple off.

It is good manners to take a little of every dish that is offered, but if it is a food you especially dislike and you are among friends, you may refuse with a polite "No, thank you." You need not give your reason for refusing a dish, but if it is an allergy or a diet, you might quietly tell your hostess so, without drawing the attention of the entire table.

WHEN TO START EATING

At a small table of two, four or even six people, it is certainly polite to wait to start eating until all have been served. Then the hostess picks up her implement and the others follow suit. If the group is larger, it is *not* necessary to wait until all have been served. The hostess, as soon as the first two or three guests have their food, says, "Please start—your dinner will only get cold if you wait"; the guests take her at her word and start immediately. If the hostess says nothing, it is perfectly correct to pick up your spoon or fork after five or six people have been served; the others will soon follow your lead. At family meals, as Mother or Father fills and passes the plates, the children say, "May I please begin?" if they are not old enough to be expected to wait.

As to which silver to use: *You always start with the implement farthest from the plate.* Starting at the outside, you work your way with each course toward the center.

USING THE KNIFE AND FORK

The proper way to use the knife and fork can best be explained by the accompanying illustrations. The American custom of "zigzag" eating (changing the fork from left to right hand after cutting meat) is perfectly correct, but unnecessarily complicated. The simpler method is to leave the fork in your

left hand, raise the meat to your mouth, after cutting it, with the fork tines down, still in the same hand, rather than turning the fork over and switching it to your right.

Dessert may be eaten with spoon or fork or both. Stewed fruit is held in place with the fork and cut and eaten with the spoon. Peaches or other very juicy fruits are peeled, then eaten with knife and fork, but dry fruits, such as apples, may be cut and then eaten with the fingers. *Never* wipe hands that have fruit juice on them on a cloth napkin without first using a fingerbowl, because fruit juices leave injurious stains.

Fingers or forks:

All juicy or soft fruit and all cake is best eaten with a fork. If you can eat a peach or ripe pear in your fingers and not let juice run down your chin or make a sucking noise, do so. But if you cannot eat something—no matter what it is—without getting it all over your fingers, use a fork and, when necessary, a spoon or a knife also.

Pushers:

A piece of dry crust is an excellent pusher. Lacking this, the knife is also correct—if properly used. Held in the left hand in the same position as it is when held in the right hand, the tip of the blade helping to guide each mouthful for the fork to lift, it is a quite acceptable pusher.

OTHER THAN THE MAIN COURSE

Soups:

Either clear soup or thick soup may be served in a cup with one handle or with handles on both sides. After taking a spoonful or two, you may pick up the cup, using both hands if it has two handles.

Both soup cups and soup plates should be served with a saucer or plate beneath them. The spoon, when not in use or when the soup is finished, is laid on the saucer when a soup cup is used, but it is left in the soup plate rather than on the dish under it.

Clear soups are often served in a soup plate. When the level of the soup gets low, lift the near edge in your left hand and tip the plate away from you. Then the soup may be spooned away from you or toward you.

Croutons are either put on the soup or else passed separately in a dish with a small serving spoon. Oyster crackers and any others are put on the bread-and-butter plate or the tablecloth —and dropped two or three pieces at a time into the soup.

Bread and butter:

Bread is broken into moderate-sized—not bite-sized—pieces with the fingers before being eaten. To butter it, hold a piece on the edge of the bread-and-butter plate, or the place plate, and spread enough butter on it for a mouthful or two at a time, with a butter knife—lacking a butter knife, use any other knife available. Never hold bread flat on the palm and butter it with the hand held in the air. Jellies and jams are spread on bread with a knife, never with a fork, though you do put butter on vegetables and jelly on meat with a fork.

Bread and gravy:

Certainly you may sop bread into gravy by putting a small piece down in the gravy and then eating it with a knife and fork.

Salad:

To cut one's salad in small pieces is eminently proper and practical, but avoid cutting up a whole plateful at a time. Anything more difficult than managing leafy salad with a fork alone is difficult to imagine. Beware of rolling the fork and wrapping springy leaves around the tines in a spiral. Since the advent of stainless steel knife blades, there has been no reason to refrain from using a knife to cut your salad.

Beverages:

Many people today use mugs instead of cups and saucers for coffee, tea or hot chocolate. Since saucers are not used with mugs, the problem arises of what to do with the spoon—which should never be left in the mug. Mugs are not proper on a formal table and are rarely seen on any table covered with a cloth, so the solution depends on the place mats. If the mats are informal, of paper or plastic, perhaps, wipe the spoon clean with the lips and lay it on the mat or on the table beside the mug. If the mats are of fine quality rest the bowl of the spoon, face down, on the edge of the butter plate or dinner plate, with the spoon handle on the table.

A smart hostess serves a coaster or saucer under a glass. If not, the procedure just mentioned for removing the spoon is correct. When dining informally one may use a clean, unused teaspoon to put a small piece of ice from the water glass into a steaming beverage to cool it slightly.

Tea bags are placed on the edge of the saucer after they are pressed gently against the side of the cup with the spoon to remove excess liquid. Should the tea be served in a glass or china mug without a saucer, you may ask for a dish on which to place the bag. Otherwise you must put it on the edge of the butter or dinner plate. In spite of an outdated idea to the contrary, tea which is too hot to drink from the cup may be sipped from the spoon, as may coffee or any other hot beverage.

When coffee spills into the saucer, replace the saucer with a clean one. If a clean saucer is not available in a restaurant or cafeteria, rather than drip coffee each time you lift the cup to your mouth, pour the liquid back into the cup and use a paper napkin (if one is available) to dry the bottom of the cup.

Salt:

If there is no spoon in the saltcellar, use the tip of a clean knife. If the saltcellar is for you alone, use your knife or take a pinch of salt with your fingers. Putting salt on the tablecloth and then pinching it between the fingers to put on food is permissible. But salt that is to be dipped into—for example, with celery or radishes—is put on the bread-and-butter plate or on the rim of whatever plate is before you.

Fruit at table:

The equipment for eating fruit at the table consists of a sharp-bladed fruit knife and fork, a fingerbowl and a napkin that fruit juice will not permanently stain. In a restaurant, when no knife is given you, ask for one.

Raw apples and pears. These are quartered with a knife, the core cut away from each quarter, and the fruit eaten in the fingers. Those who do not like the skin pare each quarter separately.

Bananas. Although it is permissible to peel the skin halfway down and eat the fruit bite by bite, it is better to peel the skin all the way off, lay the fruit on your plate, cut it in slices and eat it with a fork.

Berries. Strawberries and other berries are usually hulled ahead of time, served with cream and sugar, and eaten with a spoon. They are also served with their hulls on and sugar placed at one side of each person's plate—hold the hull of each berry in your fingers, dip the fruit in the sugar and eat it.

Cantaloupes and melons. These are served in halves or quarters and eaten with a spoon. A honeydew is cut into new-moon-shaped quarters or eighths and eaten with either spoon or knife and fork, as are Persian or Casaba melons. Watermelon is cut into large-size pieces or slices and is usually eaten in the fingers. If eaten with a fork, remove the seeds with the tines, then cut a piece with the side of the fork.

Raw cherries and plums. These are eaten in the fingers. The pit of the cherry is made as dry as possible in your mouth and dropped into your almost-closed cupped hand and thence to your plate. The plum is held in your fingers and eaten as close to the pit as possible. When you remove a pit in your fingers, do it with your thumb underneath and your first two fingers across your mouth, not with your fingertips pointing into your mouth.

Grapes. Hothouse grapes are eaten two ways: one, lay a grape on its side, hold it with the fingers of the left hand, cut into the center with the point of a knife, and remove the seeds; then put the grape in your mouth with the left hand. Or put a whole grape in your mouth, chew it, swallow the pulp and juice and drop the bare seeds into your almost-closed fist, and convey them to the plate.

Oranges. Slice the two ends of the rind off first; then stand it on the plate with the fingers of the left hand; cut the peel off in vertical strips with the knife, and cut the peeled orange in half at its equator. After this, each half is easily cut and eaten mouthful by mouthful with knife and fork together. They can also be halved, the sections loosened with a curved grapefruit knife, and then eaten with an orange spoon or teaspoon.

Peaches. A freestone peach or a nectarine is cut into the pit, then broken in half and eaten. If you mind the fuzz of a clingstone, which won't come off the pit easily, peel the peach whole and then eat it with knife and fork.

DIFFICULT FOODS

Artichoke. The leaves are eaten with the fingers. A leaf at a time is pulled off, the edible portion dipped in the sauce, then bitten off. At the center scrape the thistlelike part away with a knife and eat the heart with a knife and fork.

Asparagus. Fastidious people invariably eat it—at least in part—with the fork. Cut the stalks with the fork at the point at which they become harder, then pick up the ends in your fingers if you choose. But don't squeeze the stalks. All hard ends should be cut off asparagus before serving it at a dinner party.

Baked potato. If not otherwise prepared before serving, it is eaten by breaking it in half with the fingers, scooping all the inside of the potato onto the plate with a fork and then mixing butter, salt and pepper in it with a fork. Or you may break it in half with the fingers and lay both halves, skin down, on the plate. Mix a little butter in a small part of one half with a fork and eat that, then mix a little more, and so on, eating it out of the skin.

For those who like to eat the skin as well as the inside, cut the baked potato into two halves with the knife and fork, then again into pieces, a few at a time, of eatable size. Butter the pieces with the fork alone and eat with the fork held tines up. The skins may be eaten separately, exactly as you would bread and butter.

Bacon. Breakfast bacon is eaten, if possible, with a fork. If it is very crisp so that it scatters into fragments when broken by the fork, fingers are permitted.

Cheese. Cheese may be spread with either a knife or a fork. If eaten with a salad, with which one is using no knife, one may break off a piece of cheese and put it on lettuce or a cracker with one's fork. Runny or soft cheeses, such as Brie, Camembert or Liederkranz are always spread with a salad knife or butter knife.

Corn on the cob. Hold the ear, either broken in half or whole, by its own ends or by special little handles. Spread the butter across half the length, about two rows at a time. If the ear is not too long, spread it across the whole length of two rows, add salt and pepper, hold the ends in both hands, and eat those two rows. Repeat the buttering and eating until all is finished. When corn is served for a dinner party, it should be cut off the cobs in the kitchen and creamed or buttered.

Chicken (roast or broiled), squab, game hen. At a formal dinner, no part of a bird is picked up in the fingers. Among family and friends, however, it is permissible to eat as follows: You cut off as much meat as you can and eat it with your knife and fork. If you know how to manage very small bones, such as the joint or wing of a squab, put the piece of bone with meat on it in your mouth, eat it clean, and remove the bare bones between forefinger and thumb. Larger joints, such as the drumstick of a chicken, may be picked up after the first few easily-cut-off pieces have been eaten.

French-fried potatoes. When they are accompanying a hamburger, hot dog or other sandwich, they may be eaten in the fingers. Otherwise they are cut into reasonable lengths and eaten with a fork.

Lamb chops. At a dinner party or in a restaurant, lamb chops are eaten with knife and fork. At the family table or among an informal group of friends, the center may be cut out and eaten with the fork, and the bone picked up and eaten clean with the teeth. (This is permissible with veal or pork chops provided they are broiled without gravy or sauce.)

Lobster, broiled. Pick up the claw in its shell and pry out the meat with a lobster fork; then put the meat (and that from the main body) on your plate, cut it with a knife and eat it with the fork. (An extra napkin and a fingerbowl with hot water and lemon slices should be put at the side of each place at the table as soon as people are served and taken away when the plates are removed.)

Olives. Eat them with your fingers; don't nibble too avidly around the stone. Bite a stuffed one in half—put only a very small one in your mouth whole. (When a small olive, cherry or onion is in a cocktail: after the glass is drained, tip it and drop the olive, etc., into your mouth. Lift out a large olive with the fingers and eat it in two or three bites.)

Sandwiches. All ordinary sandwiches are eaten with the fingers. Club sandwiches are best cut in smaller portions before being picked up and held tightly in the fingers of both hands; if literally dripping with mayonnaise they should be served on a plate and eaten with a knife and fork.

Shrimp. If not too impossibly large, each shrimp in a cup should be eaten in one bite. The jumbo size is cut with the edge of the fork. Or arrange the shrimp attractively on a small plate, where they can be cut easily with knife or fork.

Spaghetti. Winding spaghetti on a fork held against a spoon is incorrect both here and in Italy. A few pieces are held against the plate with the end of the fork, which is twisted to wrap the spaghetti around the tines and then conveyed to the mouth. An extra amount of grated Parmesan cheese makes the strands less slippery.

EMBARRASSING DIFFICULTIES

If food is too hot, quickly take a swallow of water. Never, NEVER spit it out! Once food has been taken into your mouth, you must swallow it. It is offensive to take anything out of your mouth that has been put in it except dry fish bones and equally dry fruit pits or seeds. If you choke on a fish bone, cover your mouth with your napkin and leave the table quickly. If you get a bad clam or something similar, take it from your mouth in your fingers—thumb underneath and the other four fingers forming a screen over it—and wipe your fingertips on your napkin. Pits of stewed prunes or cherries that are eaten with a spoon are made as clean and dry as possible in the mouth with the tongue and teeth, then dropped into the spoon with which you are eating and conveyed to the edge of the plate. Fish bones are taken between finger and thumb and removed between compressed lips.

Spills:

If you spill jelly or other solid food on the table, pick up as much as you can with a clean spoon or the blade of your knife. If it has caused a stain, apologize to your hostess, who should assure you that "No harm was done—the cloth will be washed tomorrow in any case." If you spill wine or water at the family table or informal dinner, offer to get a cloth or sponge to mop up the liquid and help the hostess clean up in any way you can.

SOME TABLE DON'TS

Don't encircle a plate with the left arm while eating with the right hand. Don't push back your plate when finished. It remains exactly where it is until whoever is waiting on you removes it. If you wait on yourself, get up and carry it to the kitchen.

Don't lean back and announce, "I'm through"—just put your fork or spoon down.

Don't *ever* put liquid into your mouth if it is already filled with food.

Don't dunk, except in the privacy of your home.

Don't apologize if you have to blow your nose at the table. The only thing to do is to end it as quickly as possible.

Don't wipe off the tableware in a restaurant. If you find a dirty piece of silver at your place, call a waiter and ask for a clean one.

Don't, if you are a woman, wear an excessive amount of lipstick to the table (out of consideration for your hostess's napkin—it is also unattractive on the rim of a glass or on the silver).

Don't spread jelly or jam directly onto a piece of bread from the dish in which it is served. Put a small portion on your butter plate (or the rim of your dinner plate), using the spoon provided to serve the condiment. If there is no spoon with the jelly, use a clean knife to put a little on your plate.

Don't crook your finger when picking up your cup. It's an affected mannerism.

Don't—ever—leave your spoon in your cup.

Don't leave half the food on your spoon or fork to be waved about during conversation. This is often done with ice cream, but the coldness is no excuse—put less on the spoon.

Don't cut up your entire meal before you start to eat; it makes a mess on your plate.

Don't bend your head so low over the plate that you seem

to be bobbing up and down for each bite like a robin for a worm. Lean forward slightly to avoid spilling on your lap.

WHEN CHILDREN COME TO THE TABLE

No child under five can be expected to use a napkin instead of a bib, but he may be given a napkin in addition to the bib to become accustomed to using it. It is much easier to supply him with a clean bib for the next meal than to change his clothes for the next moment, so do not force the issue unduly.

Very little children usually have warming plates—a double plate with a hot water space in between—on which the food is cut up and the vegetables "fixed" in the kitchen. It is brought to them before other people at the table are served as it is hard for them to wait, and they naturally eat slowly and deliberately. As soon as they are old enough to eat everything on the table, they are served, not last, but in the regular rotation in which they come at table.

The left-handed child:

To the many who ask whether it is best to set the place at the table in reverse of usual order for a left-handed child who has to "cross over" for every implement, the answer is definitely "No!"

Nothing could turn out to be a greater handicap than letting him become accustomed to reversed place-setting. It is only by being obliged to make this maneuver at every meal at home that he becomes adept at it. If his place is set especially for him at home, he will be conspicuously as well as helplessly awkward at every meal he ever eats away from home where his place will not be so set.

Table tricks that must be corrected:

To pile mashed potato and other vegetables on top of meat on the convex side of the fork for two inches or more of its length is an ungainly habit dear to the hearts of schoolboys and sometimes of their fathers—a habit that is more easily prevented in the beginning than corrected later. Taking a big mouthful (next to smearing the face and chewing with the mouth open) is perhaps the worst offense at the table.

To sit up straight and keep their hands in their laps when not occupied with eating is hard for children, but it should be insisted upon in order to forestall careless habits of flopping this way and that and fingering whatever is in reach. Never allow the child to drum on the table, screw his napkin into a rope or make marks on the tablecloth. If he shows talent as an artist, give him pencils or modeling wax in his playroom but do not let him bite his slice of bread into the silhouette of an animal and model figures in butter at the table. And do not allow him to construct a tent out of two forks or tie the corners of his napkin into bunny-rabbit ears. Food and table implements are not playthings, nor is the dining-room table a playground.

Teach children from the time they are little not to talk at the table about what foods they like and don't like. A child who is not allowed to say anything but "No, thank you," when offered something he doesn't want at home, will not mortify his mother in public by screaming, "I *hate* spinach. I *won't* eat potato. I want ice cream and cookies!"

A child, once his feet reach the floor, should sit down in the center of his chair and draw it up to the table by holding the seat in either hand while momentarily lifting himself on his feet. Do not let him jump or rock his chair into place. In getting up from the table, he must push his chair back quietly, using his hands on either side of the chair seat, and *not* by holding on to the table edge and giving himself, chair and all, a sudden shove.

SPECIAL RESTAURANT PROBLEMS

Many accompaniments to meals in restaurants are served with paper wrappers or in cardboard containers. The question arises of what do you do with them. Crumple the sugar packets up tightly and either tuck them under the rim of your plate or place them on the edge of the saucer or butter plate. When jelly or marmalade is served in a paper container, take it out with the butter knife (or dinner knife if there is no butter knife) and put it on the butter plate. Put the top back in the empty container, which is left on the table beside the butter plate.

Vegetables brought to the table in small individual dishes may be left in the dishes or spooned onto the plate; then ask that the dishes be removed. If no serving spoon is provided, tilt the small dish over the dinner plate, and push the vegetables carefully out with the dinner fork.

Meat pies or stews are removed from the dish in which they are served with a serving spoon, taking as much as you think you will want. Ask the waiter for a spoon if one is not served with the pie container. If only one fork (or knife) is provided, and it is used for the first course, it may be placed on the butter plate when the used plate is removed, and used again for the main course. Never wipe it clean and replace it on the table.

If toothpicks are on the table or counter, help yourself, but leave the table before using them and go someplace where you will not be observed, because nothing is more disgusting to other diners than the sight of someone digging at the food stuck in his teeth!

58

In business

In the well-run business office, the more important the executive, the greater courtesy he shows to those who come to see him. If, for example, an unknown person asks to see the president of a large industry, an assistant goes out to find out what the visitor's business is. Instead of telling him bluntly that the executive can't see him and to write a letter, he not only says, "Mr. Prominent is in conference just now," but adds, "I know he wouldn't like you to be kept waiting. Can I be of service to you? I am his assistant."

The president has a courteous manner that makes every visitor feel there is nothing in the day's work half so important as what he, the client, has come to see him about. Should he be due at an appointment, his secretary comes in, a few minutes before the hour, and reminds him, "I'm sorry, Mr. Promi-

nent, but your appointment with the traffic committee is due."
Mr. Prominent uses these few minutes in an unhurried close
of the conversation, showing undiminished interest until the
end. This is neither sincerity nor insincerity, but merely bringing social knowledge into business dealing. A less experienced
man might show his eagerness to be rid of his visitor and
possibly still be late for his own appointment!

Fundamental knowledge of etiquette is no less an asset in
business or public life than it is in society. An expert at a
machine bench gives an impression of such ease as to make
his accomplishment seem to require no skill. A bungler makes
himself and everyone watching him uneasy. Inexpertness is
quite as irritating in personal as in mechanical matters. Washington was completely a gentleman—and so was Abraham
Lincoln. Though Lincoln's etiquette was self-taught, it was
no less mastered for that!

WOMEN IN BUSINESS

The ideal business woman is accurate, orderly, quick and
impersonal, whether she is a typist or the top executive of a
great concern. "Impersonal" means exactly that. Her point of
view is focused on the work in hand, not on her own reactions
to it or on anyone's reactions to her. At the top of the list of
women's business shortcomings is the inability of many of
them to achieve this impersonality. Mood, temper, jealousy,
these are the chief flaws of the woman in business. The greatest handicap to a woman's advancement in business is her inability to leave her personal feelings and affairs at home.

A woman who goes into an office because she thinks herself pretty and hopes to meet romance in the form of her employer, or at least to rise quickly because of her physical
charm, has clerkship and chorus work mixed up. A man naturally likes a girl who is attractive, but business personality
and leisure personality are two different things. Every time the
prospect of romance intrudes into a business situation, think
twice before allowing an office relationship to become a personal one.

THE PERFECT SECRETARY

The function of the perfect secretary is to complement her
employer's endeavor and not make any intrusions that would

be more likely to impede than help. A good secretary never betrays the secrets of her employer. His business dealings must be regarded as professional secrets no matter how inconsequential they may seem to her.

Business training teaches every secretary to know everything she can that will be of service to her employer, but to know as little as possible about the things that are not her concern. When sorting his mail, she leaves unopened obviously private letters—envelopes written by hand on stationery not suggestive of business—and having opened his other letters and clipped them in whatever order he likes to have them, she then clips a sheet of blank paper on the top of each pile, or puts the mail in a manila folder so that visitors or others who have access to his office will not inadvertently see them.

When a secretary enters a man's office in response to his summons, she takes a chair and places it near enough to hear him easily. He need not get up and offer her a chair or show her the sort of personal attention that a man in social life shows to a woman.

In unconventional situations:

The young woman who is a confidential secretary to an executive may be required to stay late into the evening, working with him alone, or to go with him on business trips of investigation or conference with firms in distant cities. Every professional or business woman must write her own code of propriety. She knows exactly how necessary she is or is not to the work her employer must do, his attitude toward her, hers toward him and whether she must or need not go with him.

In making business trips, it is true the business woman is free from criticism, but there are qualifying exactions that the critical world expects her to follow. In preparation for the journey, she orders whatever accommodations her employer always expects. On trains, she engages a drawing room or a roomette for him, and a roomette for herself in the same car, but in hotels she engages a suite for him, and a room and bath on another floor for herself. This is not prudishness since everyone knows that the relationship between Mr. Employer and herself is one of professional necessity. But such carefulness insures that there can never be any possible distortion of the truth about their relationship.

It is almost certain that she will lunch with him or have dinner with him—especially on trains or boats or in hotels or restaurants. On rushed days, she may have to eat in his rooms where they are working. In other words, she takes eating alone or eating with him as incidental to convenience. The danger point appears when the pleasure of dining becomes social.

Greeting visitors:

Should a secretary rise when visitors enter the office? Unless the visitors are persons of importance to her employer, it would not be expected of her, or even proper, to greet them in such a way as to encourage their talking to her at length. If she is the private secretary of an executive and part of her job is to make a pleasant impression, she would naturally leave her desk to greet a stranger or an important customer but not to greet one who comes into the office constantly. A secretary's duties do not include helping a visitor off and on with his coat, unless he actually needs help.

THE WELL-RUN OFFICE

You should take as much pride in helping to keep up the tone of the office you work in as you take pride in your own efficiency.

Do not bring your personal problems to the office. Leave them at home, or, if you must, discuss them with a friend during lunch.

In the office of a large company, the executives usually call their employees "Miss [or Mrs.] Jones" rather than "Mary," and they, in turn, call him "Mr. Smith." There are, however, varying degrees of formality in business organizations. Offices today tend to be more casual than formerly. Many employers feel that in a more relaxed atmosphere employees will be more efficient, more reliable and more loyal. The ranking executive determines the degree of formality in his office. He may, for instance, prefer to be on a first-name basis with his staff and the informality does not itself imply a too-familiar relationship. This is invariably true in a small office.

A young woman in a subordinate position does not go out to lunch with her superior or employer. If she holds a responsible position and has matters of business to discuss, she may quite properly lunch with him, provided their going out together does not become a habit.

Though a man does not rise when a woman employee comes into his office, he stands to receive a woman visitor and remains standing until she is seated. He stands again when she prepares to leave and usually goes with her to the door, opens it for her and "bows her out."

Personal messages over the telephone are at times unavoidable, but personal calls that interfere with the routine of office procedure, either incoming or outgoing, are inexcusable except in genuine emergencies.

Discourage visits from your family and friends at the office. Your baby brother may be a most enchanting child, but his place is not in the office in which you work.

Gifts from a firm to its employees are usually in the form of a bonus or a proportion of one's salary. At Christmas a man may give his personal secretary a present. (Wearing apparel is NOT suitable.) A private secretary known well to a man's wife is occasionally remembered by the wife at Christmas. Employees may give presents to their employers, but it is not common. There are exceptions: If there is a wedding in the employer's family, or if a baby is born, then the employees may all contribute and send a gift. As a group they may also send flowers to a funeral. A committee usually collects contributions and makes an appropriate selection.

SOCIAL AMENITIES

A man who is new in a company or who has been transferred to another branch does not entertain his employer until he has first been entertained. Shortly afterward, the newcomer and his wife may return the compliment, though not necessarily "in kind." Even though the employer takes a young executive and his wife to an expensive restaurant for dinner, the young couple may invite the older couple to a simple buffet supper including another couple or two if they wish. Or if the employee has known his superior for some time he might invite him over as he would any friend. Also, if he should be giving a large party—an open house or housewarming, perhaps—including all the other members of the office, it would be insulting to leave his employer out.

The most important thing for a young wife to remember

in entertaining her husband's boss is that she recognize that
he knows her situation and her means, and she need not "put
on the dog." She and her husband should do their best to relax
and act naturally, so that their guests go home thinking,
"What a charming, friendly couple—we're lucky to have them
with our company!"

STORE ETIQUETTE

The technical aspects of salesmanship are much too special-
ized for such a book as this, but aspects that depend for their
success upon tactful and pleasing manners do belong here, as
well as the good manners expected of all customers who make
any pretense to being well-bred.

The successful saleswoman:

Really great saleswomen have cultivated not only an expert
knowledge of the commodities they sell, but an equally expert
ability to appraise each of the customers to whom they sell:
whether a customer likes to be "dearied" or "madamed" or
chatted to about every topic under the sun, whether she likes
to have her mind made up for her or whether she prefers to
have her questions answered intelligently without any unasked-
for advice. The saleswoman whom an intelligent customer is
certain to like best—and return to—is one who listens to what
she says and tries to give her what she wants, instead of trying
to sell her what the store seems eager to be rid of.

For example, when you ask for something she can't supply,
the ideal saleswoman answers, "I am sorry we have nothing
like that in the color you want; but I could give you something in a small pattern of yellow"; then with certain eagerness she asks, "Have you time to let me show it to you?"
When she brings it, you are inclined to be pleased because,
though you know it is not just what you want, you are sure it
is not going to be thrust upon you. Even if you do not want
it, you will certainly come back to that saleswoman another
time when you are looking for something else.

The poorest saleswoman is the one who brushes aside what
you say you want and blandly spreads before you something
that you do NOT want, extolling its beauties or its bargain
values and capping the climax by telling you that Mrs. Uppity
thinks this is exquisite. High-pressure salesmanship never pays

in the long run and sends a customer out of the store determined not to return.

The inconsiderate customer:

An inconsiderate customer can be at her worst and cause the greatest strain on a saleswoman's good temper in the ready-to-wear clothing department. A careless customer often smears the dresses with lipstick as she pulls them on or off, tears them in her haste or sheer carelessness. And in the end she orders none, or perhaps she buys several and then returns everything looking still more shopworn the next day.

Another lack of consideration is shown by those who go shopping ten minutes before closing time. The salespeople have had a long day and have routine chores to do before they can leave.

And finally there are women who, with no thought of buying anything, will go into a dress department solely to pass an hour or so before a lunch date, and waste the time of a saleswoman who is paid at least in part by commissions on the dresses she sells—and not on the ones she shows.

59

With the handicapped

There are certain rules that apply to your behavior in regard to all handicapped people and the most important by far is this: NEVER stare or indicate that you are conscious that the person is different from others in any way. People who are getting themselves about in wheelchairs or have mastered the use of crutch or brace or can manipulate a mechanical hand dexterously take great pride in their independence and approach to normalcy. An offer to help a man in a wheelchair seeking to navigate a steep curb or an arm proffered to a lady with a cane and a leg brace trying to maneuver steps is, of course, in order. But before grabbing the wheelchair or seizing her arm, ask if, and in what way, you can be of assistance.

Never make personal remarks or ask personal questions of one with an obvious disability. Let him introduce the subject, if he wishes, but never pry into his feelings or his clinical symptoms.

Deafness and blindness are the two disabilities with which the greatest number of people come into frequent contact. Here are suggestions for those meeting deaf or blind people, and for those so handicapped.

DEAFNESS

In the case of total hearing loss, where the deaf person must depend on lip reading, speak distinctly and reasonably slowly. Don't use exaggerated mouth movements that may confuse him, as he has been taught to read normal lip movement. If he is not facing you, tap him gently on the arm or shoulder to attract his attention. Be willing to repeat or make your statement in words that are easier for him to understand.

Here are rules in conversing with someone who is partially deaf:

If you know a friend is deaf in only one ear, sit on the side of his good ear in movies, restaurants or any place where you may not be face to face.

Don't raise your voice or shout—his hearing aid is probably adjusted for a normal voice. Call him by name to attract his attention. If you must repeat, don't shout or appear annoyed. This will only embarrass him. Don't exclude him from conversation, but try to place him so that he may see you or the group. Even normal people read lips unconsciously, and being able to read another's lip movements is a great help to one handicapped by partial deafness.

If you are handicapped by deafness the following suggestions may add to your comfort and that of your friends:

DO wear a hearing aid—loss of hearing is no different from loss of sight, and few people refuse to wear glasses. Keep your aid turned on. Listen attentively and concentrate on what people are saying. (Look at the people talking to you—their expression and their lips will help you to "hear" them.)

BLINDNESS

The most important thing to remember when coming in contact with someone who is blind is that in every other respect he is exactly like you. He has a problem, but it is a problem with which one can learn to live, and most blind people have done so with considerable success. Therefore treat the blind man as you would any other person. Talk to him about the same subjects that would interest your other friends. Don't avoid the use of the word "see." Blind people use it as much as anyone else. Don't show surprise that he can dial telephone numbers, light a cigarette, dress himself or perform the daily chores that we all do. He has simply made a little more effort to learn to do them by touch or sound.

When you are with, or pass by, a blind person on a street corner, you are perfectly correct in asking if you may help him to cross, but never grasp his arm or try to give assistance without first asking whether he wishes it or not. If he does, let *him* take *your* arm. If he asks you for directions, be sure to use left and right from his viewpoint—the direction he is facing.

If you go to a restaurant with a blind person, read him the menu, including the prices if the occasion demands. Tell him quietly where the salt and pepper are and help him to the sugar and cream if he wishes. You may tell him how the items on his plate are arranged and help him cut his meat if necessary.

When he visits your home, lead him to a chair and then just place his hand on the arm or back. If he is staying with you for any length of time, tell him where the furniture is, mention it if anything is rearranged, and keep doors open or closed—never halfway.

When taking him to a strange place, tell him where the furniture is located and who is present. Before you leave him alone, be sure that he has someone to talk to with whom you feel he would be congenial.

When there is a blind person in a room you have just entered, make your presence known and tell him, if he does not recognize your voice, who you are. Tell him also when you leave.

If the blind person has a Seeing Eye dog, do not attempt to play with or distract the dog in any way. His attention must remain fully on his master, whose safety and well-being depend on his strict adherence to his training.

60

At public beaches and parks

At the beach:
When there are children to be watched, choose places near the spot where they are going to wade in and out of the water and dig canals and build sand castles. Not only is it dangerous to have little children paddling in the water far away, but when a child runs back and forth he is apt to kick sand and splash water over those sitting in his path.

Before letting Johnny make himself one of a group of strangers sitting nearby, be sure to notice whether the strangers respond to his interest. If not, call him back immediately.

When dogs are allowed in an area where there are other people, they must be kept on leash so as not to alarm anyone. If your dog is to be free to run and swim, find a more deserted part of the beach, being sure to leash him again if a stranger approaches.

Groups of athletic young men throwing a ball over, around and between the sunbathers are an all too common annoyance. Another one is an obvious display of affection, such as languid back-rubs, heads resting on stomachs, kissing and caressing. These breaches of good manners can make neighbors thoroughly uncomfortable.

The public park:

Don't crowd others if you can help it. Don't spread your picnic baskets and personal belongings over two or three tables when your share is one. Picnic tables do not grant children the privilege of eating like little savages to the distress of those nearby who cannot help but see them.

Where there is playground equipment, teach your child to take turns and be satisfied with his own share of time with the slides, swings, seesaws and any other pleasures offered to all children.

Always leave public grounds as clean or cleaner than you find them. Papers, cans, trash and broken bottles completely destroy the beauty of the loveliest landscapes.

61

For pets and people

DOGS

I could quote instances by the dozen of pleasant neighborhood friendships that have become strained and even broken by the Smith dog that barks all night, or the Pope dog that runs through flower beds and digs in them. Other dogs are brought by their owners into friends' houses and allowed to jump up on the furniture with muddy paws or sharp claws.

The behavior of a dog—like the rest of us—is seldom better out in company than it is at home. If Kiltie (bright little Scottie though he is) is allowed to run around the dinner table at home and beg, he will do the same in every other house. It is always safest in a friend's house to keep him on a short leash. He can, with patience and love, be trained to obey cer-

404 GOOD MANNERS FOR EVERY DAY

tain fundamental commands. On the street, he pays no attention to another dog unless his master releases him with a "Go run." At the command "Heel!" he takes his place at his master's side. He sits and stays when told to and never jumps up on a friend unless encouraged to.

If you are invited to stay with those who do not welcome four-footed visitors, you must stay home unless you have someone with whom you can leave the dog or a good kennel at which you can board him. On the other hand, no absolutely obedient dog has ever—as far as I know—been objected to by anyone, even as a house guest. Unless, of course, your prospective host has a pet who resents four-footed intruders.

If you cannot train your dog, there are excellent "obedience schools" who will do it for you for a modest fee.

CATS

Cats are taken visiting far less often. When your cat has the run of the neighborhood, you may have to take steps to see that he does not become an inadvertent but regular visitor at a neighbor's house. It is perfectly proper to ask your neighbors not to feed your pet, as the bad habit is hard to break and can easily become a neighborhood problem.

In your own house, you may be quite accustomed to having your cat jump into your lap without warning, but remember that your guest probably isn't. Until you know your visitor likes and is not allergic to cats, it is far safer to put Fluffy securely in another room. This also avoids a suit or dress covered with hairs and possibly snagged.

OTHER PEOPLE'S PETS

If you are one of those who have an allergy or an aversion to dogs, cats, hamsters, white mice or any of the other pets you are likely to encounter, it is only polite to tell your host or hostess so, quietly and unobtrusively. No one will wish you to suffer as a guest in his house, and a few words can usually prevent much discomfort and possibly an unpleasant misunderstanding.

If you are fond of household animals, be careful to respect their training and encourage their good habits. Don't, for example, thump the sofa beside you and invite Kiltie to jump up until you have asked whether he is allowed to sit on the furniture. Your thoughtless actions may undo months of careful training. Finally, don't ever feed an animal without his owner's permission.

62

Gifts and giving

A gift is an expression of affection; it need not be large or expensive, but it should show thoughtful consideration of the interests of the person to whom it is given. And it should be attractively wrapped with a card enclosed.

MONEY AS A WEDDING PRESENT

The custom of giving money as a wedding present is a long established tradition in Jewish communities and among various other groups. Even in those weddings where most guests give presents, close relatives and intimate friends of the bride's or groom's parents sometimes prefer to give money. The amount should depend on your affection for the receiver and the closeness of the tie between you. In some groups it is accepted that one gives five or ten or twenty dollars as a gift. If this is the custom in your area, you must go along with it or risk criticism. Otherwise, for anyone to say "You must give thus-and-so" is entirely wrong.

A check given before the wedding is made out in the bride's maiden name, or if the couple have opened a joint account, to both the bride and groom. A check presented at the reception is made out to the bride's married name or to the couple jointly.

Checks may be displayed along with other presents but

should be arranged so the amounts are hidden. When money is given at a reception, the cash or a check is placed in an envelope with the couple's first names written on the outside and handed to them as the guests go down the receiving line. The bride and groom both thank the donors, and the envelopes are put into a receptacle to be opened later. In addition to her verbal thanks, the bride writes a thank-you note.

OTHER GIFTS OF MONEY

For people who dislike the idea of giving cash or a check a gift certificate is a good compromise. One thoughtful couple bought a certificate in the leading department store of the town to which their neighbors were moving and presented it at their going-away party.

To include a request for money on the invitation to any private party such as an anniversary or open house is highly incorrect. If, however, the people giving the party have planned a special group present such as tickets for a vacation trip, a new television set or a fine painting, it is proper to enclose a short note with the invitation explaining what has been planned, and asking the guests if they would like to make a contribution in place of bringing an individual gift. Each guest who contributes signs the card accompanying the gift.

THANK-YOU LETTERS

A bride should try to write her thanks the day the wedding gifts arrive; three months should be the outside limit for acknowledging every one. Thank-you letters are not necessary for presents that have been given in person on a birthday, at a house party, a shower or other similar occasions. A note may be written but sincere verbal thanks when you receive the gift are sufficient. A thank-you or "bread-and-butter" letter is not acknowledged but a thank-you gift sent with, or in place of, a bread-and-butter letter is. Sending printed cards of thanks is inexcusable, unless a personal note is added.

When a gift is received from a married couple, the thank-you note is generally written to Mrs. Doe, but some reference to her husband is made in the text of the note: "I want you and Mr. Doe to know how much we like the. . . ." It is not incorrect, however, to address these notes to both man and wife: "Dear Mr. and Mrs. Doe." The same procedure is followed when a wife writes a thank-you letter for a gift given to both her husband and herself.

RETURNING AND EXCHANGING GIFTS

If an engagement is broken, the woman returns to her former fiancé the ring and all other gifts of value that he gave her. Gifts received from relatives or friends are also returned with a short note of explanation. Once the wedding has taken place, however, gifts are not returned, no matter how short the marriage. Strictly speaking, the presents belong to the wife, but the usual procedure is for the husband to keep those items that came from his own family and friends, and those particularly meaningful or useful to him, while the wife keeps the others.

If a gift arrives broken, return it with its wrappings to the shop where it was purchased. Any good store owner will replace the merchandise on reasonable evidence that it was received in damaged condition. Do not involve the donor in this transaction, nor even let her know what happened if you can possibly avoid doing so.

Although a bride should not change presents chosen for her by her own or her bridegroom's family—unless especially told she may do so—other duplicate wedding gifts may be exchanged. A donor never asks on a subsequent visit, "Where is that lovely bowl we gave you?" The time-honored custom permitting the exchange of duplicate wedding presents is so practical and sensible that no one should be offended by it.

A present received on another occasion is not exchanged just because it is not exactly what you want. If it is a duplicate, call the giver and say, "Mary, I happen to have two bottle warmers already. Would you mind terribly if . . . ?" Then in your thank-you note tell Mary how much you are enjoying what you got as a replacement. An exchange to correct the size of a present of clothing need not be mentioned.

OPENING PARTY GIFTS

Half the fun of giving and receiving presents at any party is to see and enjoy what everyone else brought. The nicest way to do this is to collect all the presents in one place until after everyone has arrived, at which time the guest of honor opens them. The recipient reads the cards enclosed and shows enthusiasm for each gift. Always include a card with a gift delivered personally because many people like to collect and save the cards they receive at these times as mementos of the occasion. If anybody has given money instead of a present, the amount is not mentioned but the recipient says something like, "This is a really welcome contribution toward the china we are saving for." On occasions when gifts are not necessarily expected, such as gifts for a dinner hostess, they are opened in the donor's presence but without drawing the attention of other guests.

FLOWERS AS PRESENTS

Flowers may be sent by almost everyone to almost anyone. There are certain times when sending them—if you can possibly afford it—is obligatory. They may be used in place of, or in addition to, the gifts suggested for many occasions mentioned here. Some people are timid about sending flowers because they think those they can afford are not good enough. This reminds me of our daughter who, as a teen-ager, received at times corsages and gifts of flowers. I can truthfully say the one she treasured most was a single red rose from a boy whose knowledge of how to please a girl was well in advance of his years.

SUGGESTED GIFTS FOR DIFFERENT OCCASIONS

R—Gift required

O—Gift is optional

R&O—Gift may or may not be required depending on relationship and circumstances

O *Engagements:* (Presents are expected only from close relatives and intimate friends and are almost always intended especially for the bride.) Towels for bathroom; luggage for honeymoon; blanket cover; jewelry; lingerie (negligee, slips); plastic mat set; bar or kitchen towels; table linen

R *Showers:* (Gifts are chosen to meet the specifications, including color and size, given in the invitation.) Any useful or decorative article appropriate to the particular occasion; it should not be elaborate or intended to take the place of a wedding present. Something made personally by the donor is traditional, and often the most appreciated gift of all.

R&O *Weddings:* Anything to furnish a house or apartment

including: set of folding tables on rack; mirror for an entry
or hall; leather box containing decks of cards; crystal or
china vase; planter; electric hot tray; carving set; large pepper grinder; painting or prints; glasses or china; lamps;
hors d'oeuvre tray; salad bowl; items of china or silver pattern selected by bride

R *Wedding-party attendants to bride or groom, or both:* silver
after-dinner coffee spoons, each engraved with name of one
attendant; silver tray; pitcher; or cigarette box engraved
with attendants' names

R *From bride to her bridesmaids:* small silver picture frame
with bride's picture; bracelet with disc engraved with wedding date; gold charm for bracelet

R *From bridegroom to his ushers:* monogrammed key case or
ring; initialed silver belt buckle; monogrammed stud box

R *Anniversary parties:* picture album (to be filled later if possible with pictures taken at party); picture frame with
family portrait; bottle of wine or champagne; plant—one
which may be planted outside if couple has yard
(For a list of anniversaries see pages 207–08.)

O *Farewell parties*

   I *For those permanently leaving a neighborhood:*
     scrapbook with mementos of years spent together (if you
     have the imagination and inclination); gift certificate
     from department store in future hometown

   II *Bon voyage parties:*
     books; small game; trip diary; guidebook; champagne or
     wine; money exchange guide; playing cards in case;
     small leather picture frame and family picture; travel
     kit of cleaning and laundry products; camera film

R *Housewarmings:* cigarette box; wastebasket; bookends; mag-
azine rack; leather or silver stamp holder (filled with postage
stamps); potted plant; seeds or bulbs for garden; address
book including names of recommended local services and
stores

O *New babies:* sweater, other clothing; blanket or comforter;
crib toys; baby food; bath articles; furnishing for room
(picture, little chair); spoon and fork; bibs

R *Christenings:* silver porringer; hair brush and comb; savings
bond; for a girl, one pearl or charm to be added to later;
baby's memory book album

R&O *Birthdays*

 I *For teen-agers:*

  clothing; sports equipment; records; books; money (perhaps one dollar for each year of age)

 II *For a wife or husband:*

  any little present you know he or she wants but has avoided buying because *you* think it foolish or extravagant

 III *For an older couple:*

  travel tickets for a special vacation; gift certificate; plants

 IV *For friends:*

  any foolish "gag" present. Unless very close friend, to avoid embarrassment, don't give expensive gifts

R *First Communion:* Bible; prayer book; jewelry; fine book

R *Bar mitzvah:* a gift of money is most generally given. The amount depends on the closeness of the donor to the youngster.

R&O *Graduation:* money, gift certificate, savings bond or stock; initial deposit in a new savings account; watch or bedside clock or clock-radio; desk pen and pencil set or desk lamp; books (especially those useful for chosen career or standard reference works); camera; sports equipment; stereo or hi-fi equipment; jewelry

R *For weekend visit:* gourmet hors d'oeuvres; cocktail or highball glasses; a set of good scissors; toys for young children; liquor or wine; steak or casserole dish ready for heating (check with hostess in advance); record album; flowers or plant; a new game or jigsaw puzzle (especially good if hostess has children); cookies, a cake or candy

R&O *Christmas*

 I *Girl to a boy friend:*

  key case; wallet; imprinted stationery; picture frame with her picture; something she has knitted or personalized herself, such as a sweater, mittens or golf club covers

 II *Boy to a girl friend:*

  a pair of tickets to a hit show; costume jewelry; inexpensive charm; clothing accessories (gloves, scarf, belt, etc., but not "personal" clothing); books; records; stuffed toy animal

O *To nurses, doctors and professional people in appreciation of special care:*

I *For hospital nurses:*
cookies, candy or fruit sent to nurses' desk on patient's floor

II *For doctors:*
desk set; food specialty (homemade fruitcake); liquor or wine; golf balls; carving set; contribution to his favorite charity

O *For sick people or hospital patients:* light reading matter; homemade soup; cookies or other specialty (clear all food gifts with doctor first)

GIFTS TO AVOID

Never choose a gift that might be construed as criticism. A present of a cookbook can be most welcome providing your friend knows that you know she likes to cook. This same cookbook given to someone at whose home the food is mediocre might easily be resented. Avoid giving presents requiring constant care to people who are not interested or able to give it: live birds, fish or animals, including unsolicited gifts of baby ducklings and rabbits at Easter. The well-meaning family friend who gives a young child a puppy or kitten without first clearing the matter with his parents will not long remain a family friend. Before buying any present think to yourself, "What would she do with it?" and if you can't find an answer to that, then don't buy it.

MARKING GIFTS

Before you have anything of value monogrammed, be sure you know it is wanted and that it is the right size, color and style. If you *are* sure of this, initials are a handsome addition to many gifts. Muriel Barbara Jones uses the initials "MBJ" before she plans to be married, but when she marries Henry Ross, her initials become "MJR." (Wedding presents are usually marked with her married initials or, on her flat silver, it may be just "R," the first letter of her new last name.) A man uses all three of his initials and should include "Jr." after them when applicable.

QUESTIONS

The queries below have been selected from those I am most frequently asked by my readers.

Q. Does an invitation to a wedding ceremony require that the receiver send a gift?

A. An invitation to a wedding ceremony carries no obligation, neither does a wedding announcement. People receiving invitations to a reception, however, are expected to send gifts whether they attend or not. Recipients of a church invitation or an announcement may send a present if they feel so inclined.

Q. Do engaged couples send joint or separate wedding presents?

A. It depends on their relationship to the bridal couple. If each of them knows one member of the couple well, they may wish to send separate gifts. If one is closer to the couple than the other, or if one does not know the bride or groom at all but is included on the guest list, they may send a joint present.

Q. What do you do when your neighbor arrives Christmas Eve with an unexpected Christmas present?

A. It's a wise idea to have a supply of small gifts on hand for just such an emergency. When you see something you really like, and it's not too expensive, buy half a dozen instead of one, and put the others away—later on you'll thank your lucky star for your foresight.

Q. Are the cards that accompany wedding presents displayed with the gifts?

A. There is no firm rule. Some brides feel that it is complimentary to display them, others that it invites comparisons or that some donors who could not afford to give as much as they would like dislike having the fact advertised. It is entirely up to the bride. It is correct to display cards—it is equally correct to leave them off.

Q. How can you let guests know that you do not wish gifts brought to a birthday or anniversary party?

A. You write "No gifts, please" on any invitation. If the invitations are issued by telephone, you tell the guests that you do not expect, or want, a gift. When this is indicated, the guests should respect the wish, and not say, "Oh, I'll just take some little thing."

Q. What should you say when someone asks you what you want as a present?

A. Try to help them out, although they may have shown ill judgment by putting you in an embarrassing position. Rather than saying, "I don't know," or "I'd rather you chose something yourself," attempt to make a suggestion or two. If you can't, tell them you'll let them know, and then remember to do it.

PART TWELVE

ON HOW TO DRESS

63

Women's clothes and fashions

THE WOMAN WHO IS CHIC

The woman who is chic is always a little different. Not different in being behind fashion, but always slightly apart from it. Chic (pronounced *sheek*) is a combination of sophistication and fastidious taste, and the woman who is chic adapts fashion to her own personality. This is in contrast to the woman who will merely buy the latest hat or dress and adapt herself to it, whether the fashion is suited to her or not. When it conspicuously is not, it is likely to be chi-chi (pronounced *she-she*), or a flashy imitation of chic.

ACCESSORIES

Accessories provide the accents that can vary the costume, giving it versatility as well as adding to its beauty. In planning your wardrobe, stick to a narrow range of colors, so that the same accessories may be used with a number of outfits. A simple black dress may be perfect for lunch at a restaurant when it is worn with a gold circle pin, single-pearl earrings and a daytime watch or wide gold bracelet and accompanied by black kid pumps and a plain leather pocketbook. But change these accessories to a diamond or zircon clip, a double strand of pearls, diamond (or pearl drop) earrings, a bracelet, perhaps, or a ring of glittering stones, suede pumps and a small suede purse, and you may appear at any but the most formal party that night.

Jewelry:

It has always been the rule of the well-dressed not to wear too many jewels in public places because such a display is considered ostentatious and in poor taste. But with the rise in popularity of costume jewelry, smart women all over have increased the amount of jewelry they wear in public as well as at home. Cultured pearls and semiprecious stones such as zircons, garnets or jade come in an infinite variety of colors. With the lower cost of these substitutes for expensive gems, many more women than ever before are able to wear beautiful jewelry.

Jewelry should be chosen and worn with an eye to suitability rather than to fad. A woman with stubby hands, for example, should not draw attention to them with a large flashing ring. When engaging in an active sport, jewelry of any kind is out of place. In the daytime, a gold or silver bracelet, a string of pearls and earrings unadorned by large stones are more suitable than the brilliant gems that go well with evening clothes. A pretty pin or clip to set off a dress or suit is lovely at any hour. In short, the choice of jewelry is limited only by the good taste and the budget of the wearer.

Gloves:

Gloves are worn on city streets, to luncheons, dinner parties and other social gatherings, to churches, restaurants, theaters and other public places of entertainment. At a restaurant, theater or the like, they may be removed on arrival, but they are generally left on in church except during communion or when it is very warm.

A lady never takes off her gloves to shake hands, no matter when or where, and *never* apologizes for not doing so. But she *always* removes them for dining. On formal occasions, the hostess wears gloves to shake hands with her guests—and keeps them on until food is served. Gloves are *always* worn when standing in a receiving line. When long gloves are an intrinsic part of your costume at a ball, they may be left on for dancing—otherwise they are taken off. A bracelet may be worn outside a long glove, but never a ring.

Hats:

If you look well in hats—wear them! If well chosen, a hat may add a dash and distinction to your outfit that a bare head can't possibly achieve. You must wear a hat to all Roman Catholic church ceremonies, and it is always correct at churches of every faith. At official luncheons and receptions, they are almost a requirement. A small hat or veil is appropriate, but not necessary, with a cocktail dress. Except for the necessary head covering at an evening wedding, a hat, even the smallest veil, is never worn with an evening dress.

Fur capes and stoles:

For many years ladies adhered to an arbitrary and, to me, inexplicable rule that fur capes, stoles and jackets should not be worn before five o'clock in the evening. Actually, there is no reason for a fur stole's not being worn to any "dressy" affair from noon on, if the costume the fur is worn over is of a comparable degree of elegance. Morning wear is invariably less formal, and therefore a short fur of any sort would not be in keeping. But for luncheons, receptions, weddings, etc. held at or after noon, a fur stole is quite correct. Women who have a choice might prefer to wear a cloth coat in the daytime and save their fur for evening, but those who can only have one "dress" coat, and prefer a fur to all others, may feel free to wear it at almost any hour.

Mink and other luxurious and expensive furs should never be worn with sports clothes such as wool suits or slacks.

Shoes:

The first thing to consider in buying shoes—and this cannot be stressed too strongly—is comfort. The most beautiful pair of shoes in the world will destroy the appearance of the wearer if the height of the heel causes her to teeter or the tightness of the toes causes her to stand painfully, first on one foot and then the other.

When picking out shoes, try to find colors and styles that will go with more than one dress. Red is an excellent choice for spring and summer, as it goes well with black, navy, white and many of the light summer shades.

If you are more comfortable in "flats" or low heels, stick to them.

The business girl who is on her feet much of the day should

sacrifice some smartness for comfort and choose a shoe that has a thick soft sole and gives her foot some support. A good suggestion is to keep an extra pair of shoes at your place of business, as a change in the middle of the day is very restful to the feet.

Shoes worn with more formal clothes should match or blend with the costume in color and be appropriate in material and style. Generally speaking, leather shoes such as alligator or kid, in dark colors, are correct for daytime in the winter. Black shoes go well with almost every winter costume. Suede or satin shoes in a color matching your dress are worn for more formal occasions or in the evening. Pumps or sandals in gold or silver are worn with a formal evening dress, but they are in very bad taste for daytime wear with street costumes. "Spectators" (white pumps trimmed with black, brown or navy) for daylight occasions and white linen or cotton pumps for after dark go happily with almost any summer ensemble. High heels worn with sport slacks look—and are—ridiculous.

Handbags:

Bags can now be found in a literally unlimited variety of colors, styles and materials. Decide on whatever color blends best with all of your costumes. A good quality black leather one, large enough to contain all the items you may need for a whole day, will last for years and pay for itself many times over in usefulness, durability and beauty. A straw handbag for daytime use in the summer goes with all cottons and sport clothes.

Bags with changeable covers are not inexpensive, but the cost is more than made up for by the versatility. For a winter bag of this type, the basic purse might be black leather and the covers (designed to snap on so that the result appears to be an ordinary purse) might be of brown kid, black lizard or suede. The summer bags have covers of cotton or linen and are washable!

For evening, gold metallic bags are popular or, for older people, black velvet, silk or satin. Small suede or satin bags come in pretty colors and are a good choice for cocktail time.

Corsages:

There is no rule in existence about how a woman wears a corsage. She simply stands in front of a mirror and holds the flowers against her dress in various places until she finds the spot that pleases her most. If the dress is so designed that a corsage does not go well on it, or if the wearer is afraid of crushing the flowers while dancing, they may also be pinned on a cloth evening bag. If the flower has a stem, wear it upright as the flower grows—if not, place it whichever way it looks best.

A word about slacks:

Slacks as sports wear have been accepted for a number of years. They are certainly the most practical dress for an active woman engaged in sailing, hunting, heavy housework, gardening or many other activities. However, a woman who has a weight problem or who is particularly heavy through the hips should avoid wearing slacks on all other occasions. The same is true of evening slacks and the popular "pants suits." They cannot be surpassed for comfort and for smartness when worn by the right woman, but on anyone else a long "at home" skirt, or a cocktail or dinner dress is far more appealing.

CLOTHES FOR THE BUSINESS WOMAN

The unfailing directions for clothes worn in an office are that they be neat, tailored, smart, in good taste, but in no way conspicuous. Avoid everything that interferes or catches or keeps getting out of place. Also wear clothes that properly cover you.

One important accessory for beautiful business clothes is a pair of plain sensible shoes of best quality. High-heeled, fancy sandals and heel-less slippers are inappropriate. A well-shod foot is much to be prized—and noticed.

YOUR TRAVELING WARDROBE

When you plan a wardrobe for a trip, whether it be by airplane, car, train or boat, there are two considerations—space and weight. Nothing takes up more space or weighs more than handbags and shoes. If you can plan your costumes so that one pair of the most comfortable, sturdy shoes available for sightseeing can be exchanged in the evening for a pump of the same color, your packing and overweight problems will be almost solved. The handbags with changeable covers mentioned earlier in this chapter are ideal for traveling. You may carry the bag itself onto the boat or plane and pack only the light-weight covers. For evening, pack a small flat silk or satin bag.

Dresses of wrinkleproof material are a "must." Take along a little package of cleaning powders, put up specially for travelers—a spot on a dress that forms an important part of your clothing scheme can be a disaster.

Think of the versatility of your clothes. Sweaters should go well with *all* your skirts, shorts and dresses. A skirt with a matching coat makes a stunning costume for cruise or country wear because, with a change of blouses, the skirt can give the appearance of several outfits. One rarely needs an evening dress when traveling, but a sleeveless cocktail dress with a jacket may be worn in any restaurant or theater or at any party to which you are invited.

Shorts and slacks, incidentally, are never worn by women abroad except at resorts, and therefore American women should "in Rome, do as the Romans." So if you are traveling on the Continent rather than on a cruise ship, save space by taking only those shorts needed for your day or two on the Riviera. Don't forget a bathing suit—even a wayside stream can provide a refreshing relief from the heat of southern France, Italy or Spain in summer; swimming pools and lakes are found near resort hotels all over the world.

(For clothes appropriate to special occasions, please consult the Index.)

64

Men's clothes

FORMAL DAYTIME WEAR

When it is necessary to dress formally, the cutaway or a black sack coat and striped trousers are worn at any affair that takes place before six o'clock in the evening. They are often worn at government or diplomatic receptions, but they appear most frequently on the principals in a formal afternoon wedding or when they are worn by pallbearers in a large funeral.

The cutaway:

The cutaway is the most formal afternoon attire and is rarely seen except on participants in large afternoon weddings or at official teas or receptions. For this reason, few men not in the diplomatic corps have cutaways, but they can always be rented. Make your arrangements well ahead of the date it is to be worn, so that it may be fitted to you.

The cutaway (sometimes called the morning coat)—Black or oxford gray worsted or cheviot, with peaked lapels. Edges may be bound, but plain edges are preferred. Buttons are bone or self-covered.

Waistcoat—Double-breasted. In winter, black wool to match the coat or pearl-gray fine wool. In summer, white or fawn linen or white piqué.

Trousers—Black and gray striped worsted or cheviot. Cuffless.

Shirt—White, with starched bosom and starched cuffs.

Collar—Detachable wing or starched fold collar.

Tie—For weddings, ascot, in gray, silver-gray or black silk, plain, figured or striped. Worn with wing collar. For funerals, black four-in-hand, worn with fold collar. Other occasions, a four-in-hand or bow tie with either wing or fold collar.

Socks—Black or dark gray. Any material except very heavy wool.

Shoes—Black calf oxfords.

Hat—Black silk hat. Less appropriate, a black homburg.

Topcoat—Black, dark gray or dark blue.

Gloves—Gray, any material of good quality.

Accessories—Jewelry; pearl pin with ascot, gold cuff links. With stiff shirt with bow tie, gold single stud. Boutonniere, white or red carnation. At a wedding, the groom may wear a small sprig from his bride's bouquet. Handkerchief (white linen) and white or gray silk scarf. Handkerchief initialed in white, with all initials, or that of last name only, is folded square and shows no more than ½ to 1 inch above the pocket.

The sack coat:

The sack coat, a less formal version of the cutaway, is worn by the participants in morning or afternoon weddings, large funerals, and on any daytime occasion when the formality of the cutaway is not essential.

Sack coat—Black or oxford gray worsted, single-breasted.

Waistcoat—Double-breasted. Black or oxford gray, same as the sack coat, or pearl-gray fine wool.

Trousers—Same as for cutaway.

Shirt—White, soft bosom, starched French cuffs. Starched fold collar.

Tie—Black or gray and black pattern, silk. Four-in-hand style.

Hat—Black homburg or soft black felt.

All other clothing and accessories are the same as for a cutaway.

EVENING CLOTHES

For all informal evening wear, the dark (preferably blue) suit, with white shirt, dark tie and dark socks, is the accepted outfit. For formal evenings, either full evening dress, called "white tie" or "tails" (sometimes "white tie and tails") or a dinner jacket, called "black tie" or "tuxedo," is worn. If in doubt as to what to wear, err on the side of informality. Thus, if you are not sure whether to put on your full-dress suit or your tuxedo, wear the latter. When an occasion is important, it is entirely proper for a man to call his host or his hostess on the telephone and ask, "Do I wear a black tie tonight, or a white one?" or the question may be: "Day clothes or tuxedos?"

Black tie:

To go out for the evening dressed in "black tie" means that you are wearing a dinner jacket or tuxedo. Nowadays, black tie is accepted as correct on almost every formal occasion. Therefore, while it is more practical for most to rent a "set of tails" when the occasion demands, a good quality, well-fitted tuxedo is an excellent investment. It consists of:

Jacket—In winter or summer, black or midnight blue; the material is usually tropical worsted or, if it is not shiny, one of the new blended materials. The lapels are faced with satin. In hot weather, white linen is worn for formal affairs, but for less formal parties, plaid (madras) or a solid-color cotton, Dacron or other blend is appropriate, attractive and gay. On all jackets the lapels are rolled or peaked and of whatever width current fashion demands. Dinner jackets are usually single-breasted, but a few men still prefer the double-breasted form, which requires neither waistcoat nor cummerbund.

Trousers—When a dark jacket (black or midnight blue) is worn, the trousers are always of the same material. If a colored jacket is worn, they are of good-quality black material, usually the same pair that is worn with a black jacket. In either case, they do not have cuffs and do have a single stripe of black braid or satin.

Waistcoat or cummerbund—The waistcoat is of white piqué or plain or patterned black silk. Nowadays, instead of a waistcoat, a cummerbund, usually (and most formally) of black or maroon silk, is frequently worn; it may also be plaid or figured, especially in the summertime.

Shirt—A daytime white shirt with fold collar; for a formal occasion, a piqué or pleated bosom.

Tie—Black silk bow with waistcoat or black cummerbund. If cummerbund is other than black, the tie should be of matching color and material.

Socks—Black silk or lisle.

Shoes—Black patent leather.

Hat—A black homburg or black or gray soft-brimmed fedora

in the winter, gray fedora in the spring or fall, and a panama in the summer. Many men prefer no hat.

Gloves—Gray chamois or buck.

Topcoat—Black, dark gray or navy, with or without velvet collar.

Accessories—Jewelry; pearl or mother-of-pearl or black onyx studs. Cuff links may be gold or mother-of-pearl to match the studs. White linen handkerchief, with or without initials. White silk scarf. Boutonniere, white or red carnation.

White tie:

The great majority of men rent their "tails" for the occasion. This is perfectly correct, provided the rental establishment has excellent tailors to do alterations.

A tailcoat *must* be worn by the fathers and escorts of debutantes at their coming-out parties and to any affair when the invitation reads "white tie." Otherwise, it *may* be worn to formal dinners or balls, to official or diplomatic parties or when sitting in a box at the opera or by those in charge of benefits or charity affairs.

Tailcoat—Black worsted or tropical worsted; lapels are peaked and faced in grosgrain or satin. The tails should hang to the break at the back of the knees.

Waistcoat—White piqué. Usually single-breasted, but may be double-breasted.

Trousers—Match the coat. Single stripe of satin or braid; no cuffs.

Shirt—White, made to wear with detachable wing collar. Piqué or plain linen bosom, stiffly starched. Cuffs are single, starched. Shirt may have either one or two buttonholes for studs.

Tie—White piqué bow. Current fashion favors straight ends rather than "butterfly" shape.

Socks—Black silk or nylon.

Shoes—Black patent leather pumps or oxfords.

Hat—High silk or opera hat is most formal, but a black homburg is more frequently worn. Many men prefer not to wear a hat with tails.

Topcoat—Black or dark gray or blue.

Gloves—White chamois or doeskin.

Accessories—Jewelry; pearl or mother-of-pearl studs for shirt, mother-of-pearl or platinum or white gold for the waistcoat and cuff links. White linen handkerchief and white silk scarf. Boutonniere, white carnation or small white gardenia.

COATS AND HATS

For the man who frequently wears evening clothes, a solid black, navy or dark gray coat is a necessity. For daytime wear he also requries a less formal coat in the color that goes best with his suits. The dress coat may or may not be double-breasted—the daytime sports coat, never.

For men whose wardrobe is limited, a gray felt fedora is the best choice. It can be worn with any color and in any circumstance except with full evening dress. Those who wear white tie frequently should have a black homburg or silk hat to go with it. Derbies, which used to be worn with business suits, are rarely seen and the high silk hat has almost disappeared.

Lifting or tipping the hat:

Lifting or tipping the hat means merely lifting it slightly off the forehead—by the brim of a stiff hat or by the crown of a soft one.

A gentleman does this: (1) When walking with a friend who greets a woman who is a stranger to him. (2) When a lady who is a stranger drops a glove or other article and he retrieves it for her. (3) When he passes a lady in a narrow space so that he blocks her way or in any manner obstructs her. (4) If he gets on a bus and the bus gives a lurch and throws him against a woman. (5) If an older woman or a young one carrying a baby or heavy packages enters the bus, and he rises and offers his seat (also when she thanks him). (If he is seated when a young woman enters a bus, he may keep his seat.)

If he is in the company of a woman anywhere in public, he lifts his hat to a man who offers her a seat or who picks up something she has dropped or shows her any other civility. He lifts his hat if he asks a woman a question and always if, when walking on the street with a lady, she greets another person. In short, he tips his hat to say "Excuse me," or "Thank you."

When to remove a hat and gloves:

A gentleman takes off his hat and holds it in his hand when a lady enters the elevator in an apartment house or hotel—

any building which can be classified as a dwelling. He puts it on again in the corridor—an elevator in a hotel or apartment house has the character of a room in a house and there a man does not keep his hat on in the presence of women. But in public buildings such as offices or stores or buildings that contain neither apartments nor assembly rooms, the elevator is considered as public a place as a bus or train.

When a man stops on a city street to speak to a woman of his acquaintance, should he be smoking, he transfers the cigarette or pipe to his left hand before he removes his hat. Then he pulls off his right glove and offers his hand to the lady. If they walk on together, he puts his hat on. While standing in the street talking to her, he remains hatless unless, in cold weather, she thoughtfully says, "Please put your hat on." At a formal ball or wedding, a gentleman need not remove his glove to shake hands.

An American citizen always stands with his hat off at the passing of the flag and when the national anthem is played— indoors or out-of-doors. He also takes his hat off in the presence of a funeral and in all Christian churches.

Men's jewelry:

The best rule for buying men's jewelry is to choose the simplest that can be found.

Cuff links should be of moderate size. Flashing stones in tie pins or rings in the daytime are in poor taste.

The most appropriate rings are those of gold, with initials or crest, worn on the little finger, or a seal ring of one's school or military service, which is worn on the fourth finger of either hand. Wedding rings should be of plain gold, or with the very simplest of patterns.

PART THIRTEEN

THE WELL-APPOINTED HOUSE

65

The employer-servant relationship

THE NEW EMPLOYER

If you have never kept house before and do not know what a maid should be able to do, go to a reliable employment office where the personnel will be glad to tell you about hours and wages and an average working plan. Or you may ask a friend who has a maid to help you.

When an applicant comes to you for an interview, she usually brings with her a written reference from her last employer. Read it carefully but do not put too much stock in it. Most housewives hesitate to write down derogatory comments and then give them to their ex-employees. A written reference is worthwhile only if it gives the name and telephone number of the writer. Before hiring anyone, the housewife should take advantage of that information because she will get a far more complete and honest appraisal over the phone than the note of reference can possibly give.

If the references are good, the wages you can pay meet her expectations, and you find her personality pleasing, you describe to her the schedule of both working and time-off hours. Be accurate. Misrepresentation of facts or intentions is unfair. If she is going to care for the baby, say so quite honestly. Don't say you are always prompt when you are not or that your meals will be simple if you expect her to be an expert chef. Don't say that the house is easy to take care of if it isn't. At the other extreme, don't exaggerate whatever inconveniences there may perhaps be.

HOW MUCH WORK?

Out of every twenty-four hours, every normal human being should have at least nine hours for sleeping, dressing and undressing, in addition to plenty of time for eating three meals. During the rest of the day, she must find the time for rest and recreation as well as for work, and this additional time off must be adjusted to the household routine. The maid's days off should be stated clearly and respected. If it is absolutely necessary to change a day off, she must be given ample warning so that she may change her own plans.

The maid's food and lodging, her uniforms and aprons are part of her pay so that her hours for housework would naturally on occasion run longer than ordinary business hours.

MAY SERVANTS ENTERTAIN FRIENDS?

Certainly! In every large house, there is always a sitting room furnished with comfortable chairs, a sofa, a radio, a television set and good light to read by. In a smaller house where no sitting room is possible, the kitchen table has an attractive cover put on it and a droplight and a few restful chairs are provided if there is space. Or the maid's room, especially one on the ground floor, may be furnished as a sitting room.

In homes with one servant, the use of the living room is sometimes offered the maid when the family is not at home. The man of the house may even suggest that her caller will find a soft drink in the refrigerator.

UNIFORMS

All maids' uniforms as well as aprons and collars and cuffs are furnished by the employer, with the exception of the dresses worn by a lady's maid and those worn by a cook, for whom the employer furnishes only the aprons.

AN ATTRACTIVE ROOM

Make her room as attractive as possible with a comfortable bed, attractively painted furniture and a little gay chintz. Smooth-flowing paints or enamels in beautiful colors can be applied even by an amateur. The kitchen should be equally attractive, for this is where she will spend much of her time.

COURTESY ON BOTH SIDES

In a formal household servants are addressed as James, Margaret or Katherine, rather than Jim, Maisie or Katie. A butler is called by his last name. The Worldlys' butler, for instance, is called Hastings, not John; the housekeeper is Mrs. Jones and the nurse is called by her name or a nickname such as "Nanny." In a less formal household, the maid may be called by a nickname, or if she is an older woman, she may be called Mrs. Helper.

Every courteous person says "please" in asking that something be brought her or him. "Would you mail these letters, please" or "Some bread, please." So, too, in refusing a dish at the table one says, "No, thank you."

The well-trained servant is faultlessly neat in appearance, reticent in manner, speaks in a low voice and moves silently. In answering a bell, she asks, "Did you ring, madam?" A courteous maid answers her employer, "Yes, madam," "Very good, sir," or "Yes, sir," but never "Yes," "No," "All right," or "Sure."

SUCCESS IN HOUSEHOLD MANAGEMENT

Justice is the foundation upon which every tranquil household is constructed. It is not right to be too lenient, any more than it is right to be unreasonably demanding. There is no greater example of injustice than to reprimand those about you because you happen to be in a bad humor and overlook greater offenses because you are in an amiable mood. There is also no excuse ever for correcting an employee in front of anyone else. If the lady of the house and the other members of the family show human understanding and fairness in what they exact, they are very unlikely ever to have any housekeeping difficulties.

66

Household assistants

Thanks to the conveniences and appliances in modern homes, the work that used to be done by many servants can now be done by one or two. This is not to say that there are no homes with a large staff, but the vast majority of home owners who have live-in servants have no more than one or two, and it is to these people that this chapter is devoted.

COUPLES

A satisfactory solution to the problem of household help for many families who have large houses but cannot or do not wish to employ many servants is the married couple who are hired together. The usual arrangement is for the woman to do the cooking and clean the bedroom floors, while the man waits on table, cleans the living rooms, dining rooms, halls, etc., and also does some driving and takes care of the cars. They share the work of cleaning up after meals; he may also help with their preparation, especially if the employer is entertaining.

The couple must have an apartment of at least two rooms, preferably with a private entrance, perhaps over a garage. Some employers do not object if a child lives with the parents; however, he is not allowed the run of the house except when playing with the children of the employer.

THE CHILDREN'S NURSE

A children's nurse is either the comfort or the torment of the house. Innumerable young mothers put up with inexcusable crankiness from a crotchety middle-aged woman because she is "so wonderful" to the baby. In ninety-nine cases out of a hundred, the sooner a domineering nurse—old or young—is let go, the better. When the right sort of kindly and humane person takes the tyrant's place, the mother usually finds that the child is as relieved as the rest of the family. A young child is inescapably imprisoned in the atmosphere created by the disposition of the person in charge of him and sunlight is not more essential to a plant than an atmosphere of sympathetic lightheartedness is to a child.

A nurse's references should *always* be checked by talking on the telephone with the woman who employed her last. Her moral character is of utmost concern, for she is to be the constant and inseparable companion of children whose whole lives are influenced by her example, especially if busy parents can give only a small portion of time to their children.

The nurse dresses in white in the home—the wonderful wash-and-wear fabrics available today make this entirely practical. On the street she wears a simple suit or dress and hat (the cloak and cap of the English nurse is suitable only if she actually is British).

THE REGISTERED NURSE

The social position of a registered hospital nurse is that of a deputy physician and, when on a long case, the closest of the family's friends. She always eats her meals with the family or has them served to her on a tray in a sitting room. When on duty in her patient's room or anywhere in a private house, she wears her uniform. But when going into the street, going downstairs in a hotel or traveling with her patient, she dresses as does any other lady.

THE MOTHER'S HELPER

The duties of a "mother's helper" are generally related to the care of the children—their meals, their rooms and their clothes. If there are only one or two children, her chores may also include some light housework, some laundry, some cooking and some washing up. It is essential, because of the loosely defined nature of the job, that the areas and amount of work to be done are discussed and settled upon before the position is accepted. Too often a woman is hired to "take care of the children" and, because no guidelines were laid down in the beginning, eventually finds herself taking care of the whole house as well.

The relationship of a "mother's helper" and her family is usually quite different from that of other servants and employers. She often, over a period of time, becomes almost a member of the family. In some cases she may eat her meals with them, but this can become somewhat of a strain, because every couple is entitled to their privacy and the privilege of being alone. When there are young children in the family, the ideal solution is for her to eat dinner with them at an earlier hour, except, perhaps, on Sundays and special occasions. Some perceptive "mother's helpers," in order to avoid imposing, simply say that they prefer to eat earlier, or to watch television at that hour, or make some other excuse. But she, with the children, may join the family for a while before dinner if she wishes, and once the children are in bed, her time should be her own.

A great many young girls come from abroad to fill this position, and they have their special problems. They generally contract to come for a ridiculously low salary, for a period of one year. But the housewife should realize that the wage, even though agreed upon, is often completely inadequate in our economy. Therefore if she does not voluntarily offer to pay a reasonable amount, her mother's helper may be wooed away by an offer of higher wages from one of the neighbors. These girls are often highly educated, and take the job as a means of getting to the United States. Their background is frequently the same or better than that of the people they are working for. When this is so, it is even more necessary, if the year is to be a success, and possibly to extend to more years, that her employers make every effort to make their "helper" feel at home. Although she need not be included when they are entertaining or when they are alone as a family, she should be a welcome member of the group.

THE BABY-SITTER

A baby-sitter's age may range from the early teens up to that of an elderly lady. The customary rate of the community should be observed and the sitter paid at the end of the evening. The sitter should be told that after the children are asleep he or she may use the television set or play the radio, read or do homework; in other words, what she is expected to do and what she may not do. It is thoughtful to leave a snack in the refrigerator. Be specific about where you are going—leave address and telephone number, as well as the name, address and telephone number of the children's doctor. Always tell the sitter when you expect to be back—and try to be on time. Adequate transportation must be provided for her safe return home, and this applies for sitters of any age.

PART-TIME HELP

The maid, or "cleaning woman," who comes by the hour or day, is treated with the same courtesy as the permanent servant. She is paid promptly—daily, weekly or any other way agreed upon. In the country, if the house is far from public transportation, the employer sees that she is transported to bus or train or, if she is not, that her pay is augmented to cover taxi fare. In the city, the employer pays all carfares involved. If the employer wishes her to wear uniforms, she naturally provides them for her.

The maid's duties should be carefully outlined in advance. Will there be cooking to do? Are washing and ironing expected, and what about heavy cleaning like waxing floors and washing windows? For any unusual work, to help with a dinner party, for example, the hourly rate for this extra service should be agreed upon beforehand.

67

Serving the family meals

THE TABLE

In many of today's houses and apartments, the pressures of space and expense have caused the large, formal dining room to disappear. The dining table appears in an ell or an alcove off the living room, in the end of the living room nearest the kitchen, or at one end of the kitchen itself. Whatever the location, the table should be thought of as a pleasant center of family gatherings. It should be large enough to accommodate the entire family comfortably, for young children especially need plenty of room to eat properly and crowding only encourages jostling.

A pretty cloth or attractive place mats lend an air of graciousness to even the simplest meal; a centerpiece is also pleasing. With a little help, children can pick and arrange a few flowers or make a simple table decoration. Such contributions help children recognize the importance of household appointments.

Most often, when there is no maid, mother sits nearest the kitchen door with the youngest, who may still need help from time to time, next to her. Father sits opposite her.

If there is a maid in the house, the family always eats at the dining table, where they are served simply, in whatever way best fits their preference and the capabilities of the maid.

Kitchen dining:

If possible have an end or corner of the kitchen set apart, furnished and decorated in such a way that children growing

General Electric

up in the home feel the importance of good manners at the table, just as they would if they were being served in a beautifully appointed dining room. Even a kitchen table should be charmingly set for dinner with place mats (paper doilies will do), spotless utensils and pretty plates and glasses, attractive in color and pattern.

THE PLACE SETTINGS

The main difference in setting a table for guests and setting a table for the family is that a minimum number of utensils is put at each place—only those absolutely necessary for each course. There may be no more than a fork, a knife, and a spoon or fork for dessert. At a family dinner, a separate fork for salad is not necessary, but a salad plate is, so that gravy and salad dressings do not become mixed. Bread and butter are often placed on the edge of the dinner plate, but with the convenience of an electric dishwasher, it is nicer to have a separate butter plate.

The table settings described below indicate the correct position of the articles that will be needed. No china or silver that will not actually be used needs to be put on the table —no salad forks if you are not serving salad, no bread-and-butter plate if you have no bread.

Breakfast:

There is a wide difference in the tastes of breakfast-eaters. If your daughter only eats toast and coffee, omit the fork. If your son doesn't drink coffee, you need only give him a glass for his milk.

In the informal household, a variety of cold cereals, milk, cream, sugar, salt and pepper, and jams or jellies are in the center of the table or on a convenient side table; whoever does the cooking serves the hot food directly onto the plates and places them in front of those sitting at the table. If your table is large enough, a "lazy susan" or turntable is most convenient.

Individual places are set with as many of the following articles as will be necessary: Fork at the left of the plate, knife at the right of the plate, spoon for cereal at the right of the knife, teaspoon for fruit (but not for coffee) at the right of the cereal spoon.

Butter knife across the bread-and-butter plate, which is to

the left and above the fork. Napkins at the left of the plates if fruit or fruit juice is at the places; otherwise, napkins at the center of each place.

Coffee cups have spoons lying at right of, or on, the saucers, at the right of each plate. Glasses for milk or water are to the right and above the spoons.

Lunch:

For the busy woman of today, lunch usually consists of a sandwich, a bowl of soup or a salad served at the dining-room table, if there is a maid. Otherwise, it is often brought to the living room or patio on a tray. When children are home for lunch, it can be served either at the dining table or in the kitchen, according to the preference of the family. No more than three courses are ever served for lunch; even that number is most unusual. The setting is as follows:

Salad fork at the left, next to the plate, if salad is to be served after the meat. The meat fork is at the left of the salad fork. On the right, a meat knife; and at the right of this knife, a bouillon or fruit spoon, if necessary.

The butter plate and knife are above the forks at the left.

Because dessert, if served, is brought in after the main course, the dessert fork or spoon may be brought in with the dessert plate.

Dinner:

If the food is to be passed, the dinner plates are at each place on the table when the family sits down, or in front of the head of the household if he is to serve. Many women prefer to serve the plates directly from the stove. If there is a maid in the home, she may pass the plates around as they are served by the man of the house, or, if the family is small, she may pass the dishes to each person. The table setting for dinner is similar to that for lunch with the implements necessary for each course arranged in order of their use: the one to be used first goes on the outside; that to be used last is put nearest the plate.

Next to the plate and at the left is the salad fork, then the dinner fork. (If salad is to be served first, the salad fork is farthest from the plate.) At the right, the dinner knife is next to the plate, then the soup spoon or the oyster fork or fruit spoon on the outside (if necessary).

The glass or goblet for the beverage is at the right above the knife. The butter plate is at the left with the butter knife laid on it diagonally from upper left to lower right. The dessert spoon and fork may be brought in on the dessert plate after the table is cleared; otherwise the fork goes next to the plate on the left, and the spoon immediately to the right of the knife.

THE MEALTIME TRAY

When a member of the family is ill and must remain in bed for his meals, an attractive tray with a flower in a little vase or a gay napkin and tray cloth can aid a lagging appetite. Always use a tray cloth or a doily of any sort. The setting is the same as the individual place setting at the table. The dessert plate and the coffee cup and saucer are usually brought when the main meal is finished because of lack of room. The

dinner plate should be heated and covered, if the meal is hot, to keep it warm. If you do not have a regular domed plate cover, a piece of foil laid over the food will keep it warm for several minutes.

68

The young child

Etiquette applies to everyone, old or young, and the best way to teach etiquette to children is by consistency, firmness and example.

Children can scarcely be too young to be taught the rudiments of etiquette. Any child can be taught to be well behaved with patience and perseverance, whereas to break bad habits once they are acquired is a herculean task.

FAIR PLAY

Children should be taught, even before they go to school, to "play fair," to respect each other's property and rights, to give credit to others and not to take too much credit to themselves, to share their playthings and to take good care of toys that belong to other children. A bright, observing child should never be encouraged to brag about his own achievements or to tell his or her mother how inferior other children are.

"BECAUSE EVERYONE ELSE DOES"

All young people feel a need for conformity with the activities of others of their age. This they express in their speech, their play, their choice of clothing and their relationships to each other. This conformity is quite normal and is to be respected as part of the development of individual personality as well as social responsibility.

Children should be permitted to follow the customs of their community, so as not to differ too radically from the other children in the neighborhood, but there are necessary qualifications to this advice. Parents sometimes must make a decision at the risk of having their children a little different in some particular from their friends. There are times when children should be required to set an example for others to follow, rather than be just like all the rest. There is a certain element of risk involved in this position, but there is also an element of discipline that is far more important. Precepts and lectures are never a substitute for understanding and sympathetic guidance.

EATING HABITS

When children are a year and a half to two years old, they begin to learn to feed themselves. From the very first, they can be encouraged to keep the food on the plate, taught how to hold a cup so that it will not spill, and shown the use of a bib or napkin. These skills do not come naturally, but with patient repetition and gentle insistence, they can be acquired.

As soon as the child has learned to eat well enough so that his presence at the table is not offensive, he should be allowed to eat with adults, occasionally at first, and more often as his manners improve. As a member of the family group at meals, there are more advanced lessons to be learned.

He must be clean and neat when he comes to the table, chew quietly, with his mouth closed, not overload his spoon or fork, or fidget or play with his food or the implements at his place.

He must not interrupt the adults, but he should be included in the conversation, and his mother or father from time to time should introduce a subject within his range of interests.

If he finishes before the others, he asks, "May I please be excused?" and waits for permission before leaving the table. Very young children should be given this privilege, because when their food is gone, they resort to wriggling and noise-making to pass the time.

If he refuses to be good, say nothing, but lead him quietly

from the table. The child quickly learns to be well-behaved when he understands that good behavior is the price of admission to grown-up society.

The little one's mother can help by bringing his plate to the table with the food ready for him to eat—the portions of small or moderate size, the meat and vegetables cut in small bite-size pieces. His glass or cup should have a broad base and be of plastic or pottery. If he is very small, his fork and spoon should be of appropriate size. A bib large enough so that an accidental spill will not ruin his clothes is mandatory. Let him have a high chair or put cushions on a regular chair to raise him to the proper height. If you think this is unimportant, try sometime to eat neatly while kneeling at a table that comes approximately to the level of your chin!

The child who sees his family enjoying their food and enjoying each others' company follows their example. Constant nagging and correction are as detrimental as a total lack of instruction. If older children are allowed to complain about the food and if there are continuous arguments at the table, unhappy associations will result in antagonism to food and to good manners in eating.

MONEY MATTERS

When a child is old enough to buy a candy bar or an ice cream cone for himself, he should be given a small, regular allowance in return for helping with the dishes or keeping his room neat. Extra duties—washing the dog or running an errand—deserve special consideration and are paid for separately if the parents feel that they merit a reward. Children should be permitted to use an allowance as they wish. The amount should be about the same as that given to his small friends. Some parents give the child more allowance but insist that a part be set aside for the weekly church contribution or saved for birthday presents or a special hobby or treat. This seems a wise system, as the child acquires a sense of the value of money.

As the child grows, so must his allowance and the expenses he is expected to pay for himself. As he approaches his teens, he pays for movies, cosmetics, presents or extra pieces of clothing or jewelry that are not actually necessary. To pay for such items, he has to plan ahead and give up other pleasures until he has saved a sufficient sum. This is excellent training. If he is working toward something worthwhile that he really cares about, his parents may encourage him by giving him extra chores paid for at an hourly rate and by adding to his fund with a small check for Christmas or birthday.

A CHILD'S APPEARANCE

As soon as a child shows any interest in what he is wearing, he should be allowed a voice in choosing his clothes, though naturally his mother must make the final decision. But he will thus absorb some principles of dressing well and he will also be happy to wear the clothes that are bought for him.

Don't overdress your child. If he or she is invited to a party, ask the mother of the host or hostess what type of clothing will be appropriate. Even school clothes should conform to those of the other children. If wearing ties is not required of the small boys, let your son go in a sport shirt, and if the girls all wear brown loafers, don't insist on patent-leather slippers.

Never dress your child in clothes that are too old for him. The three-year-old dressed in long gray flannels and a sport jacket looks as inappropriate as his father would going to business in shorts and an Eton jacket. Little girls should never wear even moderately high heels before they reach their teens. Nor should they wear makeup or dress their hair elaborately. Let them play at being grown up in the privacy of their rooms but never in public.

CHILDREN'S PARTIES

The span of attention of tiny children is limited, and they tire quickly, so parties for very young children, under six, let us say, should be no more than two hours long. The refreshments should be very simple. To avoid confusion and permit better organization, the guest list should be short—five or six guests for a second birthday party, and ten or twelve for a six- to eight-year-old. The formula for a successful party for the very young is as follows:

Guests arrive at four. One half hour is allowed for opening presents and letting off steam. One hour of organized games or entertainment follows. A magician is always popular; so are comedy movies. Treasure hunts, "pin-the-tail-on-the-donkey," musical chairs for the littlest children, and guessing games, a "three-legged" race for older ones are always good. At five-thirty refreshments are served: sandwich (peanut butter and jelly cannot be surpassed for popularity); ice cream and the birthday cake. In warm weather a fruit punch, soda or ice-cold milk are popular; in winter, hot chocolate is welcome.

Parties for older children may run to two and a half or three hours if enough entertainment is planned. Games are more complicated, and a short feature movie takes the place of "shorts." A scavenger hunt or a swimming pool makes a summer party successful. At the age of ten or eleven or even older, hay rides, sleigh rides, trips to baseball or football games, or circuses or rodeos become more fun than the "game party" at home. When a group is taken to this sort of entertainment, be sure the invitation makes it clear whether or not lunch or supper will be provided.

Whether they are three or ten, the essential manners for party guests are identical. They say "Hello" to their host and the host's mother when they arrive, and they shake hands and say "Good-bye, and thank you for a wonderful time" when they leave. The young host or hostess greets them when they come and, in answer to their farewell, says "Good-bye, and thanks again for the present" or "Good-bye. Thank you for coming."

PARENTS AND CHILDREN

The first outward sign of respect you can show your toddler is not to talk *down* to him. "Baby-talk" is an insult to the intelligence of a normal child.

I have found that most children are far more capable than their elders believe. If you assume that your child will react to a situation in a reasonable way, you will generally find that he will live up to your expectations. One word of warning, however: nothing frustrates Johnny more than being required to do things that he simply is not capable of handling. To scold him for not being able to do up his snaps or buttons causes him to rebel against all attempts to teach him to dress himself.

Study your child as an interesting person, increase his responsibilities as he seems able to cope with them, reprove him when he falls short, and praise him when he takes a step forward. Teach him new words, and share as many family activities with him as you can. Laugh *with* him—not at him or his mistakes. Encouragement, appreciation and lots of love are essential in a baby's happy environment.

OBEYING THE RULES

Teach your children from their earliest years that certain rules have to be obeyed, particularly those that govern the relationship between themselves and other people. Delinquency is often the result of overly permissive parents, who either think that they should not ("Oh, I wouldn't want to stunt Harvey's independent development") or are afraid to discipline their children ("But Sally won't love me if I don't let her eat her ice cream before dinner"). Young people, no matter what they may say aloud, want and need direction and correction and the more honest ones will even admit it.

The single most important thing about disciplining a child is to make your point and stick to it. If you say "No" to an extra half hour at bedtime, and then say "Yes" when Susie says "But Mommy, this is my favorite TV program," how will Susie ever know whether or not you mean what you say?

The severity of the punishment should be directly related to the seriousness of the misdeed. A minor infraction should not result in a major penalty, or the child will have no way of differentiating between an important and an unimportant offense. If possible, the punishment should be related to the error. If Johnny refuses to remove his muddy rubbers time after time, he might be forbidden to go out and play in the mud puddles the next time his best friend calls him.

Unless you can hold to them, don't make threats. When you have not followed up on a threat once, your child will pay little attention when you make another. A simple one, such as "Bobby, stop throwing the wrappers on the floor, or I will take away the rest of your chewing gum," is all right. But to say, "Karen, if you don't go to bed at once, you can't go to kindergarten for a week," when you know (as does Karen) that she will be there the next morning, only makes you appear ridiculous.

When a child has committed a serious misdeed, such as lighting matches, take the time and trouble to explain the reason for the rule. Show him, with paper or kerosene or however you can make it the most impressive, how quickly a fire can spread and explain the consequences from his point of view—his favorite toy would be burned up, his dog might be killed, etc. And then decide on the punishment: deprivation of certain privileges like watching television, or the cancellation of a longed-for treat. In extreme cases, where repeated admonitions and punishments have not brought any results, there is no substitute for a good hard spanking with the palm of Daddy's or Mother's hand.

RESPECT

If you as parents lead your youngsters to believe that your experience, your education and your attitudes are worth emulating, respect, that quality most lacking today between parents and their children, will follow of its own accord. This, in turn, will be expanded, as your children grow up, to include relatives, friends and finally, more mature people of every sort.

69

The teen-ager

THE EARLY TEENS

If parents have had a loving, intelligent relationship with their sons and daughters during childhood, with confidence and respect growing on both sides, the problems of adolescence will be greatly modified. This book is not designed to discuss the psychological aspects of the young, but rather to discuss their manners and what they should or should not do. Remember, when making a rule or saying "No" to a teen-ager, to consider the importance of the decision to him (does it really *matter* if Bob stays out a half-hour longer?), the customs of his friends and classmates, and whether it will actually help him, either from his own point of view or in the eyes of others. The last reason in the world for making a regulation is "Well, I always had to wash the dishes when I was your age!"

APPEARANCE

It sometimes seems that teen-agers *like* to be sloppy. This applies not only to themselves but to their rooms and possessions. My feeling about this general attitude is that they be allowed to dress as sloppily as they please when they are not "in public" or with adults. But at school, at meals, on any excursion with adults, on all public conveyances and at all social functions, they must be properly and neatly dressed. This does not mean that they can't go to an informal gathering without a tie and jacket. Of course they may wear a sport shirt, shorts and sweater, or whatever the favorite local costume is, but the sweater and shirt should be clean, the hair combed and shoes ON.

Young boys must constantly be reminded to wash and to shave. Many boys who are not accustomed to regular shaving do not realize that their beard is becoming heavier each year. Parents have to keep after them day in and day out until it becomes a habit.

Teen-age girls fix their hair interminably, but they need guidance as to style, length, becomingness and good hygiene. The simplest hairdo currently popular is generally the most becoming. As they get older and begin to experiment, the only restriction should be that they refrain from becoming too extreme, lest they look "cheap." A thirteen- or fourteen-year-old may wear a little light lipstick to a party. As she gets older, she uses a more vivid shade, and by the time she is sixteen or seventeen, she may choose any shade that goes well with her complexion, as well as powder, a *very light* rouge if she is pale, and inconspicuous eye makeup. Heavily made-up eyes belong only on the stage. As to style in clothing, avoid extremes: the lowest neckline, the barest bathing suit, the tightest trousers. People, young or old, who have the most delightful manners and the greatest charm are those who do not go out of their way to attract attention.

TABLE MANNERS

Slouching, tipping the chair back and fiddling all seem to be within the special province of the teen-ager. In many cases, it is not willful disregard of directions—they simply do not absorb them. Their minds are on a thousand other more interesting matters—girls, boys, parties, school, sports, ad infinitum, and the only hope of penetrating the screen is repetition in the hope that eventually your words will "sink in." By the tone of your voice and the way you say it, repeated correction can avoid the undesirable effect of "nagging."

ALLOWANCES

The question of a "clothes allowance" usually arises in the middle teens. Some youngsters can't wait to be given enough money to dress themselves and pay all their own expenses, while others cling to the security of letting their parents pay for their clothes and receiving a small weekly or monthly "daily expenses" allowance. As a general rule, the year a boy or girl enters college, or becomes of college age, is the time to give him or her financial independence.

But there is no set rule—the time might come a year or two earlier for a boy who is responsible and understands the value of money and the danger of wasting it, while the girl who has had little experience in shopping or managing a checking account might better wait longer.

A system that seems to me to be excellent is practiced by one of my neighbors. Her fourteen-year-old daughter, a sensible, intelligent girl, wanted a clothes allowance. The parents started her out with a monthly sum to cover school clothes—blouses, skirts, shoes, socks, underwear, etc.—but no expensive ones such as party dresses or overcoats. In this way she is learning to understand the handling of money, but she does not have a large sum at her disposal which might prove to be a temptation to irresponsible spending. They are increasing the sum and the variety of clothing she is expected to buy each year; by the time she finishes high school, she will be completely responsible for her clothes and incidental expenses.

If paying all their children's tuition at school and college is too severe a strain on the family budget, teen-agers should certainly help by applying for scholarships, working part-time (in the cafeteria, dormitories or library) or taking an evening job, preferably one like baby-sitting that allows the student to study during those hours. Parents should never be ashamed to discuss the need for financial assistance of this sort with their children. Young men and women, brought up with love and respect for their families, will understand and take pride in doing what they can to help.

As to the amounts for suitable allowances, it is difficult to say, because requirements vary so widely. A city child needs more—bus or subway rides cost him money; his country cousin rides the same distance on a bicycle. Movies, food and entertainment also cost more than in the country.

A possible scale for a weekly allowance, necessarily subject to change to fit the circumstances, might run something like this:

13–14 years	$1.00–2.00
15–17 years	4.00–5.00

When the teen-ager is older and it seems advisable to add a clothing allowance to his pocket money, he might receive a monthly amount something like this:

16–18 years	$25.00– 35.00
18 and over	75.00–100.00

A boy or girl receiving one hundred dollars a month would be expected to pay all expenses such as school books, cleaning bills, etc.—everything, in other words, except tuition and doctors' bills.

LEARNING TO ENTERTAIN

Youngsters who learn how to entertain their friends nicely during their adolescence will have a good background for more formal and ambitious entertaining later on. Parents who encourage a child to invite his or her friends in reasonably often and who help him to plan and prepare parties will be more than rewarded by the young person's gratitude and enthusiasm. Because girls are more inclined to give parties than boys— just as it is the wife who plans a couple's social activities—my suggestions may be of special interest to young girls and their mothers. However, a boy who is planning a party may profit from them, too.

Although the following subjects should be discussed and decided on by mother and daughter (or son) together, the word "hostess" will refer to the daughter, since the party will be hers. She may issue her invitations on colorful cards available at all stationery stores. She may add R.S.V.P. with her telephone number below it, or put "regrets only" with the number. She may also issue her invitations by telephone, but she runs the risk of her guests forgetting the date, the hour or the location of the party.

The guest list:

First she chooses congenial guests. A group of friends who all know each other well is easy and fun but not particularly interesting or stimulating. On the other hand, a group of strangers who have little in common can be a nightmare for the young hostess trying to get the party off the ground. A combination of a few friends and two or three "outsiders" works best, as long as the hostess sees that the strangers are included in conversation and activities.

The number of guests invited depends on the size of your home and the amount you can afford to spend. Discuss these questions frankly with your daughter. Overcrowded rooms and lack of space can ruin an otherwise good party.

If it is to be a "singles" party, with invitations issued to both boys and girls, the hostess sees that there are even numbers, or extra boys. If only boys or only girls are sent invitations with "bring a date" written on them, those receiving them should let the hostess know whether they are successful in finding a date, and if so, who he or she is. When a boy or girl is going steady, or has a previous date for the night of a "singles" party, it is perfectly proper to call and ask if the date may be included. But if it upsets the boy-girl ratio, the hostess refuses—politely, and with an explanation.

Since teen-agers like to get dressed up once in a while, don't be afraid to suggest a "jacket and tie" or "dress" party. Then dress up the party to suit the outfit—fancier food, prettier decorations and, perhaps, live music.

There are a few things that you should insist on, no matter how informal the party. Guests should wear shoes and socks. At VERY informal parties, they may sometimes kick them off later, but at a dance girls should not be allowed on the floor without shoes. It lowers the tone of the party, and the tone is what makes a more or less formal party rather special. The same is true of jackets and ties—at a formal party they should be kept on. When an invitation says "black tie" or "formal," a

boy out of respect for his hostess should not try to go unless he
is wearing a tuxedo or, in some communities, a dark suit.

Making a party "go":

Young people love to dance, so be sure that your youngster
has good records available and cleared floor space. The most
popular parties are those which combine the opportunity to
dance with the chance to sit around and talk and eat. A piano
is a tremendous asset if one of the group can play, and so is a
guest with a guitar. Active games such as ping-pong, pool,
carpet bowls or Twister are not to be scorned. If one or two
people start playing, the rest of the group is often quick to join.

Food and drink:

The most important consideration is quantity. It doesn't
matter too much *what* you serve—your daughter will know
the preferences of her guests. But it is a calamity to run short
before the end of the evening. For an after-dinner party, count
on the guests drinking two soft drinks apiece and add half
again as many for emergencies.

Food is generally simple: snacks like pretzels, popcorn,
corn chips, homemade cake or cookies. You and your husband
might offer to help cook up a batch of hot dogs and hamburgers around midnight; if you help serve, it gives you an
excellent opportunity to check on how things are going without
seeming to "chaperon." Other popular late-evening foods are
pancakes, pizzas or cheese fondue.

As long as there are teen-age parties, there will be boys who
try to smuggle in liquor. You and your daughter must decide
in advance how you will cope with this if it occurs. Your
daughter must keep her eyes open for signs of hidden flasks or
bottles. If she does not have the self-assurance to handle the
situation by asking the offenders to stop drinking, to remove
the liquor or to leave, she should come to you. Ask the boy or
boys to hand their liquor over to you for the duration of the
party and when it is over, if they are of legal age to drink,
return it to them before they go home. If they are not of legal
age, notify their parents. As for allowing your own teen-agers
to serve liquor in states where it is permissible, my advice is—
don't do it. If you do, be sure that there are plenty of soft
drinks available for those who want them.

Ending the party:

When your daughter sends out, or issues, her invitations, she states "eight to twelve" or whatever the hours may be. In that way, parents of nondrivers will know what time to come for their youngsters, and that will automatically start a break-up of the party. Cutting off the supply of food and drink a half-hour or so before the party should end also helps. Tell your daughter that if all else fails, and nobody seems to have the slightest intention of leaving, she may ask you to put in an appearance, and that will be a sufficient hint!

70

College years

PERSONAL POPULARITY

Attending college is a serious business. Good marks are of primary importance. But of almost equal importance is the ability to make people like you, to get on easily with others and to make friends. The best way to do this is to become interested in what interests them and to be outgoing and friendly. Most of us go through life thinking of what *we* are going to do, what we hope or fear is going to happen to *us,* instead of thinking or caring about what happens to those about us. Sensitive awareness of the reactions of others is a priceless gift. If you would be liked by those with whom you come in contact, cultivate sensitiveness of perception. Attractive looks are an asset, certainly, but a bright, responsive personality is far more friend-making than great beauty or a handsome face.

THE FRESHMAN ARRIVES AT COLLEGE

Your first days in college will be harried and hurried but also a lot of fun: learning new things, meeting new people. Orien-

tation or Welcome Week at many colleges is devoted exclusively to the freshman, helping the new student feel at home.
Group meetings explain study programs, registration routine,
the faculty-adviser system and other facts of campus life, including extracurricular activities. Faculty members meet and
talk with the new students. If you will welcome the Welcoming Committee with interest and cordiality, you will acquire
many first-of-the-year friends that will be yours for four years
and possibly for life.

DORMITORY LIFE

Consideration is the key to successful dormitory living. The
facilities of the dormitory are yours and your roommate's.
This means sharing your quarters, keeping "your side" in order, and being considerate of your roommate's sleeping and
studying habits as well as observing the quiet hours that the
dormitory imposes. Obeying the regulations of the dormitory
will not make you a "square." It will merely make the lives of
many strangers living together run more smoothly.

Avoid borrowing like the plague, but respond graciously
when asked to lend an article of yours, whether you accept or
refuse the request. Take better care of borrowed property than
of your own, and return it to the owner promptly.

Treat the house mother in a girl's dormitory with respect
and friendliness. Drop into her apartment now and then with
a few friends for a chat before dinner; this gesture will be
appreciated for its thoughtfulness. Christmas gifts to the house
mother and tips to the staff are in order. Usually a box is
passed, with a sum being collected for those on the household
staff, and a gift from all presented to the house mother; otherwise, a small remembrance can be given individually.

IN CLASS AND AFTER

The student encounters faculty members in the classroom,
at joint student-faculty committee meetings, departmental teas,
extracurricular activities and on the campus. A professor is
never addressed as "Doc" or "Prof." If a graduate assistant
himself requests it, it is all right to call him by his first name.

You will miss a lot if you don't join some of the many
extracurricular activities the college offers: history or foreign-
affairs clubs, religious organizations, student government and

any kind of athletic club. Some of them are educational; in all you will make valuable friendships. But don't overdo it to the point where you have no time left for your studies.

Fraternities and sororities are an integral feature of many campuses but are not essential to a collegiate social life. Follow your own individual tastes and needs in deciding whether to affiliate with one or remain an Independent.

THE BIG COLLEGE WEEKEND

One of the most important events of the year at college is the special annual weekend that takes place in the fall or in the spring. There may be a Friday-night informal party at the fraternity house; on Saturday, a picnic or a game to watch or perhaps a ski excursion in midwinter. Saturday night is the formal dance, often preceded by a sit-down dinner. Sunday, students and their dates may go to church together and organize an excursion or informal party. After Sunday dinner, the weekend closes.

When a girl is invited to such a weekend, she pays for her own transportation to and from the campus. As soon as she has accepted her host's written invitation, he informs her of the bus, train or plane schedules. If it is impossible for him to meet her, he arranges for a friend to be there or sees that a taxi is available.

The girl may stay in the college's chapter house of her sorority, in a dormitory made ready for the visitors, or at a local hotel, perhaps sharing a room with another "import." The man makes all the arrangements and far enough in advance to get comfortable and convenient accommodations, and to let her know where she will be staying. He assumes the financial obligations, pays for all her meals and for all transportation after she arrives at the local railroad depot.

Don'ts for girls as house party visitors:

DON'T wait until the last moment to be sure your bag is in perfect condition. Don't arrive with a shabby, down-at-the-heels suitcase with the handle half off, the lock broken and straps carelessly hanging out. Neat, compact, good-looking luggage pleases a man more than you might suspect.

DON'T forget to dress mentally as you pack. Stockings? Shoes? Slip? Dress? What goes with it? Belt, clips or other accessories, bag, etc.

DON'T make your luggage one inch bigger or one ounce heavier than necessary, unless you are driving your own car. On holiday occasions in small college towns there may not be taxis or cars for more than about one out of ten. Therefore DON'T count on being that one.

DON'T show an alive and interested manner toward the boys and total indifference toward the girls. When you are shown to the room which you are to share with another girl, DON'T claim the bed you like best by throwing your bag on it. At least make the gesture of asking the other girl if she cares which she takes. DON'T take up more than exactly your share of the closet space and drawer space. If you have brought too many things for the space that is yours, leave some of them packed in your bag and leave the bag neatly closed.

DON'T monopolize the bathroom. DON'T leave your personal belongings around on all the bedroom furniture. When you pack to leave, DON'T leave powder, smears of lipstick or bobby pins in the bureau drawer. Be sure you have not left panties or other personal items in dresser drawers. DON'T forget throughout your stay to respect the wishes of the house mother and other chaperons and to say good-bye to her and to the others and thank them for their kindness.

On the evening of your arrival you will probably all congregate before dinner when introductions are made. They are likely to be not only by first names but by nicknames: "Sally, this is Slim," or "Babs," and so on. DON'T, however, wait for introductions under the house roof. If you are shy or afraid you won't make friends, remember that nearly every other girl is feeling exactly the same!

If you don't know anything about the boy seated beside you at dinner, ask your own date, who should be seated at your left, about him first so as to know what to talk to him about. A man is rarely bored if you talk—but with some intelligence —about him. DON'T lay flattery on with a trowel.

At the dances, greet the chaperons as though you liked them. DON'T refuse to dance with anyone who cuts in, unless he is drunk or objectionable.

Throughout the days of your visit, DON'T think only of what you like to do; do whatever the majority suggest—unless what is suggested is something you think is wrong. For instance, there is no obligation to drink anywhere at any time—unless you choose to.

DON'T be jealous of every attention your date pays to another girl. DON'T show that you hate to be teased or you'll be a target for it. DON'T show chagrin or disappointment. Be blind, deaf and insensible to annoyance or disappointment. DON'T do anything that can seem unappreciative of the efforts made for your pleasure by the man who is your host. DON'T try to impress him with your powers by attracting one of his classmates; your lack of loyalty will be resented by every member of his crowd.

Above all, DON'T forget that the friendship of other girls is the crown of your own success. Trying to take their boy friends will end in ostracism. The really popular girl is popular with girls as well as boys.

71

Chaperons and dates

MODERN CHAPERONAGE

From an ethical standpoint, the only chaperon worth having in the present day is a young girl's own efficiency in chaperoning herself. She must develop expertness in handling situations herself, be able to gauge the reactions of various types of persons, particularly men, in varying circumstances, which man has the instincts of a gentleman and which does not and will try to take advantage of her.

Apart, however, from the consideration of ethics, which is concerned with what the girl herself thinks or feels or the motives behind what she says or does, there still remain the appearances to be considered. Many young people today are foolishly inclined to ignore appearances; they feel they can act independently of public opinion. But gossip still influences a world that seldom takes the trouble to sift appearance from fact.

The necessary proprieties:

If on her return from a party, a young girl finds her family is not at home, she does not invite any man to "come in for a while." If he persists, she answers casually but firmly, "Sorry, another time," and bids him good night.

Some families insist on a sensible practice. Just before leaving a dance their daughter telephones home if she plans to go on to someone's house or bring friends to her own. The daughter finds this reasonable, making her practice of telephoning a mark of respect for her mother which no one questions. As for the mother herself, she must find the middle road between too great permissiveness and overprotectiveness which hampers the child's development of responsibility.

An unmarried girl should not go on overnight trips with any young man, even with her fiancé, because convention still decrees that she may not stop in a hotel with a young man unchaperoned. However, a girl of eighteen may perfectly well go on a weekend trip with several couples to a ski resort or a beach resort without giving any cause for gossip.

The chaperon at the school dance:

Chaperons for a school dance may be recruited from among the faculty, the parents of the students, or other townspeople. They may be single persons or married couples. Chaperons are the ringside participants at the dance, responsible for the general discipline and order of those dancing without putting a damper on the fun.

A committee of one or a few may be in charge of securing the chaperons for the gala evening, chaperons who will be congenial to one another. Single persons are always invited to bring escorts. And, of course, everyone bids the chaperons good night and thanks them for having come to the dance. After the dance, the same committee writes thank-you notes to each chaperon.

The house mother as resident chaperon:

The most usual chaperon today is the house mother in preparatory boarding schools, college dormitories or metropolitan women's residence hotels. She is neither inquisitive nor interfering, except for seriously considered, valid reasons. Charm is a necessary quality, because she meets and greets the parents, girl friends, and beaux of her charges, and serves at teas or presides at luncheons, dinners and other social occasions. A house mother offers friendship to all the girls under her wing and never shows favoritism.

A young girl in her parents' home:

Whether a girl of college age or her little sister of thirteen invites friends to a party, no chaperonage is necessary other than that of her parents' presence in the house; however, they arrange to be present at some time during the party, perhaps to say "Hello" when their daughter's guests arrive. Then they leave the young people alone, returning to serve the refreshments or, at the younger girl's party, bid the guests good-bye.

A girl of sixteen may invite a boy she knows well to have dinner with her in her parents' home on an evening when they are dining out as long as they are returning shortly after dinner. She may also invite a group in under the same circumstances, provided she sees that the kitchen is left clean and her mother does not have to return to a stack of dirty dishes in the sink.

When a bachelor entertains:

The bachelor-about-town may occasionally entertain in his apartment. On such occasions, four is a better number than two for a small dinner party. A young woman visiting a man's apartment alone is still subject to criticism and a wise girl avoids a tête-à-tête in a bachelor's apartment.

Young men who live out of the metropolitan area or who have a country house may give weekend house parties to which both men and women are invited. The bachelor host should make sure that sleeping accommodations are adequate and comfortable and, if bathroom facilities are limited, that his women guests have precedence. He should also arrange for transportation into town for any guests who may wish to go to church.

DATES

The age at which a girl may go out alone with a boy in the evening, and how late she may stay out varies according to the responsibility of the girl herself and the custom of the community. Only a parent can make the exact decision. A girl of fourteen might go out with a boy as part of a group of four or more to an early movie, dinner, sports event or some other special occasion. Most of the parties she goes to will be those at the homes of friends or dances organized by her school. Her parents should at all times know where and with whom she is and at what time she will be home.

Homecoming hours:

During the early teen years, when children do not have the wisdom to recognize their own needs, the parents must set time limits on dates and see that they are kept, even though it may mean waiting up to greet the returning son or daughter. This is a simple matter of good health, as well as setting a high standard of behavior. It is wise to discuss homecoming hours with other parents and arrive at an hour on which everyone, including the children, agree.

Dates should be restricted to weekends and vacations. Even high school students who are "going steady" should not be permitted to date during the week, even to study together. Exceptions might be made if a boy were given theater tickets to an excellent difficult-to-see show or a league-winning game.

As a general rule, ten-thirty or eleven is a reasonable time for a thirteen- or fourteen-year-old to be home; or twelve o'clock for a school or club dance or other special party; a sixteen- or seventeen-year-old might stay at parties until twelve-thirty or one o'clock, but for an ordinary movie date, this group should still return by eleven o'clock or thereabouts. If they plan to go to a friend's house or a snack bar afterward, their parents should know in advance or be called on the telephone, so that they may know the whereabouts of the child and re-adjust the hour when he must be home. When a youngster reaches his late teens, his hours are regulated only by his or her own need for sleep or, if he is away at college, the rules of the university. Parents of a child living at home should realize that, were he away at college, he would be making his own rules as to hours, and allow him the same privilege. Many eighteen-year-olds live away from home, they work, they are in the armed forces and they are even married, so it seems a little ridiculous for parents, simply because they are fortunate enough to have their youngster at home, to attempt to treat him as a child, rather than an intelligent, if young, adult.

Making contact:

When a boy (or man) sees someone he thinks he would like to know, it is fairly simple for him to make contact. All he has to do is find someone who knows the girl and will introduce them. Then he can chat with her for a bit and if she is as attractive as she appeared from a distance, he may ask her for a date.

If a girl wishes to avoid giving the impression that she is chasing a boy, she must be more devious. Boys are flattered when a girl obviously wants to meet them but they are often scared by an overzealous attack. Without seeming too eager, she may: give a friendly smile and an enthusiastic "Hello" whenever they meet; persuade a mutual friend to invite them both to a small party; go to all school events in which he takes part; join school, church or community organizations to which he belongs; get a girl who knows him to arrange a blind (double) date.

After the contact is made, and it's clear that they would like to get to know each other, the boy may ask for a date by telephone, or simply when they meet. He should remember to mention the following details: what time he will call for the girl; their means of transportation; what kind of date it will be—movies, a party at a friend's, a picnic, etc.

If he forgets to offer any of this information, the girl should ask for it.

Unless a boy and girl are going steady, he should ask for a date two to four days ahead for an ordinary date; at least two weeks ahead for a formal dance; a month or more ahead for a big college weekend.

There are exceptions, such as when a party is planned on the spur of the moment, but these are good general rules.

Accepting or refusing a date:

If she wants to go, a girl need only say, "I'd love to!" promptly and enthusiastically. The worst mistake she can make is to be evasive. If she promised to baby-sit and doesn't know if she can get a substitute, or if she is not sure if the family is going to the country for the weekend, she says so. But it must be true, or he will surely know it. No one should ever say,

"Can I let you know tomorrow?" without saying why. Once a girl has accepted, she must keep the date unless a real emergency arises. One *never* breaks one date to accept another.

To refuse a date politely, a girl only need say, "I'm so sorry, but I already have a date for Saturday night." If she is no more specific, she is free to accept someone else who calls. If, however, she would really like the man to ask her again, she gives him a more detailed excuse which sounds, and is, true.

Other dating data:

A girl introduces a new friend to her parents on her first date with him. She briefs her parents a little before he arrives so that they can carry on the conversation easily. Five or ten minutes is enough for the visit and it is up to the young lady to suggest that they had better be on their way.

Men—and boys—must call for their dates at their homes. Only if he knows her well and has a good reason (such as an early dinner reservation at a restaurant) might he meet her at a more convenient spot.

Unless a couple have been going steady and have agreed to share at times, the man pays all expenses on a date. The girl helps by suggesting inexpensive entertainment—a movie instead of the theater—or choosing the lower-priced items on a menu.

It is the man's responsibility to make all the plans for the evening. Provided the activity he suggests is not one of which she does not approve, the girl should participate with enthusiasm. At the end of the evening, it is she who decides that it is time to go home.

The man should arrive for the date on time, and the woman should be ready. There is no truth in the old idea that she makes herself more desirable by keeping him waiting.

The girl should be dressed suitably, assuming the man has told her what they are going to do. If he has been vague, a simple rather than a "dressy" costume is a safer choice. Should she discover that her date is dressed for bowling when she thought they were going to a cocktail party, she excuses herself for ten minutes—no more—while she hastily changes into something more casual.

THE BLIND DATE

The "blind date" is sometimes arranged by a third person such as Mrs. Towne, who thinks that Gloria Gorgeous and

Harry Handsome would enjoy each other's company. She first makes sure that Harry would be interested in calling Gloria; then she asks Gloria if she would like to meet an attractive man. Only after both parties have indicated that they are willing to be so introduced should Mrs. Towne give Gloria's telephone number to Harry.

The date may also be arranged by a girl who is asked for a date by a boy she does not know well or does not wish to go out with alone. She might say, "Jane Ratsey is spending the night with me, so I would love to go out with you if you have a friend who would like to take her out, and we'll make it a foursome."

Another type of blind date occurs when a host or hostess arranges a date for his or her overnight guest. A girl calls a good friend and says, "Tom, Sally, who is my roommate at college, is spending the weekend with me, and I think you would like her, so how about taking her to a movie with Jim and me on Saturday night?"

A blind date may turn out to be great fun, but if not, make the best of it and act as if you were enjoying every minute. After all, you may meet other attractive people through your new acquaintance.

"GOING STEADY" and "PINNING"

"Going steady" has become a fact of American teen-age life. When a boy and girl date each other consistently, they are considered by their contemporaries to be "going steady." Usually they agree that neither is to date anyone else and this may even be formalized by an exchange of friendship rings or identification bracelets.

This is an unfortunate practice. Only by meeting many other young people of varied backgrounds and interests can a boy or girl broaden his or her own experience and gain enough insight to be capable of making a good choice of a marriage partner when the time comes.

The presentation of a fraternity badge by a college man to his girl, known as "pinning," may be merely another type of "going steady," or it may mean that the couple are "engaged to be engaged," depending on the customs of that particular college. This relationship allows them to examine their compatibility without committing themselves formally to an engagement. If the "pinned" couple "breaks up," the girl returns the pin to the young man.

72

A happy marriage

HINTS FOR THE NEWLYWEDS

I don't know why people should feel that because they have married, they may give up all pretense of good manners and treat their partner as an "old shoe." Many a marriage has failed because one or both of the partners allowed their attitude toward the other to become careless, ill-mannered or just plain bored. It takes effort to keep a good marriage going and the constant presence of good manners is more important than in any relationship with those outside the family.

The wife's part:

It's curious how the habit of careless manners and the habit of old clothes go together. And how many lovely women commit esthetic suicide by letting themselves slide down to where they feel natural in an old housecoat, not only physically but mentally. The very fact of *looking* attractive makes one feel less tired and therefore more charming and better company.

She who complains incessantly that this is wrong or that hurts or that some other thing worries or vexes her, very decidedly is getting into an old housecoat! If something is seriously wrong, if she is really ill, that is different. But of the petty things that are only remembered in order to be told to gain sympathy—beware!

The wife who smears her face with cream and rolls her

hair in curlers before going to bed is not a sight that many husbands can endure. With a handy portable drier, there is no reason that hair cannot be dried while doing chores, feeding the baby, paying the bills or during any other household duties in the morning. And the wife who sees her husband off to work in a dirty bathrobe, with hair uncombed and face unwashed, sends him off with a thoroughly unflattering picture of her in his mind. He may find his neat, efficient, pretty secretary more appealing than his unkempt, uncaring wife!

The intelligent woman listens interestedly to her husband's problems at the office. She doesn't interrupt with "Oh really? Come and see Junior's new tooth—and then please repair the stopper in the sink."

Even though a girl loathes cooking, she makes an effort to cater to her husband's likes and dislikes and to make meals appetizing and interesting. If she is on a diet, she must not feed her husband a dinner of one lamb chop and a small green salad. A little surprise now and then—something he especially likes, such as a homemade apple pie or a special cut of steak ordinarily beyond her budget—will do wonders toward making her seem a marvelous cook and clever wife.

A considerate wife always consults her husband before accepting an invitation for them both unless she knows it is something he will enjoy. If he is working very hard, it is thoughtless of her to plan a dinner party for Friday, to accept an invitation for a dance on Saturday, and to organize an all-day picnic with the children on Sunday.

If her husband enjoys an evening of poker with his friends, the smart wife cheers him on his way and even offers to provide refreshments for his gang at home when it is his turn to invite them there. She leaves everything in readiness and disappears—completely! When he brings a business acquaintance home, she is a gracious hostess. After dinner, she excuses herself, washes up quietly and goes to her room to leave them to their business discussion. (A considerate husband never, if he can avoid it, brings home unexpected guests without giving his wife some warning.)

The husband's part:
The bride generally has to make more effort to achieve a successful marriage than the groom, but it is certainly a two-

sided partnership, and she cannot do it alone. The man who rushed to open the car door or hold her coat for her when they were engaged, unfortunately too often drops these little politenesses as soon as they are married.

The worst of evenings begins when the husband—whose wife has had no one but the baby to talk to all day long—grunts and buries his nose in the newspaper when she tries to carry on a conversation.

He may have been accustomed to living alone or in a bachelor apartment where no one cared, but the new husband must learn that trousers dropped in the middle of the floor, a sink spattered with shaving soap and soggy towels on the bathroom rug can be an unpleasant shock to his bride.

Many men do not care too much for babies until they are old enough to respond or even to show interest in things about which Daddy cares. But this can be a very sore point with a young mother to whom her husband's lack of interest seems callous. If Daddy will take the time really to observe and play with his infant son or daughter, he will find himself more interested in the baby than he thought possible.

The husband who keeps his wife company in the kitchen while she is finishing the dinner preparations and gives a helping hand with the dishes after dinner, rather than retiring to the TV set or his newspaper, will find himself more than repaid by his appreciative wife.

It is important to women that their husbands remember special occasions. If the budget is limited, the remembrance need only be a card for Mother's Day, a single rose for an anniversary or a simple little gift for a birthday. It is the thought that counts, and women, generally more sentimental than men, attach tremendous importance to these little gestures.

Unless he has come to an agreement with his wife, it is selfish and stupid of a man to spend all his free time pursuing a sport or hobby that does not interest her. A Saturday golf game with his friends, and a Sunday picnic with his family, plus, perhaps, an hour's workout at the driving range one evening or two during the week can be a happy solution for the whole family.

One of the most pleasing things a man can do is to plan occasional entertainments that will appeal to her—especially a dinner at a restaurant or a trip to the theater, an overnight jaunt to some favorite spot or even an evening at the movies can be a wonderful treat to a girl who spends much of her time at home. Or he may offer to plan and cook the dinner occasionally or take her on a picnic at a beach or lake or to a free concert or museum or lecture.

AIRING THE PROBLEMS

Lesser bones of contention in many marriages are: interrupting each other, making fun of idiosyncracies, not laughing at his or her jokes, never being on time, the wife using the husband's razor—these can build up a wall of resentment. Greater ones are: basic differences of opinion on bringing up children, how to spend vacations, watching television in the bedroom, and so on—these can undermine an otherwise sound marriage. The only way to handle these problems is by bringing them into the open and keeping the lines of communication free between husband and wife. The moment that one or the other feels he cannot discuss a problem and it is left to fester and grow inside is the moment the marriage begins to dissolve. The couple who agrees not only to listen to each other's problems, but to make an effort to see the other side and to DO something to correct the situation is one hundred percent certain to stay out of the divorce courts.

IN-LAW SITUATIONS

The two most difficult situations to meet happily and successfully are those between the husband and his father-in-law and between the wife and her mother-in-law. The other relationships are easy and there is little reason for failure. In any case, the very first rule that every father-in-law—and especially every mother-in-law—must learn is DON'T INTERFERE. Never mind what small blunders your daughter or daughter-in-law or your son or son-in-law may make; remember that is their right to live and do and think as they please. If you are asked what you think, answer truthfully, of course, but don't pour good advice upon them.

When a young wife, for any one of many reasons, goes to live with her husband's people, she must in this difficult situation adapt herself not only to their mode of living, but also to the dispositions of the various members of the family. In this way alone can she herself be happy.

When a mother or father must live with a married child, the situation demands the wisdom of a Solomon and the self-control of a stoic. She or he must conscientiously practice the art of "invisibility" at frequent and lengthy intervals. The mother should have or make occupations of her own—particularly when special friends of her daughter-in-law or even old friends of her son are present. If her room is equipped with radio and television she is always free to enjoy her own favorite programs. She assists with household chores or cares for the children as much as she easily can, but she should never be made to feel like a built-in baby-sitter.

If it is physically possible, it is far better for parents to live apart from their married children. The young people should, if necessary, help to support the older ones, especially a widow, but the parents should be allowed to feel that they are handling their own affairs. Love and affection will flourish in an atmosphere of independence, supplemented by close family ties.

SEPARATION AND DIVORCE

Divorce is always painful and all too prevalent in this country. But there are cases, of course, where divorce is the best—sometimes the only—solution for everyone concerned. If two persons are truly mismated, they and perhaps their children are better off if they part. The only consideration of vital importance is that they shall not part because of a love-for-another attack that might prove to be transient.

Sometimes a period of separation can solve the problem of too-hasty divorce. A separation may be legal or it may simply be arranged by unwritten consent of both parties. It may be either a "trial" separation, or viewed from the beginning as permanent, particularly if the faith of the couple forbids divorce, as does Catholicism.

In a trial separation two people have found it increasingly difficult to live together and decide to live apart. But they want time to consider before taking the final steps toward divorce. If they find they are better off apart, and do not intend to remarry, they make the separation legal. Papers making property settlements, arrangements for children, financial support and so on are drawn up by their lawyers.

When a couple separates, there is no public announcement. Because they are still legally married, the woman continues to use her husband's name and wears her wedding ring. He quietly moves out of their home, possibly on an extended "business trip," or she may take her children for a "visit" to her family. Friends respect the situation and never invite them both to the same party without their knowledge and consent.

If they decide that life together was better than life apart, they simply move back together. For this reason, it is wise for the wife, or husband, whichever has remained there, to keep the home and other property intact, rather than selling or renting in a moment of bitterness.

When a divorce is finally and irrevocably decided upon, there is no public announcement. The woman discards her wedding ring and substitutes her maiden name for her husband's first name (Mrs. McCallum Ford). Both parties must accept the fact that their marriage no longer exists. The husband who insists on "dropping in" to see the children or the wife who keeps calling his office to ask his advice on this or that is only prolonging the agony. They must start to make new lives for themselves and leave their ex-partner to do the same.

In the happy event that the couple resolve their difficulties after the divorce is final, they remarry quietly, with only their families or closest friends as witnesses.

In the thousands of cases where children are involved, it is far better that divorced parents make every effort to remain friendly. There can be no argument with the fact that maintaining a civil relationship is desirable not only for the couple, but especially for their children.

Index

A

B

D

E

F

G

H

I

J

K

L

M

N

O

P

Q

R

S

T

U